The Cooperative Business Movement, 1950 to the Present

The United Nations declared 2012 the International Year of Cooperatives, emphasizing that there is an alternative to privately owned firms. At a time when greed and mismanagement have caused world financial and economic crises, co-ops offer another type of business for economic activities that is less exposed to aggressive capitalism. This book provides a problem-oriented overview of the development of cooperatives during the last fifty years. This worldwide study addresses the major challenges cooperatives face, such as introducing organizational innovations to acquire necessary risk capital and implementing growth-related strategies, the wave of demutualization in developed nations, and the ability of cooperative enterprise to construct an original consumer politics. The contributors to this volume discuss the successes and failures of cooperatives and ask whether the co-op is an outdated model of enterprise. They document a wave of foundations of new co-ops, new forms of collaboration between them, and a growing trend toward globalization. Generally speaking, these authors show that this special kind of business will doubtless continue to thrive and to maintain an important position in a rapidly changing world economy.

Patrizia Battilani is a professor of economic history at the University of Bologna, Italy. Battilani is coauthor of *Cooperation, Networks, Service: Innovation in Outsourcing* (with G. Bertagnoni, 2010). She has had articles published in the *Journal of Modern Italian Studies*, the *Journal of Tourism History*, and *Entreprises et Histoire*.

Harm G. Schröter is a professor of economic history at the University of Bergen, Norway. Professor Schröter is president of the European Business History Association and is on several editorial boards. His most recent book is *The European Enterprise: Historical Investigation into a Future Species* (2008).

Comparative Perspectives in Business History

In the early decades of the twenty-first century, the world economy is experiencing its most profound transformation since the Industrial Revolution. Firms, communications systems, and markets for products, services, labor, and currencies are all breaking out of national boundaries. Business enterprises today must negotiate a global environment in order to innovate and to compete in ways that will protect or enhance their market shares. Governments must respond in new ways to the periodic crises that occur in all market-centered systems. At the same time, governments and firms find it essential to understand the different perspectives growing out of local, regional, and national experiences with business and economic development. This has become a crucial competitive advantage to companies and a vital skill for those who study them. *Comparative Perspectives in Business History* explores these developments in a series of volumes that draw upon the best work of scholars from a variety of nations writing on the history of enterprise, public and private. The series encourages the use of new styles of analysis and seeks to enhance understanding of modern enterprise and its social and political relations, leaders, cultures, economic strategies, accomplishments, and failures.

Series Editors

Franco Amatori, *Bocconi University*
Louis Galambos, *The Johns Hopkins University*

Sponsors

Associazione per gli Studi Storici sull'Impresa (ASSI), Milan
Istituto di Storia Economica, Bocconi University, Milan
The Institute for Applied Economics, Global Health, and the Study of Business Enterprise, The Johns Hopkins University

Previously Published

The Rise and Fall of State-Owned Enterprise in the Western World, edited by Pier Angelo Toninelli
Business History around the World, edited by Franco Amatori and Geoffrey Jones
The Global Chemical Industry in the Age of the Petrochemical Revolution, edited by Louis Galambos, Takashi Hikino, and Vera Zamagni

The Cooperative Business Movement, 1950 to the Present

PATRIZIA BATTILANI
University of Bologna

HARM G. SCHRÖTER
University of Bergen

CAMBRIDGE
UNIVERSITY PRESS

CAMBRIDGE
UNIVERSITY PRESS

University Printing House, Cambridge CB2 8BS, United Kingdom

One Liberty Plaza, 20th Floor, New York, NY 10006, USA

477 Williamstown Road, Port Melbourne, VIC 3207, Australia

314-321, 3rd Floor, Plot 3, Splendor Forum, Jasola District Centre, New Delhi - 110025, India

103 Penang Road, #05-06/07, Visioncrest Commercial, Singapore 238467

Cambridge University Press is part of the University of Cambridge.

It furthers the University's mission by disseminating knowledge in the pursuit of education, learning and research at the highest international levels of excellence.

www.cambridge.org
Information on this title: www.cambridge.org/9781107028982

First published 2012

A catalogue record for this publication is available from the British Library

Library of Congress Cataloging in Publication data
The cooperative business movement, 1950 to the present / [edited by] Patrizia Battilani, Harm G. Schröter.
    p. cm. – (Comparative perspectives in business history)
ISBN 978-1-107-02898-2
1. Cooperative societies – History. 2. Cooperative societies – Case studies. I. Battilani, Patrizia. II. Schröter, Harm G., 1948–
HD2956.C647 2012
334–dc23   2012012293

ISBN 978-1-107-02898-2 Hardback
ISBN 978-1-107-54581-6 Paperback

Contents

Contributors

Patrizia Battilani, University of Bologna

Fabio Chaddad, University of Missouri

Michael L. Cook, University of Missouri

Espen Ekberg, University of Oslo

Katarina Friberg, Linnaeus University

Ann Hoyt, University of Wisconsin

Hongjoo Jung, Sungkyunkwan University

Peter Kramper, University of Freiburg

Ian MacPherson, University of Victoria

Tito Menzani, University of Bologna

Virginie Pérotin, Leeds University Business School

Hans Jürgen Rösner, University of Cologne

Harm G. Schröter, University of Bergen

Rachael Vorberg-Rugh, University of Liverpool

Anthony Webster, Liverpool John Moores University

John Wilson, University of Liverpool

Vera Zamagni, University of Bologna

Acknowledgments

The chapters that make up this book were discussed in a colloquium intended for the academic community that was hosted by Bocconi University in October 2010. Many colleagues involved as discussants in the conference provided us with constructive criticisms and suggestions that the authors incorporated into the final versions of their chapters. We would especially like to express our appreciation to Lou Hammond Ketilson, Giuseppe Airoldi, Eliana La Ferrara, Francesca Polese, Alberto Zevi, Mattia Granata, Dante Cracogna, Giovanni Fattore, Marcello Messori, Alessandro Zattoni, Giulio Ecchia, Giulio Napolitano, Iain MacDonald, Luca Fantacci, Matthias Kipping, Elio Borgonovi, Carlo Borzaga, Hagen Henry, Alex Turrini, Paolo Perulli, Giuseppe Soda, Alberto Martinelli, and Lanfranco Senn.

We would also like to thank Cambridge University Press's anonymous referees for their precious comments.

Our gratitude goes to Franco Amatori and Louis Galambos, the series editors behind the whole project who provided key support from both the scientific and the organizational points of view.

For this initiative, we are grateful to be able to count on the support of the Lega delle Cooperative and its Fondazione Ivano Barberini dedicated to the memory of one of the most important leaders of Italy's cooperative movement. It was the efforts of the foundation's president, Mauro Giordani, and its first director, Maurizio Brioni, that made this book possible.

Introduction: Principal Problems and General Development of Cooperative Enterprise

Patrizia Battilani and Harm G. Schröter

INTRODUCTION

How important are cooperatives in our society and economy? Are they a vanishing form of enterprise useful only in developing countries and imperfect markets? Or are they a resilient form of enterprise that parallels investor-oriented firms? We'd like to start with these questions because the main aim of this book is to offer answers to them by surveying the evolution of cooperatives (co-ops) all over the world in the last sixty years.

At first glance, the questions seem to be answered by the United Nations' declaration of the year 2012 as the "International Year of Co-operatives." This is a remarkable development, apparently establishing co-ops firmly back on the agenda of economists, politicians, and ordinary people throughout the world. The UN's declaration of the International Year of Co-operatives is particularly remarkable because the twenty to thirty years preceding 2012 seem to have been decades of stagnant progress for co-ops in many countries. Recently, however, co-ops did a remarkable job of withstanding the financial crisis that started in 2008. That alone would seem to justify a careful look at cooperatives and at their important role in the world economy.

The cooperative sector is certainly large: the world's three hundred largest co-ops do an annual business of $1.1 trillion (in U.S. dollars), which is roughly equal to Spain's gross national product (GNP).[1] In Sweden and Switzerland, co-ops provide about 20 percent of the country's GNP. In addition, a recent statistical report comparing cooperative and conventional business ownership worldwide shows that there are 328 million people who own shares, compared to 1 billion who are member-owners of cooperative enterprises.[2] These figures suggest that, yes, co-ops matter!

---

[1] For more information, go to www.global300.co-op (accessed January 12, 2012).

[2] Ed Mayo, ed., *Global Business Ownership 2012, Members and Shareholders across the World* (Manchester: The Cooperative Union, 2012). See Appendix II for a synthetic view of these new figures.

Thus, we believe, it is worthwhile to take a closer look into this special form of enterprise. However, the preceding questions also include many underlying issues that should be considered in analyzing the role played by cooperatives in today's economy and society. Have co-ops changed through time? Does a universal model of co-ops exist? What can explain deviations from it? Are the model and its deviations efficient forms of enterprise?

WHAT IS A CO-OP?

The idea of cooperative enterprise is very old; in Europe it became strong in the Middle Ages. The guilds and the trade association of the Hanseatic League were built on the idea of cooperation,[3] and the many European towns that became politically independent from aristocracy or clergy did so on the basis of this principle. It was and is today the core idea of the Swiss nation; relics of medieval commons are to be found in today's European forest cooperatives.

Although cooperative efforts of various sorts have existed since the beginning of civilization, the modern movement began primarily as a response to industrial capitalism. Then, those concerned about the problems created by industry looked to a variety of private and public efforts to provide greater security and equity to those whose lives were being shaped and reshaped by powerful economic changes.

On the one hand, the co-ops were enterprises for making money, while on the other hand they were socially oriented. Co-ops were different from investor-owned businesses (IOBs) and also different from organizations established for the benefit of the general public, such as charities or foundations. However, in some countries, co-ops and nonprofit organizations were grouped together under the definition of social economy[4] or civic economy.[5] Following the

---

[3] Hugo van Driel and Greta Devos, "Path Dependence in Ports: The Persistence of Co-operative Forms," *Business History Review* 81, no. 4 (2007), pp. 681–708.

[4] The definition of social economy dates back to Georges Fauquet who in *Le secteur co-operative* (1935) suggested cooperative enterprises as a third sector in the modern economy between public enterprises and investor-oriented firms. This concept has enjoyed a revival since the 1970s, when the definitions of *third sector* and *social economy* were widened to include other organizations. Today's definition of social economy includes "private companies that ... provide goods, services, insurance or finance, in which the distribution of surpluses and the decision-making processes are not directly linked to the share of capital of each member ...and those economic agents whose main function is to produce services not intended for sale, for particular groups of households, financed by the voluntary contributions of families." J. Barea Tejeiro, "Concepts y agentes de la economia social," *Ciriec Espana, Revista de economia publica, social y cooperative* 8 (1990), pp. 109–17, as translated by J. L. Monzon Campos in 'Contribution of the Social Economy to the General Interest,' *Annals of Public and Cooperative Economics* 68 (1997), pp. 397–408.

[5] The civic economy encompasses a diverse variety of organizations: public-private partnerships, socially responsible companies, community enterprises, cooperatives, foundations, charities, voluntary bodies, ethical investment funds, credit unions, community, banks, the informal sector (the ethical part), and nongovernment organizations. These organizations aim to serve the interests of all stakeholders involved: customers, the local community, the organization's staff, and the providers of capital.

International Co-operative Alliance (ICA), the world's top organization of all co-ops,[6] we define *co-op* as an autonomous organization of persons who meet their common economic, social, and cultural needs by voluntarily forming a jointly owned and democratically controlled enterprise.

Thus, we have a combination of several characteristics that in some quarters are said to be contradictory, such as democracy and management, or ownership and democratic control. Co-ops are exclusive. They are membership organizations, often exclusively serving their members. Membership entails investing a defined minimum sum and obtaining a voting right. In contrast to IOBs, a larger investment does not lead to more voting rights; the one and only voting right is bound to the membership, regardless of the economic weight of the respective member.[7] Thus, co-ops have applied the idea of democratic voting and democratic control to their form of enterprise: co-ops are by definition democratic firms.

Co-ops differ from nonprofit organizations because of the different attitude toward surpluses. In cooperative enterprises, surpluses may be paid to members in the form of patronage returns proportional to the business done by each member of the cooperative. Nonprofit organizations, of course, are precluded from distributing any surplus to members.

At the same time, co-ops and nonprofit organizations share in common the ideal of collaboration among citizens for the improvement of the standard of living of the whole community, or at least a significant portion of it. During the nineteenth and twentieth centuries, in many Western countries co-ops were a vehicle for the "have-nots" to improve their lives or standards of living through organized self-aid. The same could be said today for co-ops in low-income countries. That is why in some quarters co-ops and other kinds of nonprofit organizations are linked together in the definition of social economy.

Quoting Fay (1908), we can say that "Co-operation is to charity as prevention is to cure."[8] Co-ops are only a small part of the social economy, but still they are important. For instance, in 2009 there were registered in Germany 600,000 societies for self-aid (e.g., sports clubs), 14,000 associations for self-aid, but only 5,500 co-ops; thus the number of co-ops represented less than 1 percent of nonprofit organizations in that country. In 2010, in the United States there were 1,617,301 nonprofit organizations and around 30,000 co-ops, less than 2 percent. The picture is quite different in other countries: in Italy there are more than 70,000 co-ops and 236,000 nonprofit organizations; the former are almost 30 percent of the latter.

In conclusion, the core that makes an enterprise a co-op is a merger of economic activities and democratic governance. The financial engagement of members and their support or use of the respective enterprise are as important as democratic voting and control of the firm. This is called the "dual nature" of co-ops.

---

[6] The ICA, founded in 1895, has the goal of representing co-ops worldwide.
[7] In some countries, for instance, Italy, exceptions to the general rule have been introduced, and by law some cooperative shares can generate more than one voting right.
[8] Charles R. Fay, *Co-operation at Home and Abroad* (1908), p. 8.

ORIGINS AND TYPES OF CO-OPS

Although all co-ops share some characteristics, numerous types of these enterprises exist. Generally the cooperative model of enterprise can be applied to any business activity. And indeed, co-ops have existed in many fields of economic activity, including agriculture, retailing, housing, financial services, public utilities, and the production of goods. After the Second World War even more varieties of activities chose this form of organization: health and child care, tourism, car-sharing, and even philharmonic orchestras adopted the co-op form. For instance, in Italy up to 50 percent of all social services are provided by co-ops; in the United States health care through co-ops is important; in France more than 4 million children are educated in school co-ops. Consequently, we have small co-ops, sometimes just one shop, but most are medium-sized enterprises. A good example is the many cooperatives in wine-making (check your next wine bottle!), in which private growers have pooled their vinification and marketing. There are also a few very large ones, such as Co-op City in New York with more than 15,000 residential units all in one place. The world's largest co-op is, however, the Spanish Mondragon, which in 2010 employed 85,000 persons and is a transnational enterprise with production units in Europe, Asia, Africa, and America.

There are vast variations. Usually three different typologies of co-ops can be identified: customer-owned co-ops, worker co-ops, and producer-owned co-ops. Their origins are from different European countries, mainly from the UK, Germany, France, and Denmark.

One of the most important modern co-ops was the Rochdale Society of Equitable Pioneers, a consumer co-op (in our taxonomy, a customer-owned co-op), founded in 1844 in the UK. In that year a band of Rochdale weavers set up a shop where their families could buy good-quality, basic food at reasonable prices. A couple of other customer-owned co-ops existed before: in the UK (e.g., the Fenwick Weaver's Society founded in 1761), in France (the Co-operative Grocery Store of Lyon set up in 1831), and in the United States (the Philadelphia Contributorship for the Insurance of Homes from Loss by Fire dating back to 1752). What made Rochdale different was (a) its long-term success and (b) its written principles, which, with a few changes, still provide the basic ideology of all co-ops worldwide (as you can see from the ICA principles described below). From the UK, consumer co-ops spread to Switzerland (first consumer co-op in 1851), Germany (1852), Italy (1854), Japan (1879), Brazil (1887), South Africa (1892), and so on.

Another important source of co-op development was in Germany, where Hermann Schulze-Delitzsch and Friedrich Wilhelm Raiffeisen launched a movement for credit co-ops. Independent of each other, they founded institutions to provide small credits to their members. Schulze-Delitzsch, a shoemaker, started a co-op for fellow shoemakers that enabled the group to buy leather in bulk (in our taxonomy, a second kind of customer-owned co-op). Raiffeisen, a burgomaster, built a credit co-op for the support of small farmers. According to the World Council of Credit Unions, in 2010 there were 49,000 credit unions with 184 million members in 97 countries.[9] Today this tradition is carried forward in the movement for microfinance in Central Asia, highlighted by the United Nations in 2005 as the International Year of Microcredit. While Schulze-Delitzsch's ideas spread among craftspeople, Raiffeisen's had much success with peasants, both in and outside Germany.

France has been the cradle of worker co-ops. In 1834, in Paris, four workers set up the Association chrétienne des bijoutiers en doré (The Christian Association of Jewelers), inspired by Philippe Buchez, a doctor following the Saint-Simon ideals. Another source was the socialist Louis Blanc, who in his book *L'organisation du travail* (1839) launched the idea of social workshops, worker-owned enterprises based on the principle of equal benefits for the members. According to Blanc, the government should finance co-ops in their early stages by purchasing productive equipment or giving public procurement and then withdrawing its support once they become viable. The first attempt to implement this project came with the 1848 Revolution, when the provisional government and Blanc himself created the National Workshops, laboratories in which unemployed urban workers were given employment in carrying out useful public works. However, the National Workshops were more state-owned enterprises than co-ops and were closed after a few months. Nevertheless, Blanc's idea of worker co-ops for the "have-nots" who could carry out public works became an important part of the nineteenth-century European cooperative movement.

Both in Europe and in the United States, dairy and cheese cooperatives had been organized since the beginning of the nineteenth century. However, modern producer-owned cooperatives were founded in Denmark, where cooperative dairies were set up in the 1880s. These enterprises were inspired by the Lutheran theologian and bishop Nikolai Frederik Severin Grundtvig, and similar co-ops for other commodities soon followed.[10] Diffusion of Co-ops from Europe to the Rest of the World

From Europe cooperative ideas spread all over the world. They traveled to North America fast and spread quickly, and this was also true in Latin America, Japan, and South Africa, all of which were included in the movement before the end of the nineteenth century. The ideology of cooperation established surprisingly small roots in the rest of Asia and Africa, and generally speaking, the co-op ideas did not spread in the European colonies. This was true in spite of the fact that the British tried to promote co-ops in India and Eastern Africa, the French in Western Africa and Indochina, and the Belgians in Central Africa.[11] The reasons

---

[9] Home page of WOCCU: http://www.woccu.org (accessed October 26, 2011).

[10] Johnson Birchall, *The International Co-operative Movement* (Manchester: Manchester University Press, 1997).

[11] Patrick Develtere, Ignace Pollet, and Fredrick Wanyama, eds., *L'Afrique solidaire et entrepreneuriale. La renaissance du mouvement co-opératif africain* (Ilo, 2009); Vishwar Satgar and Michelle Williams, eds., *The Passion of the People: Successful Cooperative Experiences in Africa* (Copac, 2008).

are quite simple: there were no democratic traditions, nor well-defined property rights, nor indigenous movements supporting cooperative ideals. In America and Japan, where such deficits did not exist, co-ops were developed from the bottom up. In most African countries and India, the colonial rulers tried, rather unsuccessfully, to employ a top-down approach.

Because co-ops functioned well in raising living standards of the poor in Europe and America, however, after World War II they were thought to be the vehicles of choice for developing countries as well. Especially after 1960, the year most African countries became independent, the UN, the cooperative branch of the International Labour Organization (ILO), as well as the ICA tried to promote this form of enterprise for small farmers and others in Africa and Asia. Unfortunately these trials failed dismally with some important exceptions: for instance, India (Appendix II). Generally the governments of the decolonized countries strengthened the top-down approach of the former colonial powers and strictly connected co-ops to special government departments. In some cases, such as Tanzania, co-ops were nationalized. The impact of these developments figures prominently among the reasons why even today co-ops are unevenly distributed over the globe.

Nevertheless, since the 1990s, after the disruption of many co-ops that were unable to face the challenge of economic liberalization, a new phase in the history of African co-ops started. Many old co-ops were reorganized, the governments' influence was reduced, and the ICA cooperative principles became a reference point for a new generation of co-op laws.

Despite all that, today the diffusion of co-ops in this continent is relatively wide, and some African countries surpass Europe in numbers. However, the co-ops tend to be smaller and include a smaller percentage of the population (see Appendix II).

The former Asian and African colonies were not the only part of the world in which a strong and dangerous link between co-ops and the central state emerged. Indeed, after the transformation of the Russia Empire into the Soviet Union, in 1917 this new government created an anomalous type of co-op. The Soviet Union organized most agricultural production in co-ops called *kolkhozes*. After the Second World War, the other socialist European states, except Poland, followed the same policy. Eastern Europe in the 1950s and 1960s witnessed the speedy growth of state-centric cooperatives. Consequently, the number of socialist co-ops surmounted the number of all others. However, the majority of these co-ops were not set up voluntarily, and after the collapse of the USSR, their members preferred other forms of enterprise. The link between communism and co-ops left a bitter intellectual heritage: even twenty years later, peasants in the former socialist countries chose not to explore the advantages of this form of enterprise and insisted on other, in many cases less appropriate, types of organization. Therefore, the 1950s and 1960s development was followed by an equally rapid decline of co-ops after the collapse of the Soviet Union and the other socialist states in 1990–1.

Jewish settlers in Israel have developed yet another extreme form of co-op called a *kibbutz*. Buttressed by a powerful national and religious ideology, they not only work together, but they share their products, and, in some cases, even private life, equally. In other cases, cooperation coexists with private ownership. Because of the special role of religion connected to the *kibbutzim*, it is not clear if these organizations still can be called co-ops. But what is clear is the fact that most of them are economically successful even though they violate one of the Rochdale Principles: religious neutrality.

To complete the world history of co-ops we should come back to Western Europe, to the cradle of cooperative enterprises. After the Second World War two basic patterns of change emerged. In Northern Europe, in Germany and Belgium, cooperative undertakings were very successful for at least three decades; then, after the oil crises of the 1970s, co-ops entered a new phase dominated by stagnation or decline. In Mediterranean Europe, Switzerland and Austria, by contrast, the number of cooperatives has kept growing since the end of World War II. To summarize, over the last decades co-ops in the European countries seem to have shared only one single characteristic: an increase in the number of members per enterprise.

VARIATIONS IN PURPOSE

Over the decades co-ops have changed some of their ideal inspirations. In the modern age, when merchants or harbor workers set up the first cooperatives, their aim was to organize their businesses or jobs in a better way. During the second half of the nineteenth century, when the European cooperative movement spread, a new set of ideals, inspirations, and goals emerged. For instance, consumer co-ops were thought to improve the standard of living of the poor, credit unions and Raiffeisen banks were developed to stimulate small enterprises' investments in both rural and urban contexts, while worker co-ops were set up to escape from unemployment. Frequently, in Europe, there was a strong cultural link with the worker movement on the one hand and with the Catholic world on the other.

During the first half of the twentieth century and in some Western countries until the 1970s, most European co-ops continued to be enterprises for the "have-nots" and maintained a strong connection with the worker movement.

However, the deep transformation of society and economy that has characterized Western countries since the 1970s has affected co-ops in many different ways. In some countries, a strong decline of the cooperative ideals has occurred. For instance, in Germany, during the 1950s and 1960s, co-ops were still perceived as a morally superior form of business, but nothing more than a supplement to IOBs. Later, after various scandals in and about co-ops, the public began to doubt the moral aspect of the cooperative movement. Today, the movement is perceived by many as a defensive reaction, a means of protecting certain groups, such as labor, from the harshest aspects of capitalistic change.

In other Western countries, a deep change involving the redefinition of ideals, governance, and organizational models was undertaken. For instance, in Italy a new generation of members took the lead and little by little introduced both new ideals and merit-based organizational models, while the link with the worker movement waned.[12] The emergence of an affluent society changed the needs of many co-op members. Young members assigned new tasks to their co-ops, emphasizing the acquisition of an entrepreneurial attitude, a chance for upward mobility, and so on.

IDEOLOGICAL FLEXIBILITY OF CO-OPS

Though Western Europe represents the cradle of cooperative enterprise, already on this continent a multitude of models emerged. The variety of ideological contexts was great as well. E. Furlough and C. Strikwerda in 1999 defined it as the ideological flexibility of cooperatives.[13]

That is why in some countries co-ops have received political support from both left and right circles, while in others from neither. How is this possible? The answer is that both the definition and nature of cooperatives have differed in different societies at different times. As a result, various movements have found their way to co-ops, from the working class to the religious minded, from liberal to anti-corporation-oriented movements. The pattern of movements having supported cooperative ideals is quite different across countries.

Nevertheless, throughout Western Europe, working-class organizations played a crucial role in co-ops, at least until the last decades of the twentieth century. So, too, did various forms of Christianity (usually Catholic inspired in Italy and Spain, Protestant oriented in Denmark and Central Europe). In the United States, different sorts of anticorporate movements arose, including most prominently, those in agriculture.

Most of these movements have had certain characteristics in common: they usually focused on the "small people" owning little or nothing, in order to raise them from poverty through organized self-aid. The attention to the "have-nots" created a strong connection between co-ops and workers' movements in response to the first and second industrial revolutions. On the European continent, workers' movements involved four pillars: the socialist party, trade unions, organizations for recreation (e.g., sports or singing), and the co-ops. Leaders of these movements were usually convinced that co-ops were not only better institutions in a moral sense but also economically superior to any form of privately owned enterprise. Consequently, co-ops would one day finally simply

[12] This aspect has been studied in some depth for the Italian cooperatives. P. Battilani,*Il gruppo Co. ind 1961–2011: Storia di un co-packer* (Bologna: Il mulino, 2011), pp. 263–88; P. Battilani and V. Zamagni, *The Managerial Transformation of Italian Co-operative Enterprises: 1946–2010*, Business History, forthcoming.
[13] Ellen Furlough and Carl Strikwerda, eds., *Consumer Against Capitalism? Consumer Cooperation in Europe, North America and Japan 1840–1990* (Lanham, MD: Rowman & Littlefield, 1999), p. 3.

outgrow the private economic sector – a peaceful way to some kind of socialism. However, the idea of co-ops also attracted other, more well-to-do circles, which soon learned of the advantages of buying or selling in large quantities. For instance, in the United States, founders of the cooperative movement chose theoretical approaches that were consistent with American ideologies of liberal individualism. Later, cooperative theory became increasingly conservative, especially in the early twentieth century.

Also, political approaches that did not believe in the long-term survival of cooperatives have occasionally supported them. An important part of the political left understood co-ops as a short- or medium-term solution to what in the long run the state should do: run the economy. Some part of the political right supported co-ops as a short- or medium-term solution to what in the long run the market should do (but had not yet achieved).

The result has been a multitude of explanations and motivations for co-ops' development all over the world. In the end, co-ops everywhere changed their organizational structures as they adapted to the needs they were designed to satisfy, including their social goals. Besides, the distribution of numbers suggests that co-ops seem particularly well suited for the agricultural and service sectors. Finally, like business, they seem to have their own product cycle.[14]

In Western Europe and partly in the United States, co-ops for the "have-nots" flourished for more than 180 years, until the "golden years" of growth from 1948–73 generated a decent standard of living for a very high percentage of the population. Since that time, demand for co-ops has deeply changed in those countries. People who were well-to-do needed new motivations to cooperate. The organizational structures of co-ops changed and hybrid forms of the enterprise emerged. At the same time, in developing countries there was still room for "cooperation of the poor." There is thus a special kind of cooperative product cycle shaped by the changing needs of the co-ops' members as economic development proceeds.

VARIATIONS ON THE EUROPEAN MODEL

Because cooperatives have always been a world of variations in place and in time, since the 1930s the international cooperative movement has tried to outline a sort of universal model by defining a set of cooperative principles. These principles were published in 1937. However, they have a much older origin because they represented the extension of the 1844 Rochdale Pioneer bylaws.

The Rochdale Principles called for (1) open membership, (2) democratic control (one person, one vote), (3) distribution of surplus in proportion to trade, (4) payment of limited interest on capital, (5) political and religious

---

[14] Vernon suggested a life cycle for products from start, over maturity, and to aging, an idea that was transferred to other issues such as ideas, organizations, and so on. Raymond Vernon, "The Product Cycle Hypothesis in a New Environment," in *Oxford Bulletin of Economics and Statistics* 41 (1979), pp. 255–67.

neutrality, (6) cash trading (no credit extended), and (7) promotion of education. These basic rules were designed to meet the needs of their time and place and were suited above all to consumer co-ops. The rules to provide no credit and the distribution in proportion to trade were designed, for instance, to educate member-customers. Since that time, credit unions and other forms of financial co-ops have become important institutions that share the culture and many of the practices of other cooperatives.

In 1937, when the ICA for the first time provided a set of co-op principles, the Rochdale statute became the basis for this formulation. Since then ICA has accepted small revisions in 1965 and 1995, and today the following rules are considered to be the basic ones: (1) voluntary and open membership; (2) democratic member control; (3) member economic participation; (4) autonomy and independence; (5) education, training, and information; (6) cooperation among cooperatives; and (7) concern for community. Rules 4, 6, and 7 are especially worth mentioning. Autonomy and independence of the co-op was no issue in Rochdale, as it was considered to be natural, but what was considered "natural" in the nineteenth-century UK is not so in other parts of the world today. Co-ops struggle to maintain their independence and develop their democratic potential. Cooperation among different co-ops was not an important idea in 1844, but it is an important goal today. Concern for the community has also been added. Today in many countries co-ops are strong and widespread enough to play a major social role, not only for their members, but for society as a whole. During the last decades, the principles have led directly to some important issues for the movement; the most important of which are addressed in this volume: degeneration (demutualization), variation, mutual trust (also over borders), and law.

Co-ops are enterprises, and enterprises can fail and go bankrupt. Co-ops have another possibility of failure: *degeneration*. Since the beginning of theoretical reflection on co-ops, this was, and today is more than ever, a major issue. Degeneration involves deviation from the social purposes of co-ops. One of the first systematic studies of worker cooperatives[15] used the concept of degeneration to describe the process that could lead worker cooperatives to lose their democratic characteristics. Through this process, co-ops can become similar to or the same as investor-owned enterprises. This process can be internally controlled when co-ops decide to change their character (see the contribution on demutualization in this volume), or uncontrolled when democratic voting just gradually disappears. Indeed, democratic engagement has emerged as the Achilles' heel of many co-ops. In many cases members were content and did not bother to vote. This is, of course, an open invitation to management to do what it wants. In several cases managers decided to demutualize the respective co-op, and during the process acquire through their insider-knowledge the best pieces for themselves as private property. Lack of democratic practice is a long-term threat to all co-ops.

---

[15] Beatrice Webb (Potter), *The Cooperative Movement in Great Britain* (London: Swan Sonenschein, and New York: Charles Scribners' Sons, 1891).

Western managers and theorists of co-ops have often pointed to the lack of democratic practice in the communist states, and consequently claimed co-ops there not to be "real" ones. Indeed, democratic member control did not exist, which means ICA conditions 2 and 4 were not met. Similar problems have arisen also in other countries where the government played a large role in creating or eliminating co-ops (see the contribution by Zamagni in this volume). Most scholars who study co-ops would not count them as part of the movement. And if in a traditional democratic country such as the UK, out of the electorate of a co-op less than 10 percent participate in elections – is this still to be called democratic? The ICA's rules are clearly normative in character, but there are many forms of cooperation that skirt those norms.

This leads us to the *variations*. How much deviation from the Anglo-European model and the ICA's rules can be allowed in order to still call a certain enterprise a co-op? Indeed there were important voices that understood co-ops as a primarily European institution – in contrast to the rest of the world – and also in contrast to the United States. For instance, in 1957 Fritz Baade, one of the most influential German economists of his time, labeled co-ops to be the *European form* of defining the balance between order and freedom in the economy.[16] Other societies and other cultures, one then would presume, would produce different forms of cooperative action, just as they have produced different forms of capitalism. See especially the work by the sociologists Peter Hall and David Soskice.[17] When there are already substantial differences between these highly developed Western countries, where do African or East Asian ones fit in? Culture matters,[18] and we cannot presume that co-ops have an identical profile all over the world. The contributions in the book serve as an illustration of this variety.

In all cooperative social systems, trust is an important dimension. The precondition of cooperation is initial *mutual trust*, while later, through the work of the co-op, trust between members becomes enlarged and deepened. This occurs not only within the co-ops but also between members of different co-ops and even beyond. The dynamics of trust-building are of general importance because trust is the lubricant of the economy. Without trust there will be very little trade and very little division of work. The more trust, the less the transaction costs.[19]

---

[16] F. Baade, "Weltmacht Verbraucher," in Zentralverband Deutscher Konsumgenossenschaften (ed.), *Wirtschaft für den Verbraucher* (Hamburg), pp. 16–19, esp. p. 19.

[17] Peter A. Hall and David Soskice, *Varieties of Capitalism: The Institutional Foundations of Comparative Advantage* (Oxford: Oxford University Press, 2001); Alfred D. Chandler, Jr., *Scale and Scope: The Dynamics of Industrial Capitalism* (Cambridge: Cambridge University Press, 1990); Geert Hofstede, *Cultures and Organisations: Software of the Mind* (London: McGraw-Hill, 1991).

[18] The book *Culture Matters: How Values Shape Human Progress*, edited by Samuel P. Huntingdon and Lawrence E. Harrison in 2000, contains contributions discussing to what extent cultural values affect the economy. In addition to the editors, contributors include twenty other distinguished authors such as Robert B. Edgerton, Davis Landes, and Seymour Martin Lipset.

[19] M. Casson, *Entrepreneurship and Business Culture, Studies in Economic Trust*, 2 vols. (Aldershot: Edward Elgar, 1996).

For instance, the exceptionally high rate of trust in Scandinavia is one of the reasons why these countries can still export and enjoy a high standard of living in spite of extremely high wages – here again culture matters. Not least because of the trust-building potential of co-ops, economists and politicians expect more social benefits to society from co-ops than from other forms of business. Does reality meet these expectations?

Law as well as trust is an important precondition for enterprise. This applies both to the existence of appropriate laws and to the manner in which jurisdiction is applied in practice. It was only during the nineteenth century that alternatives to the sole proprietorship were allowed: innovative forms of enterprise were created in order to achieve long-term economic growth. Industrialized nations' commercial codes made it increasingly simpler to create limited liability companies. Later special laws on co-ops were passed. These laws and their application varied between countries, and for a third time we point to the importance of cultural variety. Law and legal proceedings in a wider sense are another issue addressed in the pages of this book.

LITERATURE SURVEY

Much theoretical attention was paid to cooperatives, especially during their formative years. Some of the greatest economists of that age – including Léon Walras, John Stuart Mill, and Vilfredo Pareto – felt the need to write about the form of enterprise we now call the cooperative, but which at that time was known under a variety of names: *sociétés à capitale variables, associationes populaires, equitable pioneers, industrial and prevident societies.*

John Stuart Mill defined the cooperative as an association of workers with equal rights, each being a joint owner of capital stock, working under a management that the workers themselves chose and that the workers possessed the power to dismiss.[20] Walras defined *associations populaires* as companies whose capital stock was not created by an immediate, definitive underwriting, as occurs in the case of ordinary commercial and manufacturing companies, but through a gradual process consisting of the regular payment of membership shares by the cooperative's members. Like a joint stock company, which may allow a certain amount of capital not yet paid in, co-ops often allowed their members to pay in their capital over a certain period. Often this was carried out by reinvesting the dividend, or the company would withhold a certain amount of pay until the share was paid. Walras defined these cooperatives in terms of two basic characteristics: (1) their purpose, which was the creation of capital (a sales outlet, a factory, or a bank) that would belong jointly to all members; and (2) the means that were available to them, which basically consisted in the regular, systematic withdrawal of a portion of wages and company profits, that is, of the members' overall income, for the purpose of increasing capital stock: "*Ainsi,*

---

[20] John Stuart Mill, *Principles of Political Economy*, 3rd ed., vol. II (1852).

*avènement des travailleurs à la propriété du capital par l'épargne, voilà en deux
mots tout le système des associations populaires."*[21]

The economists' debate focused on technical questions – such as the type of
company liability (limited or unlimited), the nature of invested capital (variable
or fixed), members' aims (to obtain ownership of capital through work, to
improve living standards by having access to cheaper goods, etc.) – albeit within
clearly defined cultural boundaries. The development of the cooperative movement was set against a background of pauperism (ultimate poverty) and the
"social question." Indeed, the problem of pauperism was so great that Walras
declared that "either society destroys pauperism or pauperism will destroy
society."[22] He and the other economists saw the cooperative movement as a
vehicle that would enable the poor to enter the world of production and
consumption, through the creation of shops, banks, and later factories.
Consequently, co-ops would not only solve a threatening social problem but at
the same time help increase national wealth. Frequently the essays addressing
economic issues provided useful information on cooperative enterprises in some
countries or sectors. Take, for example, Charles Gide who provided a general
overlook of the consumer cooperative in Europe,[23] and Adrien Berget who
described cooperatives in wine production.[24]

However, the first comparative study in historical perspective came to light in
1908. It was written by Charles R. Fay,[25] a student of Alfred Marshall, who had
been provided a research scholarship for that purpose at the London School of
Economics. Addressing the issue of varieties of co-ops, the book stated for the
first time the three typologies of consumer, producer, and worker cooperatives
and identified the country of origin for each of them. Two long-standing ideas
were launched by Fay: the link between cooperation and the weak group of
population on one side, and the homogeneity of members' business interests on
the other. As Marshall claimed in one of his letters, the suggestion that "the
success of any kind of co-operative in any [country] tends to vary with the
homogeneity of the class of population to which it is applicable" is "lumi-
nous."[26] The central idea of Fay's analysis was that cooperative enterprises
had been the "corner-stone in the development of modern agriculture" and
also in other sectors because they had made it possible for small-sized farmers

[21] Leon Walras, *Les associations populaires de consommation, de production et de crédit* (Paris: Dantur, 1865).
[22] Walras, p. 85.
[23] Charles Gide, *Les Sociétés cooperatives de Consommation* (Colin, 1904).
[24] Adrien Berget, *La cooperation dans la viticulture europeenne* (Lille: A. Devos, 1902); Henry W. Wolff, *Cooperation in Agriculture* (London: P.S. King & Son, 1912).
[25] Charles R. Fay, *Co-operation at Home and Abroad* (1908). In the 1920s, Fay extended his analysis to the former British colonies. Charles R. Fay, "Post-War Development of the Cooperative Movement in the Countries of the British Empire," in *American Cooperation* 1 (1928).
[26] John K. Whitaker, ed., *The Correspondence of Alfred Marshall, Economist: Towards the Close, 1903–1924*, Letter 853 (London: Cambridge University Press, 1996).

(or weak groups in general) to standardize and mechanize their undertakings and thereby exploit the economies of scale usually associated with the large enterprise. In conclusion, cooperation was "fully within the competitive system ... in such a way to temper its harshness and excess."[27] In the interwar years, Fay extended his research to Australia, Asia, and America; his book can be considered the first example of a world history of cooperative enterprises.

In addition, in the same decades national histories of the cooperative movement and enterprises began to spread. A variety of commissioned histories provided more insight on the origin and evolution of single cooperatives in the UK,[28] while Carr-Saunders provided the paramount analysis of the British consumer cooperation, and some years later G. D. H. Cole of the whole cooperative movement of that country. Likewise J. Gaumont wrote the first history of the French cooperative movement in 1924[29] while Bertrand had already provided the same for Belgian co-ops in 1903.[30] Also, Germany and Russia had been covered before 1930.[31] Outside Europe we can mention the wide literature on the U.S. agricultural cooperatives,[32] Walter Mallory's article on credit co-ops in China,[33] as well as a short pamphlet on Latin America.[34] In conclusion, the first half of the twentieth century enriched the knowledge of cooperatives within and outside Europe.

After World War II research on cooperative enterprises became multifaceted. At that time, the diffusion of this kind of enterprise could be taken for granted, in some countries as a consequence of the "rebirth" following the end of

[27] Fay, 1920, p. 348.
[28] A dozen jubilee publications bear the name William H. Brown, as the Bath Co-operative Society, Jubilee History, 1939; Brighton Equitable Co-operative Society, 1828–1938, 1938; Cambridge and District Co-operative Society, 1868–1919, 1920; Cambridge – Co-operation in a University Town: With the 70 Years Record of the Cambridge and District Co-operative Society, 1939; Eastleigh Co-operative Society, 1892–1948, 1949. An interesting list of the cooperative societies' history published between 1920 and 1960 can be found at www.chelmsford-tuc.org.uk/article124.html.
[29] A. Carr-Saunders, P. Sargat Florence, and R. Peers, *Consumers' Co-operation in Great Britain* (1938); G.D.H. Cole, *A Century of Co-operation* (London: Allen & Unwin, 1944); Jean Gaumont, *Histoire generale de la co-operation en France: Les idees et le faits, les hommes et les oeuvres* (Paris: Federation nationale des cooperatives de consommation, 1924).
[30] L. Bertrand, *Histoire de la cooperation en Belgique. Les homes, les idees, les faits* (Bruxelles, 1902–1903).
[31] Theodor Cassau, *The Consumers' Cooperative Movement in Germany*, trans. J.F. Mills (London: Fisher Unwin, and Manchester: The Cooperative Union, 1925); E.M. Kayden and A. Antsiferov, *The Cooperative Movement in Russia During the War: Consumers' Cooperation* (New Haven: Yale University Press, 1929); Elsie T. Blanc, *Co-operative Movement in Russia* (New York: Macmillan, 1924).
[32] Among others, T.R. Pirtle, *History of the Dairy Industry* (Chicago: Mojonnier Bros., 1926); George Harold Powell, *Cooperation in Agriculture* (New York: Macmillan, 1913).
[33] Walter H. Mallory, "Rural Cooperative Credit in China," *Quarterly Journal of Economics* 45, no. 3 (May 1931), pp. 484–9.
[34] A. Fabra Ribas, *The Cooperative Movement in Latin America: Its Significance in Hemisphere Solidarity* (New Mexico: University of New Mexico Press, 1943).

dictatorship, in others as a pursuance of the interwar development, and finally in command economies as an instrument of state planning and political control over the economy. In addition, as we mentioned earlier (also see endnotes 20 to 34), historical and economic literature had already provided not only a general description of the cooperative movement in most countries but also had prompted some interesting interpretations about its origin and development.

Therefore, since the 1950s the main concern of cooperative studies has not been to witness the foundation of cooperatives, but instead to investigate their ability to survive in different economic environments. The existence of structural weaknesses became a constant issue not only in economic but also in historical analyses. For example, Ward's and Vanek's seminal papers in 1958 and 1977 held that cooperatives (which they called labor-managed enterprises) have weak incentives to growth and tend to keep investments low[35] as a consequence of the democratic rule (one member, one vote). In addition, we can mention the well-known Furubotn and Pejovich article, according to which the growth potentialities of cooperatives were constrained by an inadequate capitalization because, since members were not in a position to cash the capital gains on shares when they left, they privileged strategies maximizing short-time returns.[36] Even if empirical investigation did not provide support for the conclusions of these authors, nevertheless their writing stimulated intense scientific activity;[37] however, this activity was restricted to the worker cooperative typology.

While economists explored the long-run sustainability of the cooperative form, historians got involved in discussing its social and political dimensions. The relationship between cooperation and left parties or trade unions was extensively explored in Germany, Italy, and Scandinavian countries,[38] while in the United States the focus was on the link between populism or conservative-

---

[35] This was a consequence of the fact that cooperatives' target was to maximize the income of the working members and keep as low as possible the returns to capital. J. Vanek, *The Labor-Managed Economy* (Ithaca: Cornell University Press, 1977); Ibid., ed., *Self Management: Economic Liberation of Man* (Harmondsworth: Penguin, 1975); B. Ward, "The Firm in Illyria: Market Syndicalism," *American Economic Review* 47, no. 3 (1958), pp. 566–89. Bonin, Jones, and Putterman (1993) surveyed the empirical literature on the worker cooperatives in developed economies.

[36] E. Furubotn and S. Pejovich, "Property Rights and the Behaviour of the Firm in a Socialist State," *Journal of Economic Literature* 10 (1970), pp. 430–54. Because this was in turn a consequence of the lack of a market for cooperative shares, in 2003 Dow demonstrated that this limit can be overcome. Gregory K. Dow, *Governing the Firm: Workers' Control in Theory and Practice* (Cambridge: Cambridge University Press, 2003).

[37] An interesting survey of empirical investigation is John P. Bonin, Derek C. Jones, and Louis Putterman, "Theoretical and Empirical Studies of Producer Cooperatives: Will Ever the Twain Meet?," *Journal of Economic Literature* 31, no. 3 (1993), pp. 1290–320.

[38] It is useful to mention the most important of these books: Walter Hesselbach, *Public, Trade Union and Cooperative Enterprise in Germany: The Commonweal Idea* (1976 [German ed. 1971]); R. Zangheri, G. Galasso, and V. Castronovo, *Storia del movimento co-operativo in Italia. La Lega Nazionale delle Co-operative e Mutue (1886–1986)* (Turin: Einaudi, 1987); G. W. Rhodes, *Co-operative – Labour Relations, 1900–1962*; John Earle, *The Italian Cooperative Movement: A Portrait of the Lega Nazionale delle Cooperative e Mutue* (London, 1986); Bernard H. Moss, *The*

oriented groups and cooperative ideals.[39] The analysis was usually restricted to the consumer cooperatives in Europe and to the agricultural ones in the United States, and generally in this research cooperative enterprises were considered an expression of political beliefs, with their success and failure strictly connected to the life cycle of the twentieth-century ideologies.

In the last decade of the twentieth century, two stimulating approaches deeply renewed the research on cooperatives. The first one dates back to 1996 when Henry Hansmann introduced the idea that ownership, and consequently the form of the enterprise (e.g., cooperative versus investor-oriented), should be assigned so that total transaction costs for all patrons (stakeholders) were minimized. Differently from the previous literature, the cooperative was not considered weaker or less efficient than the investor-oriented enterprise, but simply a form of enterprise that emerges when antitrust enforcement is weaker and homogeneity of interest among the patrons is high. This last suggestion brings us back to the 1908 Fay research on agricultural cooperatives in Europe. Both Hansmann's theoretical model and Fay's economic history analysis suggested that cooperatives operate more successfully when members are more homogenous (in term of interests, products, and so on).

The second approach is connected to the historians' research on consumerism and dates back to 1996 when Peter Gurney situated the analysis of the British consumer cooperatives within the framework of consumer studies. In this way the focus went to the ability of cooperatives to construct a consumer politics alternative to the investor-oriented enterprise.[40]

Despite the multifaceted scientific production of the last decades, the operation of cooperative undertakings remained most neglected, so that more than ten years ago Steven Kellor wrote: "historians of agrarian protest analyzed rural co-operatives as auxiliaries of populism; labor historians treated co-ops as supporters of the trade unions. Business historians have neglected them."[41] However, during the last decade some business histories have been written, and a handful of business historians and economists have provided insights into the characteristics and the transformation of cooperative enterprises in

Origins of the French Labor Movement 1830–1914: The Socialism of Skilled Workers (Berkeley: University of California Press, 1976), ch. 2; B. Fairbairn, "Co-operative Values and the Cold War: The Rebuilding and Undermining of the German Consumer Movement, 1945–1955," *Annals of Public and Cooperative Economics*, 71 no. 4 (2000), pp. 637–63.

[39] Lawrence Goodwyn, et al., "The Role of Co-operatives in the Development of the Movement Culture of Populism," *Journal of American History* 69, no. 4 (1983); Lawrence Goodwyn, *The Populist Moment: A Short History of the Agrarian Revolt in America* (Oxford/London/New York: Oxford University Press, 1978); Carl J. Guarneri, *The Utopian Alternative: Fourierism in Nineteenth-Century America* (Ithaca, NY: Cornell University Press, 1991); Raymond W. Miller, *A Conservative Look at Co-operatives* (Athens, OH, 1964).

[40] P. Gurney, *Co-operative Culture and the Politics of Consumption in England, 1870–1930*, (Manchester: Manchester University Press, 1996).

[41] Steven J. Kellor, *Cooperative Commonwealth. Coops in Rural Minnesota 1859–1939* (Minnesota Historical Society, 2000), p. 4.

specific countries.[42] Now we are in a position to widen the analysis and provide a worldwide comparison.

This brings us to a second aim of this book. The many issues addressed by historical and economic literature usually have been analyzed in a national perspective. Few attempts have been made to analyze cooperative enterprises worldwide as well as to offer a historical overview over the last two generations. We can mention the attempt developed by Birchall in 1997,[43] the seminal book *Consumer versus Capitalism?* edited by Carl Strikwerda and Ellen Fourlough in 1999, the proceeding of a conference on consumer cooperatives published in 2005,[44] and two recent books on the origin, failure, and success of cooperatives in Africa.[45] Thus, this book is the first attempt to provide the history of co-ops over the last sixty years in a worldwide perspective as well as in its business history dimension.

HOW THIS BOOK IS ORGANIZED

A central goal of this volume is to explore the patterns of development and to confront the great varieties of co-ops in the world. That is why the first of the two parts in which the book is organized provides a worldwide overview of cooperative enterprises. In Chapter 1, Ann Hoyt and Tito Menzani trace the evolution of cooperative businesses on different continents, bringing attention to the second half of the twentieth century. Vera Zamagni's contribution in Chapter 2 shows in which sectors cooperatives have historically flourished across the world and how the service sector has always played a fundamental role in cooperative endeavors. To shed some light on emerging countries, which

[42] P. Battilani and G. Bertagnoni, eds., *Cooperation, Networks, Service: Innovation in Outsourcing* (Preston: Crucible, 2010); José Miguel Martínez-Carrión and Francisco José Medina-Albadalejo, *Evolution and Recent Developments of Spanish Wine Sector, 1950–2008* (UHE Working Papers, 2010); Diana Hunt and Chiara Cazzuffi, "Causes and Consequences of Institutional and Governance Change in Cooperative Firms: The Case of Agricultural Processing and Marketing Cooperatives in Italy and in the US," *Imprese e storia* 37 (2009); Kostas Karantininis and Jerker Nilsson, eds., *Vertical Markets and Cooperative Hierarchies: The Role of Cooperatives in the Agri-Food Industry* (Dordrecht: Springer, 2007); G. Bertagnoni, ed., *Una storia di qualità. Il gruppo Granarolo fra valori etici e logiche di mercato* (Bologna: Il Mulino, 2004); V. Zamagni, P. Battilani, and A. Casali, *La cooperazione di consumo in Italia. Centocinquant'anni della Coop consumatori: Dal primo spaccio a leader della moderna distribuzione* (Bologna: Il Mulino, 2004); C. Clamp, *The Evolution of Management in the Mondragon Cooperatives.* Paper presented at the conference Mapping Cooperative Studies in the New Millennium, University of Victoria, May 28–31, 2003; D. Cote, *Les Holdings coopératives, Evolutions ou Transformation Définitive?* (Jalons, De Boeck, Paris, 2003).
[43] Johnson Birchall, *The International Co-operative Movement* (Manchester: Manchester University Press, 1997).
[44] *Consumerism versus Capitalism? Co-operatives Seen from an International Comparative Perspective* (Ghent: Amsab-Instituut voor Sociale Geschiedenis, 2005).
[45] The *Passion of the People,* edited by Vishwas Satgar and Michelle Williams in 2008, and *L'afrique solidaire et entrepreneurial,* edited by Patrick Develtere, Ignace Pollet, and Fredrick Wanyama in 2009.

are often marginalized in international comparisons, Hongjoo Jung and Hans Jürgen Rösner (Chapter 3) bring to our attention the origin and evolution of cooperatives in South Korea. The history of this country is particularly interesting because Korean cooperatives cannot be considered a Western offspring. As a matter of fact, they came from a native tradition and were also fostered by Japanese colonial rule. With this essay, we launch a new research topic: the extension of a native cooperative tradition outside Europe.

Despite variety in time and geography, cooperatives have shared some basic values all over the world, thanks in part to the efforts of the ICA in developing a kind of constitution, "the co-operative principles." These principles and their related ideology have been negotiated and renegotiated within the movement about every thirty years in order to accommodate to a changing political, social, and economic scenario and above all to incorporate the values of new generations of members. Ian MacPherson's essay in Chapter 4 examines the way in which the cooperative movement tried to make the connection between values and principles during the 1990s, at the time of the last revision that took place in 1995.

The first part of the book ends with a general issue affecting co-ops in general, the reasons for failure in different countries and periods. In Chapter 5, Peter Kramper analyzes two general failures (the demise of consumer co-ops in Germany and the strong decline of cooperative banks in Japan) and the wide transformation in the nature of co-ops that took place between 1980 and 2000 in the United States with the emergence of hybrid models of agricultural co-ops. He concludes that co-op longevity is highly dependent on the stability of the social groups that provide the basis for a committed membership.

Because co-ops can fail in two different ways, through normal bankruptcy or conversion into an investor-owned enterprise (IOE), an entire chapter (Chapter 6) of the book is devoted to the issue of demutualization. The essay by Patrizia Battilani and Harm Schröter addresses the demutualization process from a historical perspective. It provides some explanations for demutualization of both types, its acceleration over the last two decades, and its slowdown after the 2008 financial crisis.

As some issues do not affect the generality of the cooperatives but are specific to a particular type, the second part of book includes contributions focusing on agricultural, consumer, and worker cooperatives. In Chapter 7, Fabio Chaddad and Michael Cook bring attention to the organizational innovations introduced by the U.S. agricultural cooperatives in order to acquire necessary risk capital and implement growth-related strategies. Utilizing insights from property rights and agency theory, they discuss a wide variety of innovations, from the setting up of subsidiaries with partial public ownership to the adoption of preferred trust shares. Virginie Pérotin focuses on worker co-ops in Chapter 8. Her essay demonstrates that worker cooperatives perform well in comparison with conventional firms, and that the features that make them special – worker participation and unusual arrangements for the ownership of capital – are a crucial part of their strength. Therefore, more participatory cooperatives are also more productive.

Two contributions take into consideration consumer cooperatives. Following a comparative approach, Espen Ekberg (Chapter 9) distinguishes between federal, nonfederal, and hybrid models of organization, and discusses their roles in the development of consumer cooperation in Western Europe. His main conclusion is that many of the co-ops that abandoned the federal model and opted for full centralization experienced decline or even total collapse. The contribution in Chapter 10 by Katarina Friberg, Rachael Vorberg-Rugh, Anthony Webster, and John Wilson is dedicated to examining business strategies in an era of growing consumer spending and increased competition from larger and increasingly multinational investor-led retail corporations. By comparing Swedish and UK enterprises, the authors underline the primacy of commercial dynamics and the replacement of old managers as the essential catalysts that drove the twenty-first-century revival after the deep crisis of the earlier decades; in these instances, political environment played no role.

With this book we attempt focusing on three different perspectives. First, we provide an overview of the worldwide development of the cooperative movement for the last two generations. We combine a focus on today's problems and a brief outlook into the future with a historical perspective in order to root the future of this species firmly in its own history. Second, we put the cooperative issue on the agenda of business historians, hoping for more studies in this exciting field in which business and politics merge. Last but not least, with this edition we mark the United Nations' International Year of Cooperatives 2012, supporting the idea as such and also providing fresh information.

SECTION I

COOPERATIVE ISSUES IN A GLOBAL OVERVIEW

Does there exist a universal model of cooperative enterprise? Have cooperative firms basically the same characteristics over both time and space? Is the existence of a worldwide central organization of co-ops, the International Co-operative Alliance (ICA), along with the international acceptance of the ICA's rules on co-ops, an indicator of cast-iron stability in the movement? Many books have been published on the variety of capitalistic enterprises, but questions similar to those asked about conventional enterprises need to be asked concerning cooperatives. For example, what have been the most important issues in the development of co-ops during the last two generations? During this period, the movement has been confronted with grave, even fundamental problems of existence. These problems have been more concentrated in economically developed countries than in less developed ones. Has the cooperative form of enterprise been able to cater to the economic and social changes during the last decades? And if not, why not? Are co-ops more useful during a certain stage of a country's economic development, providing less of a contribution at a higher stage? Is it right to look at the economic side only, or do other issues, such as social and educational ones, need to be taken into account when dealing with cooperatives?

This first section of the book addresses questions such as these by offering a worldwide perspective. This approach entails an innovative and multifaceted portrait, though, of course, not a complete picture. Cooperatives used to be perceived as a Western offspring, but comprehensive research has revealed a more differentiated suggestion; for example, an indigenous tradition can be found in some Asian countries. From Europe cooperative ideas spread all over the world, but in doing that, many deviations from the original model of a co-op were initiated and further developed according to local and regional require-ments. Already in 1937 the ICA reflected this development and suggested that cooperative enterprise should be understood not so much as a cast-iron con-struction but more as a universal model described by a set of "cooperative principles," that is, be understood as operating on guidelines rather than law.

Cooperatives have been shown to be well suited for a variety of economic sectors, however, some more than others. Here, as in capitalistic enterprises, we find variety. Usually co-ops have flourished in agro-business, retailing, finance (both banking and insurance), and recently in the whole service sector, including health. In contrast, the sector missing to a large extent is the manufacturing industry. However, here we also find interesting variation: Industrial co-ops have flourished in two European regions until today: in the Basque countries in Spain and the Imola district of Italy. Like other types of enterprise, cooperatives can fail for a multitude of reasons; however, during the last thirty years or so, failure has become a general demise of a whole typology of co-ops as a consequence of bankruptcy or conversion into investor-owned enterprises (IOEs). When this happens, the true difference between co-ops and IOEs emerges. Cooperatives, a special kind of enterprise based on the one-member-one-vote principle, need a certain degree of cohesion among members to be viable. Otherwise they will fail economically or change their nature. In either case, they no longer exist as part of the co-op species.

The following contributions show that co-ops are an enduring form of enterprise that has put down roots in every continent of the world, even if to a different degree, depending on the economic policies (market or command economy), the legal environment, and the cultural tradition of the different countries, as well as on the business strategies of their members and managers.

CHAPTER I

The International Cooperative Movement: A Quiet Giant

Ann Hoyt and Tito Menzani

INTRODUCTION

Throughout the world, individuals and communities have created cooperative self-help organizations to provide an extensive array of goods and services. In numerous cases, cooperatives play a critical role in significantly improving the well-being of their members and their communities. The International Cooperative Alliance (ICA) reports that more than one billion people around the world are members of cooperatives. The tremendous variety of economic, social, and political conditions among the world's population has spawned a similar variety of cooperative experiences worldwide. This chapter gathers statistical data on the world's cooperative community during the past fifty years, and identifies trends in various regions.

The chapter begins with a caveat of sorts regarding the quality, availability, and consistency of basic data on the international cooperative movement. Not being able to discuss every country or every sector where there is cooperative activity,[1] we have chosen countries that are representative of cooperative activity at various stages of economic development. To some extent our choices of cooperatives have also been limited by availability of data for any particular country.

That said, we discuss cooperatives in four types of economies in order to highlight the similarities and differences among cooperatives depending on each country's stage in its economic development. Countries are described in terms of five development stages: developed countries in Europe that were founders of the cooperative movement (England, Germany, and Italy); three economic power-houses of the developed world (United States, Canada, and Japan); three emerging industrial giants (China, India, and Brazil); two countries making the transition from a planned economy to a market-based economy (Poland and Czechoslovakia); and developing countries in Africa and South America. The

---

[1] The International Cooperative Alliance includes cooperative members from at least one hundred countries and is aware that there cooperatives in many other countries that are not members of the organization.

chapter closes with reflections on the impact of politics and economics on cooperative enterprises.

WHAT ABOUT THE NUMBERS?

There is some hubris in attempting to describe the international cooperative movement, given the difficulty of identifying reliable comparable data on its size and scope. Our most complete data comes from the World Council of Credit Unions, which has collected data from its members annually since its founding in 1972. This data is available because credit unions are subject to government regulation and required to report basic financial information at least annually. The International Co-operative Alliance has data provided by its member cooperatives, but not all nations are members of the ICA. In most countries not all cooperatives are included in the ICA data, and there is tremendous variety in the specific data collected, the methods used to collect the data, the units of measure, and the definition of a cooperative enterprise. The ICA itself has not published a consistent collection of data during the past forty years. Other international organizations[2] collect data on cooperatives and credit unions that is specific to their mission (e.g., food, agriculture, financial services, poverty reduction, labor, gender issues). No one systematically collects data on the size and scope of cooperative business worldwide.

Commitment and capacity to collect national data on cooperative business differ widely among countries. Perhaps the most comprehensive recent national data collection effort was conducted in the United States by the University of Wisconsin-Madison with more than $1.5 million from the U.S Department of Agriculture. That effort collected cross-sectional data on the economic impact of cooperatives at one point in time. It is not clear whether that program will continue.

Within the national data, there is confusion over membership counts. It is often difficult to determine whether countries are counting memberships in specific cooperatives (we suspect that is most likely) or the number of individuals who belong to cooperatives. Since many people belong to more than one cooperative, the latter would be the more accurate measure of the percentage of a country's population that are cooperative members. However, that data is far more difficult to collect. In addition, it is often not clear whether the members being counted are individuals or households.

Difficulties with the data also include what appears to be a limited effort to determine reliability of the available data and the absence of complementary historical and contemporary data that could be used to identify trends. Furthermore, significant discontinuities in data collection exist over time due to civil unrest, natural catastrophes, budget constraints, and lack of interest.

[2] Notably the World Council of Credit Unions (WOCCU), the International Labor Organization (ILO), the Food and Agriculture Organization, and the Committee for the Promotion and Advancement of Cooperatives (COPAC).

Where data on the impact of cooperatives does exist, it is primarily anecdotal and/or limited to specific industries, locations, or issues in order to study specific hypotheses.

Notwithstanding all of these caveats, it is important to be able to give some idea of the vast size and scope of the cooperative movement. In order to provide as broad a picture as possible, we have limited our efforts to providing national data on the number of cooperatives in the country, the number of cooperative members, the economic sectors in which they operate, and, where possible, an indication of the volume of business they conduct. We have collected statistical data from a variety of sources: ICA, WOCCU, ILO, FAO, cooperative apex organizations, and individual countries. Sources for specific data are provided in the text. Although it is clear that cooperatives have significant direct and indirect economic and welfare impacts (in terms of increasing personal income and wealth, providing employment and broad-based access to markets, and increasing community welfare and sustainability), analysis of those impacts is beyond the scope of this chapter.

EUROPE: THE CRADLE OF COOPERATION

Although cooperatives are active in all economic sectors throughout Europe, national cooperative development has varied by country. In England consumer cooperatives are strong; in Germany credit cooperatives dominate. In France, Spain, and Italy manufacturing cooperation is strong, and cooperation in food processing distinguishes Scandinavia. In 2010 there were 160,000 cooperatives in Europe, serving 123 million members and providing 5.4 million jobs.[3]

By the mid nineteenth century, the Industrial Revolution was in full swing in Europe. A new society based on market transactions and mass production lured farmers to cities, moved independent craftspeople to factories, and created new classes of industrial capitalists and workers. In the midst of high levels of production, however, living standards for the working class plummeted such that it was estimated that by the end of the century "between a quarter and a third of the British population was living in poverty."[4] In response to hardships created for the urban working class, a rich cultural and economic debate and practice identified cooperation as an alternative way to do business based on democratic control by user-owners and distribution of profits based on use, not ownership of capital. Successful operating principles developed in England rapidly spread throughout Europe and North America, most commonly in agriculture, consumer goods, and access to credit. As a second Industrial Revolution took shape in the late nineteenth and twentieth centuries, the interest in the cooperative alternative became even stronger.

[3] "Cooperatives in Europe 2010," Cooperatives Europe, accessed May 23, 2011, at www.coopseurope.coop/spip.php?article828.
[4] J. Birchall, *The International Cooperative Movement* (Manchester: Manchester University Press, 1997), p. 3.

Following the Second World War there was significant growth in cooperatives in nearly all of Western Europe for two reasons. First, the entire European economy grew significantly and cooperatives participated in that growth. Second, during the war, fascist governments deliberately destroyed prewar cooperatives which were seen as tools of socialism and communism. In Germany consumer cooperation was wiped out, and forced dissolutions of cooperatives were successful in Italy and other areas of occupied Europe.

To describe trends since 1945, we provide data on countries in the northern, middle, and southern sections of Europe in Table 1.1.[5] The data show that the number of cooperatives, the number of members, and the penetration rate[6] increased for each country between 1945 and 2010. The number of members in every country increased except in the United Kingdom where there was a decrease of nearly one million members. During the same time period, changes in the number of cooperatives varied significantly. The number of cooperatives increased substantially in some nations (Norway, Germany, Austria, Italy, Switzerland, and Spain), was stable in others (France and the United Kingdom), and declined only in Denmark, even though the number of cooperative members there increased by nearly 33 percent.

In almost all the European countries, the traditional segments in which cooperatives were strong (consumer goods, food processing, and credit) experienced decreases in the number of co-ops, primarily to achieve economies of scale, but increases in the number of members and the volume of business. The significant growth in numbers of members presented a governance challenge as a result of a decrease in participation by members. Coupled with the organizational structures required by large corporations, this has spurred a widespread political and economic debate on the decline in distinction between cooperative and capitalist enterprise. In some cases (in Germany, for example), the juxtaposition of large-scale versus democratic participation contributed to the failure of large consumer cooperatives and a contraction of the cooperative movement. Often these highly visible failures led some to consider economic cooperation as a minor residual subject in the advanced economy.

Recent European cooperative experience occurred in two phases, a golden age (1945 to the 1980s) and an age of consolidation (1980s to the present). The cooperatives regained their prewar strength in commercial distribution and food processing, insurance, banking, and the production of goods and services and made important contributions to economic and social recovery from the rubble of the Second World War.[7]

---

[5] The Eastern European cooperative experience is discussed later in this chapter.

[6] The total number of members of all cooperatives divided by the total population.

[7] S. Strasser, C. McGovern, and M. Judt (eds.), *Getting and Spending: European and American Consumer Societies in the Twentieth Century* (Cambridge: Cambridge University Press, 1998); E. Furlough and C. Strikwerda (eds.), *Consumers against Capitalism? Consumer Cooperation in Europe, North America and Japan, 1840–1990* (Lanham, MD: Rowman & Littlefield, 1999).

TABLE 1.1 *Cooperatives and Membership (in Thousands) in European Countries (1945–2010)*

Country	1945–48			1985–88			1994–96			2010		
	# Co-ops	Members	% Population	# Co-ops	Members	% Population	# Co-ops	Members	% Population	# Co-ops	Members	% Population
Norway	1,001	239	7.70	950	1,415	33.8	4,259	1,597	36.4	5,348	2,040	44.1
Denmark	7,799	1,385	33.8	na	na	na	1,445	1,797	34.2	523	1,840	33.6
UK	1,100	9,745	19.8	3,638	9,322	16.5	10,656	9,652	16.6	977	8,434	13.6
Germany*	284	500		10,185	14,018	22.8	10,320	22,322	27.9	7,415	20,509	25.1
Switz.	893	516	11.6	na	na	na	1,651	3,657	50.1	1,416	3,426	43.6
Austria	30	130	1.90	na	na	na	1,485	3,839	47.9	2,339	4,866	58.23
Italy	17,624	3,824	8.40	na	na	na	38,194	7,624	13.3	41,552	13,063	21.6
Spain**	14,984	2,600	8.50	25,868	3,864	10.0	23,481	4,336	11.1	24,276	6,960	14.8
France	19,170	4,079	10.2	25,008	13,175	23.29	23,673	17,486	30.1	21,000	23,000	35.1
Russia	28,000	32,000	16.5	6,817	60,100	21.2	4,538	11,600	7.8	3,163	4,407	3.1
Poland	11,075	3,198	13.4	16,260	14,964	39.3	19,186	6,092	15.9	8,823	8,000	21.0
Czech.	10,659	3,074	23.5	2,518	4,876	31.3	2,185	1,381	13.4	1,395	898	8.6

* Western Germany, except 1996 and 2010.
** Numbers in the 1945–48 column are for 1972.
Sources: R. Rhodes, *The International Co-operative Alliance in War and Peace, 1910–1950* (Geneva: International Co-operative Alliance, 1995); J. Shaffer, *Historical Dictionary of the Cooperative Movement* (Lanham, MD: Scarecrow Press, 1999); *European Cooperatives Key Statistics 2010*.

However, as economies and opportunities grew in the 1970s and 1980s, cooperatives experienced increased competition from investor-owned firms. By the 1980s cooperatives involved broad sectors of citizens and workers through consumer networks, utilities, and housing cooperatives, which included large numbers of members. Labor and support cooperatives of small entrepreneurs (e.g., in credit and food processing), though small in number of members, could boast very high economic power in terms of turnover.[8]

Since 1980, the European cooperative movement has been distinguished by two trends. First, some large, important cooperatives – especially consumer cooperatives – went bankrupt. Although some spectacular failures gave the idea of a widespread crisis in the cooperative movement, and in some countries there was a significant drop in businesses and members between the mid-1990s and 2010, the results were actually mixed. Other factors contributed to positive trends during the period. Second, many organizations pursued a policy of consolidation, with mergers and integrations of various kinds accompanied by step-by-step development.[9] The number of cooperatives fell during the period, but both the number of members and annual turnover increased. Currently, with a population of 731 million, there are 160,000 cooperative businesses in Europe owned by 123 million members that create jobs for 5.4 million citizens.[10] In some countries (e.g., Norway, Switzerland, and Austria) the cooperative movement involves nearly one out of two citizens, while in other countries (e.g., Italy, France, Denmark, and Germany) one out of three or one out of four is a cooperative member. From a historical perspective, the countries of Southern Europe appear to be those in which cooperation registered a more positive path during the period in question, with substantial and constant increases in terms of businesses and especially members. The Mitteleuropa area demonstrates quite a similar trend, with the exception of the German and Swiss drop in recent times. It appears cooperation has not progressed much in Northern Europe, both because in certain cases it had started from a position of relative strength, and because it has had a rather faltering performance during the second half of the twentieth century. The experience of cooperatives in England, Germany, and Italy illustrate the significant differences in postwar European cooperative experience.

England

The entire world looks to England as the cradle of modern cooperation. It was there that a number of communal societies developed in the early nineteenth

---

[8] W. P. Watkins, *The International Co-operative Alliance, 1895–1970* (London: International Co-operative Alliance, 1970); S. Yeo (ed.), *New Views of Co-operation* (London: Routledge, 1988); F. Just (ed.), *Cooperatives and Farmers' Unions in Western Europe: Collaboration and Tensions* (Esbjerg: South Jutland University Press, 1990).

[9] J. Roure i Gavines, *Cooperative Structure in the European Economic Community* (Barcelona: Fundacio Roca Galès, 1987).

[10] European Cooperatives Key Statistics 2010 Report.

century and there that a group of flannel weavers developed a system of principles and practices that ensured stability and growth of the Rochdale Society of Equitable Pioneers. Although many cooperatives had operated prior to the founding of the Rochdale Society, most failed for lack of effective, efficient, and democratic operating principles. As a result, the modern cooperative movement normally dates its inception to December 1844, the founding date of the Rochdale cooperative.

The English cooperative movement was dominated by its Co-operative Wholesale Society (CWS), a procurement consortium owned by individual consumer cooperatives, with interests in food, consumer goods, banking, insurance, and production. From its beginning in the mid-1800s until 1914, consumer cooperation experienced extraordinary growth, which continued through the two wars, but at rates below those of its principal private competitors.[11] Although there were English agricultural co-ops and strong growth in the housing sector, consumer cooperatives continued to dominate the movement.[12] In 1945 consumer cooperatives involved more than eight million members in small, single-store operations usually located in rural areas and large-scale, primarily urban operations with hundreds of thousands of members. In both cases, in addition to the sales of commercial goods,[13] the cooperatives were committed to the well-being of their communities and engaged in various social and recreational activities.[14]

The postwar economic boom and growth of the consumer society created a crisis. From their beginnings, the cooperatives had focused on a rather Spartan lifestyle. They carried basic necessities at cheap prices, mainly destined for mass consumption. The products were practical, but lacked the style of abundance and modernity that postwar consumers wanted.[15] More modern retailers were creating the "spectacle of merchandise" with innovative presentations, original

[11] N. Barou (ed.), *The Co-operative Movement in Labour Britain* (London: Victor Gollancz, 1948); P. Gurney, *Co-operative Culture and the Politics of Consumption in England, 1870–1930* (Manchester: Manchester University Press, 1996); L. Black and N. Robertson (eds.), *Consumerism and the Co-operative Movement in Modern British History: Taking Stock* (Manchester: Manchester University Press, 2009).

[12] D. Clapham and K. Kintrea, *Housing Cooperatives in Britain: Achievements and Prospects* (Harlow: Longman, 1992); L. Black, "Which? Crafts in Post-war Britain: The Consumers Association and the Politics of Affluence," *Albion*, 36 (2004): 52–82.

[13] To have a *driving* role in terms of lifestyles and consumer models, the English cooperative movement developed a political arm, the Cooperative Party, in 1919. The party has often elected its representatives to Parliament. See T. Carbery, *Consumers in Politics: A History and General Review of the Co-operative Party* (Manchester: Manchester University Press, 1969).

[14] D. Flanagan, *A Centenary Story of the Co-operative Union of Great Britain and Ireland* (Manchester: Co-operative Union, 1969); J. Turnbull and J. Southern, *More than Just a Shop: A History of the Co-op in Lancashire* (Lancashire: Lancashire County Books, 1995); N. Robertson, *The Co-operative Movement and Communities in Britain, 1914–1960: Minding Their Own Business* (Farnham: Ashgate, 2010).

[15] W. Richardson, *The CWS in War and Peace, 1938–1976* (Manchester: Co-operative Wholesale Society, 1977); J. Benson, *The Rise of Consumer Society in Britain, 1880–1980* (London: Longman, 1984).

packaging, and glorification of the frivolous.[16] As a result, the inability or unwillingness to adapt to radically different postwar market demands led to a serious crisis in English consumer cooperation.[17] Between the 1960s and the 1980s, the movement experienced large declines in membership and turnover, while private competitors gained market share.[18] Nearly disastrously, British consumer cooperation was considered residual and anachronistic.

The prophesied disappearance of consumer co-ops did not, however, occur. As a result of strategic redirection, British consumer cooperatives have experienced a significant recovery. During the 1990s, the sales and marketing network was reorganized to adjust structures to changing consumer demand and competitive pressures.[19] In 2001 CWS merged with banking, insurance, and many other cooperatives to form the Co-operative Group, which now boasts nearly six million members, more than 5,000 retail outlets, and annual turnover of £13.7 bn.[20] In addition to and in concert with the consumer cooperatives' historic concern for community, health, and well-being, the Co-operative Group recently announced a major new "ethical operating plan that it hopes will set a benchmark for corporate responsibility on carbon reduction, fair trade and community involvement."[21] The plan is clearly in line with consumer cooperative sentiment about social and environmental issues and has met with great success in its first months of operation. At the same time, English cooperation was growing in another sector, where there had been little previous interest. About one hundred credit unions were founded with the help of the World Council of Credit Unions (WOCCU) and the economic support of American credit unions. With this exception, English cooperation remains centered primarily on consumption.

During the last sixty years the movement has had anything but a linear path, from growth to contraction with decreasing adequacy in meeting members' needs to regrowth following a relaunch that emphasized ethical choices, cooperative values, and modern merchandizing.

---

[16] B. Lancaster, *The Department Store: A Social History* (London: Leicester University Press, 2000).

[17] J. K. Walton, "The Post-War Decline of the British Retail Co-operative Movement: Nature, Causes and Consequences," in L. Black and J. Robertson (eds.), *Consumerism and the Co-operative Movement in Modern British History: Taking Stock* (Manchester: Manchester University Press, 2009), pp. 13–31.

[18] M. Hilton, *Consumerism in Twentieth-Century Britain: The Search for a Historical Movement* (Cambridge: Cambridge University Press, 2003).

[19] S. Yeo, *A Chapter in the Making of a Successful Co-operative Business: The Co-operative Wholesale Society 1973–2001* (Manchester: Zeebra Publishing, 2002).

[20] The Group operates businesses in fourteen sectors, the largest of which is food. They include retail food sales, travel, funeral care, legal services, financial services, and many others. Source: The Co-operative Group, 2011. *About Us.* Accessed June 3, 2011, at www.co-operative.coop/corporate/aboutus/

[21] T. Bawden, February 18, 2011, *Co-operative Group Commits to Ambitious Ethical Operating Plan*, accessed June 3, 2011, at www.guardian.co.uk/business/2011/feb/18/cooperative-group-ethical-operating-plan

Germany

As in England, the German cooperative experience is long and has had tremendous influence throughout the world. The first rural credit and savings associations (that provided the foundation for the worldwide credit union movement) were founded by Friedrich Wilhelm Raiffeisen in 1864 and were extended to urban areas by Hermann Schulze-Delitzsch. Heavily influenced by principles developed by Raiffeisen and Schulze, the German cooperative law has served as a model throughout the middle and Eastern European countries.[22] Today more than 20 million Germans (one out of four) are members of 7,415 cooperatives. The 41-fold increase in members since 1945 and the 26-fold increase in number of cooperatives masks an 8 percent decrease in the number of members and a 28 percent decrease in the number of cooperatives since 1994 (Table 1.1). Today's German cooperatives operate in five major sectors (banking; agriculture; buying, marketing, and other services for small businesses; consumer goods; and housing). More than 85 percent of cooperative members belong to cooperative banks.[23]

The German cooperative movement was profoundly altered by Nazism and World War II. Operated democratically, the cooperatives supported anti-Nazi political groups and directly competed with small shopkeepers (one of the principal groups that supported Hitler). In retaliation, they were completely destroyed by the Nazi regime. In agriculture and in credit, also strong areas of cooperation, the movement did not suffer political attacks but did suffer serious destitution as a result of the war.[24] Recovery from the war required complete reconstruction of German society and its economy. In addition, the country was divided and remained so for more than forty years.

Following the war, Germans revived and rebuilt their cooperatives, networks, and market strategies, with the decisive help of the Allied Occupation troops, who wanted to facilitate the rebirth of cooperation in the commercial distribution sector. By 1960, consumer cooperatives had regained a strong position in the large German distribution sector, with 2.6 million members.[25] Today, cooperative banking accounts for the most German cooperative memberships, while members of consumer cooperatives have fallen to 500,000.[26]

---

[22] "The German Cooperatives in Europe," DRGV, accessed June 4, 2011, www.dgrv.de/en/services/internationalrelations/publicationsinternational.html

[23] Ibid., p. 4. Membership statistic includes membership in both urban and rural cooperative banks.

[24] K. Ditt, "Le Cooperative nel Terzo Reich," in M. Degl'Innocenti (ed.), *Le imprese cooperative in Europa* (Pisa: Nistri-Lischi, 1986), pp. 282–307; P. Kramper, "Il Movimento Cooperativo Tedesco nel Periodo fra le Due Guerre," *Rivista Della Cooperazione*, 2 (2009), pp. 104–20.

[25] D. Dowe, "Le Unioni di Cooperative Commerciali, Agrarie e di Consumo in Germania nel XIX e XX Secolo," in M. Degl'Innocenti (ed.), *Il movimento cooperativo nella storia d'Europa* (Milano: Franco Angeli, 1988), pp. 275–6; K. Novy, "Cultura ed Edilizia Popolare e Cooperativa," in M. Degl'Innocenti (ed.), ibid., pp. 287–97.

[26] "The German Cooperatives in Europe."

Much has been written on why German consumer cooperatives suffered a long series of failures. They chose to represent cooperatives as an alternative movement to capitalism and closely linked them to the labor movement. As was also true in the 1960s and 1970s era in U.S. food cooperatives, rejection of capitalism often entailed rejection of business practices that were critical to survival in a market economy. In Germany the movement was not able to promote an entrepreneurial spirit and good financial management. Also, as in England, the cooperative movement did not respond to the consumer revolution of 1960–80. As a result, the co-ops found it difficult to compete against the large private groups, whose products were more modern, more convenient, better stocked, and more competitively priced.[27]

At the same time, however, other German cooperative sectors, particularly banking, continued to be important, with substantial growth in numbers of members and total assets since 1945. This growth was accompanied by a process of consolidation, with cooperative mergers creating a smaller number of businesses of larger and larger dimensions. The growth in credit cooperation was marked by the cooperatives' ability to penetrate the (previously) East German market where the existing banking system was not able to effectively meet the pent-up demand for financial services after reintegration. Thus, the German cooperative movement remains influential in many sectors despite the resounding failure of consumer cooperatives.

Italy

The Italian cooperative movement is more complex than that of England or Germany in that it involves several political parties and idealistic ambitions, many product sectors, and strong and efficient networks of cooperatives. Although there are numerous cooperatives throughout the country, the cooperative movement is strongest in the more prosperous and industrialized northern Italian provinces.[28] Unlike many other countries, as early as 1900,[29] the Italian cooperative movement was developing along three major political and religious

---

[27] B. Fairbairn, "The Rise and Fall of Consumer Cooperation in Germany," in E. Furlough and C. Strickwerda (eds.), *Consumers against Capitalism? Consumer Cooperation in Europe, North America and Japan, 1840–1990* (Lanham, MD: Rowman & Littlefield, 1999).

[28] M. Fornasari and V. Zamagni, *Il Movimento Cooperativo in Italia (1854–1992): Un Profilo Storico Economico* (Firenze: Vallecchi, 1997); P. Cafaro, *La Solidarietà Efficiente. Storia e Prospettive del Credito Cooperativo in Italia, 1883–2000* (Roma: Laterza, 2002); V. Zamagni, P. Battilani, and A. Casali, *La Cooperazione di Consumo in Italia. Centocinquant'anni della Coop Consumatori: dal Primo Spaccio a Leader della Moderna Distribuzione* (Bologna: Il Mulino, 2004); V. Zamagni, "Italy's Cooperatives from Marginality to Success," in S. Rajagopalan (ed.), *Cooperatives in the XXI Century: The Road Ahead* (Punjagutta: Icfai University Press, 2007), pp. 155–79.

[29] J. Shaffer, *Historical Dictionary of the Cooperative Movement* (Lanham, MD: Scarecrow Press, 1999), p. 270.

lines: communist/socialist; Catholic social; and liberal-democratic (or Red, White, and Green, respectively).

Fascism and World War II had a negative effect on cooperation in Italy, but less so than in Germany. "The Fascists co-opted what they could of the cooperative movement, abolished or exiled whatever they could not and restructured all to serve their political ends."[30] This was most heavily felt among laborers' cooperatives. The cooperative movement as a whole also contracted in numbers of cooperatives and members as it had in Germany during the war.[31]

The Red, White, and Green cooperatives survived the war and continue to this day, admittedly with fewer distinctive characteristics and with a strong rethinking of some characteristic ideologies. Postwar growth has been the greatest in the Emilia-Romagna (Red) and Trentino-Alto Adige (White) regions where local communities were more responsive to a collective approach to enterprise and local political parties played an important role in cooperative education and organization.[32] In addition, the movement has diversified beyond the traditional food processing, consumer, building, and credit sectors into manufacturing (e.g., cleaning, maintenance, company cafeterias, and surveillance) and social services or social cooperatives (education, health, welfare, and work integration of the disadvantaged).[33]

While the Italian economy grew at staggering rates from 1950 on, cooperation did not make much progress for the next two decades. The movement lacked the necessary human and financial capital to expand and, as in other European cases, the organizations were hard pressed to revise their political nature and think more about the market and less about their social mission.[34]

From the 1970s to 2010, however, Italian cooperatives were able to expand their social base, to build some large businesses that stand out in the Italian economy, to build new networks, and to expand their interest in new product sectors.[35] In fact, the creativity, mutual support, and strength of the many cooperative networks in Italy are some of the unique features of Italian cooperative enterprise. Italian cooperation was able to emphasize its entrepreneurial

[30] Ibid.
[31] T. Menzani, *Il Movimento Cooperativo fra le DueGguerre: Il Caso Italiano nel Contesto Europeo* (Roma: Carocci, 2009).
[32] T. Menzani, *La Cooperazione in Emilia-Romagna: Dalla Resistenza alla Svolta degli Anni Settanta* (Bologna: Il Mulino, 2007); A. Ianes, *La Cooperazione Trentina dalSsecondo Dopoguerra alle Soglie del Terzo Millennio: Economia, Mutualismo e Solidarietà in una Società in ProfondaTtrasformazione* (Trento: Edizioni 31, 2003).
[33] C. Borzaga and A. Ianes, *L'economia della Solidarietà: Storia e Prospettive della Cooperazione Sociale* (Roma: Donzelli, 2006); P. Battilani and G. Bertagnoni (eds.), *CNS: Cooperation Network Service Innovation in Outsourcing* (Lancaster: Carnegie Publishing, 2010), pp. 118–76.
[34] G. Sapelli (ed.), *Il Movimento Cooperativo in Italia. Storia e Problemi* (Torino: Einaudi, 1981); M. Granata, *Impresa Cooperativa e Politica: La DupliceNatura del Conflitto* (Milano: Bruno Mondadori, 2005).
[35] V. Zamagni and E. Felice, *Oltre il Secolo: Le Trasformazioni del Sistema Cooperativo Legacoop alla Fine del Secondo Millennio* (Bologna: Il Mulino, 2006); T. Menzani and V. Zamagni, "Cooperative Networks in the Italian Economy," *Enterprise and Society*, 11 (2010), pp. 98–127.

nature, freeing itself from the trade unions and the parties with which it had been too closely tied. In 2011 the movement was distinguished by the presence of large cooperatives, with thousands of members or employees, who worked on a national or international basis and demonstrated unquestionable organizational skills and an excellent level of effectiveness.

It cannot be denied that, during this time, help came from Italian legislation, which created various obstacles to demutualization and promoted the idea that owners of the cooperatives are not only the members of today but also those of tomorrow. Demutualization, which is one of the largest and most dangerous enemies of cooperation in the world, has had a very marginal role in Italy. On the contrary, the large size and federation into groups of many cooperatives have raised the importance of governance and hybridization in the twenty-first-century Italian cooperative movement.[36]

INSPIRED BY EUROPE, INNOVATIVE BY NECESSITY: COOPERATIVES IN THE INDUSTRIAL GIANTS

Faced with the specter of large-scale, multinational investor-owned firms, one might wonder whether cooperatives have a role to play or can be sustainable in a highly industrialized economy. The following section on the cooperative experience in the United States, Canada, and Japan highlights the remarkable story of cooperative business that not only survived, but actually thrived within these economic behemoths. The story is not one of unqualified success. There have been many cooperative failures in all three countries during the last fifty years. However, the rate of failure of cooperatives is far less than that of their investor-owned competitors.

United States and Canada

Steeped in a long tradition of informal cooperative effort needed to settle the vast frontiers of the New World, farmers and workers in the emerging industrial economies of the United States and Canada quickly learned from the Northern European cooperative models. By the opening of the twentieth century, both countries had farm marketing and supply, consumer, retailer-owned, housing, utility, insurance, credit, and service cooperatives and national organizations to represent them.[37] For the most part, North American cooperatives were started by groups of people who had a common economic interest and, like their counterparts in Europe, were acting in response to the consequences of the Industrial Revolution. Although most, but not all, of the early American cooperators were farmers rather than the working-class laborers of the early British

[36] P. Battilani, "L'impresa Cooperativa in Italia nella Seconda Metà del Novecento: Istituzione Marginale o Fattore di Modernizzazione Economica," *Imprese e Storia*, 37 (2009), pp. 9–57.
[37] J. Shaffer, *Historical Dictionary*, pp. 173–5 and 395–401; J. Birchall, *The International Cooperative Movement*, pp. 191–220.

cooperatives, they took their inspiration and cooperative principles from the Rochdale Society of Equitable Pioneers. They also modeled their cooperative structures on the hierarchical model of the British "unified" system of local cooperatives, joined together in regional and national federations with significant centralized control. Consistently, however, and much like the experience in Italy, cooperation among North American farmers became "embedded as an aspect of regional culture."[38]

Particularly in western Canada, but also on the United States prairies, farmers started cooperative grocery and clothing stores, insurance companies, health clinics, and funeral societies. Thus the cooperative became not only a business enterprise but also a social association, a duality the cooperatives shared with the European cooperatives. A great deal of the similarity between the North American and European cooperatives can be attributed to the large number of European immigrants to the shores of Canada and the United States who brought their cooperative experience to bear in their new surroundings.[39] With several significant exceptions, political parties and religious groups have not had the same impact on North American cooperatives that they have had in Europe.[40]

Although the early history of cooperatives in both countries has been turbulent with periods of growth, decline, failure, and regrowth, and no political parties have openly embraced cooperatives as a political platform, by the end of World War II both countries had enacted legislation favorable to cooperatives at the state/provincial and federal levels. Birchall attributes this support to "a uniquely American school of thought"[41] that cooperatives provided a necessary countervailing power that ensures competition in the marketplace.[42]

In spite of the large number of consumer co-op failures in the United States during the Great Depression of the 1930s and World War II, by 1945 the number of U.S. and Canadian cooperatives had grown significantly, particularly in agriculture and financial services. During the 1950s, United States agricultural cooperatives reached their peak in terms of number of cooperatives (more than 10,000) and number of members (nearly eight million). After that, rural outmigration, the increasing cost of farming, and the consolidation of small

[38] B. Fairbairn, "Social Bases of Co-operation: Historical Examples and Contemporary Questions," in M. Fulton (ed.), *Cooperative Organizations and Canadian Society: Popular Institutions and the Dilemmas of Change* (Toronto: University of Toronto Press, 1990), p. 72.

[39] Ibid., p. 75, for a detailed description of the immigrant influence on North American cooperatives.

[40] For example, in Quebec, the government has been a strong supporter of cooperatives, as co-ops have been seen as a way to create a strong and independent Francophone economy. In eastern Canada, Father Moses Coady was crucial to the development of cooperatives in Antigonish and the eventual creation of Co-op Atlantic, and African-American churches have long supported cooperative efforts, particularly in the southern United States.

[41] J. Birchall, *The International Cooperative Movement*, p. 191.

[42] R. Torgerson, et al., *Evolution of Cooperative Thought, Theory and Purpose*. Paper presented at the Food and Agricultural Marketing Consortium, Las Vegas, NV, January 16–17, 1997, accessed May 21, 2011, at www.uwcc.wisc.edu/info/torg.html

cooperatives created steady downward pressures on these numbers. Turnover for the agricultural cooperatives has climbed steadily since the 1950s.[43]

During the Depression, it became important to both make credit available to people of modest means and promote thrift. In 1934 President Roosevelt signed the Federal Credit Union Act, designed to accomplish that objective through a national system of *nonprofit, cooperative* credit unions. The act created a national system to charter and supervise federal credit unions and was extremely effective. The war years saw a substantial increase in credit unions (to nearly 9,000 in 1945) and credit union members (more than 2.8 million). That growth continued steadily over the next twenty-five years (to just over 23,000 credit unions with 25.7 million members in 1970).[44]

The same was not true for consumer goods cooperatives in the United States. With a few notable exceptions, small cooperative stores were widely dispersed geographically, were not organized into federations, received no support to speak of from the federal government (as had the agricultural and rural electric cooperatives), did not have access to significant amounts of capital for modernization and expansion, and were unable to complete with the highly capitalized, more modern supermarket chains. Cooperatives were no longer able to provide meaningful economic benefits to their members, and their downward spiral continued well into the 1960s.[45] This did not happen in Canada, where cooperatives belonged to strong unified cooperative systems that were able to garner the capital and buying power needed to compete with supermarket chains.

In 2009, Americans held nearly 351 million memberships in almost 30,000 cooperatives in a wide variety of industries. Because many Americans hold multiple cooperative memberships, it is currently estimated that about 120 million Americans (just over 37% of the population) are members of cooperatives. Although United States cooperatives account for a significant market share in a relatively few industries, they are significant because the country has so many cooperatives and so many cooperative members (see Table 1.2).

United States cooperatives experienced a significant decrease in number between 1970 and 2010, led by decreases in the number of credit unions (68%) and agricultural marketing and supply cooperatives (74%). The experiences of the two industries during this period, however, have been quite different. Although both experienced significant consolidation, credit union membership and assets grew significantly in surviving credit unions, while membership in agricultural cooperatives decreased even though revenue increased.

---

[43] J. Shaffer, *Historical Dictionary.*
[44] "History of Credit Unions," National Credit Union Administration, accessed June 26, 2011, www.ncua.gov/About/History.aspx
[45] M. Rofsky, "Unfinished Business," in Ralph Nader Task Force on European Cooperatives, *Making Change? Learning from Europe's Consumer Cooperatives* (Washington, DC: Center for Study of Responsive Law, 1985), pp. 199–251.

TABLE 1.2 *Cooperatives, Membership, and Revenue by Sector in the United States (1970–2009)*

Sector	1970[a]			1995[b]			2009[c]		
	# Co-ops	# Members (in thousands)	Turnover (in million USD)[d]	# Co-ops	# Members (in thousands)	Turnover (in million USD)[d]	# Co-ops	# Members (in thousands)	Turnover (in million USD)[d]
Credit[e]	23,098	25,697	24,599	11,880	71,382	336,392	7,381	91,991	903,809
Agriculture[f]	9,163	7,203	16,194	5,625	4,783	85,097	2,389	2,200	147,700
Housing	1,160	250	na	6,450	1,018	na	9,471	na	na
Retailing	305	515	514,958	350	324	na	290	487	865
Worker/ production[g]	na	na	na	154	na	na	300	3.5	400
Health	na	na	na	11	1,600	na	305	961	3,290
Insurance	na	na	na	1,800	50,000	na	1,497	232,969	140,038
Utilities[h]	na	na	na	1,290	26,200	na	4,525	19,682	36,399
Social services[i]	na	na	na	650	50	na	1,535	na	na
Fishery[j]	78	9.5	na	70	10.4	na	37	5.4	na

TABLE 1.2 (cont.)

Sector	1970[a]			1995[b]			2009[c]		
	# Co-ops	# Members (in thousands)	Turnover (in million USD)[d]	# Co-ops	# Members (in thousands)	Turnover (in million USD)[d]	# Co-ops	# Members (in thousands)	Turnover (in million USD)[d]
Other[k]	3,335	16,130	na	na	na	na	na	na	na
Total	na	na	na	27,599[l]	150,692[l]	na	29,322[m]	356,272[n]	652,903[m]

[a] Unless otherwise noted by sector, source: *Statistics of Affiliated Organizations: Comparative Statements 1970–1971* (Geneva: International Cooperative Alliance, 1974).

[b] Unless otherwise noted by sector, source: Schaffer, *Historical Dictionary*, p. 400.

[c] Unless otherwise noted by sector, source: University of Wisconsin Center for Cooperatives, "Research on the Economic Impact of Cooperatives," accessed May 14, 2011, from reic.uwcc.wisc.edu/impacts/

[d] For credit unions, total assets.

[e] Credit union data from Credit Union National Association, "United States Credit Union Statistics," accessed May 14, 2011, from www.cuna.org/download/longrun/us_totals.pdf. Year 1: 1972; Year 2: 1996; Year 3: 2009.

[f] Agriculture data: Year 1: 1960; Year 2: 1980; Year 3: 2010.

[g] Worker cooperatives data: Year 1: not available; Year 2: 1980; Year 3: 2010. Source: U.S. Federation of Worker Cooperatives, accessed May 14, 2011, at www.usworker.coop/aboutworkercoops

[h] 1995 figure only includes rural electric cooperatives. 2009 figure includes rural electric, rural telephone, and water. The number of cooperatives is dominated by water (3,350), revenue ($34,275,000), and memberships (16,652,000) by rural electrics.

[i] Includes child care, education, and transportation.

[j] Year 3: 2010. Source: *Annual Farmer, Rancher and Fishery Cooperative Statistics*, Rural Development, U.S. Department of Agriculture, accessed July 3, 2012, at http://www.rurdev.usda.gov/BCP_Coop_DirectoryAndData.html

[k] Other includes: biofuels, purchasing, worker, miscellaneous retail, child care, education, and transportation.

[l] Shaffer, *Historical Dictionary*, p. 439.

[m] Total U.S. cooperative data from University of Wisconsin Center for Cooperatives, "Research on the Economic Impact." Totals do not equal sum of columns because sector-specific data may come from other sources.

[n] Total number of memberships held by Americans.

During the same time period, credit unions have dominated the United States cooperative community in number of societies, number of members, and total assets. In 2008 total credit unions assets were nearly 7 percent of the total assets of banks, and the average credit union size was 6 percent of the average bank size.[46] While total assets of all United States credit unions were less than the net income for commercial banks in each of the last forty years except 2009,[47] credit unions' share of total combined assets held by depository institutions was constant between 1994 and 2004 and has changed little since then.[48]

In both the United States and Canada, agricultural co-ops suffered significant setbacks early in the twenty-first century. These included several large bankruptcies (e.g., Farmland Industries, Agway, Tri-Valley Growers in the United States) and demutualizations (e.g., Calavo and Gold Kist in the United States, and the Saskatchewan Wheat Pool in Canada).

In contrast to other developed countries, the consumer cooperative sector in the United States is small with the exception of the largest consumer cooperative in the country, Recreational Equipment, Inc. (REI), which operates more than 100 retail stores and provides more than 3.5 million members with outdoor gear.[49] The remainder of the sector is concentrated on retail food sales, through stores and informal buying groups. Apparent consistency in the number of retail cooperatives during the past forty years masks significant changes in the sector. Most of the "old-wave" stores founded in the 1930s have gone out of business while many of the stores founded in the early 1970s have grown to significant size. In 2010 retail food cooperatives operated in a niche market that specialized in natural and organic foods and emphasized local sustainability.

The Canadian Cooperatives Secretariat estimated that 40 percent of all Canadians were members of cooperatives in 2007.[50] The number of Canadian cooperative members has increased steadily since 1930 and at nearly three times the growth rate of the Canadian population.[51] As in the United States, the cooperative sector is dominated by credit unions. Housing cooperatives comprise 39.3 percent of the total nonfinancial cooperatives in Canada while agricultural co-ops make up just under 16 percent (see Table 1.3).

Canadian agricultural cooperatives are primarily engaged in marketing and supply. Several of them are very large, multinational organizations with annual

[46] "Frequently Requested U.S./Bank Credit Union Comparisons 2008," Credit Union National Association, accessed May 21, 2011, at www.cuna.org/research/download/freq_compar.pdf
[47] "Net Income FDIC-Insured Banks," Federal Deposit Insurance Corporation, accessed May 21, 2011, at www2.fdic.gov/hsob/hsobRpt.asp
[48] "Size Doesn't Matter in a Credit Union Being a Credit Union," Credit Union National Association, accessed May 21, 2011, at www.ncleague.org/www/upload/CUNA_CU_Size.pdf
[49] "The REI Story," REI, accessed June 8, 2011, at www.rei.com/jobs/story.html
[50] "About Co-ops in Canada," Cooperatives Secretariat, accessed May 22, 2011, at www.coop.gc.ca/COOP/display-afficher.do?id=1232131333489&lang=eng
[51] The number of members increased 8.8 times compared to 3.2 times for the Canadian population. "Cooperatives in Canada," Cooperatives Secretariat, accessed May 22, 2011, at www.coop.gc.ca/COOP/display-afficher.do?id=1295452952292&lang=eng#coo

TABLE 1.3 *Cooperatives, Membership, and Revenue by Sector in Canada (1960–2009)*

Sector	1975[a]			1995[b]			2007[c]		
	# Co-ops	# Members	Assets/Turnover (in millions)[d]	# Co-ops	# Members	Assets/Turnover (in millions)[d]	# Co-ops	# Members	Assets/Turnover (in millions)[d]
Credit[e]	4,214	6,520,437	6,968.8	905	4,105,738	na	877	5,056,373	256,172
Agriculture Marketing	186	1,423,000[f]	3,363.4	162	209,000	11,817.6	379[g]		
Agriculture Purchasing	572	na	1,329.7	247	347,000	20,297.6[h]	218	423,000	5,094.5
Fishery	85	9,000	54.1	56	8,000	164.6	50	7,000	198.2
Production	343[i]	27,000	43.5	461	31,000	778.1	565	39,000	381.7
Services[j]	819	439,000	82.2	3,904	932,000	1,700.9	4,183	918,000	2,072
Consumer	389[k]	na	581.2[l]	582	2,977,000	6,382.3	502	5,212,000	14,000.9
Total	2,391	2,109,000	5,542.0	5412	4,504,000	24,845.7	5,679	6,638,000	30,685

[a] J. M. Sullivan, *Co-operation in Canada 1975* (Ottawa: Information Division, Agriculture Canada, Publication No. 77/5, 1997).
[b] S. Gagné and L. McCagg, *Cooperatives in Canada (1995 Data)* (Ottawa: Co-operatives Secretariat, Government of Canada, July 1997).
[c] Rural and Co-operatives Secretariat, *Co-operatives in Canada* (Ottawa: Government of Canada, April 2010).
[d] Canadian dollars.
[e] Credit union data for 1975 and 1995: World Council of Credit Unions. Data for 2010 "System Results: March, 2011," Credit Union of Canada 11–12), accessed May 14, 2011, from www.cucentral.com/SystemResults4Q10
[f] Includes agricultural purchasing and consumer.
[g] Sum of Supply (218) and Marketing (161).
[h] Includes service revenue and other income; does not include consumer and supplies.
[i] Includes artificial insemination, grazing, fodder, farm machinery, wood-cutting, and other. J. Sullivan, *Co-operation in Canada 1975*, p. 22.
[j] Includes electricity (389 cooperatives), cold storage, cleaning, medical, transportation, water and gas utilities, housing, and other. Ibid., p. 23.
[k] Sum of food and student purchasing cooperatives. Ibid., p. 22.
[l] Sum of food products, clothing, and home furnishings. Ibid., p. 28.

revenues in excess of $1 billion Canadian (La Co-op Fédérée, Agropur, and United Farmers of Alberta Limited). As is the case in the United States, consumer cooperatives are a mix of very large and quite small businesses. Consumer cooperatives sell food products, dry goods, hardware, and petroleum. Petroleum products account for 46 percent of the total sales in this sector, and food 41 percent. Although there are relatively small independent natural food retailers in Canada, most of the sales in the sector flow through two large federations of retail stores, Federated Co-operatives Limited (FCL) and Co-op Atlantic. Of the $14 billion revenue in this sector in 2007, FCL accounted for nearly $6 billion and Co-op Atlantic $5.9 million.[52] While most of the large United States retail food cooperatives are members of a national purchasing cooperative, the National Cooperative Grocers Association (NCGA), none of them belong to a federated system similar to those in Canada.

One area in which the Canadian cooperatives are more like their European counterparts is in the presence of a strong social cooperative sector. Social cooperatives exist to provide social services such as the care of children, elderly, and disabled people, and the integration of unemployed people into the workforce.

Japan

Japan has a long history of informal rural mutual assistance groups that appeared during the Edo Period (1603–1867) among "less economically powerful individuals."[53] Just like Canadians and Americans, the Japanese were quick to understand the potential of the European cooperative model and first applied it in German Raiffeisen-inspired agricultural credit unions.[54] By 1900 many industrial cooperatives had been established voluntarily by landowners and wealthy farmers[55] but "did not develop as expected."[56]

Early in the twentieth century the Japanese government strongly encouraged multipurpose agricultural cooperatives that focused primarily on providing credit, but also provided marketing, purchasing, and management services to farmers. After a major attempt by the government to force farmers to belong to agricultural associations during the Second World War, a 1947 law was passed that supported the creation of autonomous, voluntary, and democratic cooperatives called *nokyos*. However,

---

[52] Ibid.

[53] M. Klinedinst and H. Sato, "The Japanese Cooperative Sector," *Journal of Economic Issues*, 28 (1994), p. 510.

[54] Information on the history of Japanese agricultural cooperatives is based on the Klinedinst and Sato article, ibid.

[55] K. Yamashita, "The Agricultural Cooperatives and Farming Reform in Japan," The Tokyo Foundation, accessed May 24, 2011, at www.tokyofoundation.org/en/articles/2008/the-agricultural-cooperatives-and-farming-reform-in-japan-1

[56] Klinedinst and Sato, "The Japanese Cooperative Sector."

the nokyo system differed from agricultural cooperatives in most parts of the world in that it was established by the government, encompassed all farmers throughout the country, and was comprehensive in its role, taking control of most of the economic activities of Japan's farming communities.[57]

By 1970 more than nine million farmers were members of nearly 9,000 *nokyos* that continued to provide a diversified array of services. Today the JA Group (Japan's nationwide organization of farm cooperatives) provides 9.5 million regular and associate members with credit, insurance, marketing, supply, technical assistance, and lobbying services. It is a powerful political force in Japan with significant interests in maintaining the small-holder, part-time farming system in the country.[58]

The Japanese consumer cooperative movement is one of the largest and the most innovative in the world. Unlike its counterpart in Canada, a significant portion of its volume is generated from small buying groups, *hans*, as well as from large supermarkets. One third of the total households in Japan belong to a consumer cooperative.[59] The first cooperative shops in Japan, based on the Rochdale model, began in Tokyo and Osaka in 1879. Like the Canadian and United States consumer co-ops, they have gone through several periods of growth and decline. But unlike their Western counterparts, the early cooperatives were organized among three groups of members: factory employees, worker groups associated with the radical labor movement, and middle-class citizen groups. Most of these cooperatives were destroyed during the Second World War.[60]

After the war, the Japanese reorganized consumer cooperatives in an innovative way. Instead of organizing around a physical store, small groups of housewives organized into preorder buying groups. Meeting often and discussing various common issues, these groups developed a strong social movement dimension ranging from consumerism and food safety to pacifism. In addition, the *han* groups were able to provide food to the increasing number of people living in suburbs that had not yet developed shopping facilities. Like many of the American buying groups in the 1960s and 1970s, the *han* groups were deeply dependent on a large cadre of nonworking housewives who could participate in frequent small group meetings to order and deliver groceries. The small-group nature of the Japanese cooperatives may be their most distinguishing characteristic. Although in many cases the Japanese consumer cooperatives are far larger than those in the West,[61] they have been able to maintain closer connections to their members, are able to ascertain and respond to their concerns, both

[57] K. Yamashita, "The Agricultural Cooperatives and Farming Reform in Japan."
[58] Ibid.
[59] O. Hasumi, "Consumer Co-ops in Japan: Challenges and Prospects in Transitional Stage," in *Toward Contemporary Co-operative Studies: Perspectives from Japan's Consumer Co-ops* (ed. Consumer Co-operative Institute of Japan, 2010), pp. vii–xix.
[60] A. Kurimoto, pp. 5–7.
[61] The four largest Japanese consumer co-ops each have more than 1 million members. A. Kurimoto, ibid., p. 10.

consumer and social, and have far stronger democratic participation in their governance.[62]

Between 1970 and 1990, the Japanese movement grew from two million to 14 million members and annual turnover increased tenfold.[63] Since 1990, however, many of the unusual traits of Japanese cooperation appear to be in jeopardy. Annual turnover has remained at about 2,500 billion yen. The cooperatives have been buffeted by the increasing number of women entering the workforce (and no longer able to participate in the *han* groups), competition from large and often global retailers, a prolonged recession, and the challenge of integrating the business with the social movement. They have responded by shifting joint buying to individual home delivery, extending their activities in social welfare services (e.g., child care and senior care), intensifying their effort to provide accurate consumer information, and working to develop methods to ensure democratic management (see Table 1.4).

EXTRAORDINARY CASES IN THE NEWLY EMERGING INDUSTRIAL GIANTS: CHINA, INDIA, AND BRAZIL

A discussion of the world's cooperative movement would not be complete without mention of cooperatives in China, India, and Brazil. Between them, China and India alone account for 42 percent of the world's cooperative members. The Chinese movement has a nearly one hundred year history and is large, complex, and fraught with numerous changes tied to the massive social and political transformations in the country since 1900.

China

The International Co-operative Alliance estimates there are 180 million cooperative members in China, second only to India.[64] Nearly 90 percent (160 million) of these are represented by the cooperative societies of the All China Federation of Sales and Marketing Cooperatives (ACFSMC). The vast reach of ACFSMC can be seen in Table 1.5.

The first Chinese cooperatives arose in the 1920s to supply and market agricultural products and provide credit to farmers. Yintang Du describes these as having been mostly experimental and started by local grassroots efforts, by the Kuomingtang government or by the Communist Party.[65] This period of

---

[62] A more extensive comparison of the Japanese and European consumer cooperatives can be found in A. Kurimoto, ibid., pp. 17–25.

[63] A. Kurimoto, ibid., p. 6.

[64] "Statistical Information on the Co-operative Movement," International Cooperative Alliance, accessed June 9, 2011, at www.ica.coop/coop/statistics.html

[65] Y. Du, *Cooperative's Status and Role in Rural Area of China*. Paper presented at the International Conference on Co-operative Alternatives to Capitalist Globalization, South Africa, 2006, accessed June 8, 2011, at www.iccic.org.cn/en-info-show.php?infoid=643. The history in this section comes from Y. Du unless otherwise noted.

TABLE 1.4 *Cooperatives and Membership by Sector in Japan (1970–2009)*

Sector	1970[a] # Co-ops	# Members (in thousands)	1993 # Co-ops	# Members (in thousands)	2009 # Co-ops	# Members (in millions)
Agriculture	8,834	9,033	3,204	8,844	na	9,500[b]
Fisheries	3,056	969	3,894	836	na	na
Retailing[c]	600	7,000	663	16,252	481	18,586
Credit	na	na	na	na	na	na
Worker/ production	na	na	113	6	66[d]	47
Housing	na	na	48	1,077	22	865
Insurance[e]	na	na	55	12,000	222	42,153
Services	na	na	117	1,619	116[f]	2,707
Others[g]	na	na	1,594	16,893	na	2,658[h]
Total	12,490	16,901	9,668	57,527	na	76,516

[a] *Statistics of Affiliated Organizations: Comparative Statements 1970–1971* (Geneva: International Co-operative Alliance, 1974).

[b] Total of 4.83 million regular members and 4.67 million associate members in 2008. *Source:* "JA Group Organization and Business," National Federation of Agricultural Cooperatives, accessed May 22, 2011, at www.zennoh.or.jp/about/english/index.html

[c] "Co-op 2009 Facts and Figures," Japanese Consumer Cooperative Union, accessed May 22, 2011, at http://jccu.coop/eng/public/pdf/ff_2009.pdf

[d] "Members of the Japanese Worker Cooperatives Union," JCWU, accessed May 22, 2011, at http://english.roukyou.gr.jp/profile.html

[e] Sum total of Japan CO-OP Insurance Consumers' Cooperative Federation (JCIF) and the National Federation of Workers and Consumers Insurance Cooperatives (ZENROSAI).

[f] Health care cooperatives.

[g] Includes school teachers, university, institutional, and expanded institutional co-ops.

[h] Calculated by author as a percentage of total retail co-op members.

experimentation lasted until 1949. At that time, most peasants did not own the land they farmed. They were tenant farmers or farm laborers who were farming at a subsistence level. They had no products available for sale. Most Kuomingtang cooperatives were organized to provide credit only to landlords and rich peasants. During this period, the Communist Party organized cooperatives in areas where they were strong. Land was reallocated to peasants who had previously been tenant farmers, and marketing and supply and mutual aid cooperatives were established which could exert some control over the marketing of agricultural products. Although farmers in the Communist areas "greatly welcomed" the cooperatives organized for them, the "broad masses" of farmers in other areas of the country were uninterested in cooperatives because they were not independent producers and agriculture was not commercialized. Thus the cooperatives had little to offer them.

TABLE 1.5 *Characteristics of the All China Federation of Sales and Marketing Cooperatives by the End of 2005* *

Total Assets	$57,548 billion	Market share – cotton purchase	56%
Total Profit of the Year	$815,204 million	Chain stores and business out- lets nationwide	110,000
Large leading enterprises	412	Specialized cooperatives	14,000
Exemplary farm produce bases	1,200	Various trade associations	6,000
Market share – agricultural inputs supply	60%	Market function cooperatives	113,000

* *Source:* "Reform and Development," ACFSMC, accessed June 8, 2011, at www.acfsmc.cn/ Business.asp. Currency converted from yuan as of December 31, 2005, using OANDA currency converter, accessed June 9, 2011, at www.oanda.com/currency/converter/

When the Communists gained power in 1949, they implemented reforms consistent with the successes they had had in the Communist areas during the decades prior to the war. Land was reappropriated to the peasants nationwide and the government created mutual assistance groups and agricultural production cooperatives in which the peasants were essentially forced to "use their land to become shareholding members."[66] This essentially meant the land was pooled. During the same period, Rural Credit and Supply and Marketing Cooperatives were created with the peasants as owners. In this phase, dividends were paid based on each member's "land share." In 1958 this system was discontinued in favor of collective ownership of the land and payments made on the basis of work in the collective. Nearly every farmer was forced to join the land communes in 1958. "The average size of the commune was about 5,000 households, 10,000 laborers and 10,000 acres."[67] The state took over the production, credit, and marketing and supply cooperatives, thereby disbanding mutual ownership of the agricultural cooperatives. In addition, the supply and marketing cooperatives had a monopoly on agricultural products.

As in other communist economies, the cooperatives were no longer member controlled, but were managed by the government in a centrally controlled agricultural production system. Because the state owned and controlled all facets of the system, there was limited accountability and transparency within the cooperatives. Without rewards tied to individual initiative and member control, members "lost enthusiasm for production and management." As a result, both

[66] Y. Du, *Cooperative's Status and Role*, p. 2.
[67] D. Pattison, *Agricultural Cooperatives in Selected Transitional Countries*. Discussion paper, International Cooperative Agricultural Organization, 2000, p. 30, accessed June 12, 2011, at www.acdivoca.org/acdivoca/CoopLib.nsf/dfafe3e324466c3785256d96004f15a8/1b491e21a30 094c385256efa00635250/$FILE/Agricultural%20Coops%20Transitions.pdf

efficiency and profits fell and it became clear that production had not increased under the "cooperative" system. No inroads had been made in the country's widespread rural poverty. A severe famine and production crisis forced the government to seriously consider new policies toward agriculture and the rest of the economy.

Accepting the failure of the commune system, the government began shifting the agricultural sector to a more market-oriented system in 1978. The communes were dissolved, individual households were allowed to lease land on a long-term basis (they still could not own it), and farmers were paid based on the value of their individual output. Because of the long-term leases, farmers were more willing to invest in the farm and in technological improvements. This system had a tremendous impact and agricultural production increased by one hundred million tons within six years.[68] Once the "household responsibility system" was instituted, agricultural monopolies were disbanded, and individual farmers had to learn to function in more open input and product markets. They had a need for technical market information and for a vehicle to pool their efforts to secure inputs and sell product. From 1980 through the mid-1990s, farmers themselves organized rural producers "organizations" that met these needs. Starting in the mid-1990s Chinese farmers started feeling the impact of globalization and organized farmer professional cooperatives (FPCs) that could conduct economic functions similar to those of traditional Western agricultural cooperatives. They offer more opportunity for member control, members are expected to invest in them and receive voting rights, and the government promotes them, but does not manage them. A major milestone was achieved when a law was passed to grant FPCs legal identity so that they could enter into contracts.[69]

In 2003, there were more than 100 thousand producer associations and cooperatives in China.... In June 2010, the number of FPCs was more than 310 thousand, which provided services to about 26 million farm households.... According to the insiders, at least one third of those FPCs only exist on the "paper," another one third does not strongly meet the "cooperative principles," and only the last one third are functioning properly.[70]

India

India's is the largest cooperative movement in the world. The ICA estimates more than 239 million Indians are members of cooperatives, primarily in rural areas. Cooperatives are in all rural villages (100%) and control substantial

[68] Pattison, ibid., p. 31.
[69] T. Sultan, et al., *"Learning by Doing:" Farmers Specialized Cooperative Development in China*. Paper presented at the 5th International European Forum on System Dynamics and Innovation in Food Supply Networks, Insbruck-Igls, Austria, February 2011, pp. 3–4, accessed June 9, 2011, at bscw.ilb.uni-bonn.de/fsdcommunity/bscw.cgi/d205731/Sultan%20et%20al.pdf.
[70] T. Sultan, ibid., p. 1.

shares of many markets. In 2002 they disbursed more than 46 percent of all agricultural credit, produced 59 percent of the country's sugar, owned 65 percent of the village-level agricultural storage facilities, processed and marketed 95 percent of the rubber produced, and manufactured 50 percent of the country's animal feed. That same year cooperatives employed 1.07 million people directly and generated self-employment for another 14.39 million.[71] The largest cooperative sectors in the country are credit and agriculture cooperatives. The credit cooperative system is described here because of its dominance in the Indian movement and because of the similarities that can be seen with other transitional economies (see Table 1.6).

The first Indian cooperatives were Raiffeisen-type credit cooperatives established by law in 1904 and promoted and supported by the British government. The cooperatives were an alternative to unscrupulous money lenders who were the only source of credit available when farmers had to pay taxes in cash, a cause

TABLE 1.6 *Cooperatives and Membership by Sector in India (1970–2010)*

	1970[a]		1995[b]		2010	
Sector	# Co-ops	# Members (in thousands)	# Co-ops	# Members (in thousands)	# Co-ops	# Members (in thousands)
Credit[c]	183,809	43,018	41,500	43,716	100,000	135,000
Agri-food	41,771	7,964	102,935	20,244	na	na
Consumer	14,300	4,387	23,903	11,234	na	na
Worker/ production	60,379	4,521	56,852	4,064,000	na	na
Health	na	na	na	na	na	na
Insurance	na	na	na	na	na	na
Fishery	3,994	438,737	10,763	1,122	na	na
Other	12,278	1,519	139,191	96,608	na	na
Total	319,300	61,338	446,784	182,921	na	239,000

[a]*Statistics of Affiliated Organizations: Comparative Statements 1970–1971* (Geneva: International Co-operative Alliance, 1974).
[b]J. Shaffer, *Historical Dictionary of the Cooperative Movement* (Lanham, MD: Scarecrow Press, 1999), p. 257.
[c]2009 data from H. D. Seibel, "The Rise and Fall of the Credit Cooperative System in India," p. 1, accessed June 9, 2011, at www.hf.uni-koeln.de/data/aef/File/PDF/Cooperatively-owned/India%20-%20The%20rise%20and%20fall%20of%20the%20credit%20coop.%20system,%201904–2007%20%28Seibel%202009%29.pdf.

[71] B. Das, N. K. Palai, and K. Das, *Problems and Prospects of the Cooperative Movement in India under the Globalization Regime.* Paper presented at the XIV International Economic History Congress, Helsinki Finland, 2006, pp. 4–5, accessed June 9, 2011, at www.movimentocooperativo.it/gest/uploads/coop/fileadmin/Das72.pdf.

of much rural poverty.[72] They were managed and governed by members and capitalized by members' equity, retained earnings, deposits, and commercial credit without government interference.[73] From the beginning, however, the government was heavily involved in promoting the growth of the credit union movement and building a unified banking system on the British model of primary credit societies, district cooperative banks, and state cooperative banks.

The cooperative model quickly spread to other industries. In 1912 an act was passed to allow formation of societies in areas other than credit, and by 1942 provincial governments had been given responsibility for cooperative development and the organizations could operate across state boundaries. In 1934 the Reserve Bank of India (RBI) was given responsibility to provide refinance facilities for the cooperative credit system and the agricultural marketing and supply cooperatives. By the end of the war, however, many of the rural cooperatives were deeply in debt, their assets had been frozen, and they were in danger of failing. When the RBI stepped in to renegotiate cooperative loans, it was seen as "the beginning of State interference in the management of cooperatives and the consequent erosion in the credit discipline of the members."[74] Other writers assert that government interference in the cooperatives was endemic from the beginning to the extent that "independence and self-reliance existed only on paper."[75]

By the time independence was granted in 1947, the cooperative movement had become ubiquitous in rural life and had spread to urban areas. The new government embraced cooperatives as an important vehicle for "rapid and equitable" centrally planned economic development, one that was closely tied to the ideals of socialism and democracy.[76] Indeed, one of the goals of the second five-year plan (1956–61) was to become a Socialist Cooperative Commonwealth.[77]

However, in the long run, this was not a good thing for the cooperative credit system. To ensure that the cooperatives were achieving economic development goals, the government became deeply involved in both their management and governance and provided significant equity and loans to the system to get cheap credit into rural areas. Thus began a downward spiral that continued into the 1990s. Autonomy, member control, and self-help were lost, as was the members'

[72] B. Das, ibid.
[73] C. F. Strickland, *An Introduction to Co-operation in India* (London: Oxford University Press, 1922). Quoted by H. D. Seibel, *The Rise and Fall of the Credit Cooperative System in India*, 2011, p. 2, accessed June 9, 2011, at www.mikrofinanzwiki.de/file/564/india_the_rise_and_fall_of_the_credit_coop_system_1904–2007_(seibel2009).pdf .
[74] Unknown, *Draft Final Report of the Task Force on Revival of Cooperative Credit Institutions*, Ministry of Finance, Government of India, 2006, p. 12, accessed June 9, 2011, http://finmin.nic.in/reports/BankingDivision/ReportTFCoopCrIns.asp?pageid=1.
[75] B. Das, *Problems and Prospects of the Cooperative Movement in India*, p. 7.
[76] M. R. Ingle, "Challenges before the Indian Cooperative Movement under the Globalization Era," *International Referred Research Journal*, 2 (2010), pp. 22–3.
[77] J. Shaffer, *Historical Dictionary*.

belief in the self-help nature of the cooperatives. The overall quality of the cooperatives' loan portfolios declined, as did the quality of management and credit cooperative oversight. At the same time, the government was using the cooperatives as a method to distribute subsidies to the rural poor, which tended to make them a "conduit for political patronage."[78]

As in much of the rest of the world, globalization and neo-liberal capitalism brought a new market-based consciousness to India in the 1990s. Although many changes were put in place to encourage private enterprise, attention was not directed to the needs of the rural cooperatives and the rural poor until well into the twenty-first century. However, there are many positive signs that the government is creating a supportive climate for the return of cooperatives to their original democratic, autonomous, self-help roots. New laws are in place that provide for cooperative self-reliance and a refocus on the needs of and control by members in conjunction with a withdrawal of state involvement and financial support. Nevertheless, in 2004 the old laws were still in effect and most cooperatives were continuing to function under them, which resulted in continued deterioration of the credit cooperative societies.

While cooperatives in other areas of the Indian economy were thriving, and urban cooperative banking had improved in terms of profitability, asset quality, and member growth, by 2010 the rural cooperative credit system had continued to decline. Its share of agricultural banking had fallen from a high of 65 percent in 1981–2 to just 25 percent in March of 2009, and only half of the rural credit cooperatives reported profits, most of those coming from the district cooperative banks.[79] It appears that significant effort will be needed to restore the rural cooperative credit system to viability and its original grassroots, member-centered nature.

Brazil

Among the fastest growing economies in the world, Brazil now ranks as the seventh largest.[80] The remarkable expansion of the economy as a whole has extended to that of the Brazilian cooperative economy. Brazilian cooperation has deep roots, at least to the period of colonization and, according to some scholars, as far back as pre-Columbian civilizations. The community of Thereza Cristina, a sort of agricultural *falansterio* in the Paraña region founded by the French doctor Jean Maurice Faibre in 1847, is considered the first cooperative in Brazil.

---

[78] Unknown, *Draft Final Report of the Task Force on Revival of Cooperative Credit Institutions*, p. 15.

[79] B. Yarram Raju, *Re-inventing India: Renaissance of the Rural Cooperative Credit Institutions.* Paper presented at the Skotch Foundation Conference on "Re-inventing India," March 26, 2011, accessed June 9, 2011, at skoch.org/8tw/REINVENTING%20INDIA.pdf.

[80] "Measuring Brazil's Economy: Statistics and Lies: Very Big, but Not the World's Fifth-Largest Economy Quite Yet," *The Economist* (March 10, 2011), accessed July 5, 2011, at www.economist.com/node/18333018.

During the twentieth century, cooperation developed mainly under the impetus of the state, especially in the agricultural and credit sectors. Public administration employees, soldiers, and professionals were the main membership groups.[81] European immigrants familiar with cooperatives fueled the Brazilian cooperative enterprise. Although the main political doctrines of European cooperation, Christianity and Marxism, were brought to Brazil, neither came to dominate the local movement.[82]

Cooperation was encouraged in the Brazilian inland territories, not yet fully colonized and inhabited. The new communities of immigrants who moved from the coast to the Amazonian region were often based on cooperative organizations for management of local resources, some types of consumption, or construction of new housing units.[83] Here, cooperative enterprise found a more fertile environment, rooted in a socioeconomic context that was formed from scratch, without too many barriers to entry.[84]

During the period of military dictatorships from 1964 to 1984, cooperatives represented themselves as free from political and religious ideologies, and organized only to serve members and defend them from all forms of speculation. In 1969, the Organização das Cooperativas Brasileiras (OCB), the Brazilian cooperative umbrella organization, was born with support from the Brazilian government. Creation of the OCB testified to the growing national importance of cooperative enterprise. With the return of democracy in Brazil in the late 1980s, cooperatives could gradually free themselves from the constraints placed on them by the dictatorships.[85]

In 1991 just under three million members belonged to 3,589 Brazilian cooperatives. Significant growth since then originated primarily from new cooperatives, no longer tied to the state and based on North American cooperative models. In 1998, 5,399 cooperatives with 3.7 million members (about 2.3% of Brazil's population) had significant roots in the consumer, utilities, and services sectors, in addition to agriculture and credit. By 2010, Brazilian cooperatives had nearly doubled since 1991 to 6,652, with more than nine million members and 300,000 employees. Since 2000 there has been a robust expansion in social cooperatives and a significant growth in size of individual enterprises. The increase in turnover resulted in a higher critical mass. At the same time, the movement became more competitive globally and thus more powerful. In this

---

[81] D. B. Pinho, *O Cooperativismo no Brasil* (São Paulo: Saraiva, 2004).

[82] D.W. Benecke, "Development of Co-operatives in Latin America," in E. Dulfer (ed.), *International Handbook of Co-operatives Organizations* (Göttingen: Vandenhoeck & Ruprecht, 1994).

[83] M. Ortiz Villacis, *Aspectos del problema agrario latino-americano y la organización cooperativa* (Quito: Ecce, 1968).

[84] A. Garcia, *Las coperativas agrarias en el desarollo de América Latina* (Bogotà: Colatina, 1976); S. Bialoskorski Neto, "Member Participation and Relational Contracts in Agribusiness Co-operatives in Brazil," *International Journal of Co-operative Management*, 3 (2006), pp. 20–6.

[85] S. Bialoskorski Neto, "Co-operative Development: Changes in the Brazilian Social Economy and Institutional Environment," *Review of International Co-operation*, 94, no. 1 (2001), pp. 59–65.

context, Brazilian cooperatives have become more influential in the international cooperative community.

COOPERATIVES IN TRANSITIONAL ECONOMIES: EUROPE

Cooperatives have played a unique role in transitional economies, that is, those that are evolving from central planning to a free market. Characterized by economic liberalization and privatization, economies commonly considered transitional include those of the former Soviet Union, the European Communist bloc, and many countries in the developing world, including those mentioned in the following section on cooperatives and development.

In most cases, cooperatives were one of the principal methods centrally planned economies used to organize work and business. However, membership in these cooperatives was either explicitly or virtually coerced. The state imposed cooperatives on producers; cooperatives were managed to achieve state-determined economic and social goals, often set by government bureaucrats; and the cooperatives frequently had monopoly or near monopoly positions in the market. At the very least the cooperative principles of autonomy, voluntary participation, and democratic control were violated. As a result, cooperation as a business form often fell into bad repute. Even so, during the years of the Cold War, the planned economy cooperatives were recognized by the International Co-operative Alliance, the international apex organization of the world's cooperatives.[86]

As noted in our section on African cooperatives, there was a significant decline in cooperative businesses and cooperative members following the collapse of the Communist regimes and advent of the market. As might be expected, elimination of the coercive cooperative membership brought dissolution of many cooperatives. However, as small producers struggled and often failed to survive as independent actors in a market economy, cooperatives did not.[87] In a second phase, as well, when market failures arose because of market economics, the cooperatives were once again considered an opportunity.

One of the peculiarities of Eastern Europe is the significant drop in cooperative businesses after the collapse of the Communist regimes and the advent of the market. Certainly, enormous cultural damage resulted from characterizing the cooperative as an exclusive entity of communism/socialism. Once the regimes collapsed, much of civilian society was hostile to the very concept of cooperation, not understanding that it could be a highly effective business form in market economies.[88] As a consequence, the numbers of cooperatives and members in Eastern countries in 2010 were often below the levels prior to 1989.[89]

---

[86] A. Balawyder (ed.), *Cooperative Movements in Eastern Europe* (Montclaire: Allanhead, 1980).

[87] Often under other names such as rural group businesses.

[88] L. Nemcova and V. Prucha, "The Co-operative System in Its Historical Perspective," in *XIIth International Economic History Congress* (Praga: Visoka Skola Economica v Praze, 1998, vol. II), pp. 7–40.

[89] A. Balawyder, *Cooperative Movements.*

TABLE 1.7 *Cooperatives and Membership by Sector in Poland (1988–2009)*

	1988		1996		2009	
Sector	# Co-ops	# Members	# Co-ops	# Members	# Co-ops	# Members
Agri-food	6,000	3,840,000	na	na	4,000	400,000
Manufacturing	3,000	600,000	na	na	na	na
Retailing	397	2,957,500	na	na	na	na
Credit	1,663	2,566,100	na	na	62	2,026,000
Other	5,200	5,000,000	na	na	na	na
Total	16,260	14,963,600	13,774	2,584,634	na	na

Sources: J. Shaffer, *Historical Dictionary of the Cooperative Movement* (Lanham, MD: Scarecrow Press, 1999) and *European Cooperatives Key Statistics 2010.*

Poland's case is emblematic. In 1988, there were more than 16,000 cooperatives in the country with approximately 15 million members. Eight years later, there were fewer than 14,000 cooperatives with only 2.5 million members. Exact data are not available for 2009, but in the credit sector there were more than two million members. The data of Russia and Ukraine, even though generally incomplete, confirm that between the middle of the nineties and 2010, the cooperatives had started to increase again, particularly in the banking sector (see Table 1.7).

Czechoslovakia, whose cooperative movement is old, has experienced a series of interruptions and in 2010 had similarities to other transitional economies. Czechoslovakian cooperatives originated with the Association of Foodstuffs and Savings in Prague in 1847.[90] When the Hapsburg Empire dissolved following the First World War, almost 6,000 cooperative businesses were active primarily in commerce, agriculture, credit, and housing. By the dawn of World War II, this number had doubled.[91] Then, as happened elsewhere in Europe, the Nazi occupation devastated the Czechoslovakian economy and the cooperative movement.

The cooperatives were only able to flourish again once the occupation and the war were over. However, the postwar growth was a result of the Communist nationalization of businesses and the promotion of new forms of large cooperatives, especially in the industrial sector.[92] In 1987 there were 2,518 cooperatives with 4,876,000 members in the country. Today cooperatives total just over half that number (1,395) and membership has fallen 82 percent to just 898,000. This is a veritable collapse, which stems not so much from the post-Communist

[90] G. Hauch and K. Stadler, "Le Cooperative di Consumo alle Origini del Movimento Operaio Austriaco," in M. Degl'Innocent (ed.), *Le imprese cooperative in Europa*, pp. 56–64.
[91] G. Hauch, "From Self-Help to Konzern: Consumer Cooperatives in Austria 1840–1990," in Furlough and Strickwerda, *Consumers against Capitalism?*, pp. 191–219.
[92] I. T. Sanders, *Collectivization of Agriculture in Eastern Europe* (Lexington: University of Kentucky Press, 1958); J. Stanislav, *Czechoslovak Producer Cooperatives* (Prague: Central Cooperative Council, 1966).

division of the Czech Republic and Slovakia, but rather from a deep economic and cultural crisis of cooperation itself.

COOPERATIVES IN DEVELOPING COUNTRIES: AFRICA AND LATIN AMERICA

Cooperatives have a long history in the developing countries. Many had cooperatives in place by 1910 (e.g., Kenya, Uganda, Bangladesh, Singapore, Mexico, Guatemala, and Tunisia) and most had them by 1960.[93] Nearly all of the early cooperatives were agricultural in nature and were inspired by cooperative experiences in northern Europe, Canada, and the United States. The cooperative movement in Latin America, although widespread throughout the 42 countries, has not been as strong, consistently prevalent, or as old as in the rest of the world. There are significant differences between the movements of the Caribbean and the Latin American countries, and among the countries themselves. Although comprehensive regional data are not available, the WOCCU reported there were 2,286 credit unions in the thirty-two countries for which they had data with 15.412 million members and $39.798 billion U.S. in assets.[94] In Argentina nearly 25 percent of the population (more than 9.3 million people) belongs to cooperatives, as do one third of Bolivians. The penetration rate, though far lower in other countries in the region, is not insignificant. Usually strong in agriculture and credit throughout the region, cooperatives are also significant in health care and transport in Colombia, worker-owned manufacturing in Argentina, savings in Bolivia, and milk, honey, and wheat production in Uruguay.[95]

As might be expected, because culture, politics, economics, religion, geography, and climate all have an impact on the development of cooperative business, and the developing countries are often quite distinct one from another, we have limited this section to a description of cooperative development in Africa. Reflections on the cooperative experience in Africa can, we trust, provide a useful perspective on factors for success in a globalized economy.

By 1914 nearly the entire African continent had been colonized by Europeans.[96] Driven by a desire to exploit the continent's vast natural resources, colonial powers acquired land, forced native populations into labor, introduced cash crops (even to the neglect of food crops), and disrupted many precolonial inter-African trading patterns.[97] The early cooperatives were organized primarily to benefit white farmers by providing the inputs necessary to increase production, to pool supply, or to export needed agricultural crops to rapidly

---

[93] J. Shaffer, *Historical Dictionary*, pp. 418–25.

[94] "International Credit Union System: Caribbean," World Council of Credit Unions, accessed July 5, 2011, at www.woccu.org/memberserv/intlcusystem.

[95] "Statistical Information on the Co-operative Movement."

[96] Only Ethiopia and Liberia escaped colonial rule.

[97] V. B. Khapoya, *The African Experience* (Upper Saddle River, NJ: Prentice Hall, 1998 [1994]), p. 112.

industrializing northern Europe. Over time indigenous farmers were required to join cooperatives if they wanted to market their crops. However, these cooperatives were developed to meet the economic and social priorities of the authorities, not the priorities of the farmers.[98] In addition, legislation was created that permitted significant government intervention in and control of the affairs of cooperative businesses.

Following World War II and continuing into the mid-1970s, colonial rule ended in Africa, often after long and bitter struggles for independence. Yet the colonial impact on cooperatives continued to be felt. Leaders of the newly independent nations saw great potential for cooperatives to contribute to desperately needed economic development. Because it was thought that cooperatives could be used to "to mobilize local human resources ... and transcend the existing class and/or ethnic divisions," the new governments adopted them as "part of their populist-nationalist strategy for nation building."[99]

Although the growth in cooperatives was quite significant during this period, the co-ops were not autonomous, voluntary, or member-controlled businesses. Governments established cooperative departments that intervened in cooperative affairs, and created near monopolistic privileges for cooperatives. Farmers who wanted to market their products had to join the cooperatives. In other cases farmers were coerced to join the cooperatives, ostensibly so that development could be "speeded up."[100] Eventually the cooperatives decayed into "nepotism, corruption, mismanagement and financial indiscipline" that essentially ended any contribution they might make to social and economic development.[101]

The 1990s brought an end to the Cold War, and the introduction of Structural Adjustment Programs (SAPs) to encourage movement toward more market-based economies. An influential World Bank report found that

> genuine cooperatives were significant contributors to rural development. . . . They provide their members with the advantages of economies of scale, link small- and medium-scale producers to the national economy, provide an element of competition that is often lacking in rural areas, contribute to rural stability and form an effective means of channeling assistance to women.[102]

The impact of these changes was cataclysmic for African cooperatives. As the state moved away from its role of supporting and protecting cooperatives and their markets, new participants entered markets that had previously been near monopolies for the cooperatives. Suddenly African farmers had opportunities to

---

[98] P. Develtere, I. Pollet, and F. Wanyama, *Cooperating Out of Poverty: The Renaissance of the African Cooperative Movement* (Geneva: International Labour Office, 2008), p. 8.

[99] F. Wayama, "The Invisible, but Resilient African Coooperatives: Some Concluding Remarks," in P. Develtere, I. Pollet, and F. Wanyama (eds.), *Cooperating Out of Poverty: The Renaissance of the African Cooperative Movement* (Geneva: International Labour Office, 2008), p. 368.

[100] Ibid.

[101] Ibid., p. 370.

[102] P. Develtere, I. Pollet, and F. Wanyama, *Cooperating Out of Poverty: The Renaissance of the African Cooperative Movement* (Geneva: International Labour Office, 2008), p. 23.

market their products through many channels, not just the cooperatives. At the same time, legislation was introduced to provide for the creation of "true" cooperatives that were autonomous, voluntary, and member-controlled for member benefit.

These factors might be expected to significantly reduce the presence of cooperatives in Sub-Saharan Africa, but that has not been the case. Although the data is incomplete, cooperatives have grown both in number and numbers of members. It is particularly noteworthy that numbers of members have not declined when membership is no longer actually or virtually coerced.

Wayama has noted two significant changes in the nature of the cooperative movement nearly twenty years after liberalization.[103] First, the unified hierarchical structural model of local, district, and regional cooperatives imposed on the cooperatives by the state has lost its relevance and utility for today's cooperatives. Instead they are organizing their own industry-based networks and relationships that serve their needs, rather than the needs of the state. This would be much more in line with the social economy model of the French. And second, cooperatives themselves, now member-controlled, are diversifying their activities to meet the diverse needs of their members. There are numerous examples of very successful Sub-Saharan cooperatives. In addition, there has been a tremendous growth in credit unions and credit and savings societies throughout the continent.

African cooperatives have been tremendously influenced (not always positively) by cooperative development aid from several northern European and North American cooperative movements (often with government backing). During the 1970s and 1980s, most of this aid went to training and assisting in-country cooperative development departments and, by so doing, reinforcing imposed governmental controls that would serve the social and economic development needs of the governments.

As the African nations turned toward market-based economies, cooperative developers found themselves meeting new needs. A 2003 survey of thirty-five international cooperative development agencies found that interest in cooperatives was growing in the early years of the twenty-first century and, more importantly, the focus was on "true" cooperatives that assured autonomy, voluntary membership, and democratic member control.[104] In addition, the international development agencies were "insisting on: participation by multiple actors, ... growth and local entrepreneurship; reducing poverty and social exclusion; and specialization and professionalism."[105] Projects proliferated that offered technical assistance, financial

---

[103] F. Wayama, "The Invisible, but Resilient African Cooooperatives: Some Concluding Remarks," in P. Develtere, I. Pollet, and F. Wanyama (eds.), *Cooperating Out of Poverty: The Renaissance of the African Cooperative Movement* (Geneva: International Labour Office, 2008), p. 387.

[104] I. Pollet and P. Develtere, "Cooperatives and Development: Action Speaks Louder than Words," *IRU Courier, Internationale Raiffeisen Union*, 2004, p. 1, accessed May 24, 2011, at www.caledonia.org.uk/pollet.htm.

[105] Ibid., p. 2.

support, and extensive training in cooperative governance and management. Now, there was a need for a favorable legislative environment that would support the new autonomous market-based cooperatives. For example, the Canadian Development International Desjardin (DID) helped the Central Bank of West African States prepare favorable regulations for credit and savings cooperatives in seven countries.[106] More recently the Overseas Cooperative Development Council, a consortium of eight American cooperative development agencies, instituted a CLARITY Initiative (Cooperative Law and Regulation) to "formulate and promote principles for legal and regulatory environments for cooperatives" in developing countries.[107] Large European and North American consumer cooperatives and investor-owned firms (Legacoop in Italy; the U.K. Co-op Group; SOCODEVI, a Canadian NGO; the Canadian CIDA Industrial Cooperation Program; the Norwegian NORCOOP; and the American NCBA International Programs, among others) also have fostered the developing country market-based cooperatives by supporting and purchasing fair trade and organic products.

CONCLUSIONS

This chapter is perforce only a limited account of the successes, failures, and adaptations of the international cooperative movement, but we hope it offers our readers a general insight into the breadth and depth of the "quiet giant." Although not viable in every country or every industry, the movement has experienced steady growth worldwide in number of members, number of cooperatives, and revenue generated. This record is remarkable given that the world, during this period of time, has recovered from a Great Depression, a world war, a number of "smaller" wars, and the rise and fall of the Soviet Union and the Berlin wall; has experienced several boom-bust cycles; and, most recently, has flirted with a global financial meltdown.

During the second half of the twentieth century, the cooperative movement in the industrialized countries experienced a series of significant transformations. Many cooperatives expanded to become large-scale enterprises with a sufficient number of employees and members to be able to achieve substantial economies of scale. In this context, the failures, bankruptcies, demutualizations, and poor management of some very large cooperative enterprises in the most industrialized contexts suggested that cooperative enterprise had passed its time and was an economic anachronism that was inadequate to challenge the efficiency of very large multinational corporations.[108] On the whole, however, the data show that

---

[106] Ibid., p. 6.

[107] The Cooperative Law and Regulation Initiative, *Enabling Cooperative Development: Principles for Legal Reform* (Washington, DC: Overseas Cooperative Development Council, 2011), accessed June 3, 2011, at www.ocdc.coop/clarity/report/clarity.pdf.

[108] P. Kramper, *Why Cooperatives Fail: Case Studies from Western Europe, Japan, and North America, 1950–2010.*

global cooperation has grown significantly. Interestingly, the very success of cooperatives as large, sophisticated economic competitors has spurred a widespread political and economic debate on the decline in distinction between cooperative and capitalist enterprise.

We have seen that cooperatives have risen out of two major goals: one, to correct the failures of a neo-liberal industrialized market-based economy that had marginalized members of the working class, farmers, and families with limited resources and/or failed to provide needed goods and services (in the developed economies); and the second, to consciously use cooperatives as a tool for social and economic change (in the transition and developing economies). The first goal puts cooperatives in a position of economic and psychological inferiority as an option of last resort when the market has failed. The second makes cooperatives a first-choice option when it is important to create an economy that is able to blend efficiency and productivity with equity and democracy. In that sense, the developed world cooperatives have much to learn from those of the developing world about the cooperative advantage.

The evidence presented here describes a remarkably resilient and flexible business form. Even without the strong support from government for cooperative enterprise (as in Quebec and Italy), people around the world continue to see the advantage of pooling their resources, however meager, to achieve a common economic or social purpose. Just as in the early days of the Industrial Revolution and the ensuing economic and social crises, today the world faces significant challenges that threaten the well-being and, often, survival of the world's population. The economic, social, and political challenges brought about by a globalized economy; great disparities in income and wealth between nations and among national populations; insecurity of the world's food and water supply; global climate change; a limited supply of energy resources; and environmental degradation indicate there is a need to consider alternative models of economic enterprise. Increasingly cooperatives are being seen as an attractive model. Because many co-ops have been locally owned and democratically controlled, they have provided the opportunity for people to develop their own solutions to the problems that face them and to retain the benefits from their activities in their communities.

The story told in this chapter is one of groups of ordinary people – sometimes significantly impoverished – coming together to increase their incomes, pool their resources, address their challenges as a group, and provide themselves with jobs, markets, goods, and services at lower cost or higher quality than was available without the cooperative. In addition, successful cooperatives can and do provide a level of economic security and social cohesion that would not have been attainable without this special kind of business.

Bibliography

Balawyder, A. (ed.). (1980). *Cooperative Movements in Eastern Europe* (Montclaire: Allanhead).

Barou, N. (ed.). (1948). *The Co-operative Movement in Labour Britain* (London: Victor Gollancz).

Battilani, P., and G. Bertagnoni (eds.). (2010). *CNS: Cooperation Network Service Innovation in Outsourcing* (Lancaster: Carnegie Publishing).

Battilani, P. (2009). "L'impresa Cooperativa in Italia nella Seconda Metà del Novecento: Istituzione Marginale o Fattore di Modernizzazione Economica?" *Imprese e Storia*, 37: 9–57.

Benecke, D. W. (1994). "Development of Co-operatives in Latin America," in E. Dulfer (ed.), *International Handbook of Co-operatives Organizations* (Göttingen: Vandenhoeck & Ruprecht).

Benson, J. (1984). *The Rise of Consumer Society in Britain, 1880–1980* (London: Longman).

Bialoskorski, Neto S. (2001). "Co-operative Development: Changes in the Brazilian Social Economy and Institutional Environment," *Review of International Cooperation*, 94(1): 59–65.

Bialoskorski, Neto S. (2006). "Member Participation and Relational Contracts in Agribusiness Co-operatives in Brazil," *International Journal of Co-operative Management*, 3: 20–6.

Birchall, J. (1997). *The International Cooperative Movement* (Manchester: Manchester University Press).

Black, L., and N. Robertson (eds.). (2009). *Consumerism and the Co-operative Movement in Modern British History: Taking Stock* (Manchester: Manchester University Press).

Black, L. (2004). "Which? Crafts in Post-War Britain: The Consumers Association and the Politics of Affluence," *Albion*, 36: 52–82.

Borzaga, C., and A. Ianes. (2006). *L'economia della Solidarietà: Storia e Prospettive della Cooperazione Sociale* (Roma: Donzelli).

Cafaro, P. (2002). *La Solidarietà Efficiente. Storia e Prospettive del Credito Cooperativo in Italia, 1883–2000* (Roma: Laterza).

Carbery, T. (1969). *Consumers in Politics: A History and General Review of the Co-operative Party* (Manchester: Manchester University Press).

Clapham, D., and K. Kintrea. (1992). *Housing Cooperatives in Britain: Achievements and Prospects* (Harlow: Longman).

Das, B., N. K. Palai, and K. Das. (2006). *Problems and Prospects of the Cooperative Movement in India under the Globalization Regime*. Paper presented at the XIV International Economic History Congress, Helsinki, Finland, accessed June 9, 2011, at www.movimentocooperativo.it/gest/uploads/coop/fileadmin/Das72.pdf.

Develtere, P., I. Pollet, and F. Wanyama (eds.). (2008). *Cooperating Out of Poverty: The Renaissance of the African Cooperative Movement*. (Geneva: International Labour Office).

Ditt, K. (1986). "Le Cooperative nel Terzo Reich," in M. Degl'Innocenti (ed.), *Le imprese cooperative in Europa* (Pisa: Nistri-Lischi), pp. 282–307.

Dowe, D. (1988). "Le Unioni di Cooperative Commerciali, Agrarie e di Consumo in Germania nel XIX e XX Secolo," in M. Degl'Innocenti (ed.), *Il movimento cooperativo nella storia d'Europa* (Milano: Franco Angeli).

Du, Y. (2006). *Cooperative's Status and Role in Rural Area of China*. Paper presented at the International Conference on Co-operative Alternatives to Capitalist Globalization, South Africa, accessed June 8, 2011, at www.iccic.org.cn/en-info-show.php?infoid=643.

Fairbairn, B. (1990). "Social Bases of Co-operation: Historical Examples and Contemporary Questions," in M. Fulton (ed.), *Cooperative Organizations and Canadian Society: Popular Institutions and the Dilemmas of Change* (Toronto: University of Toronto Press).

Fairbairn, B. (1999). "The Rise and Fall of Consumer Cooperation in Germany," in E. Furlough and C. Strikwerda (eds.), *Consumers against Capitalism? Consumer Cooperation in Europe, North America and Japan, 1840–1990* (Lanham, MD: Rowman & Littlefield).

Flanagan, D. (1969). *A Centenary Story of the Co-operative Union of Great Britain and Ireland* (Manchester: Co-operative Union).

Fornasari, M., and V. Zamagni. (1997). *Il Movimento Cooperativo in Italia (1854–1992): Un Profilo Storico Economico* (Firenze: Vallecchi).

Furlough, E., and C. Strikwerda (eds.). (1999). *Consumers against Capitalism? Consumer Cooperation in Europe, North America and Japan, 1840–1990* (Lanham, MD: Rowman & Littlefield).

Gagné, S., and L. McCagg. (1997, July). *Co-operatives in Canada (1995 Data)* (Ottawa: Co-operatives Secretariat, Government of Canada).

Garcia, A. (1976). *Las coperativas agrarias en el desarollo de América Latina* (Bogotà: Colatina).

Granata, M. (2005). *Impresa Cooperativa e Politica: La DupliceNatura del Conflitto* (Milano: Bruno Mondadori).

Gurney, P. (1996). *Co-operative Culture and the Politics of Consumption in England, 1870–1930* (Manchester: Manchester University Press).

Hasumi, O. (2010). "Consumer Co-ops in Japan: Challenges and Prospects in Transitional Stage," in The Consumer Co-operative Institute of Japan (ed.), *Toward Contemporary Co-operative Studies: Perspectives from Japan's Consumer Co-ops* (Tokyo: Consumer Co-operative Institute of Japan), pp. vii–xix.

Hauch, G., and K. Stadler. (1986). "Le Cooperative di Consumo alle Origini del Movimento Operaio Austriaco," in M. Degl'Innocenti (ed.), *Le imprese cooperative in Europa* (Pisa: Nistri-Lischi), pp. 56–64.

Hauch, G. (1999). "From Self-Help to Konzern: Consumer Cooperatives in Austria 1840–1990," in E. Furlough and C. Strikwerda (eds.), *Consumers against Capitalism? Consumer Cooperation in Europe, North America and Japan, 1840–1990* (Lanham, MD: Rowman & Littlefield), pp. 191–219.

Hilton, M. (2003). *Consumerism in Twentieth-Century Britain: The Search for a Historical Movement* (Cambridge: Cambridge University Press).

Ianes, A. (2003). *La Cooperazione Trentina dal Secondo Dopoguerra alle Soglie del Terzo Millennio: Economia, Mutualismo e Solidarietà in una Società in Profonda Trasformazione* (Trento: Edizioni 31).

Ingle, M. R. (2010). "Challenges before the Indian Cooperative Movement under the Globalization Era," *International Referred Research Journal*, 2: 22–3.

"International Credit Union System: Caribbean," World Council of Credit Unions, accessed July 5, 2011, at www.woccu.org/memberserv/intlcusystem.

Just, F. (ed.). (1990). *Cooperatives and Farmers' Unions in Western Europe: Collaboration and Tensions* (Esbjerg: South Jutland University Press).

Klinedinst, M., and H. Sato. (1994). "The Japanese Cooperative Sector," *Journal of Economic Issues*, 28: 510.

Kramper, P. (2009). "Il Movimento Cooperativo Tedesco nel Periodo fra le Due Guerre," *Rivista Della Cooperazione*, 2: 104–20.

Kramper, P. (2012). "Why Cooperatives Fail: Case Studies from Western Europe, Japan, and North America, 1950–2010," in P. Battilani and H. Schröter (eds.), *The Cooperative Business Movement, 1950 to the Present* (Cambridge: Cambridge University Press).

Kurimoto, A. (2010). "Evolution and Characteristics of Japanese-Type Consumer Co-ops," in The Consumer Co-operative Institute of Japan (ed.), *Toward Contemporary Co-operative Studies: Perspectives from Japan's Consumer Co-ops* (Tokyo: Consumer Co-operative Institute of Japan), pp. 3–26.

Lancaster, B. (2000). *The Department Store: A Social History* (London: Leicester University Press).

Menzani, T. (2009). *Il Movimento Cooperativo fra le Due Guerre: Il Caso Italiano nel Contesto Europeo* (Roma: Carocci).

Menzani, T. (2007). *La Cooperazione in Emilia-Romagna: Dalla Resistenza alla Svolta degli Anni Settanta* (Bologna: Il Mulino).

Menzani, T., and V. Zamagni. (2010). "Cooperative Networks in the Italian Economy," *Enterprise and Society*, 11: 98–127.

Nemcova, L., and V. Prucha. (1998). "The Co-operative System in Its Historical Perspective," in *XIIth International Economic History Congress* (Praga: Visoka Skola Economica v Praze, vol. II), pp. 7–40.

Novy, K. (1988). "Cultura ed Edilizia Popolare e Cooperativa," in M. Degl'Innocenti, *Il movimento cooperativo nella storia d'Europa* (Milano: Franco Angeli), pp. 287–97.

Ortiz Villacis, M. (1968). *Aspectos del problema agrario latino-americano y la organización cooperativa* (Quito: Ecce).

Pattison, D. (2000). *Agricultural Cooperatives in Selected Transitional Countries.* Discussion paper, International Cooperative Agricultural Organization, accessed June 12, 2011, at www.acdivoca.org/acdivoca/CoopLib.nsf/dfafe3e324466c37852 56d96004f15a8/1b491e21a30094c385256efa00635250/$FILE/Agricultural%20 Coops%20Transitions.pdf.

Pinho, D. B. (2004). *O Cooperativismo no Brasil* (São Paulo: Saraiva).

Pollet, I., and P. Develtere. (2004). "Cooperatives and Development: Action Speaks Louder than Words," *IRU Courier, Internationale Raiffeisen Union*, p. 1, accessed May 24, 2011, at www.caledonia.org.uk/pollet.htm.

Raju, B. Y. (2011, March 26). *Re-inventing India: Renaissance of the Rural Cooperative Credit Institutions.* Paper presented at the Skotch Foundation Conference on " Re-inventing India," accessed June 9, 2011, at http://skoch.org/8tw/REINVENTING% 20INDIA.pdf.

Richardson, W. (1977). *The CWS in War and Peace, 1938–1976* (Manchester: Co-operative Wholesale Society).

Robertson, N. (2010). *The Co-operative Movement and Communities in Britain, 1914–1960: Minding Their Own Business* (Farnham, Ashgate).

Rofsky, M. (1985). "Unfinished Business," in R. Nader Task Force on European Cooperatives, *Making Change? Learning from Europe's Consumer Cooperatives* (Washington, DC: Center for Study of Responsive Law), pp. 199–251.

Roure i Gavines, J. (1987). *Cooperative Structure in the European Economic Community* (Barcelona: Fundacio Roca Galès).

Sanders, I. T. (1958). *Collectivization of Agriculture in Eastern Europe* (Lexington: University of Kentucky Press).

Sapelli, G. (ed.). (1981). *Il Movimento Cooperativo in Italia. Storia e Problemi* (Torino: Einaudi).

Seibel, H. D. (2011). *The Rise and Fall of the Credit Cooperative System in India*, p. 1, accessed June 9, 2011, at www.hf.unikoeln.de/data/aef/File/PDF/Cooperatively owned/India%20%20The%20rise%20and%20fall%20of%20the%20credit%20 coop.%20system,%2019042007%20%28Seibel%202009%29.pdf.

Shaffer, J. (1999). *Historical Dictionary of the Cooperative Movement* (Lanham, MD: Scarecrow Press).

Stanislav, J. (1966). *Czechoslovak Producer Cooperatives* (Prague: Central Cooperative Council).

Strasser, S., C. McGovern, and M. Judt (eds.). (1998). *Getting and Spending: European and American Consumer Societies in the Twentieth Century* (Cambridge: Cambridge University Press).

Strickland, C. F. (1922). *An Introduction to Co-operation in India* (London: Oxford University Press).

Sullivan, J. M. (1997). *Co-operation in Canada 1975* (Ottawa: Information Division, Agriculture Canada, Publication No. 77/5).

Sultan, T., et al. (2011, February). *"Learning by Doing:" Farmers Specialized Cooperative Development in China*. Paper presented at the 5th International European Forum on System Dynamics and Innovation in Food Supply Networks, Insbruck-Igls, Austria, accessed June 9, 2011, at http://bscw.ilb.uni-bonn.de/fsdcommunity/bscw.cgi/d205731/Sultan%20et%20al.pdf.

The Consumer Co-operative Institute of Japan (ed.). (2010). *Toward Contemporary Co-operative Studies: Perspectives from Japan's Consumer Co-ops* (Tokyo: Co-operative Institute of Japan).

Torgerson, R., et al. (1997, January 16–17). *Evolution of Cooperative Thought, Theory and Purpose*. Paper presented at the Food and Agricultural Marketing Consortium, Las Vegas, NV, accessed May 21, 2011, at www.uwcc.wisc.edu/info/torg.html.

Turnbull, J., and J. Southern. (1995). *More than Just a Shop: A History of the Co-op in Lancashire* (Lancashire: Lancashire County Books).

Walton, J. K. (2009). "The Post-War Decline of the British Retail Co-operative Movement: Nature, Causes and Consequences," in L. Black and J. Robertson (eds.), *Consumerism and the Co-operative Movement in Modern British History: Taking Stock* (Manchester: Manchester University Press).

Watkins, W. P. (1970). *The International Co-operative Alliance, 1895–1970* (London: International Co-operative Alliance).

Wayama, F. (2008). "The Invisible, but Resilient African Cooperatives: Some Concluding Remarks," in P. Develtere, I. Pollet, and F. Wanyama (eds.), *Cooperating Out of Poverty: The Renaissance of the African Cooperative Movement* (Geneva: International Labour Office), pp. 366–71.

Yamashita, K. (2011). *The Agricultural Cooperatives and Farming Reform in Japan*. The Tokyo Foundation, accessed May 24, 2011, at http://www.tokyofoundation.org/en/articles/2008/the-agricultural-cooperatives-and-farming-reform-in-japan-1.

Yeo, S. (ed.). (1988). *New Views of Co-operation* (London: Routledge).

Yeo, S. (2002). *A Chapter in the Making of a Successful Co-operative Business: The Co-operative Wholesale Society 1973–2001* (Manchester: Zeebra Publishing).

Zamagni, V. (2007). "Italy's Cooperatives from Marginality to Success," in S. Rajagopalan (ed.), *Cooperatives in the XXI Century: The Road Ahead* (Punjagutta: Icfai University Press), pp. 155–79.

Zamagni, V., and E. Felice. (2006). *Oltre il Secolo: Le Trasformazioni del Sistema Cooperativo Legacoop alla Fine del Secondo Millennio* (Bologna: Il Mulino).

Zamagni, V., P. Battilani, and A. Casali. (2004). *La Cooperazione di Consumo in Italia. Centocinquant'anni della Coop Consumatori: dal Primo Spaccio a Leader della Moderna Distribuzione* (Bologna: Il Mulino).

CHAPTER 2

A World of Variations: Sectors and Forms[1]

Vera Zamagni

> It is impossible in a state of civilization under any system of labour, to secure to every individual the exact product of his individual labour, so it is impracticable to secure even to large numbers the products of their labour, by any other proposed mode of industry than that of mutual cooperation.[2]

To identify in which sectors cooperatives have historically flourished across the world is not a difficult task: agro-industry, retail, trade, and finance (both banking and insurance). In the latter part of the twentieth century, with the large increase all over the world of personal and other services, service co-ops have multiplied, mostly in health, social services, education, catering, facility management, and road transportation. There is one additional field in which there has been a generalized presence of cooperatives in the world over time: social housing. Housing co-ops are a rather peculiar type of co-op, because they generally imply short-term participation by members – the time needed to build a house (with the exception of the few cases in which two or more of the houses remain indivisible assets). Only more recently have such co-ops started including in their activities housing services, which can make membership last longer and be more stable. For lack of space and also of a coherent set of data, however, this chapter will not deal with housing cooperatives.

The fact that all over the world co-ops are rooted in the sectors mentioned, regardless of local culture and level of development, is an empirical testimony to the comparative advantages enjoyed by co-ops in these sectors.[3] The phrase *comparative advantage* is used here with an unorthodox meaning. In general, it can be argued that the economic sectors in which co-ops are predominantly

---

[1] I am grateful to Ann Hoyt for her very useful comments. Any remaining errors are my responsibility.

[2] William Thompson, "Labour Rewarded: The Claims of Labour and Capital Conciliated: Or, How to Secure to Labour the Whole Products of Its Excertions" (1827), in D. Reisman (ed.), *Ricardian Socialism* (London: Pickering & Chatto, 1997).

[3] The most comprehensive overview of the historical development of cooperatives in the world is to be found in J. Shaffer, *Historical Dictionary of the Cooperative Movement* (London: Scarecrow Press, 1999).

rooted are sectors with low profitability, but very high positive externalities, in which the management of the "commons" is crucial. This means that the "comparative advantage" of co-ops in the sectors mentioned is in the strong capability of co-ops to produce goods and services that are highly rewarded by people precisely because they are not produced with the standard capitalist instruments, namely, profit and efficiency maximization, but with instruments aimed at maximizing the collective good of members and of their communities. This is not to say that there are no cooperatives in other sectors; indeed, cooperative enterprises can be found in all types of businesses, and there are interesting country specificities, also due to historic circumstances and chance factors, which will be discussed in this chapter when relevant.

The purpose of this chapter is to offer a historical survey of the four main co-op sectors, discussing the comparative advantage of the cooperative form of enterprise in each sector and the different organizational forms developed. A final section will be devoted to a consideration of the "missing" sector – manufacturing – and will include a few examples of successful industrial cooperatives which suggest that the conditions for success of cooperation in industry have been indeed quite exceptional during the second Industrial Revolution. The conclusions point out that the postindustrial era offers a context more open to cooperative enterprises, because it creates opportunities for co-op growth in many branches of the service sector, including new ones.

COOPERATIVES IN AGRICULTURE AND FOOD PROCESSING

Cooperatives in agro-industry are by far the most numerous in the world, from the most advanced economies (the United States, France, the Scandinavian countries, Canada, Japan) to the developing ones (India, Brazil, Thailand, China,[4] etc.). In 1951, the International Co-operative Alliance (ICA) created a specialized committee (the International Co-operative Agricultural Organization, or ICAO), which holds an annual meeting. A Global 300 survey of the ICA concluded that 110 of the world's 300 largest co-ops were in agriculture, including 23 American and 21 French organizations. Interestingly, when cooperative enterprises started to become better organized by the middle of the nineteenth century, only rural credit banks were developed in the agricultural sector, while cooperatives for land cultivation and, above all, food processing started to spread toward the end of the century. They were following the Scandinavian example:[5] dairy in Denmark; forestry in Sweden and Finland; wine and dairy in Italy and France, and grain and cotton in the United States.

---

[4] China's Township and Village Enterprises (TVEs) are cooperative organizations with common ownership of capital. In 1991 there were 19 million of them, making up two-thirds of the rural output. The problem is that membership is automatic by the part of all the local residents, and therefore these organizations cannot be defined as proper cooperatives.

[5] For a general treatment of country cases, see S. Zamagni and V. Zamagni, *Cooperative Enterprise: Facing the Challenge of Globalization* (Cheltenham: Elgar, 2010).

These co-ops had thousands of followers all over the world and were involved with the most diverse crop cultivation and processing and animal rearing and meat processing.

The reason for success of cooperation in this field is pretty clear: the co-ops were able to increase the market power of farmers. There is a strong interest on the part of producers, generally small and scattered, to avoid being exploited by wholesale buyers and to be able to internalize the benefits of the industrial processing of their produce. The capital needed to start business is not large and can be accumulated as the business grows. Also, much of the machinery needed is not within the reach of each single farmer, but can be shared among many and can be bought collectively. Purchasing of inputs and marketing of the produce are also better done collectively. The tendency of these co-ops to become large is well established, especially if they deal with highly standardized commodities. The important role that these co-ops can play in supporting the income of farmers is so established that governments are often inclined to commit to cooperatives the management of the bulk of their agricultural sectors, as the cases of India and Japan show. If cooperation remains confined only to agriculture proper, however, cooperatives tend to become locked into marginal business because of mechanization, the shrinking of the labor force, and the increased size of farms, while the agri-food industry has better prospects of having a more formidable place in the national economies. Among the many interesting cases that can be illustrated, I have chosen three – the United States, Japan, and India – but it must at least be mentioned that agro-industrial coop-eratives are very strong in Europe too, where in 2008 they accounted for 35,000 co-ops with 12 million members, a turnover of 250 billion euros, and an average market share of as much as 60 percent.[6]

In the United States agricultural cooperatives have been very strong since the nineteenth century, as a result of widespread protests against national/multina-tional corporations and in support of localized development based on the "cooperative commonwealth" of farmers.[7] The main farmer organizations, the National Grange (NG) and the Farmers Alliance (FA), sponsored the foun-dation of cooperatives, mainly in the field of common purchases of inputs and collective marketing, with a modest diversification into the foodstuff industry

---

[6] Cfr. J. F. Juliá Igual and E. Martí Meliá, "Social Economy and the Co-operative Movement in Europe: Contributions to a New Vision of Agriculture and Rural Development in the Europe of the 27," *Ciriec-España*, special issue (2008), n. 62, pp. 147–77; J. Chloupková, *European Co-operative Movement: Background and Common Denominators*, Working paper 24204 of the Royal Veterinary and Agricultural University, Department of Economics and Natural Resources, Copenhagen (2002).

[7] M. Schneiberg, M. King, and T. Smith, "Social Movements and Organizational Form: Co-operative Alternatives to Corporations in the American Insurance, Dairy and Grain Industries," *American Sociological Review*, 73, no. 4 (2008), pp. 635–67 (the quotation is from p. 638). See also J. Curl, "The Co-operative Movement in Century 21," *Affinities: A Journal of Radical Theory, Culture and Action*, 4, no. 1 (2010), pp. 12–29.

and no propensity to develop community services.[8] A century later (1986) there were 5,369 agricultural co-ops in America, with 4.6 million members. Since the 1980s, there has been a strong decline in numbers (in 2005, there were 3,000 with 2.8 million members), but this was mostly due to mergers and acquisitions, a few failures, and the decline of the farm population. The market share remains steady at around one third.[9]

The largest of the American farmer co-ops is CHS (Cenex Harvest States), born out of a merger in 1998 between Cenex (1931) and Harvest States (1929). CHS is a diversified company supplying energy, crop nutrients, grain, livestock feed, food, food ingredients, and financial services. It is owned by farmers, ranchers, and cooperatives; its board consists of seventeen directors who are active farmers with a broad experience in agribusiness. American agriculture is also the birthplace of the so-called NGC (New Generation Cooperative), which is distinct from the traditional cooperatives because of the following features: (1) closed membership; (2) substantial up-front investment; (3) delivery rights and obligations; and (4) tradable shares. The delivery rights/obligations are in direct proportion to the investment made into the co-op. The price of shares to be sold to existing or new members is determined by supply and demand. These changes have been introduced primarily to allow cooperatives to achieve better size and better capitalization for investment purposes; the one-head, one-vote democratic control remains in place.[10]

In Japan, even in the pre–World War II period, agricultural cooperatives conducted various businesses connected with credit and better living conditions in the countryside. In the postwar era, they developed into multipurpose, community-based co-ops and became more democratically run. Besides organizing the vast majority of the agricultural business activities (JA has 70 percent of market share), the JA system also provides for infrastructural development, financial services (including insurance), social services (health, public care, culture, food, and agriculture education), and retail facilities in the countryside.[11] The JA was organized in a three-tier system: basic units at the municipal level, sectoral federations at the prefecture level, and the national level were there is the central union (Central Union of Agricultural Cooperatives, known as JA Zenchu).[12] Until

---

[8] The reason being the private nature of welfare in the United States.

[9] 86 percent milk, 40 percent grains, 43 percent cotton (R. C. Williams, *The Co-operative Movement. Globalization from Below* [Aldershot: Ashgate, 2007] p. 25). The general figures come from NCFC (National Council of Farmer Co-operatives).

[10] For more details, see M. Fulton, "Traditional versus New Generation Co-operatives," in N. Walzer and C. Merrett (eds.), *A Co-operative Approach to Local Economic Development* (Westport, CT: Greenwood, 2000). Group and also the chapter by F. Chaddad and M. L. Cook in this book.

[11] A. R. Rajaratne, "Roles and Effectiveness of Agricultural Co-operatives in Japan, with Special Emphasis on Organized Farm Activities," *Journal of Developments in Sustainable Agriculture*, 2, no. 2 (2007), pp. 192–8.

[12] For a general overview, see A. G. Mulgan, *The Politics of Agriculture in Japan* (London: Routledge, 2000).

the 1990s, JA was very powerful and in close contact with the Japanese Ministry of Agriculture, to enact government policies. JA also was active in supporting Japan's very high level of agricultural protectionism until the recent WTO negotiations. According to Godo's estimates,[13] this institutional setting allowed the income levels of Japanese farmers to be 15 percent above their urban counterparts from the mid-seventies to the mid-nineties. With the financial liberalization of the 1990s, these favorable conditions disappeared, and JA reacted by trying to make the system more efficient. Since 1997, the prefecture level has been eliminated to simplify the chain and the smaller cooperatives have been merged. Because of the liberalization and the diffusion of part-time farmers, however, its power is now declining.

The cooperative organization of Indian agriculture is truly impressive. Cooperation in India goes back to the British rule. The first Cooperative Society Act in 1904 enabled the formation of agricultural credit cooperatives, soon complemented by other types of cooperatives. The movement spread in the countryside, and today India has 230 million members of co-ops that are generally located in the countryside (80 percent), with 14 million employees. The movement is organized in 214 federations under the aegis of the umbrella organization NCUI (National Cooperative Union of India). The village cooperatives provide inputs for farming, storage facilities, marketing of produce and processing of various crops. But they also provide irrigation, electricity, transport and health services, and retail facilities; they are similar to the Japanese multipurpose co-ops. When India embraced central planning, cooperatives became quasi-state organizations, with little autonomy. They are now striving to recover efficiency and democratic stakeholding. They have strong market shares in rural credit (46 percent in 2006) and in the production of sugar, rubber, cotton, milk,[14] and seed oil. Consumer co-ops (with 22 percent market share) and credit unions are the only co-ops having some presence in the Indian urban environment.[15]

COOPERATIVES IN FINANCE: CREDIT UNIONS AND MUTUALS

Another sector in which cooperatives have flourished is finance, both in rural areas and in cities. In the Global 300 largest co-ops, one quarter (80) are financial co-ops, but in the 300 largest co-ops in developing countries, 80 percent

---

[13] Y. Godo, *The Changing Economic Performance and Political Significance of Japan's Agricultural Co-operatives*, Pacific Research Paper 318 (Canberra: Australia-Japan Research Center, August 2001).

[14] In the case of milk, a project was launched by the state in the 1970s – "Operation Flood" – aiming at increased milk production, fair price, and improved incomes. By the end of the project, the system comprised 43,000 village co-ops linking 4.25 million milk producers and several dairy and cattle plants (Williams, cit.).

[15] B. Das, N. K. Palai, and K. Das, "Problems and Prospects of the Co-operative Movement in India Under the Globalization Regime," in S. Rajagopalan (ed.), *Co-operatives in 21st Century: The Road Ahead* (Punjagutta: Icfai University Press, 2007), pp. 95–112.

consist of rural credit organizations. The main comparative advantages are linked to trust and local development. In the credit business, corporate banks are usually not interested in small clients, so all those who do not have substantial collateral to offer and do not need massive loans have a great incentive to come together and offer credit to each other; they thus keep charges as low as possible and internalize the benefits. Precisely because collaterals are not a prerequisite, "relational" banking becomes a necessity, and therefore the size of these credit institutions is generally small in order to keep contact with clients. Such basic cooperative units, however, can form and do form powerful networks, which can offer the asset solidity and the services specialization each single credit union is not able to supply. These networks achieve different levels of centralization and can build up colossal organizations. Cooperative banks, being owned by the same clients who are interested in their "real" activities, have a low propensity to speculate; instead, they keep finance geared to local business, investing in local development and supporting small and medium-sized enterprises (SMEs) and their local clusters. A very similar line of thinking applies to insurance companies. Cooperative insurance companies use the money advanced by their members (often other co-ops) to the benefit of the same members, avoiding intermediaries. In both cases, there is little need of external capital to start business, and assets are accumulated automatically as the numbers of members increase.

It is well known that the earliest models of cooperative credit were born in Germany (rural credit co-ops and popular banks in the cities), and from there spread all around Europe. The United States and Canada also have created their own models of credit unions. In developing countries, beside rural co-op banks, there has been in more recent times a diffusion of nonprofit banking, known as micro-credit (e.g., the Grameen Bank). These banks differ substantially from credit cooperatives in the sense that they offer funds to people who are not yet in a position to practice self-help because of lack of savings. This situation is similar to that of the Medieval pawn banks (Monti di pietà) born in Italy in the fifteenth century and spread throughout the Mediterranean basin, or the savings banks, born in Germany in the eighteenth century and spread throughout Europe and elsewhere. The German banks were nonprofit credit institutions.

The present situation of credit cooperatives in Europe is easily illustrated, because of all the fields in which co-ops are present, credit is by far the best researched one.[16] There were some 4,200 cooperative banks in the European Union in 2008, with 63,000 branches, 774,000 employees, 50 million members (10 percent of the population), 176 million clients, 5,581 billion euros of assets, and an average market share of 20 percent.[17] As time passed, major groups were

---

[16] There is an extremely large body of literature on cooperative banking, both historical and economic.

[17] See V. Boscia, A. Carretta, and P. Schwizer, *Cooperative Banking in Europe: Case Studies* (Basingstoke: Palgrave Macmillan, 2010). Figures come from the European Association of Cooperative Banks (www.eurocoopbanks.coop).

formed outside Germany, in France, in the Netherlands, in Finland, in Austria, in Italy, and in Switzerland. Outside Europe, the diffusion of credit unions in the developed world is also substantial, in the United States as well as in Canada particularly. In America in 2009 there were 7,600 credit unions, spread across all states, with $911 billion in assets and 92 million members (one third of the total population). Their market share can be estimated at around 6–7 percent.[18] In Canada credit unions (including the Caisses populaires) in 2010 numbered 877, with $256 billion of Canadian ($265 billion U.S.) assets (around 20 percent of market share) and 11 million members (35 percent of the total population).[19] In the United States, it is common to become a member of a credit union, most of which are small and focused on granting mortgages and backing credit cards. In Europe members are generally local business people, who support their investments through their co-op banks. Therefore, credit co-ops are vastly more capitalized in Europe and play a very important role in financing SMEs, but the number of their members is not as large as in the United States. The IMF has recently become very interested in cooperative banks, not only because they can be helpful in developing countries, but also because they have shown a high resilience to the recent crisis in developed countries; they are favored as a result of their nonspeculative mission and also the more efficient organization they have developed over time.[20]

Two interesting cases are those of the French *Credit Agricole* and of the Dutch *Rabobank*, to which specific attention is devoted in this chapter. In France today, cooperative banks have around 40 percent of market share and host two major institutions – Credit Agricole and Credit Mutuel – plus two networks, one of popular banks and the other of saving banks (which adopted a cooperative status in 1999). The two networks are stratified: the one of the popular banks has at the bottom 21 cooperative banks, which own a federal bank, incorporated as a public company. In turn, this Federal Bank owns the listed company Natexis, which is used for the international and financial business of the group. The other network of saving banks is organized similarly, but at the third level there is the Caisse des Depôts et Consignations (35 percent), containing a number of other financial institutions which have made the group a very composite one, with tighter relations with the government.

With some modification, the three-tier system applies to Credit Agricole as well. The local banks providing credit to agricultural activities were born in cooperative form in 1894, but during the interwar period and particularly after World War II, state control became more and more obtrusive, while the group expanded its activities outside the agricultural sector. In 1988 during the

---

[18] Figures from www.cuna.org.

[19] Figures come from Credit Union Central of Canada and include affiliated and nonaffiliated banks (www.cucentral.ca). For an account, see I. McPherson, *A Century of Co-operation* (Ottawa: Canadian Cooperative Association, 2009).

[20] See among the works of the IMF on the subject W. Fonteyne, *Co-operative Banks in Europe: Policy Issues*, IMF Working Paper/07/159 (2007).

privatization movement that saw the French State withdrawing from the financial sector, the group was reinstituted in its original cooperative form (with some modifications). At the base, the Credit Agricole group has 2,600 local cooperative banks, with around six million members. These local credit institutions are organized in 41 regional cooperative banks owned by the local credit cooperatives and by agricultural and food cooperatives. They serve 21 million clients. At the top of the system, there is Credit Agricole SA (a joint stock company), which was quoted in the stock exchange in 2001 and is controlled by the 41 regional cooperative banks. It is Credit Agricole SA that has engaged in acquisitions domestically (the most important of which was the Credit Lyonnais) and at the international level, becoming the largest bank in the European Union.[21]

Likewise, in the Dutch case, cooperative banks have a market share of around 40 percent. The pillar is the Rabobank network. Its origin dates back to 1898 when the 46 existing cooperative banks decided to give birth to two separate coordinating institutions, the Coöperatieve Centrale Raiffeisenbank, based in Utrecht and inspired by the German Protestant tradition, and the Boerenleenbank, based in Eindhoven of Catholic inspiration. Both groups increased over time the number of local cooperative banks affiliated, reaching a peak of 1,300 local bank cooperatives. In 1972 the two groups merged, giving rise to the present-day group Coöperatieve Centrale Raiffeisen Bank-Boerenleenbank (Rabobank), with two headquarters. A 1978 law made it mandatory for any new cooperative bank to affiliate with the existing central institution, so that Rabobank is the only cooperative network in the country. The system is basically a two-tier one, with the local cooperatives at the bottom and the Rabobank BA (a joint stock company) on top. There are nine Rabobank regional offices, which carry no banking activity but are there to balance, with their delegates sitting in the Rabobank assembly, the managerial superstructure at the national level. The Rabobank BA includes several other participations and companies.

A common basic approach of these co-op banking networks has developed, starting in Germany in the second half of the nineteenth century: local banks at the bottom, with a large diffusion of branches, coordinated by central institutions, often incorporated not in a cooperative form. The central organizations provide, besides coordination and clearing, specialized services and sometimes become active nationally and internationally in acquisitions of joint stock banks. Some commentators have suggested that the advantages/disadvantages of a looser/tighter organization of these networks should be a matter of more specific attention; they also have questioned the coherence of the mission of these very large groups encompassing numerous companies not incorporated as co-ops. Nevertheless, there is little doubt that in the European countries where cooperative banking is more widespread, the 2008 financial crisis has produced the

---

[21] Boscia and associates, cit.

least damage. The two European nations in which the crisis was worst – Ireland and the U.K. – do not have credit unions.

A brief mention of the widespread presence of cooperation in the insurance industry is also warranted. The information coming from the ICMIF (International Cooperative and Mutual Insurance Federation) Web site[22] reveals that one quarter of the world insurance market was cooperative in 2008, with Germany at 44 percent, France at 39 percent, Japan at 38 percent, and the United States and Canada at 30 percent. Among the twenty largest companies, ten are from the United States, four from Japan, three from France, and one each from Germany, Spain, and the Netherlands. The ICMIF was established (with a different name) already in 1922, and in 2009 it numbered 216 members (representing 600 mutual organizations and many more individual units, some of which are joint stock companies controlled by co-ops) spread in 70 countries, with $1.5 trillion in assets and an employment of around 300,000 people.

RETAILING CO-OP

This sector comprises the very well-known consumer co-ops, but also co-ops among retailers, and even workers co-ops. The literature on consumer co-ops is becoming substantial, beginning with the very famous British case that started with the twenty-eight Rochdale Equitable Pioneers in 1844.[23] The case is notable because of the remarkable early success of the cooperative shops and of the wholesale organization backing them, a success that culminated with the foundation in 1917 of a Co-operative Party. In the case of consumer co-ops, the incentive to form cooperative enterprises came from the desire to minimize retail margins and internalize whatever profit could be made in distributing goods to consumers. Additionally, when consumer co-ops became strong enough, they could also raise the leverage of consumers with reference to producers, suggesting and in some cases imposing with their own brands different standards of production and even different products. In a nutshell, consumer co-ops tend to apply in practice the "consumer sovereignty" of which economists speak in abstract. In the beginning, a consumer co-op does not need much capital, and this is an additional reason for success. But the tendency of the movement to get organized in networks of large enterprises was caused first by the need to build a large wholesale basis, next by the advent of multiples (chain stores in the United States) that could reap economies of scale and scope, and finally by the rise of super and hyper markets.

Today the most important consumer co-ops are large enterprises. Among the 300 world largest co-ops, 80 are retail co-ops (co-ops of retailers included). They are present all over the world, including the United States and Canada, where

[22] www.icmif.org.
[23] A. M. Carr Saunders, Florence P. Sargant, and R. Peers, *Consumers' Cooperation in Great Britain: An examination of the British Cooperative Movement*, 3rd ed. (London: Allen and Unwin, 1942).

consumer co-ops have important retail corporations in the nonfood sectors (e.g., REI in the United States and Mountain People, which sells outdoor gear). In Japan, there is a special kind of consumer co-op that caters to their clients in a very personal manner from orders to home delivery, with additional services often being provided. Precisely for this reason, the managerial capabilities have become vital in the running of consumer co-ops, and when this has not been adequately understood, major bankruptcies have taken place (the worst were suffered in Germany and Austria[24]). The survival of consumer cooperatives has thus been challenged.[25] The British case also has shown evidence of an incapability of preserving its market share over time, mostly as a result of slowness in anticipating new consumption patterns and in opening up to the middle class.[26] The largest British cooperative group, the Co-operative Group (formerly CWS), was in 2009 a large diversified group, with 5.5 million members, 120,000 employees, and a turnover of 18 billion £,[27] not all in retailing, but its market share is down to 6 percent. There are in Europe also some remarkable cases of success, especially in the Scandinavian countries[28] and in Italy, so that in 2010 consumer cooperatives still numbered 3,200, with 29 million members, 36,000 points of sale, 400,000 employees, and 73 billion € of turnover.[29] A more detailed picture of their localization can be found in Table 2.1. The European retail co-ops have formed a common organization – Eurocoop – the chair of which in 2010 was an Italian.

Among the most interesting cases, the Italian Co-op network is of special relevance. The Italian case has been deeply studied[30] and shows extremely interesting features: (1) it has had a city tradition since the very beginning; (2) it has a long and uninterrupted history (150 years); (3) the decision to have a common wholesale (CoopItalia) came timely in the late 1960s, in the years of booming consumption; (4) it underwent a complex process of mergers, but it still counts on a number of autonomous co-ops; (5) it was a "first mover," ready to

---

[24] Other chapters of this book are devoted to the history of these bankruptcies.

[25] E. Furlough and C. Strickwerda (eds.), *Consumers against Capitalism? Consumer Co-operation in Europe, North America and Japan, 1840–1990* (Lanham, MD: Rowman & Littlefield, 1999).

[26] See P. Gurney, *Co-operative Culture and the Politics of Consumption in England, 1870–1930* (Manchester: Manchester University Press, 1996), and P. Gurney, "Co-operation, Mass Consumerism and 'Modernity' in Interwar Britain," *Rivista della cooperazione* (2009), n. 2, pp. 13–38. For a comparison between the British and Norwegian models in the post – World War II period, see the excellent doctoral dissertation by E. Ekberg, *Consumer Co-operatives and the Transformation of Modern Food Retailing: A Comparative Study of Norwegian and British Consumer Co-operatives 1950–2002* (Oslo: University of Oslo, 2008).

[27] Figures from www.co-operative.org.

[28] These countries had tried in 2002 to merge their business into Coop Norden, but the initiative has not proved successful. A more limited version of the initiative is now envisaged, which would entail the merging only of the wholesale level.

[29] Figures from www.eurocoop.org.

[30] V. Zamagni, P. Battilani, A. Casali, *La cooperazione di consumo in Italia. Centocinquant'anni della Coop consumatori: Dal primo spaccio a leader della moderna distribuzione* (Bologna: Il Mulino, 2004).

TABLE 2.1 *Consumer Cooperatives in Europe in 2009*

Country	Cooperative Societies	Consumer Members (× 1.000)	Employees	Outlets	Turnover € (× 1,000,000)
Bulgaria	825	160	11,038	7,000	128.3
Cyprus	1	3	283	26	2.7
Czech Republic	57	241	14,893	2,924	1,028.4
Denmark	355	1,697	18,863	1,193	5,624.6
Estonia	19	82	4,201	366	368.1
Finland	32	1,888	37,764	1,598	11,687
Germany	na	na	na	na	na
Hungary	103	50	32,000	5,000	1,819.2
Italy	120	7,200	57,100	1,440	12,744
Netherlands	1	700	3,713	186	780
Norway	130	1,230	22,000	1,200	4,326.4
Portugal	na	na	na	na	na
Romania	907	27	8,942	6,523	97
Slovakia	32	198	14,193	2,305	1,197
Spain	128	2,853	59,578	3,097	10,282.5
Sweden	47	3,195	14,803	863	3,944.4
United Kingdom[*]	26	9,547	114,561	3,000	18,293
TOTAL	2,783	29,098	413,932	36,721	72,373

Source: www.eurocoop.org
[*] *Note:* It includes the British Co-operative group, which encompasses more activities besides retailing.

introduce supermarkets and hypermarkets in an Italian context that privileged small independent shops; and (6) it enjoyed an important additional source of funds through the "members' loans."[31] The co-op system in Italy is clearly the leader in the grocery market, with a share of a little less than 20 percent; its wholesale company also supplies other chains and has exceeded one quarter of the market.

As mentioned previously, cooperation in retailing goes beyond consumer co-ops. There are in fact two other forms of cooperation active in the field: cooperation among retailers and workers' cooperation. The first has given rise to important companies that are considered co-ops under all accounts, like the Italian Conad, born in 1963, which in 2010 had reached 12 percent of the Italian

---

[31] An Italian law of the 1970s allowed consumer co-ops to collect members' savings up to a ceiling, like a deposit bank; deposits were to be used in the co-ops' investment projects.

grocery market. Some of these companies[32] in 2006 created the first European law co-op.[33] Coopernic, with about 10 percent of the EU grocery market, encompasses 19,000 stores in 22 countries and is very active, among other things, in acquiring chains in the Baltic countries (Latvia and Lithuania).

Two interesting examples of retail chains that are actually workers co-ops or partnerships are the Spanish Eroski and the British John Lewis Partnership. Eroski was founded in 1969 in the Basque countries as part of the Mondragon cooperative project; it subsequently spread in other regions of Spain, reaching in 2009 8.4 billion euros of turnover and 50,600 employees. The John Lewis Partnership, technically not a co-op but substantially in line with co-op values, was organized by John Spedan Lewis who, having inherited a shop founded by his father in an initial form in 1928, entrusted the business entirely to his employees in the present form in 1948. In 2010, the partnership was active mostly in nonfood retailing, with a turnover of 8.2 billion £ and 76,500 partners.[34]

NEW DEVELOPMENTS IN SERVICES

As is well known, services are made up of a hodgepodge of activities with very different production requirements. This chapter has already dealt with two services – retailing and finance – where cooperation is strong, but not all services can be easily put into a cooperative form. There will never be the opportunity to build a railroad co-op, and civil service cannot by definition be run by cooperatives. But many other services can very well be produced by co-ops, especially personal services (health, social services, and education).

The comparative advantage of co-ops in services outside of finance and retailing is based primarily on intrinsic motivations.[35] The fact that most services postulate a direct contact of the producer with the clients – an interpersonal relationship[36] – makes the personal involvement of the producer much more essential to the good result of the process. Having "intrinsic motivations," sometimes a true passion, for what the service worker does is the best

---

[32] The Belgian Colruyt (a family-owned company quoted on the stock exchange, third largest in Belgium), the Swiss Coop (consumer co-op, second largest in Switzerland), the French Leclerc (a retailers co-op, second largest in France), the Italian Conad (co-operative of retailers, second largest group in Italy), and the German Rewe (retailers co-op, second largest in Germany).

[33] The EU produced in 2003 a special legislation providing the possibility to incorporate a European co-op.

[34] Figures from www.johnlewis.com. It must be said that there are other cases in which capitalist companies have been turned into cooperatives by their founders' ideals. The other famous case in retailing is the Swiss consumer co-op Migros, founded in 1925 by Gottlieb Duttweiler and transformed into a cooperative in 1941. Today it is the largest employer in Switzerland (80,000 employees) and has 16 percent of the grocery market.

[35] L. Becchetti, S. Castriota, and E. Tortia (2009), *Productivity, Wages and Intrinsic Motivation in Social Enterprises* (Milan: Econometica Working Paper No. 16).

[36] B. Gui and R. Sugden (eds.) (2005), *Economic and Social Interaction: Accounting for Interpersonal Relations* (Cambridge: Cambridge University Press).

prerequisite to having a satisfactory relationship with clients. Co-op members, who choose to be in a service co-op voluntarily and work in a company run by them, are in the best position to develop their talents and express their "benevolence" toward their colleagues and clients, ready to tailor their services to their real needs. Service co-ops normally are not large, precisely because of the need of customization; they rely more than other types of co-ops on networks.[37] The physical capital needed is often very modest, while human capital is extremely important.

The presence of co-ops in personal services is widespread in the world, but not yet well documented. The pioneering role was played by Italy, where in 1963 the first "social cooperative" was founded, which provided training, education, assistance, recreation, and work for disadvantaged, young, and elderly people, and for members but also for nonmembers (thus advocating an extended concept of mutual cooperation, "external" mutualism). The social cooperative is basically a workers' cooperative, but the presence in the assembly of members who are recipients and not producers of the services makes the classical form of such a cooperative a multistakeholder form, in which even representatives from the local community often have a seat in the board of directors, side by side with producers and recipients of the services. Italy has passed a special law to regulate the social cooperatives (381 in 1991). It was estimated that in 2010, as much as 50 percent of the social services produced in Italy were by the social co-ops. This model[38] has been widely emulated in France, Spain, Portugal, and Greece, but it exists elsewhere in other forms (community co-ops in the Anglo-Saxon countries and multipurpose co-ops in Japan and elsewhere). In the Italian case, the system is a four-tier one, with single, smallish, highly diversified co-ops at the bottom, coordinated by a second tier of local consortia, themselves joining in a national consortium which provides the most qualified services. On top of the national consortia, there are the sectoral associations of the national umbrella organizations, mostly providing political representation.

Services are highly diversified, and there is a presence of co-ops in other branches as well: transportation (taxis, lorries, buses), catering, facility management, logistics, theaters, and management of cultural resorts. The literature on these co-op activities is to this author's knowledge almost nonexistent. The exception is provided by Italy, where the Bologna research group on cooperatives has done a lot to unveil this co-op presence. Bologna hosts a large catering co-op, Camst,[39] which is number one in Italy, and a large facility management cooperative group (Manutencoop), which is one of the most important Italian

---

[37] See T. Menzani and V. Zamagni, "Co-operative Networks in the Italian Economy," *Enterprise and Society*, XI, no.1 (2010), pp. 98–127.

[38] The best comprehensive book on the Italian social cooperatives is C. Borzaga and A. Ianes, *L'economia della solidarietà. Storia e prospettive della cooperazione sociale* (Rome: Donzelli, 2006). For a comprehensive assessment in English, see ch. 5 in J. Restakis, *Humanizing the Economy: Co-operatives in the Age of Capital* (Gabriola Island, Canada: New Society Publishers, 2010).

[39] See V. Zamagni (ed.), *Camst: ristorazione e socialità* (Bologna: Il Mulino, 2002).

companies in the field. It also hosts a large consortium of service co-ops[40] that aim to offer clients complete sets of services produced by different co-ops and coordinated by the consortium.

THE "MISSING" SECTOR: INDUSTRY

Industrial workers co-ops[41] are the ones mostly envisaged by the nineteenth-century thinkers (Mill, Marshall, Gide, Walras) as the typical co-op form, but in fact in capitalist societies they are the exception rather than the rule.[42] Among the 300 largest world co-ops, only 19 are not active in the three sectors listed previously, and 14 of them are in the production and distribution of electricity. These are substantial and interesting co-ops, but they are consumer co-ops, present almost exclusively in the United States,[43] where almost 1,000 electricity co-ops control 40 percent of the entire nation's electricity distribution lines, covering three quarters of American territory and serving 37 million members[44] (they also own their production plants). They came into being in the 1930s, as part of the effort by the Rural Electrification Administration (REA) to promote diffusion of electricity in rural areas, but they have since developed into highly organized corporations.

Five remaining co-ops are listed in the Global 300: two are in the construction industry, and one is mixed; there are only two co-ops, one Spanish and one Italian, in manufacturing. See Table 2.2 for the listing.

Certainly there are many more industrial co-ops of smaller size; for instance, France still has an important group of artisanal co-ops (327), but their total turnover, according to the figures published by the GNC (Groupement National de la cooperation) is only one percent of the total turnover of the French cooperative enterprises.[45] There are compelling reasons to explain why industry

---

[40] P. Battilani, G. Bertagnoni, and S. Vignini, *Un'impresa di cooperatori, artigiani, camionisti. La CTA e il trasporto merci in Italia* (Bologna: Il Mulino, 2008), and P. Battilani and G. Bertagnoni (eds.), *Competizione e valorizzazione del lavoro. La rete cooperativa del Consorzio nazionale servizi* (Bologna: Il Mulino, 2007). There is a summary English version of this research: P. Battilani and G. Bertagnoni (eds.), *Co-operation Network Service: Innovation in Outsourcing* (Lancaster: Carnegie, 2010).

[41] Many agricultural co-ops and services co-ops are workers' co-ops, because members are the ones who produce the output, but in the tradition of the cooperative literature, the meaning attached to workers' co-ops is that of industrial co-ops.

[42] In some of the former communist states, particularly Yugoslavia, propaganda wanted industrial corporations to be self-managed, but in reality they were controlled by the state. This is also the reason why people in such countries are disfavoring co-op enterprises, because they identify them with state interference.

[43] Of the 14 co-ops in the production and distribution of electricity, only one is Brazilian.

[44] One of the two 2009 Nobel Prize winners for economics, Elinor Ostrom, has studied precisely the theme of how to govern "commons." See E. Ostrom, *Governing the Commons: The Evolution of Institutions for Collective Action* (Cambridge: Cambridge University Press, 1990), and E. Ostrom, *Understanding Institutional Diversity* (Princeton: Princeton University Press, 2005).

[45] See F. Bataille-Chedotel and F. Huntzinger, "Faces of Governance of Production Cooperatives: An Exploratory Study of Ten French Cooperatives," *Annals of Public and Cooperative Economics*, 75 (2004), pp. 69–111.

TABLE 2.2 *Five Industrial Co-ops Listed in the Global 300*

9	Mondragon (Basque Countries, Spain)	manufacturing
164	Sacmi (Imola, Italy)	manufacturing
209	CCC (Bologna, Italy)	construction
227	CCPL (Reggio Emilia, Italy)	mixed
261	CMC (Ravenna, Italy)	construction

has produced fewer co-ops than all other sectors. The standardization of products and Fordist processes of mass production, the huge physical capital needed, and the necessity to achieve large economies of scale all make it difficult for cooperative organizations in industry. Workers at the assembly line have to perform menial jobs, in which there is very little opportunity to exercise personal talents. The huge corporations needed by the economies of scale can only be governed through tough hierarchies, and there is certainly no scope for "democratic" management. In the industrial corporations, therefore, what predominates is capital, and managers are seen as instruments to serve capital – hence, *capitalism* is a truly expressive word.

The capitalistic production system breeds individualism: those who advance capital are generally interested only in dividends,[46] and not in the "common good" of the people working in the corporation; the investors attend only to finance. To produce the highest possible profits for the shareholders, managers squeeze workers, who organize themselves in trade unions to oppose exploitation, giving rise to the "class" struggles well known in the history of capitalist development. The only alternative to that state of affairs seemed to be to dispossess the capitalists and build a state that would control capital on behalf of workers, but this proved not to be viable over the long run. Meanwhile, in the capitalist world, the industrial corporations, unchallenged by any alternative form of conducting business, increasingly became like commodities to be bought and sold to increase profits, though often only over the short run, with even less attention to workers than in the nineteenth century; the use of finance became more and more aggressive, losing touch with its time-honored role of serving production, again with the aim of maximizing profits. The situation became so unbearable that the movement known as CSR (Corporate Social Responsibility) developed to moderate the excesses of this approach, though without transforming its roots.

There was no place for co-ops in such an environment. It was precisely in the period of diffusion of mass production and mass distribution, across the twentieth century, that economists lost interest in the cooperative form of enterprise,

---

[46] With notable exceptions of "social" entrepreneurs like Ernest Solvay, Alessandro Rossi, the Marzotto family, and many others, who distributed some of their profits in favor of their workers and of the local community, although it was done in a paternalistic way.

which was seen as a residual of agrarian societies and at best surviving in niche sectors or in marginal sections of finance and retailing, where it had an established tradition and could remain present "by inertia" carrying on a petty activity. What was entirely lost was the basic inspiration of cooperation, namely, the natural propensity by many people to work with others "cooperatively" rather than "adversarially" and the natural aspiration by people to have decent work in which they do not feel oppressed and exploited. These seemed, however, at best utopian wishes, swept away by the crude reality of capitalism, and economics became the "dismal science." Co-ops disappeared from theoretical elaboration, with a few exceptions, not least because their sustainability was studied with assumptions taken from capitalist firms.[47]

The five large co-ops mentioned earlier are a clear demonstration that it is not impossible to have co-ops in the industrial sector, but some very special conditions have to hold. The Mondragon model is the most well-known and covered in the literature for its very exceptional features: the entire place is cooperativized. Everything started in 1941, when in face of the closing down of the Mondragon Steel Works, the 26-year-old parish priest José Maria Arizmendarrieta persuaded the local workers to buy the mill and run it as a cooperative. To help fund this and other cooperative enterprises, the priest conceived the idea of creating a popular bank (the Caja Laboral Popular, 1959). Next, for the training of the workers, the Mondragon School of Technology was set up (later turned into a co-operative university), while the initial cooperative branched out in many other related fields and, in 1969, the supermarket chain Eroski was established. Every economic activity in the place was exercised in a co-op form, so that we can speak of a "cooperative community," much along the lines imagined by the early nineteenth-century British utopians. An inner crisis of the system in the 1970s necessitated a complete reorganization, first into a tight federated group and in 1991 into a vertical structure known as MCC (Mondragon Co-operative Corporation), with sectoral divisions, which is *an unicum* within the cooperative world.[48] It is one of the largest industrial groups in Spain (the seventh in 2009), employing 85,000 people with a turnover of 33 billion € and 88 percent of the employees as members. It practices wage equality, profits participation, and horizontal work organization; and it could internationalize, although doing so would present some problems.[49] Its exceptionality need not be stressed.

[47] See, for an elaboration of this argument, C. Borzaga, S. Depedri, and E. C. Tortia, *The Role of Cooperative and Social Enterprises: A Multifaceted Approach for an Economic Pluralism*, Euricse Working Paper 000/09 (2009).

[48] R. C. Williams, *The Cooperative Movement: Globalization from Below* (Aldershot: Ashgate, 2007), ch. 6.

[49] Cfr. R. Casadesus-Masanell and T. Khanna, *Globalization and Trust: Theory and Evidence from Cooperatives*, William Davidson Institute Working Paper 592 (2003), and G. MacLeod and D. Reed, in D. Reed and J. J. McMurtry (eds.), *Cooperatives in a Global Economy: The Challenges of Cooperation across Borders* (New Castle upon Tyne: Cambridge Scholars, 2009).

Also quite remarkable are the Italian cases. Italian industrial co-ops are all part of an area (Emilia Romagna) which has a high concentration of autonomous co-ops tightly interconnected in networks. Their substantial but not extremely large size is typical of the Italian "pocket multinationals," which are competitive at the world level without being very large (co-ops are no exception). Sacmi is an engineering co-op founded in 1919 by nine workers in a small town near Bologna, a place where there had been a strong cooperative tradition. Its core business is the production of machinery for the ceramic industry (which is locally quite strong)[50] and other types of machinery (for food, beverages, and plastics). Sacmi has built up in more recent times a strong international group composed by 65 companies (most of which are noncooperatives), with a consolidated turnover of around 1.5 billion € and 3,500 employees. The holding organization, the cooperative Sacmi, had in 2009 few more than 1,000 employees, of which 335 were members.

The CMC was founded in Ravenna in 1901 and has always been the largest construction co-op in Italy. Today it is a highly international company, a general contractor specialized in infrastructures (dams, electricity plants, high-velocity railway lines, water tunnels, etc.) with 700 million € turnover and almost 6,000 workers (500 tenured employees), 377 of which are members of the co-op.[51] Italy has many other substantial construction co-ops, and in the late 1990s they formed a national consortium (CCC, Consorzio Cooperative di Costruzione), which includes today 230 cooperatives with 5 billion € of yearly turnover and 20,000 workers. It is a leader in Italy in its field. Again, this is an exceptional result due to the early organization of construction co-ops in consortia and their capability to be active outside their local area. This allowed them to grow in size and compete with capitalist companies. CCPL is a more diversified group, founded in 1904 and active today; in addition to construction, it is also involved in food packaging and energy and facility management, with a turnover of 725 million euros in 2008 and 1,210 employees.

The conclusion from these examples confirms that only exceptional conditions can allow industrial cooperatives to grow large; otherwise they normally remain small. Within this context, however, an interesting, though limited, movement should be noted—namely, the conversion of capitalist enterprises into enterprises owned by their employees. In the United States, there is a specific instrument with tax benefits known as an ESOP (employee stock ownership plan), which can preside over the creation of employee-owned enterprises. ESOPs are not technically co-ops, but certainly are enterprises owned and managed by their workers. In 2004 there were 11,500 ESOPs covering 8.5

[50] M. Mazzoli and B. Benati (eds.), *Partecipazione, Ricerca, Innovazione. Un'analisi economica del gruppo Sacmi* (Imola: La Mandragora, 2009).
[51] The part of the history of CMC covering the period in which it opened up to international ventures is now reconstructed in V. Zamagni, *Da Ravenna al mondo (1952–1985)* (Bologna: Il Mulino, 2011).

million people and controlling about $500 billion in assets.[52] In Italy, there is the CFI (Cooperazione, Finanza, Impresa), which was created in the 1980s with the aim of rescuing failing enterprises by making their employees members of a newly born cooperative. Today it is supporting more than 50 such enterprises in transition.[53] In Argentina, too, there is a well-known movement of the "empresas recuperadas" (worker-recovered enterprises), which started in the 1980s and numbered around 170 companies by the beginning of the twenty-first century, with some 10,000 workers.[54] This movement to convert capitalist enterprises into enterprises owned by their employees is a phenomenon that governments should watch carefully.

CONCLUSIONS

This chapter has examined in which sectors the cooperative form of enterprise has flourished over time, concluding that three sectors account for a disproportionate share of co-ops: agro-industry, retail trade, and finance (both banking and insurance). In these sectors, the incentive to self-manage firms and their networks is especially high because, on the one hand, producers or users are numerous and they want to retain control over their business and, on the other hand, these firms need to achieve economies of scale and scope necessary to make the business sustainable. A section of the chapter has been devoted to discerning the reasons why industry has yet to be a hospitable sector for co-ops; high capital intensity, standardization of products, and the Fordist labor organization are the major causes. Even in industry, however, there are cases of successful co-ops, when the location is particularly favorable to the building up of networks and to the practice of democratic governance or (as in the case of American electrical co-ops) when capitalists do not consider the business profitable enough to attract their investments.

Finally, a section of the chapter has argued that in the service society in which we are living today, the conditions of production offer to the cooperative business paradigm wide open fields to renew its tradition in entirely different contexts. Health, education, social services, information, culture, catering, and road transportation are all economic activities in which co-ops can do very good work, because they can customize services and practice relational skills. Even in industry today it is easier to produce new co-ops, with a post-mass-production approach, in niche lines in which plants need not be too large and the "immaterial" component of the process of production is strategic.

[52] Figures from www.nceo.org.

[53] See V. Zamagni and E. Felice, *Oltre il secolo* (Bologna: Il Mulino, 2006).

[54] See M. Vieta and A. Ruggeri, "Worker-Recovered Enterprises as Workers' Cooperatives: The Conjunctures, Challenges and Innovations of Self-Management in Argentina and Latin America," in Reed and McMurtry (2009), cit., and H. Palomino, I. Bleynat, S. Garro, and C. Giacomuzzi, "The Universe of Worker Recovered Companies in Argentina (2002–2008): Continuity and Changes Inside the Movement," *Affinities: A Journal of Radical Theory, Culture and Action*, 4, no. 1 (2010), pp. 252–87.

There is reason to believe that in the future, there will be a renewed interest in the cooperative form of enterprise. The comparative advantage of cooperation lies in valuing the dignity and the relational component of people at the center of economic activity.[55] The economic agents who act in a cooperative manner aim to serve the organization's interests, but they also take into consideration the interests of others and the community. They believe that cooperative solutions to economic problems produce a more sustainable economy over the long run,[56] one in which no serious injustices are done, more peaceful societies are secured, and "public happiness"[57] is maximized. After the climax of individualism reached with financial capitalism, people are starting to see the damage an excessive reliance on the *homo oeconomicus* paradigm can do. The campaign for CSR has arisen precisely in connection with the need to bring back into capitalist corporations some attention to stakeholders other than capital owners. It is difficult to insert preoccupations different from the maximization of shareholder value into a corporate structure framed on the basis of *homo oeconomicus*. Cooperative enterprises, instead, are *by definition* corporations practicing accountability to all their stakeholders, because they are based on anthropological and ethical assumptions different from exclusive individual self-interest. They practice reciprocity and pro-social behavior, sometimes registering in their activity higher costs than those of capitalist enterprises,[58] because they deal with their stakeholders in a more equitable manner.[59] But the talents and good will of all the members of co-ops, as well as the ethical demand of many of their clients and some state support, allow co-ops to compete with capitalist enterprises.

History has shown that co-ops are able to adapt to new environments and types of business organization, but solidarity and justice will always be their inner driving force, and this is their appeal as long as there is a demand in society for such values. In the writing of John Stuart Mill, there is a famous passage on cooperation:

---

[55] This has been recognized also in the 2009 encyclical by Pope Benedict XVI *Caritas in Veritate*.

[56] See A. Tencati and L. Zsolnai, *The Collaborative Enterprise: Creating Values for a Sustainable World* (Bern: Peter Lang, 2010).

[57] The concept of "public happiness" (meaning a fair and progressive society) was cultivated by the Italian economists of the eighteenth century as against the "private happiness" (meaning the utility of a self-interested individual) proposed by Bentham. Adam Smith was very ambiguous on this, cultivating in his *Wealth of Nations* more the self-interest element and in *The Theory of Moral Sentiments* more the "benevolence" (fairness) element, without bridging the two sides of human behavior, a goal that he seemed to have had for a third book he never wrote. The "public happiness" approach has been revived by, among others, M. Kaswan, "Happiness, Politics and the Co-operative Principles," *Journal of Cooperative Studies*, XL, no. 1 (2007, April).

[58] As a result of granting proper remuneration to all participants in the production process, but also as a result of less rough work conditions.

[59] The famous founders of the first successful English consumer co-op used precisely the adjective *equitable* in the name of their company: "The Rochdale Society of Equitable Pioneers."

[T]here is no more certain incident of the progressive change taking place in society than the continual growth of the principle and practice of co-operation.[60]

The progress the great British economist had in mind is the moral progress achieved by exercising liberty, self-determination, and democracy in economic activity, a goal that is still a long way from being accomplished but that co-ops help make attainable.

---

[60] J. S. Mill, *Principles of Political Economy*, 1852, Book IV, 1.7.

CHAPTER 3

Cooperative Movements in the Republic of Korea

Hongjoo Jung and Hans Jürgen Rösner

INTRODUCTION

This article aims to explore the historical development of cooperativism in a country with cultural characteristics different from those of the Western world. Very specific but not well-known, the case of Korea has never been thoroughly examined, not even within the country. Therefore, this study had to be based on intensive literature surveys from fragmented sources. It is structured by historical sequence in order to provide deeper insight into some of the essential implications the formation of the Korean cooperative movement has had for the national economic and social development.

In search of the historic roots of cooperativism in the Republic of Korea (commonly referred to as South Korea in some countries), one could go back about a thousand years when endogenous types of ancient mutual aid and self-help were practiced in most rural communities on the peninsula, without being named cooperatives. Second, one could choose 1926 as the year when modern organizational forms of industrial cooperatives were established in Korea (then named Chosun) under Japanese colonial rule as a means to better exploit the natural resources of the protectorate. Finally, the 1960s could be chosen as a historic decade of rapid economic development when capitalism was effectively introduced. The cooperative movements of that time, however, were strictly subjected to dictatorship and military government.

Although the ancient institutions were not named cooperatives, many authentic indigenous roots of cooperativism can be traced back historically to the period of the Later Three Kingdoms (892–936) and, especially, to the period of the Chosun Dynasty (1392–1897) when the local autonomy of rural villages was strengthened by establishing a self-governing system called "Hyangyak," literally meaning "rural promise" or agreement. Inspired by Confucian thinking in Chosun culture, Hyangyak obliges every member of rural society to work toward solidarity and mutual help in reciprocal social relationships. The tradition dates back to eleventh-century China where people had to perform common work, self-help, control, and other forms of interaction in order to promote the material and social welfare of their specific village. In spite of similarities with modern cooperatives in spirit, Hyangyak was less institutionalized and presented more of a code of conduct based on moral principles.[1]

"Bobusang," another form of cooperative behavior, was comparable to the system of commercial guilds in ancient Europe. Initially, the Bobusang were traveling merchants selling fish, beans, iron, oil, fruit, and so forth from over their shoulder or back. They represented the lowest and poorest social class in Chosun and were so deprived of economic means for survival, and so looked down upon not only by aristocrats but also by farmers and handcraft workers, that the only way they could help themselves was by grouping together for mutual assistance. Later, the Bobusang, subjected to stringent bylaws, became a nationwide organization supported by government. Compared with cooperatives, however, this organization was not autonomous and membership was not voluntary.[2]

Among other ancient rural cooperative traditions of small farming communities, the most important were "Pumasi" (exchange of work), where peasants helped each other, especially in times of planting rice seedlings and of harvesting; "Dure" (collective farming), which involved all male villagers aged 16 to 55, who were obliged to common works; and, above all, the principle of "Gye" (social bond).[3] Gye, as the oldest and most popular antecedent of modern cooperative thinking in Korean society, is an organizational principle for mutual work and reciprocal aid that follows specific objectives such as collecting and administering funds which may then be used for financial assistance in case of family catastrophes or celebrations. Events such as funerals, weddings, or special birthday anniversaries (like the 60th [Hwan-gap]) of parents can be rather costly in Korea. In addition to these family-oriented forms of cooperation, there is also the village Gye in which, as an expression of solidarity, rural communities collect agreed-upon contributions or raise funds from common labor (like Dure weaving) to help members jointly install or repair common facilities, such as wells, roads, or bridges.[4] These cooperative traditions are still observable in everyday rural life and on special occasions such as wedding or funeral ceremonies, donations for natural hazard sufferers, or year-end donations. Unlike in Western countries, however, in most cases, cooperative initiatives of significant size normally are not free from governmental influence or even control.

Rooted in these long-lasting traditions of mutual aid and communal solidarity, modern forms of cooperatives also evolved in times of economic hardship, as was the case for European cooperative models in the tradition of the Rochdale

---

[1] See Kim, Jin Kyu, "A Study on Hyang-Yak in the Chosun Dynasty under the Aspects of Establishment and Development," *Jang-An Nonchong*, 29 (2009), p. 346.

[2] See Jo, Young-Ho, *A Study on the Nature and Function of Bobusang in the Late Chosun Dynasty from the Perspectives of Social Welfare.* Master's thesis, Dong Koock University, Graduate School of Social Science, 2003, p. 3.

[3] See Kwak, Hyomoon, *A Study on the Social Welfare Character of Doore in Chosun Dynasty, Jungchaek Nonchong* (Policy Review), 13, no. 1, p. 177.

[4] See Jung, Hongjoo, et al., *Society, Economy and Insurance*, SKKU Center for Insurance Culture Studies, 2011, pp. 27–31.

Pioneers or the Raiffeisen and Schulze-Delitzsch movements, found elsewhere throughout the world. However, while European cooperatives in most cases have been the answer for social and economic challenges from rapid industrialization and early "wild" capitalism, in Korea, they have been much more a reorientation to traditional self-help against poverty brought by Japanese colonial rule in times before capitalism was introduced. Thus, at the beginning of the twentieth century, we find two very different types of cooperatives in Chosun, namely, those artificially set up by the Japanese government to facilitate control and exploitation of Korean agriculture, and others as endogenous grassroots initiatives to survive and resist colonialism. Especially between 1929 and 1932, during the Great Recession, when farmers' poverty reached extreme levels in Chosun,[5] private cooperative initiatives gained popularity. After the colonial era at the end of the Second World War, Korean cooperativism developed in many economic sectors, but differently from the European model and attributable to the Japanese colonial tradition and to thirty years of military regimes since 1961. It was mostly subject to guidance and control from the side of government.

COOPERATIVES IN TIMES OF JAPANESE RULE

Cooperatives Introduced by Japanese Authorities

In 1905, the Japanese forced the Korean Empire (1897–1910), which succeeded the Chosun Dynasty, to sign the Eulsa Treaty, which made Chosun a protectorate, and in February 1906, the Japanese Resident General took outright control and pressed the Korean government to accept Japanese colonial-style policies in order to strengthen supremacy against Russia and gain control of the country. Japan, which had adopted capitalism much earlier than its neighboring countries, considered the formation of governmental cooperatives necessary to fully exploit the agricultural sector and to effectively connect it to the Japanese economy. The so-called Council for Improvement of Korean Administration of the Japanese authorities introduced in a top-down style of official cooperatives under their strict control, namely, the Financial Cooperatives in 1907 and the Industrial Cooperatives in 1926.[6] The former usually are not considered true cooperatives because of their origination and the substantial manner in which they deviated from the "autonomy and independence" as well as "democratic member control" principles. The latter, however, are often considered to be the first cooperatives in Korea that met the

---

[5] Moon, Jung-Chang, *History of Korean Agricultural Organization* (in Korean) (Iljogak Publishing Company, 1961); and Kim, Hyun-Sook, *Research on Private Cooperative Movement in Japanese Colony* (Moonhak and Jisung Publishers, 1987), pp. 208–12.

[6] Lee, Kyung-Ran, *Research on Financial Cooperative in Japanese Ruling* (Hyean Publisher, 2002), pp. 64, 252.

seven principles of modern cooperativism in spite of the serious deficiencies concerning member control.[7]

Financial cooperatives began operation in rural areas in 1907, three years prior to Chosun being completely integrated into the Japanese economy, and were extended to urban areas in 1918. Their initial role was to provide noncollateral loans mostly for farmers with no property or land in order to let them expand their traditional subsistence production and escape dependency on exploitative local moneylenders. This motive, however, was given up when policies changed toward lending money only on a collateral basis to landowner farmers.[8] Although regulation of financial cooperatives initially offered their members some leeway for establishing a general assembly and voting rights, this was soon restricted and finally abolished by the authorities. The cooperatives mainly ran credit businesses, but also performed some production and marketing functions, like common procurement, sales, and utilization.

Following their benchmarking success in mainland Japan,[9] industrial cooperatives in Chosun were reluctantly allowed to be established after 1926. This was when colonial rule was confronted with violent resistance (i.e., the 1919 Movement), increasing socialist activities and deepening poverty in agricultural areas. However, while industrial cooperatives in the home country fulfilled all four central functions, namely, procurement, sales, utilization, and finance, credit business was not allowed in Chosun, notwithstanding its indispensable meaning for sustained growth. Unlike financial cooperatives, which were fully controlled by the Japanese authorities, industrial cooperatives consisted of voluntary Korean members only and appeared to adopt democratic organization principles of modern cooperatives in spite of their being subject to regulatory restrictions concerning the prohibition of a national headquarters, necessity of the governors' permit for the election of senior managers, and the already mentioned business limitations.

Although they started with such unwilling support, the industrial cooperatives expanded rapidly, reaching 115 entities and 221,000 members at their peak in 1940. Meanwhile, the Japanese regime intensively promoted financial cooperatives, which totaled 613 entities and 3.2 million members in 1944. In the terminal stage of Japanese control, financial cooperatives were allowed to expand into production and marketing, thus undermining the economic mainstay of industrial cooperatives which subsequently experienced financial trouble and were finally dissolved or integrated into financial cooperatives prior to the end of the Second World War.[10]

---

[7] Ko, Hyunseok, "In Search of Cooperative's Root in Korea," Korean Cooperative Research Institute, *Korean Cooperative Review* (April 2009), pp. 92–5.

[8] Ibid., p. 71.

[9] Lee, Kyung-Ran, *Research on Financial Cooperative in Japanese Ruling*, pp. 248–9.

[10] Jang, Jong-Ik, *History and Current Status of Korea Cooperative*, Korea Research Institute of the Cooperatives. Unpublished working paper, 1997, pp. 4–5.

INITIATIVES FOR AUTONOMOUS COOPERATIVES

No autonomous and civil cooperatives appeared in Chosun until 1920 when a few consumer cooperatives were established in Kyungsung (now Seoul)[11] and in Mokpo (a southwestern city)[12] by some grassroots pioneers pursuing political independence through economic independence.[13] The Chosun Labor Mutual Community, the first nationwide labor community, joined patriots, socialists, and labor representatives in order to keep the employed from starving by enabling them to purchase inexpensive basic goods at consumer cooperatives set up by the Community. The 62,000-member Community of Kyungsung opened its first cooperative in 1921, and branches in other major cities soon followed but unfortunately did not last long because of internal conflicts. The consumer cooperative of Mokpo, established by local rich people with philanthropic sentiment for the poor, soon failed to sustain its operation due to its undemocratic operation and dominance by the founding members.

Not only consumer cooperatives but also agricultural cooperatives attracted the interest of local intellectuals who subsequently established organizations which can be classified as follows: (1) the Tokyo-based Korean students group, (2) the indigenous religion group (Chondokyo), and (3) a Protestant religion group (YMCA). After establishing headquarters for their cooperative movement and publishing a cooperative magazine in 1925, the Tokyo-based student group deployed a few key members to the southeast Kyungbook Province to promote their vision and to set up cooperatives there. Increased attention to prevailing poverty and agricultural issues led to the movement of its headquarters from Tokyo to Seoul, as well as to a remarkable growth reaching eighty cooperatives with 20,000 members in the southern Chosun area. The substantial growth of cooperatives attracted Japanese concern and pressure so that many leaders were imprisoned and the cooperatives did not survive after 1933.[14] The two religious groups, the Chondokyo and the Protestants, started their initiatives in 1925 in the northern Hamkyung and Pyungan Provinces and in 1926 in the middle provinces near Seoul. The two groups shared the same focus on agriculture and the religious beliefs of their members. Some of these cooperatives went bankrupt or passed to individual ownership due to unskilled management or as a result of the Great Depression; both groups were dismissed in the same year (1937) by order of the Japanese government.[15]

Although these early foundations may not be considered true cooperatives because of their lack of autonomy from government, they were the first introduced as "cooperatives" in the Korean language, with the word "Hyupdongjohap," which is a combination of Hyupdong (cooperation) and

[11] Kim, Hyun-Sook, *Research on Private Cooperative Movement in Japanese Colony*, pp. 217–18.
[12] Ibid., pp. 212–15.
[13] Ibid., pp. 210, 215.
[14] See Jang, Jong-Ik, *History and Current Status of Korea Cooperative*, pp. 2–4.
[15] See Kim, Hyun-Sook, *Research on Private Cooperative Movement in Japanese Colony*, p. 245.

Johap (union). Given the great poverty among the rural population and resulting capital shortage, as well as the usually poor profitability of cooperatives at the initial stage, it is hard to imagine how autonomous cooperatives could have started successfully without the influence of colonial rule. In Korea, state influence on the cooperative sector was to become a permanent characteristic.

EVOLUTION OF COOPERATIVES AFTER INDEPENDENCE

Cooperatives in the Agricultural Sector

After the surrender of Japan in 1945, when Korea regained its so-called Glory Independence, the United Nations first intended to set up a joint trusteeship administration of Korea by the Soviet Union and the United States. However, in 1948 the Korean peninsula became divided at the 38th parallel between the Republic of Korea in the communist north and the capitalist south, and new governments were established in both regions. The unresolved tensions of the division surfaced in the Korean War of 1950, when the military North invaded South Korea. However, concerning further development of the cooperative movement, the common experience of economic and social hardships from this war led the rural and urban populations to revive mutual self-help and initiated a resurrection of cooperativism in many forms, especially in agriculture where farmers were eager to recover land which they had been deprived of during the colonial regime and to organize and operate their own cooperatives.[16] Correspondingly, after the new government of the (South) Republic of Korea had been inaugurated in 1948, a law for agricultural cooperatives was prepared in order to encourage farmers to organize cooperatives at the village level. In 1957 the Agricultural Cooperative Law (ACL) was passed and one year later expanded to include supply and marketing functions.

In 1961, after the military takeover of the Korean government, the Agricultural Cooperatives were merged with the Agricultural Bank into a multipurpose organization from which the National Agricultural Cooperative Federation (NACF) emerged. This encompassed village cooperatives providing farm loans and the supply of fertilizer as well as county and city cooperatives which provided financial services, such as credit, insurance, and managerial advice.[17] A rigid top-down approach in cooperative development under the strong guidance of the government replaced the former Western-style bottom-up growth with emphasis on autonomous self-help. The integrated NACF, although missing member democracy and independence as basic cooperative principles, provided various real benefits for farmers, such as about a 50 percent reduction of interest burden compared with private loan sharks, enhanced distribution to the farmers' advantage, more bargaining power against

[16] Korea Cooperative Research Institute, *Introduction of Agricultural Cooperatives for Cooperative Members*, June 2010, p. 196.
[17] NACF, *Annual Report*, 2001, pp. 35, 36.

wholesalers, and access to inexpensive necessity goods.[18] In turn, the successful integration of the agricultural cooperatives contributed considerably to the growth of rice production and satisfaction of food demand in the whole country because of the enormous support on the part of the government in the form of policy loans, procurement of grain and processed goods, supply of fertilizer, and even the (formerly denied) privilege to perform both banking and credit services. There were, however, restrictions on institutional autonomy. For instance, the president of Korea had the authority to appoint the NACF president, who in turn appointed the leaders of its member cooperatives, so it could be said that the government had changed the status of NACF into a public company which it was not supposed to be. At any rate, in the 1950s and 1960s the seeds were planted for the structure of the present cooperative sectors consisting mainly of agricultural, livestock, and fishery cooperatives as well as savings and credit cooperatives.[19]

From 1971 onward, the village cooperatives turned multipurpose, taking over key businesses from county and city cooperatives. At that time, agricultural cooperatives worked in a three-tier system: primary (village) cooperatives, secondary (county and city) cooperatives, and the national federation (NACF). In 1980, however, under the revised ACL, the three-tier system was changed into a two-tier system, turning the former city and county cooperatives into branches of the national federation, while the primary cooperatives extended their business activities, operating warehouses and offering several services. Under the revised law, livestock-related activities were transferred to a national livestock cooperative federation.

Between 1987 and 1988, the democratization process in the country reached agricultural cooperatives. In 1988, the ACL was amended and adopted most of the recommendations submitted by NACF, giving cooperatives more autonomy. Clauses requiring prior consent of the Ministry for business plans and budgets and restricting self-control of cooperatives were deleted. The temporary law for the appointment of officers of agricultural cooperatives was abolished. The president of NACF, formerly appointed by the National President on the recommendation of the Minister of Agriculture and Forestry, was now elected by the presidents of the primary cooperatives. Under the new law of 1988, the business scope of cooperatives was further expanded, including brokerage related to sale of farmland, transport with own trucks, and direct investment in daughter societies. In 1990, for the first time, presidents of primary cooperatives and the NACF were elected directly.

In 1994 the ACL was revised again. Under the new law, the president of NACF had to be a member/farmer. The share of seats on the NACF board for

---

[18] Korean Cooperative Research Institute, 2010, p. 199.
[19] Here and in the following, the authors thank Professor Hans-H. Muenkner from the University of Marburg in Germany for helpful comments made in his "Korea Case Study" for the "Cooperative Government Dialogue on Co-operative Policy and Legislation in Asia-Pacific Region" in Malaysia, November 14–18, 2005 (unpublished).

presidents of member cooperatives was increased from one-half to two-thirds. The names of primary cooperatives and specialized agricultural cooperatives changed to regional cooperatives and special (later, commodity) cooperatives. Efforts were made to reform cooperative organization and operations, for example, offering farm-gate pick-up service and attracting deposits by introducing "farmers' asset formation savings." In the NACF, a distinct separation of management of banking and nonbanking business was prescribed, with separate headquarters (business units) under a common umbrella. In 1998, an agricultural marketing complex, including wholesale and distribution centers, was established. Advanced farming technologies were disseminated and rice processing complexes (RPCs) as well as drying and storage centers (DSCs) were modernized in order to emphasize food safety and environmental conservation.

Following another amendment of the ACL (Unified Agricultural Cooperative Law) in 1999, marketing/supply, livestock, and banking/finance were introduced as three independent business sectors in NACF, while the former organizational two-tier structure was in principle maintained with regional cooperatives and commodity cooperatives as the two categories of primary co-ops. On the banking side, the NACF introduced new types of financial services, new branch offices, and special savings campaigns. Local government bodies were encouraged to deposit their funds in NACF accounts. In the year 2000, NACF had become the second-largest commercial bank in terms of deposits and, together with its member cooperatives, the largest banking institution in the country. The NACF provided funds for agricultural development and offered full banking services to customers, especially to farmers and cooperatives but also to the general public. Even during the financial and foreign exchange crisis in Asia of 1997 to 1999, which drove all the major Korean banks into bankruptcy or into obliged mergers, the NACF remained financially sustainable and kept the position of a leading bank, owing to relatively small numbers of nonperforming loans and low dependency on company loans (Jaebul).[20]

The continuing success of the NACF credit division, however, was critically contrasted with stagnant core services for members from the so-called economy division in the NACF, finally leading in March 2011 to their structural separation into two holding companies under the common roof of the NACF. Until this historic organizational change, the NACF had been subject to criticism from various groups. Beginning as a request for "Reform of Cooperatives" from the Report of Development Committee for Agriculture and Fishery in 1994, the separation of credit and economy divisions has undergone long-standing debates, changing hands with three presidents of Korea. The call for separation rose initially from the economic sector, which found itself becoming less sustainable because of the falling price of agricultural products from liberalization of agricultural markets through the World Trade Organization as well as from the change of the demand structure caused by decreasing consumption of rice and

---

[20] Korea Deposit Insurance Corporation, *Gone Name and Alive Name – Remembrance of Ten Years of Restructuring 1997–2006* (Dasan Publisher, 2007), pp. 65–78.

barley as domestic products, compared to increasing demand for imported grains such as corn and flour. Claiming that the NACF was unaccountable and irresponsible, Korean farmers were urged to intervene, while the organization was spending most of its human and financial resources on running the credit business that soon became troublesome because of the Asian Financial Crisis. Despite its survival, the credit division of NACF had to face decreasing profit margins as financial markets had become more competitive after the crisis and because of increasing globalization.[21] There was also strong criticism and pressure from the side of investors, the national Fair Trade Commission, and government. Increasingly tight control of financial solvency standards threw the NACF into the worst position within the commercial banking sector of Korea, recording the lowest BIS (Bank for International Settlement) ratio among its peer banks at the end of 2008. To make things worse, in 2011 the IFRS (International Financial Reporting Standard) treated bookkeeping member fees of cooperatives not as equity but as liability, since they may have to be returned someday, which made its BIS ratio even lower.[22] In order to resolve this financial problem, the NACF needs a fresh monetary injection of about 5 trillion won, either from its members or from government – preferably from both of them. Being aware of this critical issue, both the NACF and the government reached an agreement to introduce a holding company structure inside the organization for a sustainable future and to finance the necessary amount through member and government contributions.[23]

At the end of March 2011, after seventeen years of debate, the NACF's law was amended by the national parliament and signed by the president of Korea in order to restructure NACF, focusing on education and guidance of unit cooperatives and member farmers. Under this law, two separate holding companies have been established for financial and for economic (production and marketing) business, at "arms' length from each other." The structural transformation is supposed to be completed by March 2, 2012. The amended law specifies that (1) the NACF's main responsibility is to promote distribution of agricultural and livestock products; (2) the holding companies' goal is not to make profit but rather to enhance profits for farmers and cooperatives; (3) the current capital belonging to the NACF is to be allocated to the economy division over the credit division; (4) the credit holding company is to have its several daughter companies, including banks, life insurance companies, property-casualty insurance company, and security brokerage company; (5) the two holding companies are to pay a brand loyalty fee to their mother organization, the NACF, as much as 2.5 percent of total revenue or total operating income; (6) the required capital for

---

[21] Total profit margin has diminished from 1.3 trillion won (2007) to 0.3 trillion won (2008), 0.4 trillion won (2009), 0.5 trillion won (2010). Source: Ministry for Food, Agriculture, Forestry and Fisheries, *Major Contents and Influences of Amendment of Agricultural Cooperative Law*, 2011, p. 1.

[22] Korean Cooperative Research Institute, 2010, pp. 208–9.

[23] Ministry for Food, Agriculture, Forestry and Fisheries, 2011, p. 11.

TABLE 3.1 *Development of Agricultural Cooperatives*

Year	Number of Co-ops	Total Members	Total Assets
1996	RAC 1,350	M. 1,945,046 AM 4,348,956	
	CAC 46	M 72,212 AM 101,142	
	Total 1,396	Total 2,017,258 4,450,098	
1998	RAC 1,203	M. 1,972,885 AM 5,883,242	KRW
	CAC 46	M 77,508 AM 153,843	73,843.5 billion
	Total 1,249	Total 2,050,393 6,037,085	
2000	RAC 1,350	M. 2,003,622 AM 7,236,733	KRW
	CAC 46	M 79,519 AM 210,567	92,616.8 billion
	Total 1,396	Total 2,083,141 7,447,300	
2007	RAC 1,000	Total 2,410,049	KRW
	RLC 120		240,441.482
	CAC 47		billion
	LCC 23		
	GCC 12		
	Total 1,202		
2008	RAC 987	Total 2,421,610	KRW
	RLC 118		260,376.896
	CAC 46		billion
	LCC 24		
	GCC 12		
	Total 1,187		

RAC = Regional Agricultural Cooperatives, CAC = Commodity Agricultural Cooperatives, RLC = Regional Livestock Cooperatives, LCC = Livestock Commodity Cooperatives, GCC = Ginseng Commodity Cooperatives, M = Member, AM = Associate member.
Source: NACF, *Annual Report*, 2001, pp. 62, 65, and 67; *Sustainability Report*, 2007, p. 10; *Sustainability Report*, 2009, p. 8; *Balance Sheet*, 2007–2008, p. 6.

this restructuring should be financed initially by internal sources and the remaining portion will be supplemented by the government, which will also provide tax privileges to perform this change; and (7) the election system for presidents in unit cooperatives is to be improved for better efficiency and fairness.[24] See Table 3.1.

COOPERATIVES IN THE FINANCIAL SECTOR

Credit Cooperatives

Credit cooperatives may be considered the first major grassroots cooperatives that were set up without any governmental intervention after the independence

[24] Ministry for Food, Agriculture, Forestry and Fisheries, 2011, pp. 4–8.

of Korea in 1945. The first credit union was established in 1960 in Pusan by Sister Mary Gabriella Mulherin of the Maryknoll Mission. Sister Gabriella, who had been working for Catholic Relief Services (CRS), realized that charity alone could not solve the postwar problems of economic and social dislocation in South Korea. Searching for solutions based on self-help, she learned of courses in cooperative education at the Coady Institute at St. Xavier University in Antigonish, Nova Scotia, Canada. The propagation of cooperative self-help principles through the Canadian priest and teacher Msgr. Coady (founder of the Antigonish Movement) had been strongly inspired by Alphonse Desjardins, a Canadian journalist, who in 1900 established the first Caisse d'épargne Desjardins in Lévis (Quebec), the later so-called Caisses Populaires (People's Cooperative Banks), as the first successful North American credit union. Desjardins himself drew his ideas from the initiatives for credit union organization developed by Hermann Schulze-Delitzsch and Friedrich Wilhelm Raiffeisen in Germany during the second half of the nineteenth century,[25] so one can say that the evolution of the Korean credit union movement was inspired by European origins.

In May of 1960, Sister Gabriella with the help of, among others, Augustine Joung Ryul Kang organized the Sung-Ga (Holy Family) Credit Union. There were twenty-eight original members. Kang acted as president and Sister Gabriella as treasurer–managing director of the infant association. They were both convinced that education in the democratic principles of cooperative management, and, especially, in the practical mechanics of setting up and running credit unions was necessary for successful self-help of the poor.[26] As a result of this initiative, soon two other credit unions were established. At first, the cooperatives were named credit "Gye," as this expression was already deeply rooted in the Korean tradition of mutual aid societies (see Introduction in this article). The linkage to tradition, however, also had its limitations, as Gye principles of close-knit communal voluntary aid often were not in line with modern liability as well as liquidity requirements and were difficult to apply to large numbers of participants. Therefore, the clear and juridical approved institutional checks and balances of European cooperative management soon became the organizational blueprint for setting up statutes for credit unions. The Gye tradition, however, lived on in the "common bond" philosophy of Raiffeisen,[27] namely, that union members should have a close social relationship

---

[25] Source: http://en.wikipedia.org/wiki/Alphonse_Desjardins (co-operator) (accessed March 9, 2011).

[26] Source: www.rmaf.org.ph/Awardees/Biography/BiographyKangAug.htm (accessed March 9, 2011).

[27] It has to be mentioned, however, that initially there was a strong dispute between the two German credit union pioneers over the true nature of the common bond principle. Schulze-Delitzsch maintained that members should contribute small amounts of share capital (bonds of association) into a common pool to serve as limited collective collateral; Raiffeisen held this as inappropriate for cash-strapped farmers and favored a parish-based common bond principle instead, arguing that constant communication and mutual social control within small communities would allow for the application of unlimited joint liability. At that time, the dispute ended in a tie, with Schulze-Delitzsch's approach dominating the "People's Banks" in urban settings, and Raiffeisen's agricultural cooperatives in rural ones. Today, the principle of unlimited liability is no longer in use;

through common occupation, religion, or residency, and that only within this bond should membership be open for all. To foster thrift, however, applicants had to pay a small initial fee to join as nominal "share" and were encouraged to deposit further savings regularly, which they could withdraw at any time. To generate awareness of democratic cooperation and solidarity, as well as to prevent the credit union from turning toward a profit orientation, these monies were to have a "serving function" for members only, so they were not accumulated but kept liquid for immediate availability to grant loans. No matter their amount of financial participation, each member had only one vote in cooperative decision making through the general assembly of members, when, for instance, the board of directors was elected. This board was the central control unit and responsible for operative decisions. It was conducted by a president and vice-president(s), assisted by a secretary and a treasurer. The general assembly also elected a credit committee which decided on loan applications in accordance with general directives of the cooperative statute and guidelines from the board of directors. In general, loans were to be granted at reasonable rates of interest, and dividends on shares were paid only after funds for emergencies had been secured. A supervisory committee, which could be elected by the general assembly or appointed by the board of directors, was responsible for periodic audits of the credit union's accounts and for ensuring that the charter and bylaws were followed. By unanimous vote, the supervisory committee could suspend any member of the board of directors, but members of the committee were themselves subject to suspension by a majority vote of the board. Both suspensions had to be ratified by a majority vote of the general assembly within a specified time. All elected officers served without compensation with the exception of the treasurer who also acted as executive manager, if no external professional was hired for these functions.[28]

By 1962, the number of Korean credit unions had already increased to twenty-seven, and continued growth led fifty-two credit unions in 1964 to form the Korean Credit Union League (KCUL), with headquarters in Seoul. Kang became its first president, while Sister Gabriella relinquished her position as general manager in favor of Korean credit union leaders. While dependency on the Catholic Church was gradually reduced, the league affiliated itself in 1965 with the Credit Union National Association of the United States (CUNA), which later became the World Council of Credit Unions (WOCCU), thus reaping the benefits of belonging to an international organization. Shortly afterward, the KCUL initiated the enactment of a national credit union law that was based on the cooperative principles and practices embodied in the U.S. law governing credit unions. In 1972, the Korea Credit Union Act was finally promulgated, and correspondingly the KCUL changed its name into National Credit Union Federation of Korea (NACUFOK), which was later affiliated with the

instead, member liability is restricted to the amount of their shares. See http://en.wikipedia.org/wiki/Bond_of_association (accessed March 9, 2011).

[28] Source: www.rmaf.org.ph/Awardees/Biography/BiographyKangAug.htm (accessed March 9, 2011).

Association of Asian Confederations of Credit Unions (ACCU) and with the International Raiffeisen Union (IRU) in 1974.[29]

In 1988, the structure of NACUFOK was changed from a two-tier into a three-tier system with primary credit unions, provincial leagues, and the national federation to strengthen monitoring and supervision over primary ones and also to enhance regional development.[30] In 1997, it returned to a two-tier system turning the provincial leagues into regional offices. The tasks of the regional offices are management support of primary credit unions, supervision, and inspection as well as support in interlending activities and the insurance business. After the Asian Financial Crisis of 1997, in which the Korean economy was heavily affected, the financial regulatory framework for the cooperative sector was consolidated toward a joint supervision by the Financial Supervisory Commission (FSC) of the state and the Financial Supervisory Services (FSS) of NACUFOK. Credit unions had to affiliate with the Korea Deposit Insurance Corporation (KIDC) to pay off member deposits in the event of bankruptcy, and insolvent or financially weak credit unions were advised to merge with sounder ones or be dissolved. As a result, 433 credit unions were liquidated, closed, or merged between 1998 and 2002.[31]

In 2000, an Intra-Network system was established in NACUFOK, which connected online nearly all credit unions. In 2001, NACUFOK joined the Korea Financial Telecommunications and Clearing Institute (KFTCI) and also went into the credit card business in partnership with the Industrial Bank of Korea. Online banking and online insurance services with the CUNA Mutual Group started in 2002, so that most credit unions could offer basic savings and loan services, mutual insurance products, and credit card services to their members. In addition to financial services, many credit unions have branched out into distribution networks providing fresh and ecologically safe agricultural products at a fair price, linking rural and urban areas. Furthermore, cooperatives engage in community development programs, sponsoring various social and public education activities (fitness programs, gymnasiums, auditoriums), and NACUFOK offers management consulting and training programs.[32] Because of these continuous modernization and diversification efforts, the cooperatives have been able to hold their stand in the financial sector against commercial banks and still play an important role in Korean consumer banking. See Table 3.2.

COMMUNITY CREDIT COOPERATIVES (CC)

In 1963, at the initial stage of the military regime, the first five CCs were established as part of a regional development project, to meet the local financial need for low-income people or small and medium-sized enterprises. At the end of

---

[29] Ibid.
[30] See Jang, Jong-Ik, *History and Current Status of Korea Cooperative*, p. 14.
[31] See NACUFOK, *Annual Report*, 2003, p. 13.
[32] Ibid., p. 9.

TABLE 3.2 *Development of Credit Cooperatives*

Year	Number of CUCs	Total Members	Total Assets
1992	1,461	2.8 million	KRW 6,730 billion
1995	1,665	4.2 million	KRW 13,190 billion
1996	1,671	5.2 million	KRW 16,620 billion
1998	1,592	5.0 million	KRW 20,970 billion
2000	1,317	5.3 million	KRW 20,440 billion
2002	1,233	4.7 million	KRW 19,644 billion
2004	1,066	4.8 million	KRW 22,166 billion
2006	1,027	4.7million (4,680,094)	KRW 26,300 billion
2009	982	5.2million (5,193,000)	KRW 39,699 billion

Source: NACUFOC, *Annual Reports* and *Statistics*, 2006, p. 7, and 2009, p. 5.

the year, their number had risen to 115.[33] When President Park Chung-Hee introduced the Saemaul Undong (meaning New Village Movement) in 1970, it soon became the propelling force for the establishment of even more CCs. Despite their commonality with nonprofit organizations supporting the economically poor, Saemaul credit cooperatives differed from others not only in their legal background, but even more so in their founding philosophy, driving force, and target member group. The roots of CCs are traditional mutual support agreements and precooperative organizations based on self-help and reciprocity of villagers and neighbors. Modern CCs are defined as a "financial cooperative that contributes to the development of the community as well as the nation through financial businesses, including savings, credit, insurance, and cultural welfare works, local community development projects based on principles of cooperative, and inheriting the spirit of traditional community derived from our own cooperative system such as Gye, Hyangyak and Dure."[34] Gye in particular comes close to this understanding in the form of the rotating savings and credit association (ROSCA) traditionally organized on the village or county level. As many of these former religious or civic self-help organizations had been forced to dissolve by the Japanese colonial government, there was lack of trust in the first modern cooperatives introduced by the Japanese, and this led to the rise of the CC movement.

Government support and overpromotion, however, endangered the autonomy of CCs, as many were more political demonstration projects than true self-help operations. After the Credit Union Law was promulgated in 1972, the CCs, which until then had been treated legally like other credit unions,

[33] See Jo, Sungyun, *A Research on Theory of Our Traditional Cooperation and Measures to Grow Saemaul Credit Cooperative.* Unpublished Ph.D dissertation at Jubilee International Bible College, 1995, p. 55.

[34] Korea Federation of Community Credit Co-operatives (KFCC), *Annual Report*, 2009, p. 5.

TABLE 3.3 *Development of Community Credit Cooperatives*

Year	Number of CCs	Total Members	Total Assets
1984			KRW 1 trillion
1995	2,969	8,849 thousand	KRW 20 trillion
1996	2,836	9,775 thousand	KRW 25 trillion
1998	2,590	10,140 thousand	KRW 30 trillion
2000	1,817	14,594 thousand	KRW 36 trillion
2002	1,701	12,975 thousand	KRW 40 trillion
2004	1,647	14,359 thousand	KRW 47 trillion
2007	1,543	15,763 thousand	KRW 60 trillion
2009	1,501	16,448 thousand	KRW 77 trillion

Source: KFCC, *Statistics of Community Credit Cooperatives*, 2005, pp. 33, 37, 52, and *Annual Report*, 2009, pp. 3, 10.

became affiliated to the Korea Federation of Community Credit Co-operatives (KFCC) under a separate law established in 1975. After the political turbulence of 1979–80, a separate Community Credit Cooperative Law was promulgated in 1983. By this point the general Credit Cooperative Law had been applied to the community organizations for more than ten years.[35] The independent legal base enabled the community organizations to be solely governed by the Ministry of Internal Affairs, freeing them from the Ministry of Finance which formerly had controlled them. After changing their role from a financial service organization to a citizens' organization, the cooperatives had undergone a profound restructuring process resulting in economies of scale and efficiency gains through mergers and acquisition. Under guidance and supervision of the KFCC, faltering CCs were liquidated, and small-sized CCs were consolidated and encouraged to merge. Because of these measures, the CCs changed significantly as well in number of memberships and in their assets from 1979 to 1984.[36] See Table 3.3.

OTHER COOPERATIVES INITIATIVES

Fishery Cooperatives

Fishery cooperatives underwent a fate similar to that of agricultural cooperatives before and after the end of the Second World War. In 1911, one year after Japan

[35] See Kim, Okgi, *Introduction to the Saemaul Credit Cooperative Law* (Daewang Publishing Company, 1987), pp. 26–8; and KFCC, *Twenty-Five Years of the Community Credit Cooperatives*, 1989, p. 321.
[36] From 1979 to 1983, the number of members, cooperatives, and their total assets changed from 8.5 million, 39,265, and 120 billion KRW to 3.8 million, 5,360, and 884 billion KRW, respectively. KFCC, ibid., pp. 273–5.

completed acquisition of Chosun, a decree restricted the setup of fishery cooperatives without permission of the government. Nevertheless, their number rapidly grew to 206 cooperatives with 156,000 members at the end of 1941.[37]

Fishery cooperatives differed from other industrial cooperatives in that they consisted of both Korean and Japanese members, and were run for the protection and benefit of Japanese interests. Aiming at an eventual monopoly, in 1940 all fishery-related organizations were forced to integrate under a single institutional umbrella, which after independence was turned into the National Federation of Fishery Cooperatives (NFFC, "Suhyop" in Korean) in 1962, as ordered by President Park Chung-Hee. The NFFC not only contributed to economic growth in Korea but also conducted many projects to improve the living conditions of fishermen by upgrading their economic and social status. These projects included three service programs: "General Service," dedicated to supporting, training, and educating fishermen; "Marketing Service," dedicated to the joint marketing of fishery products and to price-stabilizing programs; and finally "Banking Service," to organize the Fisheries Fund and finance management.[38] The NFFC is relatively small among Korean cooperative organizations with only 92 member cooperatives.[39]

NATIONAL FORESTRY COOPERATIVE FEDERATION (NFCF)

Originating from the Pine Tree Kye in Chosun, modern forestry cooperatives such as forest unions, local forest unions, and the National Federation of Forest Unions were officially established in 1949. With the Forestry Law enacted in 1962, all forest unions joined the newly named Korea Federation of Forestry Cooperatives (KFFC) with subordinate cooperatives at provincial and village levels.[40] The KFFC's mission is to protect the rights of forest owners and cooperative members and to promote sustainable forestry practices. Since the inception of the federation, severely denuded mountains have been reforested within a short time period.[41] In 1980, when the new military regime led by President Chun Doo-Hwan took power, the KFFC was renamed as the National Federation of Forestry Cooperatives (NFFC); correspondingly, the former Forestry Law was replaced by the Forestry Cooperatives Law, and a direct election system was introduced in 1989 for the NFFC and subordinate associations. The organization changed to its current name, the National Forestry Cooperative Federation (NFCF), in 2000.[42]

In 2011, the NFCF consisted of two million cooperative members and citizens devoted to Korea's reforestation, and the federation was still growing as forest

[37] See Jang, Jong-Ik, *History and Current Status of Korea Cooperative*, p. 6.
[38] www.suhyup.co.kr/eng/eintro/ceoMessage.jsp (accessed April 2011).
[39] www.suhyup.co.kr/intro/association.jsp (accessed April 2011).
[40] http://eng.nfcf.or.kr/forest/user.tdf?a=user.indexApp&c=1003&mc=ENG (accessed April 2011).
[41] www.nfcf.or.kr (accessed April 2011).
[42] www. 100.naver.com/100.nhn?docid=514279 (accessed April 2011).

owners and managers participated in various programs and projects such as forest management extension programs, forest resource base building projects, marketing both major and minor forest products, building logging roads and infrastructure for sustainable forest management, banking and financing services, and overseas forestry development projects. Thus, the NFCF is not only oriented toward economic goals but also plays a role in increasing quality of life and creating new value for forested mountain regions where most forest-dependent communities are located.[43]

CONSUMER COOPERATIVES

Similar to credit cooperatives, consumer cooperatives grew not out of governmental initiative but from grassroots efforts; the former stimulated the growth of the latter. In 1973, common organizations for the purchasing of necessities were formed in rural areas to supplement severe shortages in basic needs. This became the basis for consumer cooperatives.[44] The first was the Shin-ri consumer cooperative, established in 1979 as a subproject of regional development of the Shin-ri credit cooperative.[45] After rapid growth, representatives of 52 consumer cooperatives established a common headquarters in 1983.[46] The first university consumer cooperative was set up by students of the Sogang University in the mid-1980s, and although no longer in existence, it set the benchmark for the next one established at Chosun University in 1990. It was comprised of students, university employees, and teaching staff and, in turn, was followed by many other university cooperatives.[47]

Sponsored by a few foreign organizations, many early-stage consumer cooperatives provided only a simple common marketplace, mostly in rural areas, and failed to survive intensified competition from private for-profit distributors. Orders for organic and other health-safe agricultural products continued, however, and consumer cooperatives without outlets (such as the Hansalim Community and a few others) still flourished. In 1988 consumer cooperatives started direct transactions of organic agricultural products between sellers and buyers, and the enactment of a legal status regarding these cooperatives was discussed in the 1990s.[48] Finally in 1999, the Law of Consumers' Cooperatives was enacted after several years of debate and concerns raised by large-sized distributors, in particular over issues of nonmember business and compliance with market requirements.[49] The law divided cooperatives into community co-ops, group co-ops, school co-ops, institutional co-ops, and many others. Any

---

[43] http://eng.nfcf.or.kr/forest/user.tdf?a=user.indexAPP&c=1003&mc=ENG (accessed April 2011).
[44] www.co-op.or.kr/english/korea_2.htm (accessed April 2011).
[45] Ibid.
[46] Ibid.
[47] Ibid.
[48] Jang, Jong-Ik, *History and Current Status of Korea Cooperative*, p. 18.
[49] Ibid.

TABLE 3.4 *Recent Development of Consumer Cooperatives*

		2008(a)	2009(b)	2010(c)	Growth rate (in percentage) a→b	b→c
Sales volume (in billion Korean won)	Hansalim	1,334	1,594	1,909	19.5	19.8
	iCOOP Federation	1,301	2,053	2,800	57.7	36.4
	Dure Federation	405	555	702	37.1	26.4
	Women Minwoo	113	153	2,052	35.5	33.6
	Etc.	238	283	335	19.0	18.3
	Total	3,393	4,640	5,952	36.8	28.3
Number of members (in thousands)	Hansallim	171	207	2,430	21.2	17.3
	iCOOP Federation	55	786	1,100	43.9	40.0
	Dure Federation	483	666	850	37.7	27.6
	Women Minwoo	172	196	249	13.9	27.2
	Etc.	374	431	496	15.0	15.3
	Total	3,284	4,150	5,124	26.4	23/5

Source: Jo, Wan-Hyung (2010, July). "Past, Present and Key Challenges of Consumer Cooperative in Korea," *Quarterly Cooperative Network*, Korea Cooperative Research Institute, p. 78.

cooperative with more than 300 members and a starting investment of 30 million won could be established.[50] Because of fierce competition and often failing managerial expertise and competence, of 231 cooperatives in 1983, only 154 were left in 2003. In 2010, the National Federation of Consumer Cooperatives had 60 affiliated primary cooperatives as members.[51] See Table 3.4.

KOREA FEDERATION OF SMALL AND MEDIUM BUSINESS (KFSB)

Similar to other major cooperative federations, the KFSB was founded in 1962 under the Small Business Cooperative Act. Although it takes the name cooperative, in fact it is more like a state-sponsored and state-controlled nonprofit

[50] www.co-op.or.kr/english/english.htm (accessed April 2011).
[51] Ibid.

organization or association aimed at protecting the rights and interests of small and medium-sized enterprises (SME). These enterprises are by far the largest employment sectors in the Korean economy. In 2011, the KFSB served 25 national federations, 203 nationwide cooperatives (17,121 members), 391 business cooperatives (17,252 cooperatives) and 391 cooperative federations, and 14 small business-related organizations (558,959 members), totaling 972 cooperatives and 623,765 members.[52] The KFSB offers its members a variety of services and programs such as the Collective Contract System, the Mutual Assistance Fund, and Joint Purchase/Sales. Because many young Korean students and workers prefer big companies like the traditional Chaebol conglomerates, there is a constant labor shortage for the SMEs. Therefore, in 1993 the KFSB set up the Alien Training Cooperation Corps in order to provide and qualify foreign workers; since 2007, it has been licensed to issue work permits to foreign workers from lesser developed countries on behalf of the Ministry of Labor, a division of the Korean government.[53]

HOUSING COOPERATIVES

The definition of *housing cooperative* in Korea is different from that in European countries. In Korea, the term generally refers to persons who share the financing, construction, and sales risk of real estate, whereas in other countries it generally refers to the common use of such properties.[54] Thus, a Korean housing cooperative is a legal entity (usually a corporation) that owns real estate, consisting of one or more residential buildings.[55] Each shareholder is granted the right to occupy one housing unit, sometimes subject to an occupancy agreement, which is similar to a lease. The occupancy agreement is specified in the cooperative's rules (tenure model). The term *cooperative* is also used, however, to describe a nonshareholder cooperative model in which fee-paying members obtain the right to occupy one bedroom, for example, and share the common amenities of a house that is owned by a cooperative organization. This arrangement is similar to student cooperatives in some college communities in the United States.

Membership in a housing cooperative, divided between regional or workplace membership categories, is a privilege in Korea, awarded by the government to enable members to designate a contractor to construct, for example, an apartment complex for the cooperative at a lower-than-market price determined by the construction company. This regulation was introduced in 1977 to help lower-income people purchase homes at a cost about 15 percent lower than normal, at the expense of taking some risks in the construction process. Thus, the

---

[52] http://johap.kbiz.or.kr/common/home.jsp (accessed April 2011).
[53] http://fes.kbiz.or.kr/ (accessed April 2011).
[54] Apartment in Korea does not mean one for rental, but for ownership. Compared to other countries, Korea has few rental apartments. Thus, an apartment in Korea is the same as a mansion or condominium in other countries.
[55] http://en.wikipedia.org/wiki/Housing_cooperative (accessed April 2011).

housing cooperative system has led to a sufficient supply of housing, mostly apartments, through cooperation between members and construction companies that otherwise would have had to bear the whole risk burden by themselves. The popularity of housing cooperatives can be explained partially by the fact that real estate property is considered a critical determinant of the individual wealth level in Korea. Expectations of price increase and actual demand have interacted so much that cause and effect cannot be easily identified, but the relationship may be partially attributable to the agricultural tradition which esteems home ownership over rental situations.[56]

Naturally, not all housing cooperatives have been successful, and some have even ended up with a bad reputation and negative results. In preparation for the Olympic Games in 1989, for example, the government launched a program of slum clearance and redevelopment around Seoul. Joint redevelopment, devised by the City Planning Secretariat of Seoul City, encouraged home owners to enter into agreements with construction companies to carry out the redevelopment. The implementation of this policy counted on market mechanisms and resulted in growing numbers of urban poor without decent shelter. The redevelopment policy pursued between 1983 and 1989 aimed to demolish traditional one-story houses and to replace them with twelve- to fifteen-story apartment buildings. Because three families usually lived in the old houses, one as home owner and two as tenants, this arrangement affected mostly poor people, which caused international organizations to put pressure on the Korean government to end evictions. In reaction, home owners of redevelopment areas were urged to form cooperatives that would be responsible for selecting a construction company and deciding on the type of new apartments desired. The cooperatives would also manage administrative and financial matters, with responsibility being shared by the cooperative and the construction company.

In practice, however, these cooperatives consisted largely of real estate people and were controlled by the construction companies. Tenants were not eligible for membership in the cooperatives or for residency in the apartments in the new buildings. They were offered "moving expenses" or were entitled to buy one third of a new apartment. Apart from the negative cultural and social consequences of destruction of urban poor communities, the demolition of the old houses left many people without shelter, so many of the evicted tenants settled in clusters of illegal settlements at the periphery of the city and had to look for work in the informal sector.[57] Thus, although housing cooperatives helped to increase the supply of houses in Korea on the one hand, they also aggravated housing

---

[56] In Korea, a housing price index, which is a per-capita income divided by average house price, is 12, whereas the index in other countries ranges from 3 to 5 in most cases. Jung, Hee-Shoo, *Housing Policy in Industrialized Countries*, Policy Brief No. 16, Kangwon Development Research Institute (in Korean), 2007.

[57] See Yoo, Che-Dong, *Research on Improvement Method for Housing Policy Changes and Housing Rehabilitation – Focus on Policy Change of Reconstruction and Remodeling.* Unpublished master's thesis, Sungkyunkwan University, 2004, p. 22.

problems for low-income tenants because of price increases and environmental damages.

WORKER COOPERATIVES

The Asian Financial Crisis of 1997 to 1999 also affected Korea, requiring many high-leveraged domestic companies to liquidate or to be sold, resulting in an unprecedented high unemployment rate. Additionally, the information technology revolution and Chinese entry to a market economy swept away numbers of mid-level managerial jobs and low-paying workplaces. Since then, in spite of increased GDP growth, the unemployment rate has remained critically high in Korea, especially among the young. This phenomenon of jobless growth has led to workers occupying or purchasing their collapsing firms in order to run them on their own. In 2007, the Ministry of Employment and Labor[58] developed the Social Enterprise accreditation system to boost these worker initiatives through financial support and tax benefits. Because some of these social enterprises have internal structures similar to cooperatives, the Korean Association of Social Economy Enterprises (KASEE) has become a member of the International Cooperative Alliance, and strives to expand employment in such areas as cleaning, recycling, and housekeeping services at competitive prices.[59]

SUMMARY AND CONCLUSIONS

As the first complete review of the development of cooperativism in Korea, this research shows that the historical beginning of cooperative enterprise is hard to identify exactly because of its amazingly long history and widespread lack of autonomy and democracy, in spite of the omnipresent popularity of such organizations. It remains an open question when the first cooperative movement developed on the Korean peninsula, but one may say that it had much to do with the traditional spirit of mutual aid and self-help,[60] Japanese colonization, and government-centered economic development. Although the Koreans developed and maintained various autochthonous types of self-help organizations based in religion or custom very early in history, modern-style cooperatives and industrial cooperatives were introduced only during Japanese colonial rule. The industrial cooperative, while created under a colonial regime and in the non-capitalistic environment of colonial Chosun in the early twentieth century, has dominated since independence and under democratic management. If one considers capitalism to be a precondition of cooperative movements, it can be said that until economic development plans in Korea introduced capitalism in the

---

[58] Recognizing both the difficulty and importance of employment, the Ministry of Labor changed its name to Ministry of Employment and Labor in July 2010.

[59] National Assembly Secretariat, "A Research on Ways to Enact the Principal Law of Cooperatives in Korea." Policy Project Report, 2010, pp. 34–5.

[60] See Sohn, Insoo, *A Study on the Korean Traditional Practice for Mutual Aids*, 1984, pp. 231–3.

1960s, there was no European-style cooperative movement in place to tackle the poverty of the low-income classes. Therefore, depending on viewpoint, one may regard either type of early cooperativism as a fountainhead for the later development of modern cooperatives in South Korea.

Since the 1960s, the cooperative sector has grown rapidly, corresponding to the general economic growth in terms of size and direction. In 2010, the Korean economy ranked twelfth in the world, and the National Agricultural Cooperative Federation (NACF) ranked fifth largest among cooperatives in the world. In addition, the cooperative sector is contributing to structural change in that cooperative development has expanded less in agriculture and more in financial services and consumption. Financial cooperatives have been a major source of funding for small and medium-sized enterprises (especially during the financial crisis of 2008–9), while consumer cooperatives are drawing recognition and popularity with the growing preference of Korean consumers for goods with higher health safety.

Cooperation among the different cooperative groups, however, is still scarce. Instead, in the sector of savings and credit cooperatives, there is a strong separation between the agricultural cooperatives of the NACF, CUs, and CCs, although they share similar goals and guiding principles, have overlapping membership, and are facing the same stiff competition from commercial banks. One reason for this lack of cooperation may stem from the fact that these cooperative groups are regulated by three different laws and governmental ministries; another reason is the absence of any effective national apex organization that can act as an integrating force and common lobby organization in negotiations with the government. There is no national cooperative council that effectively fulfills these coordinating functions, nor is there a single backbone law covering all organizations of the cooperative sector. Recently, however, significant changes have been initiated; in 2010, a single law regarding cooperatives was in discussion.[61] This law has been in response to the noticeable contribution of the cooperative sector in absorbing the consequences of the global financial crisis, an accomplishment that has encouraged a positive reaction to the call for changes in the legal framework for cooperatives.[62]

On the other hand, the cooperative sector appears to be somewhat over-regulated. Korean lawmakers may need to concentrate on offering cooperatives a lasting legal framework (the ACL has been amended seventeen times) that defines the essential features of a cooperative organization as institutional benchmarks, and leave the details for self-regulation through cooperative bylaws. This approach would give cooperative leaders more incentives and opportunities in their daily work to practice and strengthen cooperative values among their members. The same can be said regarding the ongoing trend of "commercialization" of cooperatives and the resulting dominance of business

---

[61] National Assembly Secretariat, "A Research on Ways to Enact the Principal Law of Cooperatives in Korea," Policy Project Report, 2010.

[62] The United Nations designated the year 2012 as the International Year of Cooperatives.

thinking and business speech over cooperative democracy and membership values. From an economic standpoint, it might be more efficient to merge smaller local cooperatives in order to create more competitive units, although this could further weaken the already endangered spirit of community and affect the feeling of belonging among members. In addition, expanded commercial relations with nonmembers make the advantages of joining the cooperative less visible. Mergers inevitably lead to more heterogeneity in membership and thus weaken the common bond; they further increase geographical (and often also mental) distance of service relations, causing loss of "regionality" as a unique feature offered by locally present cooperatives.

All of these factors may at least partially explain cooperative members' growing indifference toward a more active participation. In addition, the traditional spirit of self-help, mutual aid, and communal solidarity, while still vivid in the countryside, has been weakened by general trends of growing individualism, urbanization of rural areas, and increased mobility of citizens. Demography is another factor endangering this spirit of community; decreasing birth rates lead to smaller families and weaken the traditional bonds between generations. Undoubtedly, however, the Korean cooperative movement has contributed substantially to the remarkable economic and political success the country has achieved today.

Literature

Research Articles

Jang, Jong-Ik. (1997). *History and Current Status of Korea Cooperative*. Korea Research Institute of the Cooperatives, unpublished working paper.

Jo, Young-Ho. (2003). *A Study on the Nature and Function of Bobusang in the Late Chosun Dynasty from the Perspective of Social Welfare*. Master's thesis, DongKook University, Graduate School of Social Science (Social Welfare major).

Jung, Hee-Shoo. (2007). *Housing Policy in Industrialized Countries*. Policy Brief No. 16, Kangwon Development Research Institute (in Korean).

Jung, Hongjoo, et al. (2011). *Society, Economy and Insurance*. SKKU Center for Insurance Culture Studies.

Kim, Hyun-Sook. (1961). *Research on Private Cooperative Movement in Japanese Colony* (Moonhak and Jisung Publishers, 1987).

Kim, JinKyu. (2009). "A Study on Hyang-Yak in the Chosun Dynasty under the Aspects of Establishment and Development," *Jang-An Nonchong*, 29.

Ko, Hyunseok. (2009, April). "In Search of Cooperative's Root in Korea," *Korean Cooperative Review*, Korean Cooperative Research Institute.

Korea Cooperative Research Institute. (2010, June). *Introduction of Agricultural Cooperatives for Cooperative Members*.

Korea Deposit Insurance Corporation. (2007). *Gone Name and Alive Name – Remembrance of Ten Years of Restructuring 1997–2006* (Dasan Publisher).

Kwak, Hyomoon. "A Study on the Social Welfare Character of Doore in Chosun Dynasty," *Jungchaek Nonchong* (Policy Review), 13, no. 1.

Lee, Kyung-Ran. (2002). *Research on Financial Cooperative in Japanese Ruling* (Hyean Publisher).

Ministry for Food, Agriculture, Forestry and Fisheries. (2011). *Major Contents and Influences of Amendment of Agricultural Cooperative Law.*

Moon, Jung-Chang. (1961). *History of Korean Agricultural Organization* (in Korean) (Iljogak Publishing).

Muenkner, Hans-H. (2005, November 14–18). "Korea Case Study," for the "Co-operative Government Dialogue on Co-operative Policy and Legislation in Asia-Pacific Region" in Malaysia.

National Assembly Secretariat. (2010). "A Research on Ways to Enact the Principal Law of Cooperatives in Korea." Policy Project Report.

Sohn, Insoo. (1984). *A Study on the Korean Traditional Practice for Mutual Aids.*

Yoo, Che-Dong. (2004). *Research on Improvement Method for Housing Policy Changes and Housing Rehabilitation – Focus on Policy Change of Reconstruction and Remodelling.* Unpublished master's thesis, Sungkyunkwan University.

Statistics

KFCC, *Statistics of Community Credit Cooperatives* and *Annual Reports.*
NACF, *Annual Reports* and Sustainability Report, 2007 and 2009.
NACUFOC, *Annual Reports* and Statistics, 2006 and 2009.

Internet Sources

www.co-op.or.kr/english/english.htm (accessed April 2011).
www.fes.kbiz.or.kr/ (accessed April 2011).
http://eng.nfcf.or.kr/forest/user.tdf?a=user.indexApp&c=1003&mc=ENG (accessed April 2011).
www.nfcf.or.kr (accessed April 2011).
http://johap.kbiz.or.kr/common/home.jsp (accessed April 2011).
www.kbiz.or.kr/cms/content_eng.jsp?site=www.kbiz.or.kr&ch=english (accessed April 20, 2011).
www.100.naver.com/100.nhn?docid=514279 (accessed April 2011).
www.rmaf.org.ph/Awardees/Biography/BiographyKangAug.htm (accessed March 9, 2011).
www.suhyup.co.kr/eng/eintro/ceoMessage.jsp (accessed April 20, 2011).
http://en.wikipedia.org/wiki/Bond_of_association (accessed March 9, 2011).
http://en.wikipedia.org/wiki/Alphonse_Desjardins_(co-operator) (accessed March 9, 2011).
http://en.wikipedia.org/wiki/Housing_cooperative (accessed April 20, 2011).

CHAPTER 4

"… What Is the End Purpose of It All?": The Centrality of Values for Cooperative Success in the Marketplace

Ian MacPherson

What makes cooperatives unique and valuable in meeting economic and social purposes? A common answer is that it is their cooperative principles. This chapter discusses that answer and proposes that what is ultimately more important are the values that underlie these principles. It considers some of the issues associated with an exclusive reliance on the principles, followed by an overview of the complicated historical background from which cooperative values are derived. It then discusses the efforts to reach consensus on the international cooperative values during the 1990s, exploring the immediate background to them and discussing the process whereby a common core of values was identified. It concludes with a discussion of those values as they were included in the *Statement on the Co-operative Identity* adopted by the International Co-operative Alliance at its Manchester Congress in 1995.

THE PROBLEMS WITH PRINCIPLES

There are good reasons for the emphasis usually placed on the cooperative principles. As defined by the International Co-operative Alliance (ICA), they form the basis for the legal frameworks under which cooperatives are incorporated around the world. In most jurisdictions an organization wishing to incorporate as a cooperative has to conform to requirements derived (in part or in total) from the principles.[1] People wishing to explain a cooperative's unique structures or its distribution of surpluses (what are more commonly called profits) typically refer to the principles in doing so. Many local cooperatives feature the principles in point form on their membership information materials and advertising programs, thereby cementing their

---

[1] For a very useful discussion of the relationship between the cooperative principles and legislation, see Hans-H. Münkner, *Co-operative Principles and Co-operative Law* (Marburg: University of Marburg, Institute for Co-operation in Developing Countries, Papers and Reports No. 5, 1974), particularly pp. 8–21.

importance.[2] Most cooperative apex organizations (regional, national, and international) promote them vigorously.[3]

There are, however, some problems with this emphasis on the movement's accepted principles. First, collectively, the principles can seem to be a rather long-winded explanation for a kind of organization readily found in many parts of the world and engaged in so many kinds of activities by so many people.[4] The current principles on democratic member control, member economic participation, and autonomy and independence, for example, are not easily abbreviated without losing some of their key aspects (see Appendix I for the current ICA principles).

Second, the simple reiteration of the principles undervalues a point made in the ICA's *Statement on the Co-operative Identity* of 1995 – that they are "guidelines" for action. They are the way in which cooperators and cooperatives try to "put their values into action."[5] In other words, the principles are to some extent external manifestations of thought and commitments that run deeper.

Third, the principles need to be understood as an integrated package. As one thinks about them seriously – and, more importantly, seeks to apply them creatively – they are remarkably interconnected and mutually supportive. A list, which by its nature tends to separate the points it includes, does not suggest that kind of synergy. It too easily becomes just a checklist for organizational behavior to be ticked off during annual operational cycles or when specific activities are undertaken. That is hardly enough: they need to be seen in the context of the values that inform them.

Fourth, the listing of cooperative principles, in both the current and earlier ICA versions, seems to suggest uniform institutions across the movement. This is obviously at odds with reality: a few parents operating a child care co-op are running an institution significantly different from the complex organizations managing large worker or consumer cooperatives, cooperative insurance companies, and multibranch financial co-ops. The existing (general) principles can be useful "guides" for all these kinds of organizations, but the differences are dramatic. That is why people involved in cooperatives need to review the principles as their co-ops grow larger or otherwise change significantly. How

[2] Some examples from the Canadian context: Vancity Savings Credit Union (www.vancity.com/ AboutUs/OurValues/CooperativePrinciples/); Manitoba credit unions (www.creditunion.mb.ca/ about/index.htm); Calgary Co-op (www.calgarycoop.com/about_us/) and the Metro Student Living Co-operative, Toronto (www.metrostudentcoop.org/). It is not difficult to demonstrate this kind of usage in many other jurisdictions.

[3] For example, using the Canadian context, see Canadian Co-operative Association (www.coops-canada.coop/en/about_co-operative/about_co-ops); and the Co-operative Housing Federation, British Columbia (www.chf.bc.ca/pages/about3.asp). It is not difficult to demonstrate this kind of usage in many other jurisdictions.

[4] Today, the ICA has 223 member organizations from 87 countries; they represent more than 800,000,000 members. See ICA Web site (www.ica.coop/ica/index.html). The United Nations estimates that the movement in one way or another significantly serves 3 billion people, or one half of the global population. See the ICA Web site (www.ica.coop/coop/statistics.html).

[5] See ICA Web site (www.ica.coop/coop/principles.html).

does rapid growth affect their practices? What is the impact as they create subsidiaries or multinational businesses? What is the impact of significant communications changes? of the formation of federations and new alliances? The answers to such questions usually (or should) raise issues about values.

These kinds of questions led the people involved with the research into values and their principles during the 1990s to argue for operating principles for each kind of co-op. While recognizing the importance of general principles, they believed it was necessary to develop more specific principles to cover such variables as the type and size of cooperatives being considered. The raising of capital, for example, is vastly different across the cooperative movement, as is the nature of managerial and elected leadership required. Responding to such differences requires considerable thought to ensure that the decisions that are made do not undermine the distinctly cooperative quality of an organization. In the end, it is up to each local cooperative to work out how the general principles apply, given its situation, and to decide on what operating principles will best suit its circumstances. The general cooperative principles are not cookie cutters; they are guides.

Fifth, cooperative principles change, confusing enough for those (within and without the movement) who see principles as being essential and permanent truths. The reality, however, is that the cooperative principles, though they should always conform to the movement's underlying values, are subject to incremental change. There have been three editions of the ICA principles. The first one was created in 1937 – some forty years after the ICA's formation. It had taken that long to create such a list because there was so much disagreement over what should be included. And, even then, the list could be described as "minimalist" because it included only some of the most obvious common denominators. These principles were modestly revised some thirty years later in 1966[6] and again in 1995.[7]

It would appear, therefore, that cooperative principles are open for renegotiation within the movement every thirty years – or, put more meaningfully, as a new generation of leaders emerges or as major social, economic, and political shifts seem to require it. Such gradual but meaningful evolution can hardly be surprising, given the varied and deep changes of the last 200 years. Nor would it be surprising today if, amid the frantic pace of contemporary economic, social, political, and communication changes, the international movement revised its principles even more frequently. Perhaps that is the most important reason why it is essential to think more seriously about the importance of the cooperative values underlying the principles.

[6] See W. P. Watkins, *Co-operative Principles, Today and Tomorrow* (Manchester: Holyoake Books, 1986).
[7] See Ian MacPherson, *Co-operative Principles for the 21st Century* (Geneva: International Co-operative Alliance, 1995).

THE COMPLICATED VALUES INHERITANCE

Strictly speaking, specific discussions about the basic values of the international movement are a recent phenomenon. That does not mean, however, that "values" have not been discussed constantly throughout the movement's history.[8] Quite the contrary, cooperative discourse has always been heavily laden with value considerations, a major reason for today's complexities.

People have formed cooperatives to ameliorate the pressures emanating from unrelenting market forces, the hardships of industrialism, the growth of large urban slums, and rapid transitions in rural communities. Urban and rural people created co-ops to use the resources, financial and human, that the individual could not amass. These co-ops reflected the values characteristic of the working and agrarian classes of the nineteenth century.[9] They were also influenced by middle-class – even aristocratic[10] – concerns over the Social Question: how amid so much prosperity could poverty continue to exist, and even expand? The origins of cooperatives are diverse and complex. There is no simple, single story; no single taproot.

In addition to this diverse socioeconomic background, the international movement has been significantly affected by many national perspectives, beginning with its early development in Europe. In the formative years of the late nineteenth and early twentieth centuries, the cooperative movements of the United Kingdom, Germany, France, Denmark, Russia, and Italy were particularly important.[11] In the early twentieth century, the movements in Eastern Europe and along the Mediterranean coast became increasingly significant. During the twentieth century the situation was further complicated as the movement spread to the Americas, Africa, and Asia, creating numerous movements shaped by the values and myths of their national experiences.

---

[8] A discussion about cooperative ideas and what we would call values can be found in W. P. Watkins, *The International Co-operative Alliance, 1895–1970* (London: International Co-operative Alliance, 1970). An argument can be made that values were important aspects of the discussions at all the ICA congresses since 1945: Zurich (1946), Prague (1948), Paris (1954), Stockholm (1957), and especially Lausanne (1960).

[9] There is a particularly rich and growing recent literature on the subtle ways in which the British working class adopted cooperative approaches, particularly in meeting their food needs. See Peter Gurney, *Co-operative Culture and the Politics of Consumption in England, 1870–1930* (New York: Manchester University Press, 1996); and Stephen Yeo, *Who Was J.T.W. Mitchell?* (Manchester: CWS Membership Services, 1995). For examples of the rural dimension, see Lawrence Goodwyn, *The Populist Moment: A Short History of Populist Revolt in America* (Oxford: Oxford University Press, 1976); and Bradford James Rennie, *The Rise of Agrarian Democracy: The United Farmers and Farm Women of Alberta, 1909–1921* (Toronto: University of Toronto Press, 2000).

[10] See Rita Rhodes, "Paternalism in the Early British Consumer Co-operative Movement," in Ian MacPherson and Erin McLaughlin-Jenkins, *Integrating Diversities within a Complex Heritage* (Victoria: New Rochdale Press, 2008), pp. 129–50.

[11] See Johnston Birchall, *The International Co-operative Movement* (Manchester: University of Manchester, 1997), pp. 1–34; and W. P. Watkins, *The International Co-operative Alliance, 1895–1970*, pp. 1–95.

Moreover, the cooperative movement, particularly in its early years, was frequently influenced by the values of various political movements usually (but not always) on the ideological Left during what has been called the Age of Ideologies.[12] Those associations encouraged class loyalties and the distrust of "trusts" within cooperative circles in the early years. They helped emphasize the importance of the values of democracy, solidarity, and caring for others.

As European settlers migrated around the world they developed numerous co-ops, particularly agricultural and financial cooperatives. Although they reflected European values in doing so, they also were affected by the pressures and needs of the settlement process and by the dominant cultures of the countries where they settled. In some instances, they were affected by the cooperative traditions and values of Indigenous people.[13] The cooperatives in other lands are not just extensions of the European cooperative experience and value systems.

In the last half of the twentieth century, the widespread struggles for independence within the southern colonies brought new emphases and priorities to the developing international cooperative world. Some of the most passionate proponents of cooperatives were among the leaders of those movements, including such figures as Ghandi, Nehru, Williams, Nkrumah, and Sukarno.[14] Although they differed in their approaches to cooperatives, they saw them as important development tools for the future. They also saw them as embracing values and perspectives that resonated with their peoples' past, their culture and basic values.

Most of the southern movements emphasized cooperatives that could help create market-oriented agriculture and sustainable rural communities. This emphasis on rural cooperatives meant engaging diverse rural cultures intricately intertwined with kin associations and village relationships as well as purely economic considerations. It also tended to raise questions about religion. How best to understand the attitudes and values of cooperators in the various Buddhist and Hindu traditions? What was the impact of Roman Catholic Social Justice and Liberation theology initiatives? How important were the enthusiasms generated by the Social Gospel, mostly among Protestants?[15]

---

[12] For Age of Ideologies, see John Schwartzmantel, *The Age of Ideologies: Political Ideologies from the American Revolution to Postmodern Times* (New York: New York University Press, 1998).

[13] For an example of some of the issues involved when Indigenous peoples develop cooperatives, see Isobel Findlay, "Putting Co-operative Principles into Practice," *Review of International Co-operation*, 99, no. 1 (2006), pp. 44–52.

[14] See W. P. Watkins, *The International Co-operative Alliance, 1895–1970*, pp. 283–6; and J. Birchall, *The International Co-operative Movement*, which has chapters dealing with Africa, Asia and the Pacific Rim, and the Americas. The role of cooperatives within independence movements in each of these regions is considered in passing in each of these chapters.

[15] See Ian MacPherson, *Hands Around the Globe: A History of the International Credit Union Movement and the Role and Development of the World Council of Credit Unions* (Madison: World Council if Credit Unions, 1999), pp. 1–31 and pp. 69–95.

Whatever the answers, there can be no doubt they involved deep and important value considerations.

From the 1960s onward, as the urgent needs of some southern nations (and the growing pockets of poverty in the North) became more obvious and unacceptable, many governments and nongovernment organizations embraced cooperative development. Their records of achievement were mixed, not least because there was often a mismatching of underlying values. Within international cooperative development, for example, the (mostly) northern developers often brought their own sets of values related to family and community, to economic development and business efficiency, and to the roles of the state. They had their own ideas of what constituted democratic practice and effective social commitment. They did not always easily fit.

Thus, although the world of cooperative development during the last fifty years has achieved many notable successes, it also has been fraught with challenges. It has, however, been an important location for debates within the movement over similar but different sets of values associated with community, family, and sharing. In fact, it arguably has been where such issues have been best explored.

There is one other major inherited complexity: the controversial legacy of cooperatives within the centrally planned economies of the Union of Soviet Socialist Republics and China – and their satellite states. Although many from outside those countries questioned the *bona fides* of the cooperatives that were formed, their governments – and key people involved – always claimed they were cooperatives. It was a significant issue partly because of the size of the cooperatives involved. They included some of the large collective farms, huge housing projects, powerful networks for moving farm produce to the cities, and large consumer co-ops. The issue was important, too, because many southern countries copied the Soviet/Chinese models in whole or in part in building their movements. They sent people from their co-ops to the cooperative training facilities in the USSR and China, and they welcomed technical support from the two countries. Their legacy remains.

The debates over the cooperatives in the centrally planned economies rocked the international cooperative world from 1917 until the 1990s. One might even say that the serious, direct discussion of cooperative values could take place only when those debates seemed to dissipate as Perestroika occurred.

All of these complexities suggest why it is has been challenging to create a cohesive viewpoint on the values of the international movement. For decades, the best the ICA could do (and it was not insignificant) was to present "rules" or principles for the operation of cooperative organizations. Initially, it did so by emphasizing the heritage of the Rochdale Pioneers in the United Kingdom. Their contribution to the consumer cooperative movement in their own and in many other countries was substantial. The "rules" they developed for their store were very effective and were adapted by many other kinds of cooperatives. Perhaps most importantly as any factor, their work had been popularized by a series of very effective writers.[16] As a result, it became the basis for the work done by ICA Principles Committees in the 1930s and 1960s. The only problem was that they stood alone, their context not well explained – and even when it was, the connection between a Lancashire situation long over a century ago and much of the world today was not always clear.

THE BACKGROUND TO THE 1990S' DISCUSSION OF CO-OPERATIVE VALUES

The last revision of the principles, in the 1990s, differed from the earlier approaches because the ICA tried to situate the principles within the context of basic values. The origins of this effort can be traced back to 1978, when delegates to the ICA's Copenhagen Congress wondered if their movement was really speaking effectively to modern circumstances. Following the Congress, the ICA commissioned Alex Laidlaw of Canada to prepare a background paper to reflect on the state of the international movement.

Laidlaw presented his lengthy paper, *Co-operatives in the Year 2000*, at the Moscow Congress of 1980. In it, he expressed considerable concern for the older, established movement, which he believed was developing a crisis of identity. He saw deepening worries about questionable democratic practices, increasing member apathy, and weakening cooperative education. He raised such questions as: "What is going to be the status of co-operatives confronted by the intervention and growing power of governments all over the world? . . . what is the end purpose of it all? What is expected of co-operatives? How is success of co-operative enterprise to be measured? By the same criteria by which other business is judged? If not the same, then what criteria?"[17]

Although Laidlaw's focus was on cooperative institutions, he demonstrated throughout his widely read paper the importance of cooperative thought and, though he seldom used the words, what could be called cooperative values. He sought to find the "principles behind the principles" and called out for the identification of the "basic moral and ideological pillars of the co-operative system."[18] He was suspicious of tendencies within the movement to become fixated on short-term economic success: for him, being "profitable" was important, but it should not be an end in itself. He was very impressed by the deep commitments of the people creating new cooperatives addressing global food issues, the creation of productive labor, the building of what was then commonly

---

[16] G. J. Holyoake, *Self-Help by the People: The History of the Rochdale Pioneers* (London: George Allen and Unwin, 1857); S. and B. Webb, *The Consumers Co-operative Movement* (London: Longmans, 1921); G. D. H. Cole, *A Century of Co-operation* (London: George Allen and Unwin, 1944); A. Bonner, *British Co-operation* (Manchester: Co-operative Union, 1970, revised edition); J. Birchall, *Co-op: The People's Business* (Manchester: University of Manchester, 1994).

[17] A. F. Laidlaw, *Co-operatives in the Year 2000: A Paper prepared for the 27th Congress of the International Co-operative Alliance* (Ottawa: Co-operative Union of Canada, n.d.), p. 8.

[18] Laidlaw, *Co-operatives in the Year 2000*, p. 33.

called a "conserver society," and the development of more cooperative communities.

In 1984, the ICA's Hamburg Congress discussed at length the need for the international movement to address global issues more effectively, particularly peace, food security, better energy practices, environmental protection, and international cooperative development. Some of the most prominent leaders arguing for this expanded perspective came from the Soviet Union, particularly M. P. Trunov, the President of Centrosoyus, the very large wholesale organization for the Soviet consumer movement. Trunov chaired the committee that prepared a report for the Congress on "Global Problems and Co-operation."[19] Alhough his participation tended to mean that the discussion was clouded by the rhetoric and mistrust of the Cold War, the report sparked a vital debate: it deepened the questions Laidlaw had raised about what cooperatives should do in the face of unfolding global problems, notably growing poverty, hunger, war, and pollution. The discussion at Hamburg moved the discussion beyond the principles, as then accepted, and into more theoretical and challenging terrain.

At the next Congress, in Stockholm in 1988, the ICA adopted as one of its themes "Co-operatives and Basic Values." In some ways, it was a remarkable decision in that it was developed before such discussions were common in the general business world. The movement was a decade or more ahead of the "competition." The issue had emerged because of the apparently unstoppable rise of capitalist or market economies. As Lars Marcus, President of the ICA, put it:

There is clear evidence that co-operatives have been harmfully influenced by [the rapid upswing in the capitalist market economies]. In many countries the original and unique character of co-operatives has been eroded by the predominant forms of economic life, such as the shareholding companies. Nowhere is this more true than in some of the biggest, strongest and oldest member countries of the ICA.[20]

Marcus went on to itemize several other fundamental challenges then confronting the international movement: the weakness, even the failure, of some national movements, the declining effectiveness of cooperative democratic practices, the lack of multinational cooperative institutions, and declining member commitment across the movement. He called for increased attention to cooperative ideas, arguing that discussions about them had tended to lie "fallow" for some years. He argued that "co-operatives ... started from basic values,"[21] and that it was the duty of cooperators "to analyze [their] basic identity regularly and profoundly."[22] Cooperators needed to tend to their intellectual as well as their

[19] *International Co-operative Alliance, XXVIII Congress, Hamburg, 15–18 October, 1984* (Geneva: International Co-operative Alliance, n.d.), pp. 63–75.
[20] Lars Marcus, *Co-operatives and Basic Values: A Report to the ICA Congress, Stockholm 1988, XXIX Congress, Stockholm, July 1988, Agenda & Reports* (Geneva: International Co-operative Alliance, 1988), p. 95.
[21] Lars Marcus, *Co-operatives and Basic Values: A Report to the ICA Congress*, p. 99.
[22] Ibid., p. 108.

economic and institutional health if they were to address effectively many contemporary issues.

Following Marcus's report, the Congress created a committee to conduct an international study of the basic values of the global movement. It was chaired by Sven Åke Böök, the former director of the Swedish Co-operative Institute. With the assistance of a large international committee,[23] he spent three years assembling information and perspectives on what the international movement believed its basic values were. Employing what he called an "action and dialogue" approach, he and his committee worked largely through seminars, conferences, lectures, and interviews.[24] Their meetings ultimately engaged some 10,000 people around the world. It was the ICA's first sustained international dialog on a major issue; its first efforts to develop a grassroots approach to developing a consensus on cooperative thought.

Böök was nearly overwhelmed by the richness and complexity of what he and the other members of the committee saw and heard. They saw cooperatives and talked with cooperators in many different places around the world, such as Japanese fishing villages, Australian cities, northern Italy, Danish farms, rural Tanzania, the German countryside, Atlantic Canada, Greek communities, Indian farms, and the center of Singapore. They listened to a wide cross section of cooperators – older and younger, females as well as male – reflecting on their cooperatives at the time and wondering about the future.

It fell on Böök's shoulders to bring order to the abundance of insights that had been gathered. The book he prepared in doing so (as edited by Margaret Prickett and Mary Tracey of the ICA) was a valiant effort to synthesize what had been heard. In it he appealed to the international movement to reflect upon, and to apply, its basic values much more vigorously than it had in recent decades. He shared the (by then) long-standing concern of many cooperative leaders that the movement, despite its considerable growth,[25] was not making the headway that it should. He shared Laidlaw's beliefs that some older cooperatives were losing their way and that some new cooperatives were being ignored, even though they had much to offer.[26] He particularly stressed the threats and the possibilities offered by the global trends of the day, notably the gathering problems of food production and the threat of environmental disaster. He believed they offered fertile ground for extensive and very useful cooperative development.

---

[23] The committee, which played an active role in the consultative process, was remarkable for its international engagement. It included Raija Itkonen (Finland), Lloyd Wilkinson (U.K.), Igor Vyroulev (USSR/Russia), André Chomel (France), Janos Juhasz (Hungary), Philip Chilomo (Zambia), Masao Ohya (Japan), Edwin Morley-Fletcher (Italy), Hans Münkner (Germany), Dante Craogna (Argentina), Ian MacPherson (Canada), Yehudah Paz (Israel), and Dionyssos Mavrogiannis (Greece).

[24] Sven Åke Böök (edited by Margaret Prickett and Mary Tracey), *Co-operative Values in a Changing World*, Report to the ICA Congress, Tokyo, October, 1992 (Geneva: International Co-operative Alliance, 1992), p. 8.

[25] Sven Åke Böök, *Co-operative Values in a Changing World*, pp. 21–3.

[26] Ibid., pp. 82–6.

Böök devoted most of his book to a complicated discussion of the varieties of values he had discussed with numerous people. He organized them in several ways. The first was what he called traditional basic values – Equality (democracy) and Equality; Voluntary and Mutual Self-Help; Social and Economic Emancipation – arguing that they were strongly influenced by values of Honesty, Caring, Pluralism (democratic approach), and Constructiveness (faith in the cooperative way).[27] He then examined values he believed important for shaping cooperative organizations, including relations with communities, members, and other cooperatives locally, nationally, and internationally.[28] He also devoted considerable attention to what he called "cooperative ideas," though perhaps not always making clear the distinction between values and ideas. Finally, he recommended several changes in the cooperative principles, including addressing issues of capital formation, the inclusion of employees in the administration of cooperatives, and increased emphasis on cooperative autonomy, particularly as it related to governments.

IDENTIFYING THE CO-OPERATIVE VALUES

Böök's study was one of the more important discussions of cooperative thought in the twentieth century. It was also one of the most complicated, largely because of the wide range of sources he had consulted, the vast range of cooperative experiences, contemporary and historical, and the circuitous logic he tended to employ. Following its distribution and discussion at the Tokyo Congress of 1992, the ICA's challenge was to translate it into a more easily digested form, not only for cooperators but also for public servants, politicians, the general public, and people interested in developing cooperatives. That task was given to others, a new Principles Resource Group chaired by the author,[29] and supported by a Consultative Committee consisting of some fifty international cooperative leaders and thinkers.

Following considerable discussion and the distribution of a questionnaire to the Consultative Committee, the Group decided that the main need, for several reasons, was to demonstrate the unique qualities of cooperative organizations. First, they recognized that, despite its size and global importance,[30] the movement was being overwhelmed by the growing strength of capitalist organizations; it was overlooked in the media, and was rarely considered in universities.

The second reason emerged because of the collapse of the centrally planned economies in Central and Eastern Europe. By 1992 their cooperative movements

---

[27] Ibid., p. 13.
[28] Ibid., pp. 33–9.
[29] The other members of the Resource Committee were: Hans Münkner (Germany), Yehudah Paz (Israel), Masahiko Shiraishi (Japan), Hans-Detlief Wülker (Germany), and Bruce Thordarson (Executive Director of the ICA).
[30] In 1995, there were just over 750,000,000 individual memberships in the cooperatives in the organizations affiliated with the ICA. *XXXI ICA Congress, Manchester, Agenda and Reports* (Geneva: International Co-operative Alliance, 1995), p. 117.

were largely in disarray. They needed a clear understanding of cooperative enterprise, one they could use as their economies were reformed.

Third, some movements in former colonies, particularly in Africa, were also reeling because they had depended upon considerable state aid for their development and operations. That support was being withdrawn as economic situations worsened and outside forces, such as the International Monetary Fund, pressured governments to curtail direct involvement in the economy. As with Central and Eastern Europe, the pressing need was to reiterate the centrality of membership and the importance of being independent of the state.

The Resource Group responded to these challenges by developing a clear statement on cooperative values. It became the basis for a definition of a cooperative and for the reconsideration of the cooperative principles. The order was important. In carrying out its work, the Group undertook considerably more consultation. It did not assume – as was very tempting – the roles of prophet and preacher. It embraced a widely consultative process approach, one that involved as many people as practicable. It worked through no fewer than fourteen drafts. It organized discussions that, as in the case of the values project, involved some 10,000 people. Bruce Thordarson, the ICA's Executive Director, and his staff organized the movement's regular international and regional meetings to make this kind of consultation possible, as did leaders in several national movements, particularly in Asia, as they developed their annual gatherings.

The Group ultimately prepared two lists of values, the first of which addressed the ways in which cooperatives are commonly organized.

Co-operatives are based on the values of self-help, self-responsibility, democracy, equality, equity and solidarity.[31]

There are at least four important points to note concerning this list. The first is the emphasis on member engagement and control, in part a way to respond to the tendency to rely too much on government support. The second is the stress on democratic operations, one of the most important ways in which cooperatives differ from capitalist firms. Third, the insistence on equality and equity, two historic cooperative values, took on special meaning in the 1990s, given the attention being paid to gender equality. The fourth dimension – solidarity – caused some controversies at the time, a few finding it too closely tied to historic left-wing appeals, notably from the trade union movement. Ultimately, though, most people in the movement agreed with its inclusion.

The second list identified the values that should characterize the operation of cooperatives. Aware of the burden (and the benefits) of history that most cooperative movements share, the Group phrased this list as follows:

In the tradition of their founders, co-operative members believe in the ethical values of honesty, openness, social responsibility and caring for others.

---

[31] ICA Web site (www.ica.coop/coop/principles.html).

This list stimulated many fascinating discussions and seems to have led to considerable change within some cooperatives. For example, the consideration of honesty went far beyond the "truth in advertising" kind of discussion that might immediately come to mind. It included discussions about what "honesty" means for relationships among all the groups involved in cooperatives – members, elected leaders, managers, staff, communities, and regulators. It is a more complicated topic than one might assume. Similarly, the discussion on "openness" meant more than it often suggests in conventional business: it included frequent, accurate, and useful reporting to members and full discussions of actions to be taken with staff – if not their involvement in deciding upon them.

The inclusion of values on social responsibility and caring for others was how the Group recognized the movement's engagement with many of the large issues of the day. It acknowledged the community and social objectives of cooperatives, in the case of most sectors evident since the nineteenth century – the days of the founders. They include, for example, the community objectives of the Rochdale Pioneers, the rural concerns of most agricultural movements, the social concerns of Raiffeisen, the communal traditions of the worker cooperative movement, and the widespread, though underacknowledged, impact of cooperative intentional communities. It also acknowledged the social cooperative sector, traditionally most commonly represented by housing cooperatives, but increasingly more evident in health and child care cooperatives.

Obviously, these values are open ended. One can only press consistently and progressively toward "self-help, self-responsibility, democracy, equality, equity and solidarity."[32] One can only strive for more "honesty, openness, social responsibility, and caring for others" as integral aspects of a cooperative's activities. One can never expect to achieve perfection, only steadily improving performance.

It is partly because of this open-ended quality that the values were seen as "guides" to the principles. The application of the values and principles must be the subject for periodic reevaluation within a given cooperative or movement, including the international movement generally. Cooperators will consistently challenge and improve their organization's application of democratic practice, moving beyond the sometimes ritualized democracy of annual elections to develop meaningful two-way member communications. They will strive constantly to improve their cooperative's commitment to equality by ensuring that everyone feels included and that all groups – men, women, youth, ethnic groups, new members as well as old – are able to participate. They will hold the cooperative to a high standard of honesty and ensure that its involvement in social responsibility and caring for others is significant and not just a passing market strategy. The values provide a kind of "situation ethics" derived from the movement's history and enduring goals.

---

[32] As an example of the kinds of issues that these values can raise, see Stephen Yeo, "Co-operation, Mutuality, and the Democratic Deficit or Re-membering Democracy," in Ian MacPherson and Erin McLaughlin-Jenkins, *Integrating Diversities within a Complex Heritage*, pp. 223–78.

The development of a definition acceptable across the movement followed from the identification of values. There had been several attempts to prepare such a definition, going back to the nineteenth century. They had floundered because of the varying perspectives associated with different kinds of cooperatives, the multiple national backgrounds from which they came, and the ideological debates of the times. After considerable consultation, the Group came up with the following definition, which had as its central premise the importance of autonomy, voluntary membership, breadth of possible activities, and democratic structure, all of which had their basis in cooperative values:

A co-operative is an autonomous association of persons united voluntarily to meet their common economic, social, and cultural needs and aspirations through a jointly-owned and democratically-controlled enterprise.[33]

The definition was well received and fortunately was subsequently also adopted by the International Labour Organization, a very important step in helping to develop international cooperative consistency.

The Group's work on the principles was a mixture of informed history, movement politics, and values application. It was a challenging but stimulating task. For all the reasons discussed earlier in this chapter, it was not easy to identify basic principles within the international movement. For older organizations and cooperators, the principles often defined the nature of their commitment. For people who had recently learned the principles as they became involved in the movement, substantial changes could be confusing. In 1995, as in 1967, the changes that were possible, therefore, might at first glance be seen as being mostly incremental.

The *Statement on the Co-operative Identity*, however, represents an attempt to create a unified document ultimately infused by the values that had been identified. The values were reflected in slight revisions of the older principles so as to emphasize the centrality of membership engagement: as much as possible they were stated from the perspective of members so as to place responsibility for cooperative development ultimately where it belongs. The "democracy," "equality," "equity" values obviously informed the principles on Voluntary and Open Membership (#1), Democratic Member Control (#2), and Member Economic Participation (#3).

An important addition, in the Voluntary and Open Membership principle, postulated that cooperatives should be genuinely open to all kinds of people. Given the different attitudes toward gender equality around the world at the time, this was not achieved without debate, particularly in some southern countries. Similarly, the idea that race should not count was not always easily accepted in places where it demonstrably and historically was counted. The result was a rather elaborate principle directly emphasizing access to membership "without gender, social, racial, political or religious discrimination." It reflected the values that the movement had long harbored.

---

[33] ICA Web site (www.ica.coop/coop/principles.html).

The centrality of member control was reflected in the development of an Autonomy and Independence principle (#4). It was obviously important for cooperators in the former centrally planned economies and in the South, where government influence had been too great. It was not unimportant in the industrialized North, however, for new co-ops overly reliant on government grants or for larger co-ops entering into alliances that could be too restrictive with capitalist firms or governments.

The solidarity value was the basis for the 6th principle, Co-operation among Co-operatives. It did not meet the wishes of some who wanted the movement to be more open to supporting like-minded organizations and causes. The debate was intense but the *Statement on the Co-operative Identity* as it was adopted reflected a long-standing concern about being co-opted by other movements. It was also felt that such collaborative decisions should be made by local co-ops, as long as their members were demonstrably in agreement. It was not the solution many community activists wished, but it was in keeping with maintaining cooperative autonomy.

The values of honesty and openness were at least partly reflected in the principle on Education, Training and Information (#5), and in the Democratic Member Control principle (#2). In the final analysis, however, it is difficult to legislate honesty and openness: they are a matter of everyday practice, as much an accumulation of little things done properly as grand gestures performed occasionally.

It is crucially important to realize, though, that the result of emphasizing the values that inform the principles does not induce tidy uniformity. The "democracy" value, aside from the similarities in conducting elections (only one part of a healthy democratic culture), will vary in its application: the sense of ownership control is very different in an Inuit cooperative in northern Canada, a large multiline insurance cooperative in Singapore, a co-op dairy in Texas, and a housing cooperative in Amsterdam. The fostering of steadily greater equity in a cooperative will face different challenges in a community credit union in Los Angeles, a consumer co-op in Sapporo, a sugar co-op in Nigeria, a Muslim cooperative bank in Iran, a marketing cooperative in Mexico, and a two-million-member outdoor cooperative based in Canada. Equity becomes more complex as cooperatives move beyond their local communities and especially as they become national. Likewise, "caring for community" takes on different hues in a wealthy housing co-op in New York, areas caught in the turmoil of the Middle East, villages devastated by earthquakes, neighborhoods with large immigrant populations, and towns where the primary industry has closed. "Solidarity" means something different to members of a worker co-op in France than it does to farmers in Argentina, consumers in Leeds, villagers in Gujarat, and farmer-members of poultry cooperatives in Colombia. The application of "honesty" can vary across different cultures and kinds of cooperatives. "Openness" depends as much on social relations within a given society and the management culture of a given cooperative as it does on generally accepted accounting standards. The point is that values, while they can have some similar characteristics around the world, vary greatly in kinds of understanding and ways of being expressed. The cooperative identity has multiple personalities.

CONTINUING CONCERNS

The *Statement on the Co-operative Identity* is not a perfect document. What is ultimately important about it, however, is that it attempts to meld values with principles and to provide as clear a picture of cooperative enterprise as the great variety and global reach of the movement allows. It raises issues and perspectives from the long and deep history of the movement; it suggests that mere conformity with the minimum requirement of rules, a too common tendency in the movement, is not enough. It also shows that a decade before "values-based business" became fashionable, cooperators and cooperative organizations were starting to grapple with the kinds of issues and perspectives it raised. They did so by delving into their history and experience, by engaging in a global discussion over the possibilities, and by developing consensus statements on how values progressively create their identity.[34]

That does not mean that there were not useful and constructive regrets and criticisms when the task was done. The work on cooperative values and principles is a matter of fulfilling an ongoing social contract across generations of cooperators, not in achieving a statement for the ages. No one preparing such a document can expect universal or unending acclaim. The most common criticism at the time was that the *Statement on the Co-operative Identity* did not address adequately some "business" dimensions of cooperative activity, and perhaps there could have been some ways that it might have done so had there been will within the movement to do so.

The variations in purpose, type, size, economic context, and cultural influences, however, make it very difficult to generalize about the operation of cooperative enterprise. That is why at the beginning of the process a distinction was made between operating principles and general principles. The hope was that each type of cooperative, perhaps as represented in the Sectoral organizations of the ICA, would carry the work further, dealing more directly with such issues as capital formation, managerial responsibilities, employee involvement, marketing practices, subsidiaries, and alliances (with cooperatives and non-cooperatives).

The issue from among this list of operational matters that was the most discussed throughout both the values and the identity statement projects concerned the roles of employees. The discussions this issue stimulated raised a long-standing and difficult debate within the movement, one that historically – and today – stimulates very different views. In fact, one might hypothesize that it was the main difference preventing early efforts at achieving an international

---

[34] For some remarkable insights into how the ICA and international cooperative leaders worked within the context of *The Co-operative Identity Statement*, see Ivano Barberini, *How the Bumblebee Flies: Cooperation, Ethics and Development* (Milan: Baldini Castoldi Dalai, 2009).

consensus. Even in the 1990s, it was not an issue on which the movement could achieve a useful consensus. That did not mean, however, that individual cooperatives or cooperative movements could not extend considerable influence to their workers. In general, new cooperatives were much more sympathetic to the idea of involving employees in the administration of cooperatives. In some jurisdictions they could do so formally through stakeholder or "solidarity" co-ops. More importantly, worker cooperatives, which found their own ways in which to operate under cooperative laws, were primarily devoted to worker empowerment and they formed one of the most rapidly expanding sectors in the world. The issue was very much in the forefront of many cooperative endeavors and no doubt will reappear whenever future revision of the values statement and the principles occurs.

Still others wished to have greater recognition given to managers, most particularly by having them serve automatically as members of the board,[35] as they do in many capitalist firms. This suggestion came forward just as the Group, following considerable consultation, had decided that there was not a consensus on including a principle on employee participation in governance. That timing was unfortunate. There were, however, some more substantial considerations.

Deciding upon the appropriate roles for managers has always been a central (though rarely openly discussed) dimension of cooperative enterprise. The challenge has always been to decide upon the balance of power among members, elected leaders, and managers. It is an issue that grows as co-ops expand; as technological, communication, and managerial systems become more complicated; and as professionals (e.g., accountants, marketing experts, human resource specialists) become more important. The movement's original perception of managers as servants – an idea similar to the concept of the public servant as it had developed in the nineteenth century – has been transformed to echo the idea of leadership as celebrated in the private sector and within most business schools. It has been influenced by the contemporary common capitalist perspective of the manager as the chief catalyst, the essential force in any organization, sometimes even "the white knight" – the reason why they are so celebrated in the media, why they are remunerated so well, and arguably why they tend in self-interest to emphasize short-term prosperity over future stability. That perception of leadership should not fit within cooperative enterprise.

For many in the 1990s, the chief risk was not that managers had too little influence, but that they could so easily have too much. That unease will not change until more is learned about the nature of cooperative management, one of the more challenging tasks of the field of Cooperative Studies.

Another debate that did not die out was over "mutuality," a value held particularly strongly in France, the Mediterranean countries, and Japan. For those strongly supporting it, mutuality encapsulated the cooperative

---

[35] Peter Davis of the University of Leicester has argued this perspective most vigorously. For example, see his "The Governance of Co-operatives under Competitive Conditions: Issues, Processes and Culture," *Corporate Governance*, 1, no. 4 (2001), pp. 28–39.

commitment to working together for common benefit. It was more appropriate than the increasingly common emphasis on reciprocity, another widely supported value and one more in keeping with the prevailing dominant economic paradigm. Mutuality advocated advancing together and not just on the basis of "I scratch your back and you scratch mine." In an age when human beings collectively face immense challenges from environmental degradation, food problems, water crises, and energy crises – all challenges common to us all and to which cooperatives can provide at least partial answers – perhaps consideration should be given again to the importance of mutuality as a basic value. One other major issue emerged during the 1990s: a widespread concern over the environment. The cooperative record on the environment was mixed at that time. On the one hand, many cooperatives were addressing environmental issues very effectively. The organic food and Fair Trade industries in many parts of the world were largely run through cooperatives. Cooperative development projects rarely supported large-scale, intrusive projects; they were concentrating more and more on small-scale, village-based activities that had less impact on the environment. Electric co-ops were beginning to turn to wind and sun energy.

On the other hand, many of the old-order co-ops were developed during the time when environmental issues were not considered important. Many of them had fostered what had become conventional agricultural practices, including deep cultivation, specialized agriculture, and the indiscriminate use of chemicals. For them – and their members – the rapid transition to new forms of agriculture was not an academic exercise but a deep incursion into everyday life. For them change could occur, but it would have to be gradual.

The Group, trying to respond to these two perspectives, both deeply held, took a gradualist approach. As with other dimensions of the *Statement on the Co-operative Identity* – with, for example, the issues of democracy, member engagement, and education – it sought to encourage definite and progressive change. It emphasized the importance of cooperatives annually considering such questions as the following: What specific progress was made this year in addressing environmental concerns? What specific progress can we make next year?

Furthermore, the Group believed that environmentalism was central to the 7th, or Concern for Community, principle. It called for cooperatives to "work for the sustainable development of their communities through policies approved by their members." This approach, however, understandably did not completely satisfy the strongest advocates of environmentalism, people who believed that an abrupt change in practices was necessary for cooperatives – as for all other organizations – if the world was to meet its environmental challenges.

The approach in 1995 may have helped. In the years since then, perhaps partly because of the 7th principle, the international movement has demonstrated a deepening commitment to environmental issues.[36] International

---

[36] For example, see The Co-operative Group (U.K.) (www.co-operative.coop/corporate/aboutus/our-ethics/); Canadian Co-operative Association (www.coopscanada.coop/en/about_co-operative/Environmental-Sustainability); the Alberta Federation of Rural Electrification Associations

cooperative development in the South has embraced steadily better environmental practice. The Fair Trade movement, which contains substantial co-op involvement, from production through processing to consumption, has consistently emphasized environmental issues.[37] In the global North, issues of food security have encouraged expanded intensive agriculture and "slow food" production, much of it organized through formal and informal cooperative networks. New kinds of cooperatives delivering wind power and encouraging the use of bicycles and the cooperative ownership/leasing of automobiles have been developed. Large co-ops have reduced their carbon footprint by using more electronic media, reducing the use of paper, and constructing energy-efficient buildings. All the co-op sectors, in fact, are demonstrating increased concern about environmental issues to varying but significant degrees.

REFLECTIONS

Most cooperatives are effective businesses. That is attested to by the age of many cooperatives around the world and by the rapid growth of new cooperatives. There is some evidence that cooperatives have a better survival rate than capital-driven enterprise.[38] The capacity of the cooperative model to be applied in many different contexts and in pursuit of many kinds of business is remarkable; its ability to strengthen local economies is a much-needed strength in a globalizing world. The potential of the international cooperative movement to create an alternative, people-based economic system is one of its most promising possibilities.

This success, this potential, is not an accident. It is not explained by arguing that cooperatives are niche businesses filling voids when the conventional market fails.[39] Despite current tendencies within some cooperatives to ape the methods of capitalist enterprise, cooperatives have developed their own effective – if understudied – ways of conducting business. One of the many great tasks of the field of Cooperative Studies is to understand these methods more completely and to show that cooperatives were social enterprises long before some business theorists alarmed over the growing and obvious shortcomings of

(www.afrea.ca/how-green-your-co-op); and The Co-operators (www.cooperators.ca/en/aboutus/sustainability/2_8_0_1.html).

[37] The cooperative engagement with Fair Trade is remarkable, and there is a large and growing literature on the subject. For example, see "Fair Trade" on the Web sites of: The Co-operative Group in the United Kingdom (www.co-operative.coop/food/); the Ontario Co-operative Association (www.ontario.coop/pages/index.php?main_id=273); the Fair Trade Foundation (www.fairtrade.org.uk/products/retail_products/product_browse.aspx?comps=CAKES+%26+BROWNIES); and Equal Exchange (www.equalexchange.coop/). There are many more Web sites that capture aspects of this subject.

[38] For example, see "Survival Rates of Co-operatives in Quebec," Research Report, Co-operatives Secretariat, Government of Canada.

[39] For a particularly stimulating discussion of the cooperatives and market failure argument, see Claudia Sanchez Bajo and Bruno Roelantz, *Capital and the Debt Trap: Learning from Co-operatives in the Global Crisis* (Basingstoke: Palgrave Macmillan, forthcoming).

conventional capitalism popularized that term.[40] Because of their principles, their structures, and their values, cooperatives have always been "social" if they have been true to their values.

This chapter has examined the way in which the international organized cooperative movement tried during the 1990s to make the connection between values and principles. It has argued that, while principles are fundamentally important for the development of cooperatives, values are even more so. The sources for the cooperative values are very complex, derived from history, many community situations, cultural understandings, bodies of thought, and economic circumstances. The initial work of the 1990s, however, demonstrated that there are commonalities in the values accepted throughout the international movement. Subsequent work has demonstrated that the connection of established values to principles can be readily established. The connections, though, have been and still are always changing incrementally in light of social, economic, and political pressures. That is one of the great strengths of cooperatives, although some people find it confusing, and the relatively slow pace of collective change will not always satisfy everyone.

In the end, values emerge from reflections about lived experiences, and people and groups with similar convictions can naturally develop different degrees of emphasis on what they believe. The "examined life" is different for everyone, but the possibility of mutual understanding and acceptance – "I understand, I can accept" – is always present in a cooperative environment. In many ways that was what happened when the international movement sought to come to terms with cooperative values in the 1990s. That process reaffirmed what many cooperators already instinctively know: that the "end purpose of it all" has to be found through reflecting upon, agreeing upon, and, above all, acting upon the basic cooperative values as each generation applies them.

---

[40] For example, see Michael E. Porter and Mark R. Kramer, "Rethinking Capitalism," *Harvard Business Review* (January–February 2011) (http://hbr.org/archive-toc/BR1101); and "The Law of Success 2.0: An Interview with Henry Mintzberg" (http://lawofsuccess2.blogspot.com/2010/09/interview-with-henry-mintzberg_08.html).

CHAPTER 5

Why Cooperatives Fail: Case Studies from Europe, Japan, and the United States, 1950–2010

Peter Kramper

INTRODUCTION

Cooperatives are indeed "a special kind of business" – so special in fact that ever since they first appeared, their ability to survive in a capitalist environment has been severely contested. In the nineteenth century alone, a host of authors ranging from Karl Marx to Franz Oppenheimer and Beatrice Webb expressed considerable skepticism in this regard. Their points of view have been echoed by many twentieth-century researchers, and the question of the permanent viability of cooperatives has become one of the most pertinent issues in the debate about this type of organization.[1]

Surprisingly, however, few have questioned why cooperatives actually fail. To be sure, the debate that I have just referred to contains a great deal of implicit theoretical insight into this problem. With only, one or two prominent exceptions, however, the issue rarely has been stated explicitly.[2] Consequently, both theoretical arguments and empirical investigations which address this question head-on are in short supply. It is the aim of this chapter to attempt to close these gaps – that is, to identify some of the factors that have determined the failure of cooperatives in the postwar period and to find out whether they add up to any sort of pattern, rule, or theoretical model.

Cooperatives can and do fail in two ways: they either go bankrupt or transform into investor-owned businesses (IOBs).[3] From the little research that has been conducted, it is perhaps fair to say that there are three different approaches which can be applied to the question of why this happens. The first one has been

---

[1] See the second section of this paper for a more detailed discussion.
[2] The exceptions concern the case of European consumer cooperatives presented in the third section of this paper.
[3] Some economists argue that the conversion of cooperatives into IOBs can be to the advantage of prior members and thus should not be regarded as failure. However, this point overlooks the fact that cooperative democracy has to be regarded as an aim sui generis which cannot be provided by an IOB.

tried out, for example, by Attwood and Baviskar,[4] who have compared both failures and successes of cooperative enterprises in one specific industry over a limited period of time and thus identified a number of factors that affected their viability in that given context. Although the results of their research are certainly significant, they are not entirely in line with the question that is to be pursued in this chapter. It is clear that cooperatives – just like any other type of business – can fail for any number reasons, such as lack of capital, incompetent management, organizational deficiencies, and so on. A focus on these proximate causes of failure, however, does not address the question of the specific strengths or weaknesses of this *type* of organization. Consequently, I will not be concerned with the question of why some cooperatives fail while others flourish; rather, I will focus on the question of whether cooperatives as a *genre* fail for specific reasons or under specific circumstances.

This question has been addressed before, and the respective work constitutes the second approach to the issue of failure that has to be mentioned. Notably some Anglo-American sociologists, on a broad statistical basis, have compared the performance of certain types of cooperatives to other, comparable businesses over a long period of time and have found that, on the whole, they have fared equally well or only slightly worse than IOBs. It is evident from this research that instances of failure are in no way more common among cooperatives than they are among other forms of enterprise.[5] Although this type of analysis is illuminating with regard to the scale and comparative frequency of cooperative failures, it is rather less convincing with regard to their causes, primarily because statistical comparisons have tended to depict businesses as if they were acting in a static environment. Hence, these papers have offered some explanations for failure, but they have rarely connected the failure to the wider economic, social, or cultural background.

This observation brings us to the third strategy, namely, the historical case studies.[6] This methodology is typically better at detailing the dynamics of change; however, *individual* case studies are often "of uncertain generalizability,"[7] and they rarely allow for comparisons with other types of enterprises. Nevertheless, both of these problems can, at least partially, be avoided by focusing not on cases

---

[4] D. M. Attwood and B. S. Baviskar, "Why Do Some Co-operatives Work But Not Others? A Comparative Analysis of Sugar Co-operatives in India," *Economic and Political Weekly*, 22 (S. 1987), pp. A38–A56.

[5] Chris Cornforth, "Some Factors Affecting the Success or Failure of Worker Co-operatives: A Review of Empirical Research in the United Kingdom," *Economic and Industrial Democracy*, 4 (1983), pp. 163–90; Chris Cornforth, "Patterns of Cooperative Management: Beyond the Degeneration Thesis," *Economic and Industrial Democracy*, 15 (1995), pp. 487–523; and Udo Staber, "Age-Dependence and Historical Effects on the Failure Rates of Worker Cooperatives: An Event-History Analysis," *Economic and Industrial Democracy*, 10 (1989), pp. 59–80.

[6] For a general discussion of this approach from the perspective of management theory, see the seminal paper by Kathleen M. Eisenhardt, "Building Theories from Case Study Research," *Academy of Management Review*, 14, no. 4 (1989), pp. 532–50.

[7] Cornforth, 1995, p. 496.

of *individual*, but rather on cases of *collective*, failure – cases in which large numbers of cooperatives fared particularly badly and were prone to failure to a higher degree than before or after the specific period under review.

This chapter will employ precisely this strategy. I identify three historical cases of cumulative failure of cooperatives. After a discussion of the main theoretical perspectives on the issue, the paper will investigate and compare (1) the demise of Western European consumer cooperatives between 1960 and 1985, with particular reference to West Germany; (2) the failure of Japanese credit cooperatives, which had their roots in the 1970s and 1980s and came to a head during the 1990s; and (3) the large-scale transformations that affected agricultural co-ops in the United States in the last twenty years or so.

Although at first sight this may seem like a rather motley assembly of cases, the broad perspective that comes with it has certain advantages. First, it includes a range of cooperatives in different sectors. Second, it covers almost the entire postwar period and captures many of its specifics. And third, it goes some way toward addressing the problem of generalizability. For example, the selected cases integrate a considerable portion of the industrialized world; they concern areas of business in which cooperatives, rather than being marginal phenomena, have occupied center stage; and because of the fact that in all of them, *some* organizations survived largely intact, they also offer the opportunity to compare different patterns *within* the field of cooperatives. These characteristics should make it possible to isolate the relevance of the one factor they have in common – the cooperative form of organization.

WHY COOPERATIVES FAIL: THEORETICAL PERSPECTIVES

What does the debate concerning the viability of cooperatives have to offer with regard to the question of failure? Before I can address this issue, it seems important to point out that much of the relevant literature is concerned with a special type of cooperative organization, namely, with workers' cooperatives. It will be clear from the introduction that this chapter does not include this type of business but rather focuses on agricultural, credit, and consumer cooperatives. This is mainly because workers' cooperatives historically have been confined to few niches, while the organizations that will be treated here all have played a considerable role in their respective economies.

Still, it is worthwhile to begin with a look at the long-standing debate on workers' cooperatives, as these were the organizations whose ability to survive was the focal point of the early skepticism mentioned in the introduction to this chapter. This skepticism is well phrased in Franz Oppenheimer's so-called "Law of Transformation," which he formulated in 1896: "Only very rarely," he wrote, "does a producer cooperative flourish. But if it does, it ceases to be a producer cooperative."[8] A very simplistic rationale for this view has been put

---

[8] Franz Oppenheimer, *Die Siedlungsgenossenschaft* (Leipzig, 1896), p. 45 (my translation).

forward by Marxist analysis. The main thrust of its argument is "that isolated worker cooperatives cannot change the wider forces and relations of production that have developed under capitalism, and will be subject to them. In particular the need to survive in a competitive market will force them to seek to maximize profit in the same way as other capitalist businesses, and to adopt the same forms of organization."[9] Perhaps somewhat surprisingly, this is essentially the same argument that standard economic theory has developed since the 1950s. In a well-known paper, Benjamin Ward has argued that workers' cooperatives could not survive in a neoclassical environment, because their objective of maximizing net income per unit of labor would – *ceteris paribus* – result in a negatively sloped short-term supply curve and in a "wrong" response to changing market conditions.[10]

These arguments, however, have since been largely abandoned – partly because they are not immune to methodological concerns, and partly because they do not hold up to empirical scrutiny.[11] Not all of the early skepticism toward workers' cooperatives has been affected by these criticisms; both Beatrice Webb and Franz Oppenheimer focused their analyses not so much on external pressures but rather on internal factors. And it is true that, in this regard, cooperatives differ fundamentally from IOBs, particularly concerning the pattern of ownership and the concomitant pledge to democratic control that is typically identified with the traditional formula of "one member, one vote." Building on these differences, Beatrice Webb claimed that management by workers would lead to a lack of discipline and a resistance to technological innovation, thus affecting the viability of such enterprises.[12] Oppenheimer argued similarly, but additionally pointed to the problem of raising capital.[13] And Robert Michels added another element by stating his "iron law of oligarchy," which suggests that any democracy will sooner or later be undermined by the emergence of a dominant elite, and Michels explicitly included cooperatives in this analysis.[14]

Although some of these observations have been dismissed as unfounded,[15] it is striking that many of them, in the last quarter of the twentieth century, found their way into modern economic theory – under the guise of New Institutional Economics and, particularly, the concept of property rights. The basic insight of

[9] Cornforth, 1995, p. 489.

[10] Benjamin Ward, "The Firm in Illyria: Market Syndicalism," *American Economic Review*, 48 (1958), pp. 566–89.

[11] For the methodological issues, see Jacques Drèze, *Labour Management, Contracts and Capital Markets: A General Equilibrium Approach* (Oxford, 1989). The empirical side is covered by the works mentioned in note 5.

[12] Sidney Webb and Beatrice Webb, "Special Supplement on Co-operative Production and Profit Sharing," *New Statesman*, 2 (1914, Nr. 45), p. 20 ff.

[13] Oppenheimer, 1896, p. 61.

[14] Robert Michels, *Zur Soziologie des Parteienwesens in der modernen Demokratie. Untersuchungen über die oligarchischen Tendenzen des Gruppenlebens* (Leipzig, 1925).

[15] Cornforth, 1995, p. 489 ff.

this school of thought is that inefficiencies in cooperatives arise "because property rights ... are not well defined and because co-operatives are often formed to pursue multiple objectives."[16] Interestingly, this rephrasing has shown that many of the problems that the "internalists" of the older literature attributed to workers' cooperatives were not, in fact, restricted to them but did, in principle, affect all cooperatives equally. For example, Michael L. Cook (see Chapter 7 in this book) has argued that the issue of raising capital is a result of the "one member, one vote" system common to all of these organizations. In his view, this system generates a free-rider problem, thus reducing the incentive to invest.[17] A similar diagnosis applies to difficulties of control resulting from a possible divergence of interests between members and managers; to problems arising from the insufficient tradability of shares and the dual role of members as owners and users; and an apparently inevitable cooperative "conservatism." In neo-institutional terms, this has been termed the "horizon problem," as it is said to be accounted for by the "limited patronage horizon of co-operative members. Since members can only receive a return on their investment through patronage refunds when they actually use the co-operative, they will tend to support activities that maximize short-term rather than long-term returns."[18]

So the property rights approaches have brought together a range of problems, reformulated them, and demonstrated that they apply not only to workers' cooperatives, but to all forms of cooperative organizations. What is more, they have highlighted the fact that these weaknesses do not immediately result in failure, but that there are some circumstances under which they matter more than under others. For example, Cook and, following up on his work, Murray Fulton have tried to fit the emergence of these weaknesses into "life-cycle" models of cooperative growth. In the early stages of development, both suggest, the problems mentioned previously can be overcome by a strong ideological commitment of members. However, "as the co-ops grow older and larger and members became [sic] more diverse and adopt new attitudes (often as a result of generational change), the property rights issues become more salient."[19]

One the one hand, it is easy to criticize this view; for example, it is unclear what triggers the transition from one stage to the next, and relevant factors will, in any case, be highly contingent on historical circumstances. On the other hand, however, these models do offer an important starting point for a discussion. In order to recognize this, one has to turn to the neo-institutional answer to the question of why cooperatives emerged in the first place – despite their alleged inefficiencies. The answer, in this perspective, is typically that the emergence of

[16] Murray E. Fulton, "Traditional versus New Generation Cooperatives," in Christopher D. Merrett and Norman Walzer (eds.), *A Cooperative Approach to Local Economic Development* (Westport, 2001), pp. 11–24, here p. 19.

[17] Michael L. Cook, "The Future of U.S. Agricultural Cooperatives: A Neo-Institutional Approach," *American Journal of Agricultural Economics*, 77 (1995), pp. 1153–9, here p. 1156.

[18] Fulton, 2001, p. 20.

[19] Ibid., p. 16. For Cook's version, see Cook, 1995, p. 1155 ff.

cooperatives was a response to some kind of market failure. Cooperatives, it is said, "arise in response to the inability of private corporations and public enterprises to meet certain social needs or resolve certain crisis situations."[20] Under these circumstances, they may be the only way to provide certain goods or services, and their disadvantages vis-à-vis IOBs are consequently of no importance. Many economists, however, believe that market failures are the exception to the rule; sooner or later, most markets will gradually approach the ideal of perfect competition. In these situations, IOBs will enter the scene, compete with cooperatives, and unveil their inherent weaknesses. Before long, the co-ops will either go bankrupt or transform into IOBs themselves. So cooperative failure, in this view, is a logical consequence of competitive markets, and co-ops are seen as "by their very nature ... transitory projects."[21]

This may, at first sight, seem like a very stringent model of failure, and it has been severely criticized from some quarters, notably from within the cooperative movement. The main argument that has been brought up against it is that this view reduces the cooperative idea to its economic function. Cooperatives, so the counterargument goes, cannot be assessed by the yardstick of economic efficiency alone; they also serve social and political needs, such as the strengthening of community values, mutual solidarity, and democracy, which cannot be provided by IOBs. Consequently, while the mainstream argument previously outlined emphasizes the importance of demand – co-ops fail if demand for them subsides – this alternative perspective focuses on the supply side and holds that cooperatives are "formed and kept alive by the decision of people who put positive liberty ... at the top of their scale of values."[22] The implications of this view for the question of failure are clear: co-ops fail because the people and values that keep them afloat are in short supply. This shortage can have different causes which typically relate not primarily to economic, but rather to wider social and cultural, issues – such as the dissolution of a previously tight social milieu or the lack of a cultural background that is conducive to cooperative values. The consequences can be played out in a variety of ways: for example, a co-op may have a diminishing membership, thus depriving the cooperative of capital. Alternatively, supply-side shortages can result in what has been termed the "attenuation of cooperative spirit": because members do not care about cooperative values any more, they focus on the economic functions of their organization. In any case, such factors, sooner or later, will cause cooperatives to either transform into IOBs or fail – often spectacularly, because their supervisory structure crucially depends on members' involvement.

It is clear that the two views outlined here are not entirely contradictory. For example, since cooperative organization typically involves an identity of users

---

[20] Stefano Zamagni and Vera Zamagni, *Cooperative Enterprise: Facing the Challenge of Globalization* (Cheltenham and Northampton: Edward Elgar 2010), p. 28.

[21] Robert Grott, "Why Co-ops Die: An Historical Analysis," *Cooperative Grocer*, 9 (1987) (without pagination).

[22] Zamagni and Zamagni, 2010, p. 28.

and owners, one might expect that there will be close links between the supply and the demand for co-ops. More importantly still, this dichotomy does not cover the entire range of possible influences. For example, the question of political support for cooperatives or the lack thereof has often been mentioned as an important factor, even though it can probably only partially be factored into the supply side of the equation; in many cases, it will be more useful to classify this aspect as an external influence. Still, the distinction between supply-side and demand-side explanations of failure is analytically useful because it highlights the double nature of co-ops, and it makes sure that the discussion of cooperative failure is connected both to economic considerations and to the wider social and cultural background. Consequently, it should be borne in mind as we now turn to the historical case studies.

CASE 1: CENTRAL AND WESTERN EUROPEAN CONSUMER COOPERATIVES (1960–1985)

The first case of collective failure is the decline and partial collapse of what might be termed "the Western European model of consumer cooperation."[23] Beginning in the late 1950s and early 1960s, consumer cooperatives in some Western European countries – notably the Netherlands, France, Belgium, Austria, West Germany, and, to a lesser extent, the United Kingdom – started to contract, lost market shares, and, in many cases, eventually either failed or transformed into IOBs.[24] This process was particularly pronounced during the late 1960s and the 1970s, and was mostly completed by the mid-1980s. The most extreme case was West Germany: there, a once proud movement which in 1960 boasted 2.6 million members was reduced to a handful of regionally limited organizations with only about 600,000 members in 1990.[25] Additionally, a major scandal engulfed a successor organization of former cooperatives in the mid-1980s, and ultimately destroyed the credibility of the idea of consumer cooperation as a whole. The other countries mentioned fared slightly better, and in some cases – notably the U.K. – even saw a certain revival of cooperatives after the mid-1990s (see Chapter 10 in this book). Still, the basic point is well established: although cooperatives had constituted an integral part of the Western European retailing sector as late as 1960, by the mid-1980s they were confined to the margins while other types of businesses continued to flourish.

[23] The phrase is based upon Brett Fairbairn, "Konsumgenossenschaften in internationaler Perspektive: ein historischer Überblick," in Michael Prinz (ed.), *Der lange Weg in den Überfluß. Anfänge und Entwicklung der Konsumgesellschaft seit der Vormoderne* (Forschungen zur Regionalgeschichte, Vol. 43); Paderborn, et al., 2003), pp. 437–461, here p. 442.

[24] For reasons that will be explained later in the chapter, this process did not affect *all* Western European countries but only the ones mentioned. Like Fairbairn, ibid., I am therefore using the term "Western Europe" not in its geographical sense but rather to denote this specific group.

[25] Gunther Aschoff and Eckart Henningsen, *Das deutsche Genossenschaftswesen. Entwicklung, Struktur, wirtschaftliche Potentiale* (Frankfurt a. M., 1995), p. 131.

Why did cooperatives fare so badly? There are basically three schools of thought on this issue. The first one stresses the adverse political environment – particularly the liberal economic regime and, in the German case, the consequences of the Nazi dictatorship. A second school concentrates on organizational inefficiencies that resulted from a changing economic environment – a demand-side view, we might say. And a third set of authors emphasize supply-side factors such as changes in values and social milieus both within and outside the cooperatives. I will discuss each of these arguments in turn.

The first school of thought has taken the case of West Germany as its point of departure. Here, the argument goes, political influences on consumer cooperatives took on two different forms. At first, immediately after the end of the Second World War, the allied and particularly the British military administration shaped the structure of these organizations. Intent on reestablishing grassroots democracy, the British decided to rebuild consumer cooperatives from the bottom to the top, thus dismantling the partial "rationalization" that had been achieved during the Third Reich. They also did away with some of the obstacles that had been hampering consumer cooperatives in previous decades – particularly a clause which prohibited selling to nonmembers.[26]

These positive influences, however, increasingly came under threat after the end of the occupation, when West Germany turned toward a social market economy that heavily relied on the political support of medium-sized businesses among which private retailers played an important role. Because of their political clout, they managed to make life difficult for cooperatives. Although they did not succeed in their attempt to reintroduce the prohibition against selling to nonmembers, in 1954, they persuaded the federal government to limit cooperative rebates to 3 percent. After this decision, the argument goes, it was virtually impossible to convince potential members of the advantages of cooperation; the membership base shrank considerably, and cooperatives were forced to merge in order to keep up their viability. Eventually the highly concentrated trust which was formed from the remains of cooperatives in the 1970s came under the influence of an unscrupulous management that committed an almost "perfect crime"[27] and thus ruined what was still left of the cooperative idea. This argument is often the corollary of the "political influence" school of thought.

Although this line of argument is still quite popular in some quarters, it has been found wanting on several counts. First, it is anything but clear that the limitation of rebates did, in fact, have the immediate impact suggested. It certainly did not help the cooperatives, but they did still manage to grow throughout the 1950s, and membership peaked only in 1961.[28] Second, it has been argued that although this limitation may have given consumer cooperatives

[26] Brett Fairbairn, "Wiederaufbau und Untergang der Konsumgenossenschaften in der DDR und in der Bundesrepublik 1945 bis 1990," *IWK*, 34 (1998), pp. 171–98, here p. 186.
[27] Ibid., p. 195.
[28] Erwin Hasselmann, *Geschichte der deutschen Konsumgenossenschaften* (Frankfurt a. M., 1971), p. 711.

a hard time, the general political climate in the 1950s was on the whole a lot more favorable than during the Empire and the Weimar Republic, when cooperatives flourished. And third, even though similar political restrictions existed in some other countries as well, they were notably absent from others that nevertheless also saw consumer cooperatives failing on a large scale. In Britain, for example, the growth of the movement hit a ceiling at exactly the same time as it did in Germany, and there were no *direct* political influences on this process to speak of.[29] So although this factor may go some way toward explaining the scale of cooperative failure in West Germany, it obviously does not go to the heart of the matter.

What about economic weaknesses and inefficiencies? The starting point for this argument is the "retailing revolution" of the late 1950s to early 1970s. At the heart of this revolution lay the concept of self-service and, in its suite, the supermarket. Beginning in the late 1940s, a simple organizational change imported from the United States – taking away the counter and introducing payment upon checkout – cleared the way for a fundamental restructuring of the retailing sector. Once shops "had dispensed with counter service, they could become much bigger, limited only by the willingness of the customers to walk around carrying a basket."[30] At the same time, rising incomes during Europe's "Golden Age" of growth caused an increased and differentiated demand for consumer goods, thus generating economies of scale; and the increasing availability of refrigerators and cars worked in the same direction, enabling people to go shopping in supermarkets once a week rather than pop into the corner shop for a teabag twice a day.

It should not be forgotten that some consumer cooperatives were, in fact, vanguards of these changes. For example, the first self-service shop in West Germany was opened by a cooperative, and of the fifty British supermarkets operating in 1950, twenty were run by such organizations.[31] However, despite these promising beginnings, the "retailing revolution" posed considerable challenges for this type of business. The trend toward larger outlets increased the capital requirements for the running of a retail house and thus raised the issue of accessing capital for investment. Although cooperatives, on this count, were initially better placed than single shopkeepers, they could not maintain this lead vis-à-vis the large, investor-owned chain stores that emerged in the late 1950s.[32] The new environment put a premium on competitive pricing. Because of

---

[29] Johnston Birchall, *Co-op: The People's Business* (Manchester, 1994), p. 146; and John K. Walton, "The Post-War Decline of the British Retail Co-operative Movement. Nature, Causes and Consequences," in Lawrence Black and Nicole Robertson (eds.), *Consumerism and the Co-operative Movement in Modern British History: Taking Stock* (Manchester and New York, 2009), pp. 13–31, here p. 22 ff.

[30] Birchall, 1994, p. 144.

[31] Ibid.

[32] Michael Prinz, "Das Ende der Konsumvereine in der Bundesrepublik Deutschland. Traditionelle Konsumentenorganisation in der historischen Kontinuität," *Jahrbuch für Wirtschaftsgeschichte* (1993/1), pp. 159–88, here p. 182.

the economies of scale that the retailing sector generated, investor-owned supermarkets were soon much better at offering discount prices than cooperatives. This was all the more problematic because pricing traditionally had been one of the strongholds of consumer cooperatives. The differentiation of demand that came with rising incomes also generated economies of scope and, again, favored large supermarkets which could maintain a broader variety of goods than a small shop; it also ran counter to the business model of cooperatives which had traditionally focused on the availability of certain goods rather than on choice.[33]

Again, these issues were especially relevant to the German case where they triggered a process of concentration among consumer cooperatives which saw their number decline by 50 percent during the 1960s alone. These radical amalgamations, in turn, resulted in a process of "managerialization" that was in conflict with the traditional identity of cooperative organizations. The result was a classic agency problem: a structural confrontation between a membership which still had a very strong hand in the decision-making processes and a group of managers who emphasized the economic aspects of cooperative performance. Because of the continuing pressures of competition, the managers eventually prevailed; the cooperatives were duly transformed into IOBs and integrated into large, trade union-owned concerns in 1974. The scandal of the 1980s had its root causes in the firm grip that managers established over this new form of enterprise which lacked the controls that previously had been provided by cooperative democracy.[34]

So it is true that, much as the "demand" school of failure suggests, consumer cooperatives had been viable solutions for a type of market failure which was prevalent in European societies before the age of mass consumption, and that, as soon as this was remedied, they came under pressure from other types of business. Still, this explanation is incomplete. For while large-scale cooperative failure was a distinctly Western European phenomenon, the rise of mass consumption and the "supermarket revolution" extended also to other countries, for example, in Scandinavia and in Southern Europe. In some of these countries, however – notably in Norway, Finland, Italy, and Switzerland – cooperatives managed to eschew the apparently irresistible drive of competition and retained a sizeable share of their respective markets.[35] This was partly due to differences in market structure that were beyond the influence of management decisions, but it still suggests that there was nothing inevitable about the failures of cooperatives in Western Europe. So where did they go wrong?

[33] Harm Schröter, "Der Verlust der 'europäischen Form des Zusammenspiels von Ordnung und Freiheit.' Vom Untergang der deutschen Konsumgenossenschaften," *Vierteljahrschrift für Sozial- und Wirtschaftsgeschichte*, 87 (2000), pp. 442–67, here p. 453.

[34] Ibid., p. 461 f.; Achim von Loesch, *Die gemeinwirtschaftlichen Unternehmen der deutschen Gewerkschaften. Entstehung – Funktionen – Probleme* (Köln, 1979), p. 174; and Fairbairn, 1998, p. 194 ff.

[35] Espen Ekberg, "Consumer Co-operation and the Transformation of Modern Food Retailing: The British and Norwegian Consumer Co-operative Movement in Comparison, 1950–2002," in Black and Robertson, 2009, pp. 51–66, here p. 51.

In order to answer this question, it is important to look beyond the economic aspects of cooperative decision making and to recognize the social and cultural preconditions of cooperative enterprise. Take, for example, the initial assessment of the "retailing revolution" by consumer cooperatives in Germany. It is clear that, although some of them were quick to take up innovations, in general, they were reluctant to go down the path of self-service and large-scale business. Harm Schröter has argued that this was not a matter of financial or organizational weaknesses but due to the fact that cooperatives were trapped in their own cultural traditions. Because they still regarded themselves as a *Gegenmacht* – a countervailing power – they considered economic competition to be of secondary importance. Rather, they interpreted it as an outgrowth of political and cultural power. Therefore, they argued, it was much more important to provide the *social* functions of a cooperative, such as mutual solidarity and self-help, and to promote concomitant values such as thrift and simplicity. Consequently, these consumer cooperatives tried to establish alternatives to self-service and focused on their traditional milieus.[36] However, as cooperative members were increasingly lured to supermarkets – because of lower prices and the greater range of goods – this strategy became unsustainable. When cooperatives eventually did take up the challenge of competition, it was too late; the only way to secure the survival of their businesses was to dramatically overhaul the organizational structure, which eventually resulted in the demise of cooperative principles.

Why was this focus on the social functions of cooperatives so strong, and why was it stronger in some places than in others? Here, it is time to mention the common feature of consumer cooperatives in those countries in which they fared badly: in all of those countries, the cooperatives were closely associated with the labor movement. In Germany, for example, these links had been strong since the end of the nineteenth century, and they were made even stronger by the reorganization of cooperatives under British control as it drew on the resources of local trade union cells. These organizations were thus firmly rooted in the labor milieu; even in the late 1950s, they defined themselves exclusively as advocates of the working population, and they were part and parcel of working-class culture.[37]

The problem was that, with rising incomes, mass consumption, and, eventually, the beginnings of deindustrialization, the social basis of this culture began to erode. More importantly, ideas of togetherness, mutual support, and solidarity started to wane as increasing affluence, the effects of the welfare state, and the spread of individualistic mentalities seemed to render them superfluous.[38] Consequently, the supply of committed member-customers dried up – just at the

[36] Schröter, 2000, p. 458 ff.

[37] Ibid., p. 456.

[38] Carl Strikwerda, "'Alternative Visions' and Working-Class Culture: The Political Economy of Consumer Cooperation in Belgium, 1860–1980," in Ellen Furlough and Carl Strikwerda (eds.), *Consumers against Capitalism? Consumer Cooperation in Europe, North America, and Japan, 1840–1990* (Lanham, et al., 1999), pp. 67–91, has demonstrated the relevance of these factors to the Belgian case.

same moment in which the economic environment would have made a reliable social background more rather than less important.

In this situation, Western European consumer cooperatives tried to stick to their roots, and they probably had no alternative to that: the idea that they were a central component of the labor movement was not just a self-image but also a widespread attribution by others. In contrast, consumer cooperatives in other countries that were not so exclusively identified with working-class culture found it easier to tackle the "retailing revolution" because they could react more flexibly to changing economic, social, and cultural conditions. So, in the final analysis, although demand-side logic, which suggests that the decline of cooperatives was a consequence of the resolution of market failure, does contain more than just a kernel of truth, it is also important to recognize the role of social and cultural factors that precluded these organizations from following alternative strategies. Ultimately, therefore, Western European consumer cooperatives failed because their social and cultural basis was neither large enough to sustain them nor small enough to be easily ignored.

CASE 2: JAPAN'S CREDIT COOPERATIVES (1970–2000)

A second case of collective failure can be seen in the fate of Japan's cooperative banks during the 1990s. It is clear that this case is in marked difference to the previous one as the "lost decade" was a period of outright crisis in which most of the Japanese banking system failed. There are several indications, however, that cooperatives fared even worse than investor-owned banks. First, even before the crisis began, they were widely regarded as the weakest link in the financial system.[39] Second, this fear was borne out by the fact that cooperative banks were the first to fail, preceding the fully fledged banking crisis of 1997 by two years. In early 1995, two smaller credit cooperatives, *Tokyo Kyowa* and *Tokyo Anzen*, collapsed; in July of that year, *Cosmo*, Japan's fifth largest credit cooperative, followed suit, causing Japan's first bank run since 1962; and in August, *Kizu Credit Union*, the country's largest credit cooperative, also crumbled under a massive burden of bad debt.[40] Third, while the entire banking sector has been radically restructured in the wake of the crisis, this process arguably has been most pronounced in the case of cooperatives. For example, the number of *Shinkin* banks – the term will be explained later – was reduced from about 450 in 1990 to 300 in 2005.[41]

Even though cooperative banks, by and large, retained their market share during that period because of massive state intervention, it is fair to regard this episode as a case of failure. It is an unusual one, though, not just because many

[39] Mark Klinedinst and Hitomi Sato, "The Japanese Cooperative Sector," *Journal of Economic Issues*, 28 (1994), pp. 509–17, here p. 515.
[40] Michael Ehrke, *Japan. Der verwaltete Stillstand (FES-Analyse)* (Bonn, 1996), p. 11 ff.
[41] Kaoru Hosono, Koji Sakai, and Kotaro Tsuru, *Consolidation of Cooperative Banks (Shinkin) in Japan: Motives and Consequences*, *RIETI Discussion Paper Series 06-E-034* (2006), pp. 3 and 4.

banks survived with the help of taxpayers' money, but also because experience from other financial crises shows that in such circumstances, cooperative banks often perform comparatively well, since they are usually conservative in their strategies. Why was the Japanese case different? As this question has been much less researched than the decline of European consumer cooperatives, it is impossible to answer it by discussing different schools of thought. Rather, my approach is to chronicle the course of events and then draw out the theoretical implications.

The history and structure of credit cooperatives in Japan is a complex one indeed. With some simplification, the cooperatives can be divided into three groups. The first comprises agricultural and fishery cooperatives. During its heyday in the 1930s, this group was made up of about 15,000 organizations which involved around 70 percent of Japanese farmers.[42] Typically, they followed several purposes of which the provision of credit was only one, albeit a very important one. After an authoritarian interlude, they were reorganized in the late 1940s under American influence, resulting by and large in a reinstatement of the prewar pattern. The credit branches were united in associations at the prefectural level, and the *Norinchukin* bank at the national level.

The second tier of the Japanese system of credit cooperatives consisted of the so-called *Shinkin* banks. These had their origins in urban credit unions which also dated back to the interwar period but were not particularly widespread at the time. After the *Shinkin* banking law of 1951, however, their importance increased considerably, primarily because, among other factors, their membership consisted not only of private individuals, but also of small and medium-sized enterprises whose growth they financed. Furthermore, although they offered credit only to their members, they were free to accept deposits from outsiders, thus building an economic basis that, to some degree, was independent from their membership. By 1990, *Shinkin* banks made up almost half of the business volume of Japan's credit cooperatives, relegating agricultural cooperatives, which accounted for about a third of transactions, to second place.[43]

Most of the remainder was made up by the third group, the credit unions, collectively referred to as *Shinkumi* banks. The main differences between these and the *Shinkin* banks were that the amount of credit they could hand out was very limited, and they were not allowed to accept deposits from nonmembers. Although both of these factors contributed to the fact that the cooperative character of these banks was rather stronger than that of *Shinkin* banks, they also were responsible for the slower expansion of these banks.[44] A fourth type of

[42] Massaya Sumimoto and Yumiko Jino, "Struktur und Entwicklungstendenzen des japanischen Kreditgenossenschaftswesens," *Zeitschrift für das gesamte Genossenschaftswesen*, 41 (1991), pp. 216–24, here p. 217.

[43] Ibid., p. 219.

[44] Tadashi Saito, *Zustand und Perspektiven der japanischen Genossenschaftsbanken* (Arbeitspapiere der Forschungsstelle für Genossenschaftswesen an der Universität Hohenheim, Nr. 13) (Stuttgart, 1996), p. 3.

cooperative comprising labor credit unions was not particularly important and is not relevant to the following discussion.

During the 1950s and 1960s, all types of credit cooperatives flourished. Especially *Shinkin* banks and also *Shinkumi* banks benefited from a type of market failure: the fact that strong growth made liquidity an issue. As large private banks concentrated on the provision of credit for big enterprises, they neglected small and medium-sized businesses, which consequently turned to cooperative organization for meeting their credit needs. Agricultural credit cooperatives profited from similar circumstances and additionally from various forms of state intervention.[45]

In hindsight, it is clear that this pattern could not be sustained forever. For one thing, growth itself brought about structural changes that affected the social basis of cooperatives. For example, the role of agriculture declined while industrialization and rising property values in previously rural areas more or less automatically dragged agricultural cooperatives into new areas of business; they increasingly became dependent on deposits from nonagricultural activities. In a different way, structural change also affected the *Shinkin* banks. Many of the small and medium-sized enterprises that had provided their backbone simply outgrew the size restrictions which had been imposed on the *Shinkin* by law, thus threatening to erode their social basis.[46] In this situation, cooperative banks tried to develop new business activities and were, in fact, encouraged to do so by the state. For example, in 1968, the law governing *Shinkin* banks was changed so as to encourage mergers. More importantly still, the *Shinkin* were hitherto allowed to give loans to nonmembers as long as these did not surpass 20 percent of their total loans.[47]

The economic slowdown that began during the 1970s added a new twist to this strategy of widening business activities, as it marked the end of tight credit conditions. Large enterprises now needed less capital than previously to finance their more limited growth. This meant, however, that city banks increasingly turned to other markets and started to compete with credit cooperatives for private customers and smaller businesses. This trend was massively accelerated during the early 1980s, when international pressure led to a sea change in the regulatory framework of the Japanese economy. In this context, the banking sector was subject to a number of liberalizing measures that further increased competition and consequently exerted a downward pressure on profit margins.[48]

Cooperative banks reacted by speeding up their search for new market opportunities. Against this backdrop, they managed to engineer a further relaxation of the restrictions to which they were subjected – partly because of the general trend toward deregulation, and partly because of their political clout

---

[45] Sumimoto and Jino, 1991, p. 221.
[46] Ibid., p. 222.
[47] Saito, 1996, p. 13 f.; and Hosono, Sakai, and Tsuru, 2006, p. 4.
[48] Sumimoto and Jino, 1991, p. 222 f.

(particularly the agricultural cooperatives, which were strongly represented in the governing Liberal Democratic Party). So, in 1981, "agricultural, fishery and credit cooperatives saw an increase in their lending ceilings to non-members."[49] When the positive macroeconomic environment of the second half of the 1980s led to "a marked upward adjustment in growth expectations, boosted asset prices and fuel[l]ed rapid credit expansion,"[50] cooperative banks were virtually free to participate in the ensuing property bubble. They were particularly active in financing the so-called *jusen* companies which played an important role in real estate lending. It is thus fair to say that "these cooperatives had in the 1980s expanded their business so rapidly ... that by the time of their closure they had become de facto full range banks."[51]

This statement was not true, however, with respect to the internal organization of the cooperatives. On the contrary, while their external image conformed increasingly to that of IOBs, their internal regulations did not keep up with this transformation. For example, the supervisory boards of credit cooperatives traditionally had been very restricted in their competencies, as it was assumed that the actual control of the management would be in the hands of the assembly of members. This framework was evidently tailored to the needs of small organizations with a limited range of activities, not to the needs of large banks with sizeable operations in the real estate business, and yet it remained unchanged, thus giving the management considerable leeway. A similar story applies to the principle of "one member, one vote," which always had been handled in a rather negligent way, as it ran counter to some Japanese peculiarities of business organization. For example, it was customary to give large shareholders a representation on the management board, and this also applied to cooperatives: in fact, many *Shinkin* banks were run part-time by managers of large member firms. These imbalances in cooperative democracy became further pronounced when, with the increasing role of providing credit to nonmembers, some nonmember creditors also entered the board, creating yet another agency problem.[52]

Nor were such problems compensated for by external regulation. The supervisory system hinged on regional federations of credit cooperatives and was very weak indeed – partly because it originally had been formed with small, local businesses in mind, and partly because the links between management boards and supervisory associations were rather stronger than they should have been.[53] Just how important this lack of controls was can be demonstrated by the case of the *Tokyo Kyowa*, the first of the credit cooperatives to fail in 1995. Not only

---

[49] Akihiro Kanaya and David Woo, *The Japanese Banking Crisis of the 1990s: Sources and Lessons*, IMF Working Paper No. 00/7 (Washington, 2000), p. 6; and Hosonmo, Sakai, and Tsuru, 2006, p. 4.

[50] Kanaya and Woo, 2000, p. 5.

[51] Ibid., p. 25.

[52] Saito, 1996, p. 12 f.

[53] Kanaya and Woo, 2000, p. 25.

had this bank circumvented the interdiction of lending more than 20 percent of its capital to a single debtor, but it also had handed out huge loans to a single real estate company owned by Harunori Takahashi, its own director, and had covered this action by bribing auditors and politicians.[54] Although it is clear that the criminal intent of individuals played an important role in this case, there is no doubt that the lack of supervision – both internal and external – facilitated this type of behavior. Similar, if less extreme, cases of overambitious lending enabled by lack of control were behind all of the failures described earlier, and other cooperatives with the same problem were saved from the same fate only by mergers or tax money.

On the whole, therefore, it is fair to conclude that "regulatory arbitrage"[55] was the main factor behind the failure of credit cooperatives. But it is also clear that sole reference to this formula would be too simple. Regulatory arbitrage had a long-term origin. By the end of the 1960s, cooperative banks had lost both their original social basis and their original markets. In this situation, they were partly pushed to and partly opted for new areas of business which outwardly converted them into "normal" banks. This conversion, however, was not complete; it did not comprise important aspects of internal organization and the regulatory framework. So, while in some sense regulatory arbitrage was a consequence of the fact that Japan's credit cooperatives had left behind their roots, in another sense it was due to the fact that this process had not gone far enough. In this respect, at least, the crisis partially remedied the banks' weaknesses: while outwardly seeming to exist in much the same form as before, credit cooperatives, in almost every respect, were run and supervised like "normal" banks. Why, in that case, they should still be cooperatives at all is an open question that continues to affect their credibility.[56]

How do these findings connect to the theoretical perspectives outlined previously in this chapter? Again, it is clear that the demand-side view of failure contains a good deal of insight. Cooperatives were successful under conditions of fragmented markets, and their problems resulted from the policies they pursued when they were exposed to the competition of IOBs. But, as before, this view does not tell the full story. Although the role of supply-side factors is not as obvious in this case as it is with regard to European consumer cooperatives, it does seem plausible to argue that with a stronger grassroots culture, Japan's credit cooperatives might not have gone down the road of imitating other banks quite so easily. Whether this would have resulted in a more viable strategy or just another type of failure is a question that has to be left unanswered. But the fact that cooperative democracy played an inferior role from the very beginning and was further weakened by the transformation of its original

[54] Ehrke, 1996, p. 11.
[55] Kanaya and Woo, 2000, p. 25.
[56] Christian M. Ringle and Takumi Kiyota, "Der genossenschaftliche Bankensektor in Japan. Gegenwärtiger Stand und Perspektiven," *Zeitschrift für das gesamte Bank- und Börsenwesen*, 54 (2006), pp. 161–6, here p. 165.

social context was certainly highly significant for the course of events during the 1980s and 1990s.

CASE 3: AGRICULTURAL COOPERATIVES IN THE UNITED STATES (1990–2010)

The third case to be discussed in this chapter concerns the structural changes of agricultural cooperatives in the United States in the first decade of the twenty-first century. After 2000, "a number of large co-ops filed for bankruptcy or converted to investor-owned firms (IOF) to remain financially viable."[57] Until now, the total number of businesses affected by this development was comparatively small, and it is important to highlight the fact that, at the same time, many other cooperatives – particularly a certain, newly emerging type that will be described in detail later – fared rather well.[58] Even this limited occurrence of failures, however, marks a significant departure from previous periods when cooperative conversions or bankruptcies were almost completely unheard of, and it is closely connected to the more positive developments that I have just mentioned. This will become clear in the following analysis, which, again, proceeds in chronological fashion, with a discussion of the theoretical implications at the end.

Agricultural cooperatives have traditionally played an important role in American rural life. Their origins stretch back to the second half of the nineteenth century, and the number of cooperatives reached its peak in the early 1930s, when there were approximately 12,000 such organizations. Given the fact that the role of agriculture in the economy has been sharply reduced in the postwar period, it is hardly surprising that their number has decreased continuously ever since, hitting 6,000 in the mid-1980s. However, it is clear that until the mid-1980s, this decrease could not be interpreted in terms of "decline." Hardly any cooperatives actually failed; most of them were merged with others, so that the concentration into large organizations became one of the hallmarks of that period. The decline in membership followed the decline in the number of farms with only a twenty-year lag, suggesting that farmers in fact benefited from these enterprises. The market shares of agricultural cooperatives showed a consistent upward trend after the beginning of the 1950s. For example, in supply of farming equipment, which accounted for 24 percent of cooperative business in 1987, the market share increased from 13 percent in 1951 to 26 percent in 1985, whereas in the marketing of farm products – responsible for 73 percent of

---

[57] Murray E. Fulton and Brent Hueth, "Cooperative Conversions, Failures and Restructurings: An Overview," *Journal of Cooperatives*, 23 (2009), pp. i–xi, here p. i.

[58] Precise numbers are hard to come by. Ibid., p. iii; and Fabio R. Chaddad and Michael L. Cook, "Conversions and Other Forms of Exit in U.S. Agricultural Cooperatives," in Kostas Karantininis and Jerker Nilsson (eds.), *Vertical Markets and Cooperative Hierarchies: The Role of Cooperatives in the Agri-Food Industry* (Dordrecht, 2007), pp. 61–72, here p. 62 f., list a total of twenty examples, but do not aim at completeness.

co-ops' business in 1987 – the market share climbed from 20 percent in 1951 to 30 percent in 1981, with a slight decline to 28 percent in 1985.[59]

So although agricultural cooperatives did well during the 1960s and the 1970s, after the mid-1980s, and increasingly in the 1990s, they ran into difficulties. The obvious source for this were the changes that have been referred to as the "industrialization of agriculture" – a slightly misleading term perhaps for its nineteenth-century connotations; "information-age agriculture" might be a more accurate description. In brief, these changes comprise "the application of modern industrial manufacturing, production, procurement, distribution, and coordination concepts to the food and industrial product chain."[60] Whereas agriculture in the postwar period had been marked by a focus on individual commodities that were sold by farms to independent processing firms, information-age agriculture defined farms as part of an interdependent *system* – a value chain – that focused on the production of a final good.

These changes posed considerable challenges not only to individual farmers, but also to cooperatives, particularly those involved in the marketing of agricultural produce. In order to keep up with the new situation, they needed to provide for vertical integration – which means they had to grow and, above all, find the money for this much more capital-intensive type of production. One initial response to these requirements was the formation of "New Generation Cooperatives" (NGCs). An early example was the Dakota Growers Pasta Company (DGPC), founded in 1991, which was set up by wheat farmers and specialized in the processing of durum wheat for the production of pasta. This setup in itself – producers engaging in the value-added processing of their commodities – was characteristic of the strategy of NGCs. In this context, the DGPC developed a host of new organizational measures. The most important ones were the tying of members' rights to deliver their products to the buying of equity shares (other than the basic membership right); the concomitant *obligation* to deliver an amount of produce proportional to their shares; and the right to trade these shares and delivery rights among members.[61] Each of these changes addressed one of the problems that had been raised or exacerbated by the rise of information-age agriculture: the link between delivery and equity shares was designed to overcome the problem of raising capital; the obligation to deliver was a consequence of the integration of the production system; and the right to trade shares was a response to the problem of controlling or realizing the value and thus the performance of the cooperative.

Straightforward as these changes may seem, it would be rather too simple to view them as a smooth adaptation to a changing economic environment. For

[59] Werner Klohn, "Die Farmer-Genossenschaften in den USA," *Zeitschrift für das gesamte Genossenschaftswesen*, 41 (1991), pp. 48–61, here pp. 50 and 56.

[60] Michael D. Boehlje, "Industrialization of Agriculture: What Are the Implications?," *Choices: The Magazine on Food, Farm and Resource Issues*, 4 (1996), pp. 30–3, here p. 30.

[61] Michael Boland and Gregory J. McKee, "The Restructuring of Dakota Growers Pasta Company," *Journal of Cooperatives*, 23 (2009), pp. 141–51, here p. 141 f.

example, in the 1970s, some cooperatives had engaged in the processing of agricultural goods, suggesting that even back then there was some scope for vertical integration. Nevertheless, at least one reason why such policies did not catch on at the time was the fear of farmers that they would endanger cooperative democracy. It was only during the 1980s that this kind of resistance to high-level integration subsided – a process that several authors have attributed to generational change. Older farmers, the argument goes, still had vivid memories of the severe crises of agriculture during the 1930s. At that time, the formation of cooperatives had played a vital role in providing mutual assistance and thus in overcoming economic hardship. Consequently, those who still had living memories of this period valued cooperative solidarity much more than those who were born later. Opinion polls suggest that this intergenerational change had made considerable headway by the late 1980s; since then, the majority of farmers have based decisions about where to buy their equipment and where to sell their produce on purely economic considerations.[62]

These supply-side changes played an important role in paving the way for the NGCs. In fact, they made it possible for this form of organization to experience a substantial boom and be widely adopted by agricultural cooperatives across the United States during the 1990s – so much so that this transformation has even been credited with bringing about a new flourishing of the cooperative movement. How, then, does this apparent success story tie in with the increasing number of bankruptcies and transformations after the early 2000s? Why did these failures occur?

Putting aside cases of evident management mishaps, it seems plausible to divide the discussion into two parts. The first focus is on co-ops that have been slow to take up NGC-style innovations, for example, the Tri Valley Growers Cooperative and the Rice Growers' Association, both of California. These firms accepted the challenge posed by information-age agriculture and believed that it "required them to redefine their business operations and to integrate further along the value chain."[63] Because they by and large relied on their traditional organization, however, they soon encountered severe shortages of capital. Rather than reorganize corporate structures, their managements both opted for debt financing. As a short-term strategy, this might have been a viable option. However, since the root cause of the need for integration was a structural transformation of the agrarian economy that increased rather than decreased in speed and thoroughness over time, this strategy was doomed to failure. Co-ops simply could not grow fast enough without entering the risk of spiraling debt. So, "the result ... was that the co-ops were unable to survive financially and they either declared bankruptcy or were acquired by or converted to an IOF."[64]

---

[62] Klohn, 1991, p. 58 f.
[63] Fulton and Hueth, 2009, p. vii.
[64] Ibid.

Could these failures have been avoided by an earlier and more complete transformation along NGC lines? In one sense, the answer can only be a resounding "yes," because the NGC model provided an answer for the exact problems that caused failures like the ones mentioned. This is not the complete story, however, because despite the overall success of this organizational innovation, some NGCs still incurred serious difficulties that ultimately resulted in failure. Take the example of DGPC, one of the pioneers of the NGC structure. Although its strategy can be considered successful both in terms of capital raised and in terms of integrating along the value chain, these successes came up against other problems caused by what still remained of the cooperative structure. For example, the rapid economic expansion "resulted in the grower's original investment significantly appreciating in value. However, under the DGPC's cooperative structure, it was not possible to realize this value."[65] Other issues also were involved, such as changes in wheat production and the fact that, again, raising capital was not a one-time issue but rather a long-term problem, but the conversion of DGPC to a publicly traded corporation in 2002 owed much to the "horizon problem" – the fact that the property rights structure of cooperatives does not allow members to fully participate in the rising value of their enterprise. A similar problem was encountered by the Californian Diamond Walnut Growers Cooperative which additionally suffered from agency problems – again one of the aspects of cooperative organization which had *not* been addressed by the changes introduced under the label "NGC."

So while cooperatives that tried to adapt to information-age agriculture without changing their traditional structure were prone to entering a "debt spiral," some of the organizations that adopted the NGC model ran the risk of encountering a "transformation spiral": whenever they removed one obstacle posed by cooperative organization, the next one was already waiting in the wings – a process which eventually pushed them toward demutualization. This diagnosis fits neatly with the demand-side view of failure: as market conditions become more competitive, the property rights issues of cooperatives come to a head and lead them either to bankruptcy or to transformation. However, it is clear that this explanation is incomplete, simply because the majority of American agricultural cooperatives managed to adapt to changing conditions without encountering either of the two variants of failure. Which factors, then, determined the likelihood of any given cooperative being adversely affected by these developments?

An important clue for answering this question can be taken from the fact that virtually all of the cases mentioned so far – bankruptcies of traditional cooperatives and transformations of NGCs alike – were concentrated among marketing cooperatives and, more specifically, among *large* marketing cooperatives with an annual sales volume of more than $100 million.[66] It was precisely

---

[65] Boland and McKee, 2009, p. 142.
[66] See the individual case studies assembled in "Cooperative Conversions, Failures and Restructurings," *Journal of Cooperatives*, 23 (2009, Special Edition).

these businesses that were the main proponents of the drive toward vertical integration, whereas smaller cooperatives typically followed rather more modest strategies. An example is provided by the case of ProFac, a cooperative which "concluded that its best strategy was not to participate in the value-added processing and marketing segments of its industry, but instead to retrench and focus its activities much nearer the farm level."[67] This was certainly not an option for all cooperatives, and ProFac experienced its own share of difficulties in following this plan. The example, however, shows that many cooperatives could and did survive changing market conditions as long as they were able to draw on a committed membership and a solid social basis, such as the circumstances that kept ProFac economically viable despite the comparatively low profitability of its activities.

Conversely, supply-side factors played an important role in the instances of failure as well. A case in point is the issue of changing members' expectations. As mentioned before, farmers from the mid-1980s onward increasingly assessed cooperatives in terms of return on investment rather than social benefits. While smaller businesses were often able to counter this impulse by offering integrative incentives such as a high degree of control, larger cooperatives found it difficult to follow such strategies – mainly because of the "member heterogeneity"[68] that came with their size. Consequently, they were under greater pressure to focus on cost-effectiveness and thus more willing to follow reputedly profitable strategies. This, in turn, raised the problems of accessing capital or removing cooperative "obstacles" described previously. It is, therefore, no coincidence that "very large cooperatives with heterogeneous memberships" were particularly prominent among cases of outright bankruptcies or else turned into "serious candidates for conversion, unless they implement[ed] tight governance mechanisms to safeguard member control."[69]

Thus, the way in which cooperatives dealt with the long-run, large-scale shift in the social structure and cultural attitudes of American farmers determined how likely it was that they would fail. It is difficult to say what might have happened if the old social context of agricultural cooperatives had been preserved, but it seems possible that the emphasis on the economic aspects of their functions, which lay at the heart of their problems, would have been much diminished. Whether this would have resulted in a viable alternative strategy, however, is a matter of speculation.

CONCLUSION

This chapter has aimed to determine why cooperatives failed in the period between 1950 and 2010 and to analyze these failures with a view to establishing whether there are "rules" to which they were subjected. After a theoretical

---

[67] Fulton and Hueth, 2009, p. vii.
[68] Chaddad and Cook, 2007, p. 62.
[69] Ibid., p. 67.

discussion that established two basic perspectives on the issue, the chapter compared three corresponding cases: the decline of Western European consumer cooperatives between 1960 and 1985; the failure of Japanese credit cooperatives in the 1990s; and the restructuring of American agricultural cooperatives between 1990 and 2010.

In the case of Western Europe, the findings suggest that the decline of consumer cooperatives followed closely the hypotheses that have been put forward by the "demand" school of thought. In that view, cooperatives were viable as long as they filled in the gaps left by conventional businesses, but as soon as market conditions changed with the "retailing revolution," investor-owned businesses entered the fray and exposed the economic inefficiencies that property rights theory has identified, especially the issue of raising capital for further growth. It is evident, however, that this was by no means an automatic process. On the contrary, it was highly contingent on decisions made by individual cooperatives, and these were influenced by the social milieu and cultural values of the labor movement which thought of itself as a countervailing power to the market economy. Therefore, the cooperatives were slow to react to the changing environment and opted to stick with their roots. The social and cultural base that made this strategy viable until the 1950s, however, began to erode in the 1960s and eventually became too weak and small. Consequently, the cooperatives in question either failed or tried to avoid failure by transformation.

A very different story, but with some common elements, emerged from the Japanese case. In this story, apparently none of the familiar issues such as lack of capital or the "horizon problem" played a role; rather, the failures were ostensibly caused by a lack of controls. By digging deeper into the causes of this problem, however, we saw that this lack of controls was the consequence of an incomplete process of transformation that, from the end of the 1960s onward, had turned Japan's credit cooperatives into fully fledged banks – without, however, instituting an adequate regulatory framework. The reason why cooperatives undertook this transformation in the first place was because investor-owned banks had increasingly entered their traditional market. The issues in this case, however, were also more complex than the simple story of market failure and its removal suggested: the fact that the more risky strategy of cooperatives since the end of the 1960s had been possible at all was itself a consequence of their weak social roots and democratic values. While particularly the latter had been compromised by some aspects of Japan's corporate culture all along, the dissolving milieus of small enterprises and local farming communities contributed notably to a further attenuation of cooperative solidarity. So the credit cooperatives failed because they had left both their original social context and their original markets behind without fully adapting to their new environment.

This latter statement also rings true in the third case, that of American agricultural cooperatives. Again, the immediate causes of failure were consistent with the demand-side view: while cooperatives had been successful in an environment in which they had offered a solution to a certain type of market failure, changing conditions made them susceptible to the competition of investor-owned businesses – and this competitive setting exposed cooperative inefficiencies, particularly with regard to raising capital. In these circumstances, cooperatives either hung on to their structure and, consequently, sooner or later went bankrupt, or they tried to change their organizational framework, solved some of their problems, but soon encountered others and were eventually pushed toward transformation. This dynamic, however, described only the very large cooperatives that had consciously entered the competitive environment of IOBs; others that stuck to activities close to the farm gate were able to remain economically viable while safeguarding their organizational structure. The reason why some larger cooperatives could not follow this route was that they had been rid of their social meaning long before: while they had been regarded as reservoirs of solidarity by many farmers in the 1950s and 1960s, by the 1980s, the milieus that had provided the supply of these ideals had, by and large, been dissolved. As a consequence, an increasing number of large cooperatives received their sole legitimacy from the fulfillment of their economic functions, and this made them susceptible to demutualization.

So what about the "rules" of cooperative failure? The cases we have examined suggest that there are some common elements. All of the failures were connected to changing economic conditions that may be described as transitions from situations of market failure to competitive environments – often as a consequence of technological and organizational change, but sometimes as a corollary of shrinking markets and deregulation. Cooperatives performed well as long as they were not, or were only partially, challenged by other types of businesses, and as long as capital requirements were relatively limited – but under the new conditions, their organizational characteristics rendered them less efficient than IOBs, and ultimately resulted in their bankruptcy or transformation.

The case studies, however, also show that this is not the complete story. After all, many cooperatives did manage to adapt to changing circumstances and competitive conditions, which implies that economic disadvantages were typically only the proximate causes of cooperative failure – they could, under certain circumstances, be overcome. What were these circumstances, and why did they not hold in the cases under review? It is tempting to argue that cooperatives could remain economically viable as long as there was a strong social milieu to "make up" for their deficits. In fact, the functioning of cooperatives in all of the cases presented relied on this factor (even though the German example shows that a coherent basis alone does not suffice; rather, it is important to strike a balance between cohesiveness, on the one hand, and size or reach on the other). However, this way of formulating the issue can and should be criticized for the imbalance it implies between the social and economic functions of cooperatives. A different view is that the social and cultural context was not in any way "making up" for any deficit, but was rather part and parcel of the rationale for cooperatives. The point is that the ability to fill this aspect of cooperative organization with life was highly dependent on the stability of the social groups that provided the basis for a committed membership. Thus, it is no coincidence that the decline of cooperatives in all of the cases investigated here was intimately related to large-scale shifts in the social structure of the respective countries – to the transition from industrial to postindustrial patterns of stratification in Western Europe and, albeit less directly, in Japan, and to generational change and increasing social differentiation in the American case.

This view does not mean that in the newly emerging social and cultural configurations, there is no room for cooperatives. Large-scale structural change may create as many opportunities as it destroys, as can be gauged, for example, by the growth of social cooperatives in Italy and France since the mid-1980s.[70] It does suggest, however, that periods of rapid social transformation can dislocate the rationale for *previously existing* cooperatives profoundly. Consequently, these may be situations in which they have to radically rethink their basis, their aims, and their markets. If they focus on their economic viability alone, this will eventually heighten the probability of failure, whereas a consequent and early repositioning might avoid such a fate. It is, of course, extremely hard to overcome organizational inertia in any kind of business, and cooperatives are no exception. But sometimes taking a back seat may be wiser than reaching for the stars – particularly if the double mission of cooperatives, that of providing both mutual solidarity and economic benefit, is to be taken seriously.

[70] Alessandra Mancino and Antonio Thomas, "An Italian Pattern of Social Enterprise: The Social Cooperative," *Nonprofit Management and Leadership*, 15 (2005), pp. 357–69, here p. 358.

CHAPTER 6

Demutualization and Its Problems

Patrizia Battilani and Harm G. Schröter

INTRODUCTION

During the last decades, the world economy has undergone far-reaching changes which have shaped the current framework of international capitalism. Gerald Epstein summarized those developments in three words: *neoliberalism, globalization,* and *financialization.*[1] These processes have deeply affected not only the strategies but also the governance of firms. All forms of enterprise facing these new challenges have, in some way, changed their organizational structures as well as their business strategies. Financial strategies, in particular, have been transformed by the new global market for currencies and new forms of financial instruments.

Cooperatives have been no exception to this rule. They have experienced a substantial wave of innovations, and as a result, new forms of cooperative enterprises have emerged. In the United States and Canada, these new forms are commonly referred to as *new generation cooperatives* (NGCs); in Italy and Spain, they are called *cooperative groups* or *networks of cooperatives.* One of the main features of these new organizational structures is the attempt to take some of the advantages of the investor-oriented firm (above all, in capital-raising activities) while retaining the mutual/cooperative status. As Chaddad and Cook will make clear in Chapter 7, the new organizations can be considered hybrid institutions like the publicly listed cooperative (Nilsson, 2001; Chaddad and Cook, 2004; Bekkum, O. F. van, and J. Bijman, 2006).

There is no doubt that these innovations in structures and organizational models have been the salient feature of co-ops at the turn of the twenty-first century. Many of the changes have been undertaken to facilitate the growth of the enterprises both in the domestic market and abroad. As historians, we are not in a position to say whether what is now emerging will be the dominant cooperation form of the twenty-first century, but certainly we are justified in naming the last three decades the age of hybridization. At the end of this

---

[1] Gerald Epstein, *Financialization and the World Economy* (Aldershot: Edward Elgar Publishing, 2005).

transformation, an entirely new paradigm with a new set of values and reference models could well emerge.

In some cases, the search for new structures has gone so far as to assume the aspect of conversion of mutuals into stock firms. This chapter will deal with that aspect later when we focus on cooperatives that have opted for conversion or demutualization instead of hybridization.

Historically, demutualization (see the next section of this chapter for the definition) is mainly a problem of the last few decades. Consequently, we will survey the period following the Second World War. The process started earlier in some countries and was taken over in others later. A main thesis of this chapter is that all this forging ahead by some and falling behind by others was not a process of coincidence. As Fabio Chaddad has observed: "most notably Australia, Great Britain, South Africa and the USA" were the early movers (Chaddad, 2004, p. 576). Alfred Chandler and many other historians have suggested that the United States has long been particularly attuned to a competitive, market-oriented economy (Chandler, 1990). It was, after all, in America that the "Chicago school" of economists flourished and later influenced the whole world. Privatization and deregulation started in Britain and the United States, and it was thus not by chance that the United States acted as a path-breaker in the case of demutualization. On a broad scale, the movement started in the United States, spread first to the Anglo-Saxon countries along with other aspects of "Americanization," and later influenced decision making in all parts of the world. There were only a few countries in which demutualization was not put on the agenda; usually this happened where legislation placed restrictions on conversion. France opted for a different path. Indeed, in the same years in which co-ops demutualized worldwide, the French government mutualized the 34 regional savings banks with a new law on financial security.[2] We could also say that the map of countries that did not follow the U.S. model was not due to coincidence.

Most persons engaged in demutualization were trying to do the right thing, especially to ease capital constraints of their respective firms and, by doing so, enrich the old and new owners. This was accomplished not so much by exploiting customers but through better organization, improved management and decision making, and so on. Many persons involved considered co-ops to be a more or less outdated form of enterprise. Although by 2010 demutualization could be questioned, decision makers in the previous two decades usually had

---

[2] During the 1990s, 186 French Saving Banks were reorganized into 34 regional-based banks and one national bank which operated as one group (the market share was around 10 percent). After this reorganization, the regional savings banks were mutualized by the Law No. 25 of June 1999. A pyramid scheme was set up. At the basis were 451 local savings societies that held all the shares of the savings banks to which they were attached. Among other things, the mutualization made it possible to project the merger between the savings bank group and the credit unions. So, in 2006, the Banques Populaires and the Caisses d'Epargne began the process with the creation of their joint subsidiary, Natixis; and in 2009, the two groups merged their central institutions, giving birth to the second-largest French banking group.

the best intentions when demutualizing their co-ops and did so in good conscience.

The aim of this chapter is to address the demutualization process in a historical perspective and provide some explanations for its acceleration during the last two decades, as well as its slowdown after the 2008 financial crisis.

Among others, three crucial questions deserve an answer:

- Why was demutualization a worldwide process?
- What drove demutualization?
- Did demutualization take place in the public interest?

DEMUTUALIZATION AS A WORLDWIDE PROCESS

Before analyzing the different phases of demutualization, it is necessary to provide some definition of it and, above all, reveal our choice of definition. As a matter of fact, demutualization has been defined in at least three different ways by scholars and practitioners: the first one focusing on ownership structure (Chaddad, 2004; Birchall, 1998),[3] the second taking into consideration the deviation from traditional cooperatives (Zvi Galor, 2007),[4] and the third one based on the co-op values (Griffith, 2004; Barberini, 2007).[5]

The main differences among the various definitions concern the attitude toward the institutional innovation characterizing the cooperative enterprises in recent decades. The mergers of co-ops in order to create a new one, the purchases of companies by co-ops, the creation of companies owned by cooperatives, and the creation of a new cooperative group are examples of demutualization in the view of Galor; however, they are not all examples according to Chaddad. In other words, the definition of demutualization is intimately

[3] This definition dates back to the 1990s and has been clearly restated by Chaddad and Cook in 2004 and 2007: "it is a change in the ownership structure of user owned and controlled organizations from a mutual to a for-profit, proprietary organization. As a result of demutualization, residual claim and control rights are reassigned among stakeholders with implications to firm behaviour and performance. In particular, cooperative membership rights are converted to unrestricted common stock ownership rights in a corporate organization."

[4] According to Zvi Galor, the great part of the new forms of cooperatives – like the NGC in the United States and Canada or the cooperative group in Italy – should be classified as examples of demutualization.

[5] Griffiths in 2004 claimed that "the origin of demutualization is when the cooperative has lost its cooperative identity and what distinguishes it from investor-oriented companies." This view was shared also by the ICA president of that time, Ivano Barberini, a former manager of the Italian consumer cooperation, who in 2007 claimed: "The economic value of cooperation is the result of the implementation of its social values for the benefit of members and of the community in which the cooperatives operate. Nevertheless, on occasion this has not been the case, and changes have taken a direction that is anything but the right one. In diverse parts of the world, certain major cooperative groups have favoured the logic of pure financial gain and market dynamics, to the detriment of the characteristic identity of cooperation. In certain situations, decisions of this kind have led to the complete "demutualization" of cooperative enterprises" (Barberini, 2007).

connected with the debate on traditional versus new co-ops. We will come back to this issue later in the chapter.

In the following section of this chapter, however, we will use the Chaddad definition, which means that the deep changes in structure and organization experienced by many cooperative movements during the last thirty years all over the world will not be considered a sort of demutualization. Instead, they will be classified as institutional innovation aimed at facing increasing competition and globalization.

Conversion of co-ops or mutuals into investor-oriented enterprises, and vice versa, dates back to the origin of the cooperative movement[6] (Mayers and Smith, 1986; Carson, Forster, and McNamara, 1998; De Bonis, Manzone, and Trento, 1994). Nevertheless, it is possible to identify decades in which demutualization has trended to spread, as well as periods characterized by an opposite trend.Although there is a lack of data on demutualization, the issue has been researched carefully for the United States. Fitzgerald lists 105 cases up to 1968, beginning around 1900 or even earlier. From 1968–87, he lists another 40 cases, though without providing the exact years in all instances. From this information and from that in Tables 6.1 and 6.2 in this chapter, we can infer two points. First, demutualization took place in the United States during all that time, and second, the numbers went up during the last decades. Although we have no special information, we can presume that the phenomenon was not unknown to European and other countries. The lack of interest in such a move in other countries, however, may be a hint that it was not of particular significance elsewhere. Nevertheless demutualization has become a significant issue during the last two decades. Although further investigation is needed, available data suggest that, for both the United States and Europe since the late 1980s, demutualization has entered a new phase, characterized by a substantial intensification. There is also indication of its spread to South Africa and Japan before the outbreak of the financial crisis in 2008. Demutualization has been unevenly spread, involving especially insurance and banking as well as agricultural cooperatives, and only occasionally other sectors. The largest wave of demutualization, involving more than 100 million persons, was the dismantling of agricultural co-ops in the socialist world, which took place mainly during the 1990s (although, in some cases, it still has not been carried out); its timing provides another proof for the thesis of a new phase that is about two decades old.

At the turn of the twenty-first century, after many years of demutualization, especially in the insurance sector in the United States, the U.K., and Australia, the phenomenon started to spread in other countries, including Canada, South Africa, Japan, and Ireland. Even if conversions seemed to be restricted to two sectors, agriculture and finance, nevertheless the leaders of the international cooperative movement started to become more and more worried. The ICA

---

[6] The nineteenth-century debate, known in Sweden as "the big battle about principles," provides an example.

TABLE 6.1 *The Conversion of Mutuals in Investor-Oriented Firms in the USA, 1900–2000*

Years	Carson-Foster-McNamara 1998 data (life insurers)	John F. Fitzgerald 1987 data (insurance companies)	Viswanathan and Cummins 2003 data (propriety liability, life health insurers)	Mayers and Smith 2002 data (propriety-casualty company insurance)
1900–10	5			
1911–20	2			
1921–30	8			12
1931–40	2			3
1941–50	3			9
1951–60	2			7
1961–70	3	5		29
1971–80	3	10		14
1981–90	–	3	21	22
1991–2000	–		51	–

Source: K. S. Viswanathan and J. D. Cummins, "Ownership Structure Changes in the Insurance Industry: An Analysis of Demutualization," *Journal of Risk and Insurance*, 70 (2003), 401–32; D. Mayers and C. W. Smith, "Ownership Structure and Control: Property-Casualty Insurer Conversions to Stock Charter," *Journal of Financial Services Research*, 21 (2002), pp. 117–44; J. M. Carson, M. D. Forster, and M. J. McNamara, "Changes in Ownership" (1998).

TABLE 6.2 *Demutualization in Some Countries during 1980–2010*

Country	First Demutualization	Other Demutualization
United Kingdom	1989 Abbey National (building society)	1995–9: 18 building societies and 4 farmer coops
Australia	1970s generalized phenomenon (farmer's coops)	1990–9: 10 building societies and 60 general cooperatives (agriculture, taxi, stock exchange)
Canada	1999	
South Africa	1998 Sanlam (mutual life insurance)	
Japan	2000 Daido Life (life insurance)	2000–10: 39 life insurance
Former socialist countries	1990s agricultural coops	

Source: Cummins and Venard (2007); Cronan (1995, 1999); Birchall (1998); and Reserve Bank of Australia, Bulletin January (1999).

organized a Web page on this issue and, in 2007, called for the creation of a committee of scholars to investigate this threatening development.

Then suddenly, with the outbreak of the financial crisis in 2008, the interest in demutualization came to an end. The financial crisis put new issues on the agenda. In some countries, like the U.K., the failures of demutualized societies, including Northern Rock and Bradford & Bingley, led consumers to transfer their business back to the mutual holding societies. In the midst of financial insecurity, there was a new interest in mutualization. In September 2009, the Building Societies Association published a report from the Oxford Centre for Mutual & Employee-Owned Business, Kellogg College, titled *Converting Failed Financial Institutions into Mutual Organizations*. Northern Rock was a cooperative British building society which had been converted into a company in 1992. During the financial crisis, government saved it from bankruptcy and later turned it back into public ownership. Remutualization was a way to dispose of Northern Rock (and of state-owned enterprises in general), quite a new sort of privatization. The main goals of Northern Rock's conversion were to repay taxpayers, strengthen competition in the financial market, and create a more diversified financial sector by the diffusion of low-risk enterprises like mutuals (All-Party Parliamentary Group for Building Societies and Financial Mutuals, 2006). It is not for historians to predict a reversal of the demutualization trend, but we think it is important to witness the emergence of this new attitude toward mutuals and cooperatives. It is also important that demutualization is no longer perceived to be a one-way road. Remutualization of a previously demutualized co-op is an option.

In other countries, however, the demutualizing process has continued. In April 2010, the Japanese Dai-ichi Life converted into an investor-oriented company. At the time of this writing, the other three major Japanese life insurance companies have not shown any interest in demutualizing into stock companies, but an economic recovery in Japan might bring further conversions.

Still one issue remains unexplained: why was demutualization first widespread in the United States and the Anglo-Saxon world, and only later spread to other countries? Here the cultural concept of Americanization may help: demutualization fit very well into the basic concept of American competitive capitalism; thus, it is no surprise that it mushroomed in America during the last decades. At the same time, this is exactly the period of the third wave of Americanization in the world economy (Schröter, 2005). In effect, globalization took on the form of Americanization. During this phase, enterprises from abroad looked to the United States for new and improved forms, primarily in the fields of finance, corporate organization, and government. With the 2008 financial collapse, however, this model has become less attractive, a change that surely has repercussions on the question of demutualization.

WHAT DROVE DEMUTUALIZATION?

Many reasons have been advanced to explain the demutualization process of the last decades. We can collect them into five groups. Except for the fifth, all of these approaches can boast of a long-standing tradition in economic and sociological literature. We will address all of them, one by one.

1. *Organizational isomorphism.* According to this approach, conversion into investor-oriented enterprises would be the final stage of a noncongruent isomorphic trend aimed to get legitimacy from society, from markets, or from financial institutions (Hawley, 1968; Meyer, 1979; Fennell, 1980).
2. *Cultural reasons.* The same cultural environment that supported privatization from the 1980s onward created a sympathetic attitude to the process of demutualization (Birchall, 1998).
3. *Expropriation by managers* (Hind, 1997; Mayers and Smith, 1986).
4. *Political reasons.* The dismantling of the socialist system in Europe entailed a widespread demutualization, simply because people perceived cooperatives as part of socialism and wanted to do away with them. During the antisocialist wave that swept through the countries during the 1990s, people in many quarters thought demutualization to be in the public interest in order to liquidate possible pockets of socialist resistance (Wegren, 2009; Ameline, 2002).
5. *Inefficiency or lack of growth perspectives.* The starting point of this approach is the conviction that, for some reasons (vaguely defined property rights, financial constraints, limited horizon of cooperative members), the cooperative structure limits or even inhibits growth and the viability of an enterprise (Schrader, 1989; Collins, 1991; Fulton, 1995; Cook, 1995; Holmström, 1999).

Organizational Isomorphism. The convergence of organizational forms, not only of enterprises but also of political and social institutions, is the main concern of the isomorphic approach. In 1968, Hawley defined isomorphism as a process that forces one unit in a population to resemble other units that face the same set of environmental conditions. As a consequence, the organizational structure will stepwise modify in the direction of increasing comparability with the environmental characteristics and with the other organizations. Since his pioneer paper, a lot of research has been undertaken to identify forces behind the isomorphic processes. A decade later, Meyer (1979) and Fennell (1980) identified two types of isomorphism: competitive and institutional. According to the former, the need for efficiency and competition will be the driving force of organizational innovation and will explain the growing homogeneity of organizations. This is the view usually taken by economists, even those following the property rights approach. However, "highly structured organizational fields provide a context in which individual efforts to deal rationally with uncertainty and constraint often lead, in the aggregate, to homogeneity in structure, culture, and output" (Di Maggio and Powel, 1983, p. 147). Organizations compete not just for resources and customers, but for political power and institutional legitimacy, because the latter can be the route to social as well as economic success. Thus, institutional isomorphism can proceed without increasing internal organizational efficiency.

Further research by Paul J. Di Maggio and Walter W. Powell identified three mechanisms that promote isomorphic change: coercive, mimetic, and normative. Coercive isomorphism results from the enforcement of laws and regulations or from the compulsory adoption of standard operating procedures. Mimetic isomorphism occurs in the absence of any coercive authority, but when uncertainty and the lack of appropriate human capital suggest imitation as the most viable solution. The last one, normative isomorphism, is driven by formal education in institutions, both general and vocational, and is accelerated by networks of professionals and the filtering of personnel.

Even if similarity can make it easier for organizations to transact with each other, to attract staff with a better curriculum, to be acknowledged as legitimate and reputable, nothing can ensure that these characteristics create conformist organizations more efficiently than their deviant peers. This conclusion explains why institutional isomorphism is so different from the competitive one.

The isomorphic approach has been applied to cooperative studies since the beginning of the 1990s. The first important contribution came from Bager in 1994. By using *population ecology*, he tried to explain why cooperatives may gradually lose their identity. Bager distinguished between "congruent isomorphism as the one which homogenizes the population (or subpopulation) of cooperatives and non-congruent isomorphism which homogenizes cooperatives with non-cooperatives" (1994, p. 43). In his view, cooperatives constitute one population of formal organizations within an economy and an industry. During the movement's initial decades, the number of cooperatives was so large that they formed a tightly connected group, and hence there was "congruent isomorphism." During the last decades, technological and economic transformations drove cooperatives to imitate the practices of privately owned enterprise; therefore, noncongruent isomorphism has become dominant. In summary, when tempted to improve their competitiveness by assimilating routines or even strategies of successful privately owned enterprises, cooperatives take the risk of losing their identity. In an international economy which strongly focuses on capital, we can expect conversion of cooperatives into privately owned enterprises. During the last twenty years, many researchers have related the organizational transformation of co-ops to institutional isomorphism, especially the mimetic and normative kinds. In this perspective, increasing competition and globalization as well as the collapse of the communist movement in the last few decades have created an external environment dominated by uncertainty. Several cooperatives all over the world have answered this new challenge by copying private enterprises' procedures and strategies. A new generation of managers, sometime coming from private enterprises, but always with a formal education, has stimulated the adoption of more market-oriented operating routines and procedures, while toning down solidarity values (Battilani, 2009; Battilani and Bertagnoni, 2010). The emergence of large-scale cooperatives has reshaped the relationship between members and managers, strengthening the role of the latter (Cazzuffi and Hunt, 2009).

If it is assumed that isomorphism can provide part or maybe all of the explanation of institutional change that has characterized co-ops during the last decades, the question we must ask is: can it also explain *demutualization*? This is a question primarily because demutualization has remained restricted to some sectors and countries, whereas the convergence between co-ops and investor-owned enterprises has seemed to be a more general trend. So it remains for scholars to explain why in some countries isomorphism reached its highest stage by conversion, but the process did not take place in all countries. Or, in other words, why did social or economic legitimacy apparently require demutualization in some sectors or in some countries, while in others it did not?

Cultural Reasons. Strictly connected to institutional isomorphism is a cultural hypothesis, according to which demutualization would be a sort of by-product of privatization of publicly owned enterprise. In analyzing the U.K. experience, Birchall claimed in 1998 that the same cultural values and beliefs supporting privatization fostered the demutualization of co-ops. So when privatization came to an end, demutualization began. At the time, many scholars and professionals in the media predicted that mutual organizations would soon be extinct, simply because the ownership structure of mutuals is too inflexible for a rapidly changing financial world. Trying to apply this model to the Australian case, in 1999 Garry Cronan came to the conclusion that even if the conversion trend coexists with privatization, the latter followed the former.

In any case, several arguments in support of privatization have been used in support of demutualization too. Connecting the cultural transformation that accompanied and supported privatization with the institutional isomorphism analysis, we could conclude that demutualization occurred where the new ideas of increased competition spread both quickly and deeply.

Expropriation by Managers. The focus on management permits us to introduce the expropriation hypothesis. This line of reasoning indicates that demutualization may be motivated by the chance of transferring wealth to management at the expense of the members. The starting point is the entrance of a new generation of managers with formal education, very similar to the one received by the executives of the investor-oriented enterprises. Combining these changes with principal–agent theory, some scholars have focused on the conflict between managers and members. Mayers and Smith (1986) analyzed the conversion (in this case, a *mutualization*) of U.S. insurers and suggested that wealth expropriation provides a possible explanation for conversion; they identified a number of potential wealth transfers that could occur in both directions: from members to managers, and vice versa. In 1969, Hetherington had already suggested this kind of interpretation, claiming that demutualization could be motivated by the self-interest of managers. Hind claimed in 1999 that in the later stages of an organizational life cycle, agricultural cooperatives, now being larger and more market-oriented, were stimulated to realize the aspirations of the managers, rather than those of the farmers. In 2003, Tayler's research on the demutualization of U.K. building societies concluded that, in many cases, management played an active role in transforming their organizations. Based on this evidence, he suggested demutualization to be inevitable when management no longer defends mutuality.

Cook and colleagues (2001) gave several examples of senior managers of financial mutuals making large short-term financial gains as a result of a demutualization, in the form of payouts, increased salaries in the new enterprise, and a disproportionate number of shares that had been set aside for the managers and directors from those issued to the members. Stephens (2001) cites several examples where demutualizations have created huge wealth for directors and limited benefit for the members (especially those members who at the time of the demutualization were unable to afford their entitlement of shares and, thus, effectively received nothing).

Indeed, there have been several cases where management, by pursuing its own interest, led co-ops into demutualization. One is the famous case of Abbey National Building Society, which is famous because it was the first (1989) as well as one of the largest of the U.K. demutualizations in this sector.[7] A large part of its membership actively fought management over this issue. Afterward, a court ruled against the proceedings of management, but it was too late (Perks, 1991, p. 487). In 1951, intentional fraud was carried out by five directors of Madison Mutual Fire Insurance Company. The directors demutualized, enriched themselves, and let the new company go bust. Because there was no law against it, they got away with it (Fitzgerald, 1990). The impact of another fraud was much larger: Neue Heimat, at the time the largest building society in Europe, owning more than 300,000 apartments and houses, was forced to demutualize in 1986 because top management had enriched itself at the expense of the cooperative.

Political Reasons. In terms of number of people affected, the most important wave of demutualization took place in the former socialist countries. Although hardly taken into account in Western publications dealing with research on co-ops, this wave affected more than 100 million people. It can be argued that the co-ops under socialist rule were not "real" co-ops, but they did have the potential for it. In fact, great efforts were made by various Western institutions to introduce Western-style co-ops. Why did these attempts fail to a large extent, and why did co-ops in Central and Eastern Europe (CEE) demutualize?

Prior to 1990, only 4 percent of cultivated land was private farmland in the CEE countries. Except in Poland, Romania, and parts of Slovakia, co-ops and state farms dominated (Millns, p. 4). In addition to the agricultural co-ops, others existed such as those for fishing, forestry, as well as all sorts of crafts. Theoretically, such structures were better prepared for the transition to capitalism than the rest of the economy. Also, politicians should have been interested because self-aid (and learning it) is a necessary means to construct a middle-class, without which a market economy cannot survive (Steding and Kramer, pp. 16, 86).

[7] The second reason is a curiosity: Abbey headquarters was set up in 219–229 Baker Street, London. This included 221 B Baker Street, the fictive home of Sherlock Holmes. Abbey used to answer letters addressed to him!

Nevertheless, demutualization took place and the number of co-ops fell sharply. This was due to two factors: governments wanted to reintegrate agriculture into mainstream Western market development and thought privatization to be the best way to do so. Farmers themselves were extremely skeptical toward co-ops; they could not imagine their functioning in a manner different from the traditional way without democracy: "attitude studies across the region in the mid 1990s showed that almost 60% of farmers saw voluntary cooperation as an unnecessary variant of former socialist structures" (FAO, 2006, p. 10). In spite of massive attempts by the International Co-operative Alliance (ICA) and the International Labour Organization (ILO) to teach farmers otherwise, the farmers preferred to split up the land. Even attempts involving substantial transfer of know-how and human power, as in Kosovo, failed, because farmers equated co-ops with socialism (Egger and Tomanek, 2009).

There were, however, variations. Privatization led to tiny private plots, for instance, 1.3 hectares in Albania and 1.6 ha in Moldova (FAO, 2006, p. 4). In many cases, the owners leased such plots to others who formed large or very large agrarian firms. After twenty years of transition, the situation in Russia is still unclear and complicated. Officially, privatization was carried through, but in 2011, property rights still remained unclear. The number of private farms increased tremendously, from only 4,400 in 1991 to 267,000 in 2007, but the quantity of land only doubled (from 3.2 to 7.0 million ha; Wegren, 2009, p. 21). Private farmers' share of all land was only 0.4 percent in 2008. Today many forms of agrarian enterprise exist in Russia with undefined characteristics varying between co-ops and private farms. Very few are probably organized as a Western-style co-op, and include democracy, responsibility of management, and defined ownership. In fact, we have no information on their existence. Persons in all quarters agree that demutualization generally did not achieve its goals (Amelina, 2002).

Some countries took a different path. Slovakia and Eastern Germany (formerly the GDR) provide an exception to the past-socialist demutualization wave. There, most of the land stayed with co-ops, which transformed themselves into Western-style ones. These large enterprises, using between 1,000 and 6,000 hectares, have become highly competitive. They avoided demutualization and became profitable.

Inefficiency or Lack of Growth Perspectives. All previous approaches are united by the consideration that the key driver of demutualization is not the search for a more efficient organization. However, the efficiency hypothesis has been tested more than any other, especially in the sector of insurance. The rationale behind this hypothesis is that insurers have changed their organizational structure in an effort to improve financial and operational performance, given the costs and benefits inherent in each type of organizational structure.

During the seventies and the eighties, many of the cross-sectional studies of mutual and stock financial institutions pointed out the inefficiency of the mutual enterprises. For example, Spiller (1972) and Verbrugge and Goldstein (1981) showed that the rate of asset growth was higher for stock organizations than for mutual organizations, and Frech (1980) and O'Hara (1981) found that mutual organizations had higher expenses than stock organizations.

Two sources of inefficiency usually have been recognized. The first one is capital constraints that inhibit growth and the possibility of developing new products or expanding into new geographical markets. John F. Fitzgerald (1990, p. 297) suggested: "Demutualization is the only practicable way for raising additional capital." Viswanathan and Cummins (2003), analyzing seventy-two conversions that occurred during 1981–99, concluded their research by writing: "converting firms form a unique subset of mutuals that require additional capital to sustain their current activities." However, it is worth noting that various forms of hybridization have obtained the same result without giving up the cooperative status.

The second feature favoring stock companies over mutuals is the absence or an inferior control of managers. The rationale behind this claim is that various control mechanisms are present for stock-owned firms but not in their mutual counterparts. Oliver Hart and John More (1996) demonstrated that cooperative ownership is prone to this sort of inefficiency.

Therefore, in the initial years of the demutualization wave, many economists advocated demutualization, especially for financial institutions. In an effort to examine the validity of this reason, a number of authors have set out to compare the efficiency of particular organizations before and after demutualization; several papers on this subject were published between 1986 and 2007. Nilsson, Kihlén, and Norell (2009) have outlined the most important of these in Table 6.3.

In 1991, John Kay, a leading British economist, edited a special volume of *Annales de l'économie publique, sociale et cooperative* on demutualization of financial institutions. Without taking into consideration the special social characteristics of cooperatives, he concentrated on the economic dimension only: "The objective of any business activity is to create such added value (or economic rent). In the long run an organization which fails to do this has no rationale" (pp. 310–12). According to the author, enterprises differ only in the way they "distribute the value they add." Of course, what he writes is correct, but it eliminates from consideration goals such as democratic control. Kay claimed the whole question of demutualization focused on relative efficiency.

As the literature indicates, demutualization can provide solutions for real problems, as do various forms of hybridization. The choice between these options is complex and may at times involve matters of managerial self-interest as well as efficiency and ideology.

So what was – and still is – driving demutualization? In generalizing some suggestions by Roger Buckland and Bernard Thion (1991), and based on the evidence put forward thus far in this chapter, we have identified three sources which can, but need not, work together to make demutualization imminent: (1) traditional incentives for mutual aid on the basis of membership have become watered down (when the respective co-op has lost its ideological and cultural characteristics), (2) governments have provided incentives to demutualize, and

TABLE 6.3 *A Selection of Theoretical Approaches to Explain Why Large and Complex Traditional Cooperatives May Face Problems*

Author	Core Concept	Driving Forces	Ends
Cook (1995)	Vaguely defined property rights	Large size of operations is necessary but then members will free-ride, become uninterested, etc.	Exit, conversions to IOFs or reorientation to individualized structures
Fulton (1995)	Property rights theory	Technological advancements change the locus of power in the value chain	The cooperative's power is reduced
Bager (1996)	Population ecology	Techno-economic and institutional changes induce the cooperatives to imitate other businesses	Conversions, or at least the loss of a specific cooperative identity
Harte (1997)	Transaction cost and agency theory	Markets are becoming more open, more transparent and larger	Conversions into IOFs or Hybrid forms
Holmstrom (1999)	Corporate governance, capital markets	As the capital markets function better, the cooperatives' investment portfolios becomes suboptimal	Traditional cooperative are increasingly inefficient
Hogeland (2006)	The economic culture	Industrialization of agriculture, processing becomes large scale and capital intensive	Traditional cooperatives face difficulties due to ignorant members

Source: Jerker Nilsson, Anna Kihlén, and Lennart Norell (2009).

(3) alternative visions of how to improve future prospects have become more attractive than the traditional ones. All of those things have happened, especially in the last two decades.

The Role of the Legal Framework

The institutional contest played a crucial role in drawing the map of demutualization as well as hybridization. As a matter of fact, in many countries, the conversion of co-ops into investor-owned enterprises is not legal. In the E.U. more than half of the states make it possible for cooperatives to abandon their cooperative status by converting into a commercial company. The countries in which this is possible are the U.K., the Netherlands, France, Finland, Germany,

Spain, Belgium, and, in certain cases, also Luxemburg and Denmark. In other countries, however, such a move is illegal.

Nevertheless, a substantial hesitation about conversion has been observed. Although the U.K., with section 84 of its "Friendly Societies Act 1974," theoretically enabled demutualization, it took fifteen more years until the first friendly society set its foot on this path. "Time Assurance Society" thus became "Templeton Life" in 1990, but not during the 1970s (McLean, 1991). Our hypothesis is that during the 1970s, cooperative values were still vivid in the U.K., but they became watered down during the 1980s. Although this thesis needs substantiation, the periodization is in line with similar observations presented earlier in the chapter, and with the thesis of Americanization.

In America, demutualization provisions vary by state. Some states require approval by state regulatory authorities and the majority of co-op members (in some cases, a simple majority, but in other states, two-thirds or three-fourths of the votes), while other states place additional restrictions on the process or expressly prohibit conversion. In 1988, New York ended a sixty-six-year prohibition against demutualization. Two years later, the Equitable Life Assurance Society, a New York – based mutual and one of the nation's largest life insurers, announced plans to begin the demutualization process. The 1988 New York statute served as a model for demutualization statutes in other states. See Table 6.4.

In 1999, Canada encouraged and regulated demutualization. Consequently four of the largest mutuals of Canada demutualized. In 1995, Japan enabled the process of demutualization through the Insurance Business Law and a subsequent amendment of 2000, which further modified the articles in order to solve practical issues associated with demutualization. It was only after the approval of that amendment that the first demutualization was completed.

The legal framework played a crucial role not only in allowing or interdicting demutualization, but also in creating an environment that makes demutualization appealing. Almost everywhere conversions were preceded by institutional innovation, namely, the approval of laws reshaping a more competitive framework of the financial or other sectors. As Chaddad and Cook claimed in their 2004 contribution, demutualization occurred "after disruptive institutional changes which increase industry rivalry and negatively affect profits." In many cases, the same law that allowed mutuals to demutualize also reshaped the competitive environment. The U.K. building societies were deregulated in 1986 as a response to a wish for increased competition in the financial services sector. Their U.S. equivalent, the savings and loan associations, were deregulated earlier in 1980 after a fall in interest rates left them unable to attract funds (Barnes and Ward, 1999). This kind of law was approved in Australia in 1992, and in Japan in 1995. Throughout, we find that demutualization needed a suitable legal framework and was stimulated by the changes in that part of the economic framework.

TABLE 6.4 *Statutory Authority for Property-Casualty Insurance Company Conversions to Stock Charter*

States That Have Adopted Conversion Statutes

Alabama	Arizona	Arkansas
California	Delaware	Florida
Georgia	Indiana	Kansas
Kentucky	Louisiana	Maine
Maryland	Michigan	Minnesota
Montana	Nebraska	Nevada
New Jersey	New Mexico	New York
Ohio	Oklahoma	Pennsylvania
South Carolina	South Dakota	Tennessee
Utah	Vermont	Virginia
Washington	West Virginia	Wisconsin

States With No Conversion Statutes

Colorado	Connecticut	District of Columbia
Illinois	Iowa	Massachusetts
Mississippi	Missouri	New Hampshire
North Carolina	North Dakota	Oregon
Rhode Island	Texas	

States Prohibiting Conversions

Alaska	Hawaii	Idaho

Source: Mayer and Smith (2002).

Demutualization and Public Interest

Two questions remain unsolved. First, did demutualization take place in the public interest? We define public interest as a good or, in our case, after demutualization, superior economic performance. This brings us back to the topics of efficiency and a proper functioning of the market. In general, enterprise uses institutional change as a tool of improving efficiency. So we can ask: at the end, do converted enterprises show a better profitability, that is, higher return for investors and better prices for customers (regardless of the reasons that drove their demutualization)? Until now, the answers have been multifaceted. It is worth quoting some results.

The first affirmative answer was proposed by Masulis in 1987, who, after analyzing 205 completed conversions of savings and loan associations between 1974 and 1983, claimed that conversion improved organizational efficiency due to the injection of new equity capital, distribution of managerial stock options, and decreased risk of insolvency.

The 2004 Chaddad and Cook survey of the empirical studies on demutualization in the United States also suggested that ownership structure changed the U.S. insurance industry and was in general efficiency-enhancing. Some years later, Lai, McNamara, and Tong Yu (2008), investigating underpricing and postconversion long-run stock performance of U.S.-converted mutual, suggested that "there is more 'money left on the table' for demutualized insurers than for non-demutualized insurers" (p. 1).

In contrast, in 2007, Vivian Jeng, Gene C. Lai, and Michael J. McNamara concluded that demutualized U.S. insurers in the 1980s and 1990s failed to improve efficiency after demutualization, when a value-added approach is used. Some months before, in November 2006, Lal C. Chugh and Joseph W. Meador, after examining eleven fully converted former mutuals, summarized their study by claiming that long-run market returns of demutualized companies had outperformed various market indexes, including the NASDAQ Insurance Company Index, and had indeed created economic value. According to the authors, management in those companies had successfully implemented a strategy based on higher growth, greater profitability, improved cost-efficiency, and innovations in product offerings.

Apparently, the results of demutualization have been varied according to the country involved, although the most sophisticated analyses have remained confined to the United States and Canada, and therefore it is difficult to generalize the results. The worst results have been recorded in the U.K. where, in a decade, all the converted building societies lost their independent status either because they were purchased by other banks (Abbey National and Alliance & Leicester by Bank Santander) or because they failed and were taken into public ownership (Northern Rock and Bradford & Bingley, Converted 2009). Similarly, Baris Serifsoy, basing his research on twenty-eight stock exchanges, found nothing "to support the view that an outsider-owned exchange enhances the efficiency of the exchange" (p. 329). He explicitly challenged Hart and More, suggesting that the advantages of an IPO of a stock exchange lie mainly with the directly involved personnel of the institution and with a few large financial enterprises to the detriment of the majority of the membership, the small local brokers. He thus hinted that different interests achieved different rewards. In 1991 David Llewellyn and Mark Holmes maintained that "mutuals need not necessarily be any more constrained than public limited companies in achieving objectives related to growth and diversification" (p. 481).

We find the evidence mixed. The mainstream view of economists suggests that co-ops suffer from inefficiency and a lack of growth perspectives, especially in the financial sector. On the other hand, there are those scholars who find just the opposite. For the case of stock exchanges, both sides have produced quantitative evidence supporting their different conclusions. We do not believe the case is settled and would like to have more practical evidence, especially from non–stock exchange financial institutions. How did the many demutualized insurance and housing societies fare? One may guess that – as with privatization of public ownership, a much better researched topic – the economic results are mixed.

Several authors, looking for practical evidence for the thesis that demutualization leads to a better performance, have presented disappointing results: their findings were at best mixed or the expected improvement simply did not take place. The few definite winners of such a move were the economic advisers and banks involved, and managers who, now in private business, could ask for higher pay. We conclude: at the business level, there are no clear and general advantages from demutualization, beyond the traditional one of shake-ups that may improve the performance of any commercial organization.

In general support of mutuality, Llewellyn and Holmes concluded that any national sector of finance would be much more stable when it included a substantial number of mutuals. Co-ops are more attuned to long-term planning and much less risk oriented (1991, p. 346). Practical evidence during the financial crisis of 2008 showed their prediction to be true in the case of Germany's cooperative *Volksbanken*. The same is true for savings banks in Germany, which, through their ties to local authorities, are also obliged to serve the public welfare. However, the *Landesbanken*, also obligated, turned out to have been one of the worst risk-takers or speculators in the whole financial sector. The same applies to the majority of Spanish savings banks. Thus, only financial institutions under tight member-owner control were able to stabilize financial markets. For politicians this provides an argument for not demutualizing financial institutions. The public interest in stability – a goal well appreciated since 2008 – will probably be better served by maintaining a substantial number of cooperatives in any capitalist economy. We can say less about social capital because of the lack of relevant studies, but we rather assume that co-ops are favored in this regard to because of their strong orientation toward service to their communities.

The last of our questions is about the connection between hybridization and demutualization. As we mentioned at the beginning of the chapter, during the last three decades, cooperatives have experienced acceleration of institutional innovation with the introduction of many variations to the reference model. It is certainly not surprising that co-ops, like other forms of enterprise, have changed their organizational structure over time to face the challenges of the world economy. Therefore, hybridization can be considered an important part of the co-ops' answer to the financialization and the globalization processes that accelerated at the end of the twentieth century.In each country, hybridization took on special connotations. In France, Spain, and Italy, it proceeded quite slowly and was usually accompanied by the development of new concepts such as "social economy," "mutuality extended to outsiders," and so on. In other countries, for instance the U.K. and Australia, hybridization took on the appearance of deregulation aiming to mimic key aspects of investor-oriented enterprise and consequently often was followed by a complete demutualization of many co-ops. Still, in other countries, such as Germany, the cooperative movement remained tied to past models and there was a different kind of failure, namely, bankruptcy.

In the process of hybridization, some co-ops have changed too little and lost positions or exited the market, while others have changed too much and demutualized. Thus, hybridization can be placed in between these two extremes. In our view, demutualization has been the dark side of hybridization, an outcome that has weakened a cooperative movement that has and continues to be a significant part of the world economic history.

SUMMARY

Demutualization has been happening nearly since the beginning of the co-op-movement. After the Second World War, however, demutualization was no longer carried out in a very few and exceptional cases but turned into a much more widespread process, even becoming some kind of a wave during the last two decades. A substantial amount of demutualization is to be found in the United States since the 1960s. It grew first in North America, then in the U.K., and later spread to many developed countries in the world. Legal issues have played an important role. Some countries (or single states of the United States) have facilitated demutualization by new lawmaking, while others, such as France, have interdicted it in general. The types of co-ops that have chosen to demutualize have been quite unevenly distributed. Mainly co-ops for financial aims have demutualized, though building societies and other fields of economic activities have been affected as well. The spread of demutualization, especially after the 1990s, was abruptly stopped by the outbreak of the financial crisis in 2008. The reason for this stoppage is quite clear: co-ops are generally much less risk-seeking forms of business than private enterprise. Therefore, co-ops are considered safer than other types of firms.It is interesting to compare the wave of demutualizations with the wave of Americanization, expressed through privatization, deregulation, shareholder value, and the takeover of American standards in financial activities more or less all over the world. This wave of Americanization started and ended parallel to our wave of demutualization. This gives us a hint why demutualization came about and ended: it was driven by basically the same ideas as the economy in general during this period. An indicator of the end of this wave of demutualization is a case of a reversal: Northern Rock, a U.K. building enterprise that for decades grew as a cooperative, became demutualized and then, after immense financial problems, became remutualized in 2010.

We have listed five clusters of reasons for demutualization: (1) organizational isomorphism as a trend to make all things more alike; (2) cultural reasons as a trend to apply the same ideas to co-ops as to private enterprise; (3) expropriation by managers, wishing to enrich themselves at the expense of the co-op members; (4) political preferences, especially in the countries of the former socialist states, where cooperatives have carried connotations of the communist regime; and, last but not least, (5) problems of growth and raising additional financial means with which co-ops, especially in the financial sector, have been confronted.

Finally, the question of whether demutualization has been in the interest of the public could not be solved. Literature has provided several contradicting answers; both sides have put forward their arguments with emphasis and fervor. It seems that more qualitative and quantitative research is needed on this question. These authors, however, will not hide their personal impression: we think demutualization has been, in most cases, negative and that both co-op members as well as society in general would have received better financial and nonfinancial results without demutualization.

References

All Party-Parliamentary Group (APPG) for Building Societies and Financial Mutuals, www.mutuo.co.uk/wp-content/uploads/2011/09/Fostering-diversity-APPG-Report.pdf.

Amelina, Maria. (2002). "What Turns a *Kolkhoz* into a Firm? Regional Politics and the Elasticity of Budget Constraints," in David J. O'Brien and Stephen K. Wegren (eds.), *Rural Reform in Post-Soviet Russia* (Baltimore: Johns Hopkins University Press), pp. 264–81.

Bager, T. (1994, January). "Isomorphic Processes and the Transformation of Cooperatives," *Annals of Public and Cooperative Economics*, 65(1): 35–54.

Barberini, I. (2009). "Preface," in P. Battilani and G. Bertagnoni, *Cooperation, Network, Service: Innovation in Outsourcing* (Preston: Crucible).

Battilani, P. (2009). "L'impresa cooperativa in Italia nella seconda metà del Novecento: istituzione marginale o fattore di modernizzazione economica?" *Imprese e storia*.

Battilani P., and G. Bertagnoni. (2009). *Cooperation, Network, Service: Innovation in Outsourcing* (Preston: Crucible).

Bekkum, O. F. van, and J. Bijman. (2006, May 31–June 2). *Innovations in Cooperative Ownership: Converted and Hybrid Listed Cooperatives*. Paper presented at the 7th International Conference on Management in AgriFood Chains and Networks, Ede, The Netherlands.

Birchall, J. (1998). *The Future of Cooperative and Mutual Business*. Research and report, Meiji University.

De Bonis, R., B. Manzone, and S. Trento. (1994). "La proprietà cooperativa: Teoria, storia e il caso delle banche popolari," in *Temi di discussione del servizio della Banca d'italia*, n. 238.

Buckland, Roger, and Bernard Thion. (1991). "Organizational Structure, Objectives and Agency Relationships in Banking Services: The Cases of the Crédit Agricole and Trustee Savings Banks," in *Annales de l'économie publique, sociale et cooperative*, 62(3): 355–91.

Carson J.M., M.D. Forster, and M.J. McNamara. (1998). "Changes in Ownership Structure: Theory and Evidence from Life Insurer Demutualizations," *Journal of Insurance Issues*, 21: 1–22.

Cazzuffi, C., and D. Hunt. (2009). "Causes and Consequences of Institutional and Governance Change in Cooperative Firms: The Case of Agricultural Processing and Marketing Cooperatives in Italy and in the US," *Imprese e storia*.

Chaddad, F., and M. Cook. (2004). "The Economics of Organization Structure Changes: An Us Perspective on Demutualization," *Annales de l'économie publique, sociale et coopérative*, 75(4): 575–94.

Chaddad, F. and M. Cook. (2007). "Conversion and Other Forms of Exit in US Agricultural Cooperatives," in K. Karantininis and J. Nilsson (eds.), *Vertical Markets and Cooperative Hierarchies: The Role of Cooperatives in the Agri-Food Industry* (Dordrecht: Springer).

Chandler, Alfred D., Jr. (1990). *Scale and Scope: The Dynamics of Industrial Capitalism* (Cambridge: Cambridge University Press).

Chugh, Lal C., and Joseph W. Meador. (2006, Winter). "Demutualization in the Life Insurance Industry: A Study of Effectiveness," *Review of Business*, 27(1): 10–17.

Clemens, Richard G., "A New Look at Demutualization of Mutual Insurers," *Partner*, Sidley & Austin, mimeo.

Collins, Robert A. (1991). "The Conversion of Cooperatives to Publicly Held Corporations: A Financial Analysis of Limited Evidence," *Western Journal of Agricultural Economics*, 16(2): 326–30.

Converting Failed Financial Institutions into Mutual Organizations. (2009, September). Report from Oxford Centre for Mutual and Employee-Owned Business, Kellogg College, University of Oxford. Published for The Building Societies Association.

Cook, J., S. Deakin, and A. Hughes. (2001, June). *Mutuality and Corporate Governance: The Evolution of UK Building Societies Following Deregulation*. Working Paper 205, ESCR Center for Business Research, University of Cambridge.

Cook, Michael. (1995). "The Future of U.S. Agricultural Co-operatives: A Neo-Institutional Approach," *American Journal of Agricultural Economics*, 77: 1153–9.

Cronan, Garry. (1995). *The Conversion Syndrome – A Review of the Conversion of Australian Cooperatives into Investor Owned Firms*. Published by the International Co-operative Alliance, Regional Office for the Asia and the Pacific.

Cronan, Garry. (1999). "Something for Nothing – It's Fabulous": An Australian Perspective of Demutualization, mimeo.

Cummins, J. David and Venard, Bertrand (eds.). (2007). *Handbooks of International Insurance between Global Dynamics and Local Contingencies* (Dordrecht: Springer).

Demutualization in Australia. (1999, January). Reserve Bank of Australia bulletin.

Di Maggio, Paul J., and Walter W. Powell. (1983, April). "The Iron Cage Revisited: Institutional Isomorphism and Collective Rationality in Organizational Fields," *American Sociological Review*, 48(2): 147–60.

Egger, Astrid, and Peter Tomanek. (2009). "Entwicklungsbeiträge von Genossenschaften im Kossovo," in Hans Jürgen Rösner and Frank Schulz-Nieswand (eds.), *Beiträge der genossenschaftlichen Selbsthilfe zur wirtschaftlichen und sozialen Entwicklung* (Berlin: Lit Verlag), pp. 543–75.

FAO. (ed.). (2006). *Promoting Farmer Entrepreneurship through Producer Organizations in Central and Eastern Europe*. Prepared by John Millns, Rome.

Fauquet, G. (1951). *The Cooperative Sector* (Manchester: The Co-operative Union).

Fennell, Mary L. (1980). "The Effects of Environmental Characteristics on the Structure of Hospital Clusters." *Administrative Science Quarterly* 25: 484–510.

Fitzgerald, John F. (1990, December). "Demutualization Case Studies: A 20 Years History," *Journal of Insurance Regulation*, 9(2): 287–310.

Fulton, Murray. (1995). "The Future of Co-operatives in Canada: A Property Rights Approach," *American Journal of Agricultural Economics*, 77: 1144–52.

Griffiths, David. (2004, July). *Should Our Cooperative Demutualise?* From the Australia. coop Web portal.

Hart, Oliver, and John Moore. (1996). "The Governance of Exchanges: Members' Cooperatives versus Outside Ownership," *Oxford Review of Economic Policy*, 12(4): 53–69.

Hawley, Amos. (1968). "Human Ecology," in David L. Sills (ed.), *International Encyclopedia of the Social Sciences* (New York: Macmillan), pp. 328–37.

Hetherington, J. A. C. (1969). "Fact vs. Fiction: Who Owns Mutual Life Insurance Companies?" *Wisconsin Law Review*, 4: 1068–1103.

Holstrom, Bengt. (1999). "Future of Cooperatives: A Corporate Perspective," *TLA*, 4.

Jeng, Vivian, Gene C. Lai, and Michael J. McNamara. (2007). "Efficiency and Demutualization: Evidence from the U.S. Life Insurance Industry in the 1980s and 1990s," *Journal of Risk and Insurance*, 74(3): 683–711.

Kay, John A. (1991). "The Economics of Mutuality," in *Annales de l'économie publique, sociale et coopérative*, Bd. 62(3): S.309–18.

Keneley, M. J., and G. Verhoef. "The Decision to Demutualise: An Analysis of the Pressures for Change," in *The Case of Life Insurers in Australia and South Africa: A Comparative Perspective*, mimeo.

Kramper, Peter, NEUE HEIMAT. (2008). *Unternehmenspolitik und Unternehmensentwicklung im gewerkschaftlichen Wohnungs- und Städtebau 1950–1982* (Stuttgart: Franz Steiner Verlag).

Kunz, Andreas. (2002). Die Akte Neue Heimat. *Krise und Abwicklung des größten Wohnungsbaukonzerns Europas, 1982–1998* (Frankfurt: Campus Verlag).

Lai, Gene C., Michael J. McNamara, and Tong Yu. (2008). "The Wealth Effect of Demutualization: Evidence from the U.S Property-Liability and Life Insurance Industries," *Journal of Risk and Insurance*, 75(1), pp. 125–44.

Levi, Y., and P. Davis. (2008). "Cooperatives as the 'Enfants Terribles' of Economics: Some Implications for the Social Economy," *Journal of Socio-Economics*, 37: 2178–88.

Llewellyn, David T., and Mark J. Holmes. (1991). "In Defence of Mutuality: A Redress to an Emerging Conventional Wisdom," *Annales de l'économie publique, sociale et coopérative*, 62(3): 319–54.

Llwellyn, D. T. (2004). Issues in the Governance of Mutuals in the Financial Sector. Paper commissioned for the Myners enquiry into Governance of Life Mutuals, London, HM Treasury, U.K., available from www.hmtreasury.gov.uk/media/E/C/minersllewellyn.

Masulis, R. W. (1987). "Changes in Ownership Structure: Conversions of Mutual Savings and Loans to Stock Charter," *Journal of Financial Economics*, 18: 29–59.

Mayers, D., and Clifford. W. Smith. (1986). "Ownership Structure and Control: The Mutualization of Stock Life Insurance Companies," *Journal of Financial Economics*, 16: 73–98.

Mayers, D., and C. W. Smith. (2002). "Ownership Structure and Control: Property-Casualty Insurer Conversions to Stock Charter," *Journal of Financial Services Research*, 21: 117–44.

McLean, Colin. (1991). "From Time Assurance to Templeton Life: A Case Study," *Demutualization of Financial Institutions: Annales de l'économie publique, sociale et coopérative, Bruxelle*, 62(3): 455–78.

McNamara, Michael J., and S. Ghon Rhee. (1992, June). "Ownership Structure and Performance: The Demutualization of Life Insurers," *Journal of Risk and Insurance*, 59(2): 221–38.

Meyer, John W. (1979). "The Impact of the Centralization of Educational Funding and Control on State and Local Organizational Governance." Program Report No. 79-B20, Institute for Research on Educational Finance and Governance, Stanford University, Stanford, CA.

Jerker Nilsson, Anna Kihlén, and Lennart Norell. (2009). "Are Traditional Cooperatives an Endangered Species? About Shrinking Satisfaction, Involvement and Trust," *International Food and Agribusiness Management Review*, 12(4): 101–22.

Perks, Robert. (1991). "The Fight to Stay Mutual: Abbey Members against Flotation versus Abbey National Building Society," *Annales de l'économie publique, sociale et coopérative*, 62(3): 393–429.

Schrader L. F. (1989). "Equity Capital and Restructuring of Cooperatives as Investor-Oriented Firms," *Journal of Agricultural Cooperation*, 4: 41–53.

Schröter, Harm. (2005). *Americanization of the European Economy: A Compact Survey of American Economic Influence in Europe since the 1880s* (Dordrecht: Springer).

Schröter, Harm. (2000). "Der Verlust der 'europäischen Form des Zusammenspiels von Ordnung und Freiheit.' Vom Untergang der deutschen Konsumgenossenschaften," *Vierteljahrschrift für Sozial- und Wirtschaftsgeschichte*, 87(4): 442–67.

Serifsoy, Baris. (2008). "Demutualization, Outsider Ownership, and Stock Exchange Performance: Empirical Evidence," *Economics for Governance*, 9(1): 305–29.

Spear, Roger. *The Community Interest Company (CIC): A New Form of UK Social Enterprise*, mimeo.

Spiller, R. (1972). "Ownership and Performance: Stock and Mutual Life Insurance Companies," *Journal of Risk and Insurance*, 39: 17–26.

Steding, Rolf, and Jost W. Kramer. (1998). *Konturen der Genossenschaftsentwicklung in den europäischen Transformationslä* (Berlin: Edition Sigma).

Stephens, M. (2001). "Building Society Demutualization in the UK," *Housing Studies*, 16 (3): 335–52.

Tayler, G. (2003, October). "UK Building Society Demutualization Motives," *Business Ethics: A European Review*, 12(4): 394–402.

Treptow, Felix. (2006). *The Economics of Demutualization: An Empirical Analysis of the Securities Exchange Industry* (Wiesbaden: Deutscher Universitäts-Verlag).

Verbrugge, James A., and Steven Goldstein. (1981). "Risk, Return, and Managerial Objectives: Some Evidence from the Savings and Loan Industry," *Journal of Financial Research*, 4: 45–58.

Viswanathan, K. S., and J. D. Cummins. (2003). "Ownership Structure Changes in the Insurance Industry: An Analysis of Demutualization," *Journal of Risk and Insurance*, 70: 401–32.

Webb, Beatrice Potter. (1891). *The Cooperative Movement in Great Britain* (London: Swan Sonenschein & Co.; New York: Charles Scribners' Sons).

Wegren, Stephen K. (2009). *Land Reform in Russia: Institutional Design and Behavioural Response* (New Haven, CT: Yale University Press).

SELECTED CORE ISSUES OF COOPERATIVE ENTERPRISE IN A HISTORICAL PERSPECTIVE

As mentioned in the introduction to this volume, during the last decades, the literature on cooperative enterprise has addressed three main issues: financial constraints and disadvantages suffered by co-ops with respect to investor-owned enterprises (IOEs); the role played by property rights in the viability of co-ops; and the ability or inability of cooperative enterprise to construct its own, original consumer politics. With each typology of co-op, one of these has been more pressing than the others. For instance, the research on workers' cooperatives has usually brought attention to the financial constraints of co-ops and the suggested disadvantages of the one-member-one-vote principle in terms of investment strategies. Producer cooperatives (usually in the agricultural sector) have been one of the most important research fields for the property rights approach. Finally, consumer studies have chosen the politics of consumer cooperatives for their analysis.

The reasons for these choices in research focus can be found in one of the distinguishing features of cooperative enterprises, the members' economic participation as stated by the third cooperative principle. Because the transactions between members and their co-ops are different for each co-op-type – members in consumer co-ops shop in their outlets, members in workers' co-ops work within the enterprise they own, and members in producer co-ops provide raw materials – the problems faced by the types of co-ops are usually different.

Hence, the essays presented in this section address the main issues regarding cooperative enterprise within the context of a specific co-op type. The advantages and disadvantages of co-ops in terms of productivity and rates of survival are analyzed with a focus on workers' co-ops worldwide. The property rights approach provides the theoretical background to analyze the evolution of the ownership structure of agricultural co-ops in the United States. And consumer politics and the more or less decentralized organizational model are studied in reference to Western European consumer cooperatives.

CHAPTER 7

Legal Frameworks and Property Rights in U.S. Agricultural Cooperatives: The Hybridization of Cooperative Structures

Fabio Chaddad and Michael L. Cook

The cooperative movement in the United States has been informed by multiple waves of ideas, social movements, varying economic conditions, foresighted leaders, and institutional path dependencies – thus time and space preclude a comprehensive review. Consequently, we limit our exploration to the formation of agricultural cooperatives, their institutional roots, their diverse legal offspring, and subsequent evolution since 1950. Our major finding is: U.S. agricultural cooperatives were born and formally institutionalized as a combination of cooperative principles and corporate pragmatism – a unique form of organizational hybrid. One might call them a certain variation of a "special kind of business." The legal and organizational evolution of the dominant current means of agricultural producer collaboration in the United States can be divided into three distinct periods: pre-1925; 1925 to 1985; and post-1985. In most democratic countries, institutional environments and organizational arrangements are path dependent.[1] This is the case in the United States as well.

PRE-1925 PERIOD: COEVOLUTION OF COOPERATIVE STATUTES

The development of cooperatives and cooperative principles in the United States can be linked directly to the Rochdale experience in Great Britain during the 1840s. By 1860, the Rochdale Society's rules of conduct and characteristics of organization had evolved to a point where they were itemized in the Rochdale

---

[1] Based on the path-breaking ideas of Douglass North on institutions and institutional change and Walter Powell and Paul DiMaggio on the process of institutionalization, the structure and behavior of organizations and institutions are increasingly explained with the help of process theories, which espouse the view that history and sequencing matter. Among them, the notion of path dependence has gained prominence. See, for example, Georg Schreyögg and Jörg Sydow, "Organizational Path Dependence: A Process View," *Organization Studies*, 32, no. 3 (2011), pp. 321–35; and Thomas B. Lawrence, Monika I. Winn, and P. Devereaux Jennings, "The Temporal Dynamics of Institutionalization," *Academy of Management Review*, 26, no. 4 (2001), pp. 624–44.

Annual Almanac.[2] The property rights elements discussed in this chapter, as laid down in the *Almanac*, were as follows:

1. Capital should be of their own providing and should bear a fixed rate of interest.
2. Market prices should be charged and no credit given or asked.
3. "Profits" should be divided pro rata upon the amount of purchases made by each member.
4. The principle of "one-member, one-vote" should be obtained in government and the equality of the sexes in membership.[3]

These principles were transferred to the United States and translated into three "hard-core" fundamentals. First, increased efficiency or reduced cost of service is to be achieved by reduced competition and volunteer help. Second, distribution of savings or profits results from paying a minimum interest rate to invested capital and making stock-owning patron-members the proper claimants to any surplus generated from the cooperative. Third, democratic control is achieved by allowing each member to vote as an individual.[4] Above all, the Rochdale Pioneers sought to establish the concept of an "equitable association" of persons involved in an economic undertaking.[5]

During the first half of the nineteenth century, various experiments in cooperation were undertaken in the United States. These attempts at cooperation were characterized by independent group efforts and informal organization. There was no coordinated leadership, and most efforts were restricted to local community cooperation. None of these was successful, nor did they leave behind a legal foundation for cooperation.

The first organized effort at cooperation was launched by the National Grange Association between 1870 and 1890. During this time, the Grange organized hundreds of marketing and purchasing cooperatives.[6] Before 1875, the Grange advocated no specific principles of cooperation. However, at its 1875 annual convention, the Grange adopted a recommendation endorsing the Rochdale Principles. As a result, the Rochdale Principles became widely dispersed after 1875 and were especially familiar to farmers in the Northeast and Midwest.

Despite the fact that the Grange had endorsed the Rochdale Principles, there continued to be no legal basis for their use in cooperative organizations. As a

[2] George J. Holyoake, *The History of the Rochdale Pioneers* (London: George Allen and Unwin, 1893).

[3] Catherine Webb, *Industrial Cooperation – The Story of a Peaceful Revolution* (Manchester: Co-operative Union, 1912).

[4] Edwin G. Nourse, "The Economic Philosophy of Cooperation," *American Economic Review*, 12 (December 1922), pp. 577–97. (See also today's ICA principles in Appendix I of this book.)

[5] Edwin G. Nourse, "From Dogma to Science in Cooperative Thinking," in *American Cooperation* (Washington, DC: American Institute of Cooperation, 1946), pp. 6–13.

[6] Marvin Schaars, *Cooperatives: Principles and Practices* (University of Wisconsin-Extension Service, 1980).

result, a general consensus emerged that some form of legal statute was needed for associations operating under the Rochdale Principles. Three reasons for such a statute were cited:

1. State corporation law stipulated voting only on a regular share basis.
2. A mechanism was needed to require cooperative businesses to conform to the Rochdale Principles.
3. There would be a greater likelihood that government would foster cooperatives if they had a legal standing.[7]

The first cooperative-enabling laws were basically revisions of the general corporation laws. All of these legal statutes considered capital stock an integral part of cooperative organization. In many ways, the concept of capital stock as a fundamental component of cooperatives was consistent with the types of agricultural cooperatives most common during the last decades of the 1800s and the first decade of the 1900s, that is, creameries, cheese factories, and grain elevators. All were capital-intensive endeavors; therefore, the incorporation of capital stock seemed a natural component of cooperative law.[8]

The provisions of some of the early cooperative statutes were brief and very similar in content. Further, they were primarily instigated by consumer and worker cooperative groups. The first cooperative statute was enacted in 1865 in Michigan. Other states followed suit in adopting cooperative laws: Massachusetts in 1886; Wisconsin, Kansas, and Pennsylvania in 1887. The basic provisions of these laws mirrored the Rochdale Principles. Some of the common provisions included: cooperatives could issue shares but could limit the number of shares held by each member; voting was on the basis of members, not shares; each member had one vote; the basis of distributing earnings was established by individual cooperatives. The Pennsylvania law encompassed several new provisions concerning capital stock. Specifically, it allowed for a cooperative to issue both permanent stock and ordinary stock. Every member would have to purchase a set amount of permanent stock and, thereby, have a permanent investment in the capital of the association. The holding of permanent stock conferred one vote on the holder. Ordinary stock, on the other hand, could be bought and sold and conferred no voting rights on its holder.[9] These provisions are interesting because they are forerunners to some of the stock options observed today in cooperatives as managers try to generate and reward capital.

Edwin Nourse characterized this type of cooperative law up until 1911 as the Rochdale pattern of cooperative organization. This form of cooperative law attempted merely to modify somewhat the ordinary corporate structure and procedures in order to secure a more democratic distribution of control

[7] Edwin G. Nourse, *The Legal Status of Agricultural Cooperation* (New York: Macmillan, 1928).
[8] Henry H. Bakken and Marvin A. Schaars, *The Economics of Cooperative Marketing* (New York: McGraw-Hill, 1937).
[9] Edwin G. Nourse, *The Legal Status of Agricultural Cooperation* (New York: Macmillan, 1928).

and to identify earnings with patronage rather than with the contribution of capital.[10]

This Rochdale pattern of cooperative organization was characterized by a form of association where prices of cooperative goods were established competitively in local markets. By charging competitive prices, a cooperative earned a profit from operations. A portion of this profit was distributed to the members; the remaining amount accrued to the cooperative in the form of working and equity capital. This method of pricing led to the accumulation of capital by the cooperative from current operations. As a result, patron-members were able to measure the financial benefits that accrued to them from their transactions with the cooperative, both in terms of their enhanced wealth and of the increased capital value of the cooperative.

A NON-ROCHDALIAN VIEW

Many organizers of cooperative marketing activities during this period did not like the capital stock associations fostered by cooperative laws that emerged in the late 1800s and early 1900s. Their dislike was based on four premises. First, they felt that this form of cooperative organization was just a modified type of profit-sharing corporation. Second, services of cooperatives, as currently operating, were not restricted to members. Third, critics disliked the fact that in some situations stock could be sold to persons other than producers. Fourth, they disliked the fact that profits (or losses) on nonmember business accrued to the benefit (or detriment) of bona fide members.[11]

Some cooperative laws in the period following 1911 sought to remedy these perceived problems and to create a "pure" form of cooperative. This "pure" form of cooperative took the generic name of "non-stock cooperative organization." There were three basic objectives of the non-stock laws that emerged primarily between 1911 and 1920. First, these laws sought to avoid capital stock by putting all invested capital on a loan basis. Throughout the Rochdale period, membership had been identified with the ownership of capital stock. In other words, the member was deemed the residual claimant. This practice had the benefit of emphasizing the cooperative principle that the contribution of invested capital was one of the obligations of members of the cooperative. However, critics proposed two drawbacks to this practice: (1) it could lead to the under-capitalization of a cooperative if members viewed the amount of capital to be purchased as discretionary; and (2) it would perpetuate the ordinary corporate idea that capital stock was the primary claimant to benefits generated by the association. The non-stock cooperative would supposedly remedy these problems by identifying all invested capital as loan funds. Capital would be raised by

---

[10] Edwin G. Nourse, ibid.

[11] Henry H. Bakken and Marvin A. Schaars, *The Economics of Cooperative Marketing* (New York: McGraw-Hill, 1937).

levying fees in proportion to the amount of business conducted with a cooperative rather than through the use of an attractive interest rate.[12]

A second objective of non-stock statutes was to eliminate the use of market prices in pricing cooperative goods. Rather, goods would be priced at cost plus a marginal fee to cover operating costs. This would eliminate positive or negative profits from cooperative operations. Cooperatives would carry on the business of members for a service charge. Proponents of this concept viewed it as a move toward the principle of service at cost in cooperative operations. In a sense, the cooperative was to become the selling or buying representative of members. The purpose of this proposal was to delineate the group whose common interests were to be advanced by the association. A third objective was to develop personal and responsible membership that would foster loyalty to the cooperative and simultaneously give the cooperative greater control over member actions. Cooperatives were to become purely a membership type of organization reflecting a "fraternal idea, that is, recognition of a joint group interest arising from common participation in some particular type of economic enterprise."[13] This was in contrast to the Rochdale period where membership was identified with the ownership of capital stock and restrictions were placed on the transferability of capital.

A primary impetus for the principle of the non-stock movement was the Farmers' Alliance of 1887–90. The Farmers' Alliance adopted a cooperative philosophy that was radically different from that of the Grange or Rochdale. This group advocated no joint-stock features. It espoused a doctrine of a cooperative not being a business for profit but rather an entity supplemental to farming efforts; it advocated a fraternal concept of cooperative membership and solidarity; and it urged that cooperatives benefit members by maintaining a low-price policy rather than through patronage dividends.[14] Thus, the seeds of the non-stock "pure" cooperative movement were planted by the Farmers' Alliance and non-stock laws of the early 1900s.

Three independent sources of non-stock laws emerged: (1) the California laws of 1895 and 1909, (2) the Alabama law of 1909, and (3) the Texas law of 1917. The California non-stock law of 1895 represented a new departure in cooperative legislation. Its membership provisions were especially significant. They stated that: one member equals one vote; membership is personal; and the rights of all members are equal. Further, the membership provisions implied that a cooperative was not a company of shareholders, but rather an association of persons engaged in a like undertaking, specifically qualifying for membership and accepting the discipline of the association. Although the 1895 California law followed the Rochdale principle of equal suffrage, the 1909 law was made significantly different by allowing for proportional and proxy voting. The

---

[12] Edwin G. Nourse, *The Legal Status of Agricultural Cooperation* (New York: Macmillan, 1928).
[13] Ibid., p. 28.
[14] Joseph G. Knapp, *The Rise of American Cooperative Enterprise: 1620–1920* (Danville, IL: Interstate Printers & Publishers, 1969).

Alabama law of 1909 emphasized the members' contractual obligation to the cooperative. The Texas law of 1917 had two key provisions. First, membership was nontransferable. Second, members were limited to those persons directly engaged in a particular industry.[15] Thus, these two laws reinforced the fraternal concept of non-stock law.

The push toward non-stock cooperative entities was aided in 1914 by the passage of the Clayton Act. Since the 1890 enactment of the Sherman Antitrust Act, cooperatives had a precarious standing under the law and could be adjudged as combinations in restraint of trade. Cooperative leaders desired a definite legal statement that would exempt their organizations from the provisions of the Sherman Act. In 1914, the Clayton Act exempted "agricultural or horticultural organizations instituted for the purposes of mutual help, and not having capital stock or conducted for profit" from the Sherman Antitrust Act.[16] Although the Clayton Act clarified the status of non-stock cooperatives, it left relatively unchanged the status of stock cooperatives under the law.

During the "purist" period when non-stock cooperative law came to the forefront, a shift in emphasis took place concerning cooperative principles. Coincidently, the non-stock movement occurred during the period of the founding of the socialist movement in the United States. The move away from capital stock reinforced the principle of limited return on capital and the categorization of equity capital as synonymous with loan funds. All of the non-stock laws of this period solidified the principle of democratic control and changed cooperative membership into a fraternal, personal matter as opposed to a business relationship. Finally, the non-stock movement shifted the focus of cooperatives from an economic endeavor that made "profits" for its members and paid dividends to them to a more service-driven arrangement between members and cooperatives that stressed principle of service at cost (and thus sought to avoid principal–agent problems). Thus, the non-stock movement solidified what became known as the "hard-core" cooperative principles.

BIRTH OF A HYBRID

By 1917, it was evident that some uniformity was needed in cooperative law in order to clarify the confusion caused by the differences in various cooperative laws. As a means of bringing about uniformity in state and federal laws, the U.S. Department of Agriculture (USDA) drafted a department bill in 1917 suggested as a model for states enacting cooperative legislation. The bill included provisions that allowed incorporation as either capital stock or non-stock associations, provided for marketing agreements, and suggested penalties in the event of breach of contract. Further, the voting and membership provisions of this document followed the pattern established in non-stock laws. The bill was readily

[15] Edwin G. Nourse, *The Legal Status of Agricultural Cooperation* (New York: Macmillan, 1928).
[16] Henry H. Bakken and Marvin A. Schaars, *The Economics of Cooperative Marketing* (New York: McGraw-Hill, 1937), pp. 279–80.

accepted by numerous states between 1917 and 1921, after which the Sapiro model bill became better known.[17]

The draft bill developed by Aaron Sapiro became the dominant model for state cooperative law between 1921 and 1925. The Bingham Act, enacted by the Kentucky legislature in 1922, represented the embodiment of the Sapiro law. By 1925, all but eight states had adopted legislation incorporating the chief features of the Bingham Act. The provisions of these laws closely resembled the tenets of the non-stock cooperative statutes and the commodity marketing movement. Two provisions in the Bingham Act are of special interest. One component of the membership provision stipulated that products of nonmembers were taken for storage only, precluding cooperatives from doing business with nonmembers. Further, a provision of the Kentucky law defined *nonprofit* in more explicit terms. It stated that cooperatives were not organized to make a profit for the association or for their members, but for "their members as producers."[18] This reinforced the service-at-cost principle of cooperative association.

At the same time that the USDA draft bill and the Sapiro law were shaping state statutes to conform to a more restrictive and pure interpretation of cooperation, federal legislation was enacted that actually broadened the definition of cooperatives. In 1922, the U.S. Congress passed the Capper-Volstead Act. The provisions of the act, in many ways, reflected the basic principles of the Rochdale period of cooperative law, which was dominant prior to 1911. This law was different from the Clayton Act in that it definitely authorized the association of agricultural producers and it removed the uncertainty concerning capital stock associations.[19] The primary features of the Capper-Volstead Act were:

1. Each member had one vote, or dividends on stock would be limited to 8 percent or less.
2. Nonmember business could not make up more than 50 percent of a cooperative's total business.

[17] Henry H. Bakken and Marvin A. Schaars, *The Economics of Cooperative Marketing* (New York: McGraw-Hill, 1937).

[18] Edwin G. Nourse, *The Legal Status of Agricultural Cooperation* (New York: Macmillan, 1928), pp. 100–3.

[19] With Section 6 of the Clayton Act of 1914 and later the Capper-Volstead Act of 1922, the U.S. Congress exempted agricultural marketing cooperatives from significant portions of the antitrust laws. These exemptions do not totally exempt agricultural cooperatives from the antitrust laws, and cooperatives must meet certain statutory requirements to qualify for these exemptions. Fundamentally, these exemptions enable agricultural producers to act as a single entity to bargain, further process, or market the products of their members without violating Section 1 of the Sherman Antitrust Act. The exemptions became necessary because, soon after the enactment of the Sherman Act, both farmer cooperatives and labor unions were challenged as illegal price-fixing conspiracies. Congress responded by exempting both labor unions and agricultural organizations from the strictures of the antitrust. For more details on the Capper-Volstead Act and antitrust laws in the United States, refer to the report "Antitrust Status of Farmer Cooperatives: The Story of the Capper-Volstead Act," Cooperative Information Report 59, Rural Business Cooperative Service (Washington, DC: U.S. Department of Agriculture, September 2002).

3. Cooperative associations were to operate for the benefit of their members.
4. Cooperative associations with or without capital stock were legal.

An examination of the provisions of Capper-Volstead indicates that it was significantly more liberal than the non-stock laws in several ways. First, by permitting cooperatives to pay as large a dividend on stock as desired, as long as voting was on a one-member, one-vote basis, Capper-Volstead weakened the nonprofit interpretation of cooperatives espoused by the proponents of non-stock laws. Second, the fact that up to 50 percent of a cooperative's business could be conducted with nonmembers liberalized the view of what really constitutes cooperation. Further, the possibility of making net profits on this non-member business and of having such profits accrue to the benefit of members alone placed the cooperative in somewhat the same category as that of an investor-oriented firm.[20]

1925–1985 PERIOD: COOPERATIVE GROWTH

By the mid-1920s, U.S. agricultural cooperative law had evolved to a point where federal and state statutes had taken somewhat different paths. State law had become increasingly narrow in its interpretation of proper cooperative behavior and principles. On the other hand, federal law, as embodied in the Capper-Volstead Act, had become more liberal in its definition and principles of cooperation. Thus, in hindsight, it would seem that the development of stock/non-stock laws partially laid the foundation for the user- versus investor-driven conflict in cooperatives that is observed today. We present diagrams later in this chapter to clarify this conflict. The state stock statutes provided for a more investor-oriented mentality in cooperatives, while the state non-stock statutes eliminated stock and profits and emphasized instead user benefits based on patronage. Federal law, on the other hand, allowed either form of cooperative organization, was less restrictive regarding the benefit clauses, and granted antitrust immunity to both.[21]

The conflict in cooperative legislation was due, in part, to the fact that cooperative laws have tried to chase ideology. Variation in the cooperative ideology and in the emphasis placed on components of this ideological underpinning has resulted in conflicting legal provisions both among state laws and between state and federal legislation. Consequently, instead of a well-defined, standardized national cooperative organization in the United States, there exist more than one hundred different state incorporation statutes that vary widely in their content and requirements. Most states have more than one cooperative law (usually one that incorporates stock cooperatives and one that incorporates non-

[20] Henry H. Bakken and Marvin A. Schaars, *The Economics of Cooperative Marketing* (New York: McGraw-Hill, 1937).
[21] D. R. Suhler and M. L. Cook, "Origins of a Current Conflict? An Examination of Stock-Non-stock Cooperative Law," *Journal of Agricultural Cooperation*, 8 (1993), pp. 54–62.

stock cooperatives), giving rise not only to interstate but also intrastate variation in cooperative legal provisions.[22]

The resulting practical dilemma for cooperatives in the post-1925 period has been threefold. First, cooperatives must incorporate under state law, which in most cases is more restrictive than federal law. Therefore, cooperatives have had difficulty taking advantage of the more liberal provisions of federal law that would help them in dealing with their capital problems and in adapting to different market settings. Second, the unwritten guiding principles of cooperation, that is, the "hard-core" principles and variations of these that have evolved in the post-1925 period, tend to reinforce more strongly the principles incorporated in non-stock laws rather than those of stock laws. Third, the variation in state laws results in a low degree of uniformity in cooperative organization and in confusion among cooperative members and decision makers concerning proper cooperative behavior. The conflict between stock and non-stock laws seems to have been one contributing factor to these dilemmas. The end result of these three dilemmas is that cooperative leadership is often challenged by the complexity of their legal and ideological contexts.

Yet these conflicts seem to have bothered cooperative leaders little during the Depression and the market share growth periods of U.S. agricultural cooperation between 1925 and the mid-1980s. However, the economic crisis of the mid-1980s in the agricultural sector brought new stresses to those who managed and governed agricultural cooperation. Combined with the forces of globalization, industrialization, and quantum advances in technology, the agricultural depression of 1983–7 decreased gross and net margins at the agricultural production, agricultural processing, and agricultural input levels. New producer-owned strategies and structures emerged, resulting in alternative organizational forms.[23]

POST-1985 PERIOD

Following the agricultural crisis of the 1980s, U.S. agricultural cooperatives embarked on a structural change process leading to the emergence of nontraditional models. Simultaneously, new frameworks in social science were gaining traction in the academic world. Advances in new institutional economics and new institutional sociology provided concepts and tools that allowed complex organizational arrangements such as cooperatives to be described and analyzed in new ways. A brief review of these advances will inform our analysis of the nontraditional cooperative ownership models that emerged after the mid-1980s.

[22] James Baarda, "State Incorporation Statutes for Farmer Cooperatives," ACS Cooperative Information Report 30 (Washington, DC: USDA, October 1982).

[23] M.L. Cook, "The Future of US Agricultural Cooperatives: A Neo-Institutional Approach," *American Journal of Agricultural Economics*, 77, no. 5 (1995), pp. 1153–9.

PROPERTY RIGHTS, OWNERSHIP COSTS, AND
ORGANIZATIONAL EFFICIENCY

Alternative ownership forms – for example, investor-owned, patron-owned, or mutual firms – are characterized by the way property rights are assigned to "owners." Several authors have argued that aligning residual rights of control with residual claimant rights leads to an efficient use of assets.[24] Residual claimants are those able to receive the net income generated by an asset or bundle of assets such as a firm. Residual control refers to the rights to make any decision concerning an asset's use that are not explicitly specified by law or assigned to another party by contract. They act as the default rules to the use of an asset. By pursuing their own self-interest, residual claimants tend to make efficient residual decisions regarding the use of the firm's resources because they bear the full wealth effects of their decisions.

However, when one party is assigned control of property rights that affect another party's wealth, decision makers do not bear the full wealth effect of their decisions. This creates the opportunity for conflicts of interest. Cook and Hansmann[25] provide complementary frameworks for our understanding of these conflicts of interest and the consequent costs of ownership[26] in patron-owned firms. Cook's life-cycle approach to the evolution of agricultural cooperatives focuses on the conflicts that commonly arise between members pursuing different strategies to maximize their farm wealth within traditionally structured cooperative organizations. Worldwide, variants of the traditional structure are the most common form of cooperation in agriculture. The traditional structure consists of open membership; nonappreciable, nontransferable, and (partly) redeemable shares; and capital accumulation via retained earnings.

One major cost of ownership in patron-owned organizations (i.e., cooperatives) is related to risk bearing, that is, "the cost of bearing important risks associated with the enterprise, since those risks are often reflected in the firm's residual earnings."[27] The higher these risk-bearing costs are, the more difficulty the organization has in raising risk capital from owners (i.e., patrons or members) to fund investment. The capital constraint problem in user-owned

---

[24] See, for example, P. Milgrom and J. Roberts, *Economics, Organization and Management* (Englewood Cliffs, NJ: Prentice-Hall, 1992); and O. D. Hart, *Firms, Contracts and Financial Structure* (Oxford: Clarendon, 1995).

[25] M. L. Cook, "The Future of US Agricultural Cooperatives: A Neo-Institutional Approach," *American Journal of Agricultural Economics*, 77, no. 5, pp. 1153–9; H. Hansmann, *The Ownership of Enterprise* (Cambridge: Belknap Press of Harvard University Press, 1996).

[26] According to Hansmann (1996, p. 21), "ownership involves costs. Some of these costs are what might be called governance costs; they include the costs of making collective decisions among the owners, the costs of monitoring managers, and the costs of the poor decisions and excessive managerial discretion. Another cost is the risk bearing associated with receipt of residual earnings."

[27] H. Hansmann, *The Ownership of Enterprise* (Cambridge: Belknap Press of Harvard University Press, 1996), p. 44.

organizations – that is, their inability to acquire sufficient risk capital to finance investment projects – is usually explained on the basis of the following arguments: (1) cooperative residual claims are restricted; (2) cooperative members do not have appropriate incentives to invest; (3) equity capital acquisition in traditional cooperatives is tied to member patronage (with consequent dependence on internally generated capital); and (4) cooperative equity capital is not permanent.

As a consequence of the nature of their residual claims, cooperatives may incur relatively high risk-bearing costs and therefore be constrained in acquiring risk capital for investment purposes. That is, the nature of residual claims in cooperatives can be a source of organizational inefficiency – that is, higher ownership costs – relative to competing forms of ownership. Recent empirical evidence suggests the presence of financial constraints in a sample of U.S. agricultural cooperatives with traditional ownership structure.[28]

Utilizing these insights from property rights and agency theories, we observe an increasingly industrialized and globalized food system where agricultural cooperatives are faced with survival challenges influenced by their legal and organizational uniqueness. Competitive strategies pursued by agricultural cooperatives in response to environmental and structural changes in the food system, including value-added processing, brand name development, and entry into international markets, require substantial capital investments. In order to acquire the necessary risk capital to implement these growth-related strategies and remain competitive, agricultural cooperatives are using organizational innovations to adapt to globalized agricultural industrialization. These organizational innovations include but are not limited to new generation cooperatives, base capital plans, subsidiaries with partial public ownership, preferred trust shares, equity-seeking joint ventures, combined limited liability company–cooperative strategic alliances, and permanent capital equity plans. These organizational and capital formation experiments have created considerable conflict and interest among producer leaders, cooperative management, finance institutions, and organization scholars. The basic issues in examining these new models can be reduced to an examination of ownership and control rights.

Building upon property rights and incomplete contract theories of the firm, we adopt a broad definition of ownership rights that encompasses both residual claim and control rights. We argue that alternative cooperative models differ in how ownership rights are defined and assigned to the economic agents tied contractually to the firm – in particular, members, patrons, and investors. Chaddad and Cook[29] propose a typology of discrete organizational models, in which the traditional cooperative structure and the investor-oriented firm (IOF)

---

[28] F. R. Chaddad, M. L. Cook, and T. Heckelei, "Testing for the Presence of Financial Constraints in US Agricultural Cooperatives: An Investment Behaviour Approach," *Journal of Agricultural Economics*, 56, no. 3 (2005), pp. 385–97.

[29] F. R. Chaddad and M. L. Cook, "Understanding New Cooperative Models: An Ownership-Control Rights Typology," *Review of Agricultural Economics*, 26, no. 3 (2004), pp. 348–60.

are characterized as polar forms. Additionally, we identify five nontraditional cooperative models that user-owned organizations may adopt to ameliorate perceived financial constraint problems.

TYPOLOGY OF OWNERSHIP RIGHTS IN NEW COOPERATIVE MODELS

Many economists agree that ownership in the form of secure property rights is the most effective mechanism for providing economic agents with appropriate incentives to create, maintain, and improve assets. But what does "ownership" mean? The economic analysis of ownership has concentrated on two distinct concepts: residual returns (or claims) and residual rights of control. Residual rights of control emerge from the impossibility of crafting, implementing, and enforcing complete contracts, especially in the case of complex, dynamic transactions. Since all contracts are unavoidably incomplete, the residual right of control over an asset defines who "owns" it.[30] According to the incomplete contract theory of the firm, the assignment of control rights (and hence ownership) is dictated by ex ante investment incentives of contracting parties. The theory predicts that residual rights of control are assigned to agents making relationship-specific investments whose quasi-rents are under risk from hold-up behavior.

Economists define residual claims as the rights to the net income generated by the firm – that is, the amount left over after all promised payments to fixed claim holders (e.g., employees, debtors). Additionally, residual claimants are considered the residual risk bearers of the firm because net cash flows are uncertain and eventually negative. The "owners" of the firm are the residual claimants according to property rights scholars.[31]

Drawing from the property rights theory of the firm, Chaddad and Cook[32] proposed a typology of discrete organizational arrangements (i.e., cooperative models) based upon a broad definition of ownership rights comprising both residual return and control rights (Figure 7.1). They define the traditional cooperative structure as having the following property rights attributes: ownership rights are restricted to member-patrons; residual return rights are nontransferable, nonappreciable, and redeemable; and benefits are distributed among members in proportion to patronage. As a result of this "vaguely defined" property rights structure, traditional cooperatives are subject to investment and governance constraints.[33]

---

[30] S. J. Grossman and O. D. Hart, "The Costs and Benefits of Ownership: A Theory of Vertical and Lateral Integration," *Journal of Political Economy*, 94 (1986), pp. 691–719.

[31] E. F. Fama and M. C. Jensen, "Agency Problems and Residual Claims," *Journal of Law and Economics*, 26 (1983) pp. 327–49.

[32] F. R. Chaddad and M. L. Cook, "Understanding New Cooperative Models: An Ownership-Control Rights Typology," *Review of Agricultural Economics*, 26, no. 3 (2004), pp. 348–60.

[33] M. L. Cook, "The Future of US Agricultural Cooperatives: A Neo-Institutional Approach," *American Journal of Agricultural Economics*, 77, no. 5 (1995), pp. 1153–9.

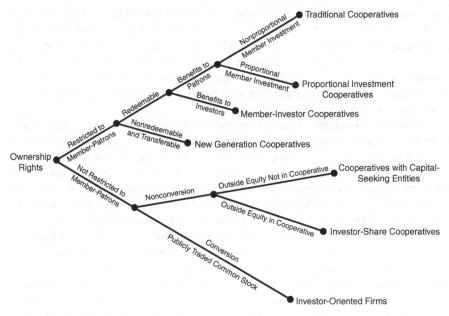

FIGURE 7.1 Alternative cooperative models: an ownership rights perspective

In addition to these polar forms of organization, Figure 7.1 identifies five nontraditional cooperative models. In the upward-egressing branch of Figure 7.1, three nontraditional models with ownership rights restricted to member-patrons are described: proportional investment cooperative, member-investor cooperative, and new generation cooperative. In the proportional investment cooperative model, ownership rights are restricted to members, nontransferable, nonappreciable, and redeemable, but members are expected to invest in the cooperative in proportion to patronage. Proportional investment cooperatives adopt capital management policies to ensure proportionality of internally generated capital, including separate capital pools and base capital plans. In member-investor cooperatives, returns to members are distributed in proportion to shareholdings in addition to patronage. This is done either with dividend distribution in proportion to shares and/or appreciability of cooperative shares. In the new generation cooperative model, ownership rights are in the form of tradable and appreciable delivery rights restricted to current member-patrons. In addition, member-patrons are required to acquire delivery rights on the basis of expected patronage so that usage and capital investment are perfectly aligned.

In the downward-egressing branch of Figure 7.1, ownership rights are not restricted to member-patrons. Consequently, the cooperative is able to acquire risk capital from nonmember sources. However, members may have to share profits and eventually control rights with outside investors who are not necessarily patrons of the cooperative and thus may have diverging interests. Conflicting goals between maximizing returns to investors and member-patrons may occur as a result. The more radical model in this branch – conversion to IOF – is an exit strategy adopted by cooperatives that choose not to continue operating as a user-owned and -controlled organization. Alternatively, cooperatives may acquire risk capital from outside investors with capital-seeking entities or investor-shares. These alternatives can generate substantial conflicts of interest between patrons and investors over cooperative structure and process (see, for instance, Chapter 5 in this book).

In the first model, investors acquire ownership rights in a separate legal entity wholly or partly owned by the cooperative. In other words, outside investor capital is not directly introduced in the cooperative firm, but rather in trust companies, strategic alliances, or subsidiaries. In investor-share cooperatives, investors receive ownership rights in the cooperative in addition to the traditional cooperative ownership rights held by member-patrons. That is, the cooperative issues more than one class of shares assigned to different "owner" groups.

Further empirical analysis has led to refinement of the original Chaddad-Cook typology (see Figure 7.2). Numerous traditional cooperatives, both stock and non-stock, while maintaining ownership rights "restricted to members only," have developed vertical investment structures by investing in limited liability companies, joint ventures, or other forms of strategic alliances. Local multipurpose cooperatives, traditional marketing cooperatives, and the majority of traditional regional multipurpose cooperatives are engaged in the vertical investment structures denoted at the top of Figure 7.2.

The next model, shown in Figure 7.2 as second from the top, is the proportional investment model. In this model, ownership rights are restricted to members, nontransferable, nonappreciable, and redeemable, but members are expected to invest in the cooperative in proportion to patronage. This is the original "pure" form of U.S. agricultural cooperative organizational design. For stock cooperatives, equity capital is considered member stock or allocated patronage, and in non-stock cooperatives working capital is called "retains" and nonmember business earnings are called permanent capital. As membership

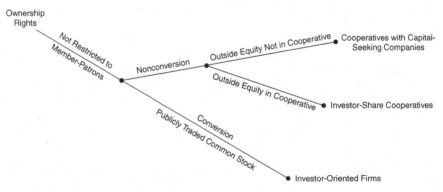

FIGURE 7.2 Emerging forms of cooperatives from an ownership rights approach
Source: Cook and Chaddad (2004).

becomes more heterogeneous, the degree of vaguely defined property rights increases, thus moving the proportionally organized cooperative to the traditional cooperative status. Recognizing the dynamic shift to misalignment of control, investment, and benefits, proportional investment cooperatives (PICs) adopt capital management policies to ensure proportionality of internally generated capital including separate capital pools and base capital plans. In member-investor cooperatives, returns to members are distributed in proportion to shareholdings in addition to patronage. This is done either with dividend distribution in proportion to shares and/or appreciability of cooperative shares.

The lowest major branch in Figure 7.2 is the new generation cooperative (NGC) model. In the classic NGC model, ownership rights are in the form of tradable and appreciable delivery rights restricted to current member-patrons. In addition, member-patrons are required to purchase delivery rights on the basis of expected patronage such that usage and capital investment are proportionately aligned. These ownership rights, generally, are not redeemable. An increasing number of NGCs are pursuing the vertical investment structure-strategy form. For example, many of the emerging ethanol ventures are limited liability corporations with an NGC being the primary investor. Another NGC ownership structure is called the collaborative model. In this model a traditional, proportional, or member investment cooperative has an equity interest in the NGC or the NGC has an equity interest in another cooperative. The authors have observed and documented an increasing number of these nontraditional cooperatives emerging in other advanced agricultural countries from Europe to South America to Oceania.

Figure 7.3 represents emerging cooperative models where ownership rights are not restricted to member-patrons. This set of models consists of cooperatives with

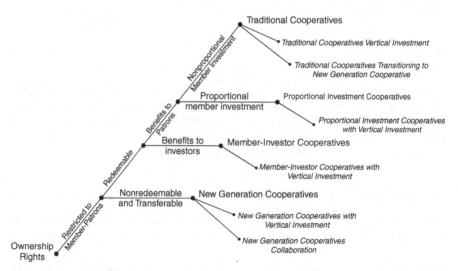

FIGURE 7.3 Emerging forms of cooperatives where ownership rights are not restricted to member-patrons
Source: Cook and Chaddad (2004).

capital-seeking companies, investor-share cooperatives, and cooperatives converting to an investor-driven ownership structure. In a capital-seeking company, investors acquire ownership rights in a separate legal entity wholly or partly owned by the cooperative. In other words, outside investor capital is not directly introduced in the cooperative firm, but in trust companies, strategic alliances, or subsidiaries. This model differs from the Figure 7.1 and Figure 7.2 vertical investment models by degree of control conceded and by the importance of the contributed permanent capital. In investor-share cooperatives, investors receive ownership rights in the cooperative in addition to the traditional cooperative ownership rights held by member-patrons. That is, the cooperative issues more than one class of shares to different "owner" groups (e.g., nonvoting fixed-returns preferred stock and nonvoting publicly tradable common stock, among others).

The conversion to a corporate or an IOF model is an exit from agricultural cooperative status (and is frequently referred to as demutualization). Notwithstanding vaguely defined property rights constraints, increased member heterogeneity, and competitive pressures from the business environment, until 2000 there had been few cases of agricultural cooperative conversions to a corporate structure in the United States. This phenomenon, however, had become quite widespread in Australia and parts of Latin America. Starting in 2000, however, a number of the legacy cooperatives in the United States and Canada filed for bankruptcy or converted to IOFs to remain financially viable. Several scholars have inferred this was a tipping point in the evolution of the agricultural cooperative model in North America.[34] These concerns reintroduce previous questions about the optimal organizational form of an agribusiness entity and whether agricultural structure is becoming less stable in this rapidly changing environment.

OBSERVATIONS

These observations might be considered general hypotheses generated from the examination of the emergence of the hybrid[35] form of U.S. agricultural cooperatives. The legal diversity and complexity in state incorporation laws of the United States have led to a multiplicity of organizational forms that primarily differ in the residual claims legal domain. Consequently, most of the following observations address the remnant of the hybrid form.

OBSERVATION 1: "TO PROTECT" OR "TO ADD" VALUE

It might be hypothesized that the generic reason producers form cooperatives is to "protect" the current and future value of farm assets. This cooperative

---

[34] M. E. Fulton and B. Hueth, "Cooperative Conversions, Failures and Restructurings: An Overview," *Journal of Cooperatives*, 23 (2009), pp. i–xi.

[35] *Hybrid* is defined in this chapter as a shift in ownership rights from purely user-oriented to a structure where formal ownership rights are shared between related user and investor interests.

formation reasoning can be defined as defensive. Alternatively, producers might organize with the primary objective being to "add" to the value of their assets. This can be thought of as an offensive reason for formation or continuance. The plethora of organizational forms that has emerged since the early 1990s has been largely offensive. The growing number of organizational structures observed below the proportional model in Figures 7.1, 7.2, and 7.3 suggests that offensive structures are becoming more common. As cooperatives grow and invest in organization-specific assets – including intangible assets – their ownership structures become realigned. As a result, they either seek to reduce members' capital contributions through permanent capital accumulation by expanding nonmember business, through required capital contributions on member business to increase the growth capital base, or to leverage partners' balance sheets into more opportune offensive strategies.

OBSERVATION 2: RESIDUAL CLAIM – RESIDUAL CONTROL TRADE-OFFS

As noncontrolled heterogeneity increases in a cooperative's membership and given no change in selective incentives, there is a tendency for cooperative investment and control constraints to be exacerbated. Resultant investment disincentives and misaligned control rights can lead to financial stagnation and member apathy. When investment constraints (internal free-rider, horizon, and portfolio problems) are realigned, control constraints in the form of agency and influence costs eventually emerge.

OBSERVATION 3: BUILDING THE BALANCE SHEET

Cooperatives rely on internally generated capital as their primary source of equity capital. Traditional cooperatives, however, depend on patronage-based methods for acquiring risk capital, particularly retained patronage refunds and per-unit capital retains. As a result, approximately 60 percent of equity capital in U.S. agricultural cooperatives is in the form of equity certificates and credits.[36] In other words, equity capital in a cooperative's balance sheet generally is allocated to individual members, representing a claim/promise against the cooperative by present and former members. This claim is partially redeemable, with the ultimate decision at the discretion of the board of directors. Because redeeming equity is a cash outlay, a large portion of the cooperative's equity capital stock is not considered permanent. Cooperatives seeking to build a permanent source of equity capital are experimenting with nontraditional capital acquisition approaches, including nonredeemable member-investor shares, capital-seeking strategic alliances, and nonvoting preferred shares. Non-stock cooperatives have relied more heavily on nonmember business earnings to generate unallocated

---

[36] D.S. Chesnick, *Top 100 Cooperatives 1999 Financial Profile* (Washington, DC: USDA Rural Business Cooperative Services, 2000).

reserves (permanent capital in the United States and collective capital in many European countries).

OBSERVATION 4: EXIT – CONVERSION

Since the early 2000s, a number of large North American and Australian cooperatives have filed for bankruptcy or converted to an IOF form. Member heterogeneity and suboptimization of multiple objectives appear to have been influential in this decision-making process. Ownership rights were misaligned with use, control, investment incentives, and benefit distribution. The high degree of misalignment violated most laws of optimal organizational design. This observation does not suggest there were no other external and internal forces which might have led to the financial failure of these member-owned and member-controlled organizations; we are only saying that the organizational architecture was misaligned. The study of organizational failure in producer-owned organizations seldom includes intrafirm coordination incentives and disincentives. It is also interesting that most of the conversions to IOFs took place in the original "non-stock" cooperatives.

OBSERVATION 5: ORGANIZATIONAL FORM DYNAMICS

Utilizing the ownership rights framework, it is tempting to hypothesize a sequential path commencing at the proportional investment cooperative level and progressing downward as a cooperative becomes more risk capital seeking. As each step downward on the typology figure is adopted, an ownership rights attribution is relaxed. The question then arises as to whether this framework suggests that, in an industrialized food system, the agricultural cooperative is a transitional form of business organization. Is the cooperative a business form moving from a group of producers with homogeneous user interest to a set of heterogeneous users who have evolved to a homogeneous economic state only through the bonding attraction to the return-on-investment metric?

This evolution has not been without considerable debate within the cooperative world. The debate reminds us of the aforementioned examples from the 1920s where the cooperative "purists" (non-stock oriented) objected to the more user-investor arguments proffered by the so-called pragmatists. Even after public hearings sponsored by the U.S. federal government in 2009–10, the debate has not generated a significant amount of serious discussion outside of the cooperative system.

OBSERVATION 6: CONTINUED INSTITUTIONAL ADAPTATION

Recently the demand to organize "offensive" types of cooperatives has evolved from the cooperative leaders' quest to realign structure and incentive systems with offense-driven strategies to a more externally oriented public policy discussion. In the mid-1990s, Iowa adopted Chapter 501 allowing formation of cooperatives exempt from rather restrictive corporate farming laws. In 2001, the Wyoming legislature passed a cooperative statute allowing a cooperative to be organized with both patron and nonpatron ownership rights. During the 2003 legislative session, Minnesota created a new cooperative law, which authorizes outside equity in cooperatives in return for limited voting rights in order to facilitate more flexible financing alternatives. In 2005 the Wisconsin legislature adopted a similar cooperative law. Numerous other states have similar legislation under study, suggesting that the institutional environment relating to producer collective action in the United States is experiencing substantial change.

OBSERVATION 7: HYBRID FORMATION

Producers are restructuring and redesigning their traditional cooperatives through realignment of ownership rights and vertical investment; they are also forming producer-controlled hybrid organizations. These hybrids, in the form of limited liability corporations (LLCs), limited liability partnerships, guilds, and subchapter S firms, have many of the organizational advantages of traditional or new generation cooperatives (with the exception of accessing Cooperative Bank debt financing and limited immunity to antitrust offered by Capper-Volstead) and provide more flexible risk capital acquisition mechanisms. Self-employment tax benefits, access to nonfarm investors, and tax credit pass-through provisions are the reasons why producers have chosen the LLC option of organizational form.

OBSERVATION 8: FILLING A VOID?

Cooperatives can be viewed as symptomatic of an underlying problem with investor ownership. Some cooperative observers believe cooperatives exist in the economy to fill gaps in the provision of goods and services, and to counteract business market power. According to this view, the cooperative business structure is a corrective measure, but can be a costly one to be avoided if it is not needed. Cooperatives are costly because they must be financed and governed. This view suggests at least two potential causes of pressure to convert from cooperative to investor ownership. First, the existence and structure of any given market evolves over time with changes in technology, consumer preferences, the institutional framework supporting the market (e.g., antitrust enforcement), and relevant state, federal, and international policy that may affect supply and demand conditions. If the underlying problem with investor ownership is, to some extent, remedied by these changes, a cooperative operating in this market may lose its relevance to an increasingly apathetic membership. The second potential cause of pressure to convert may emerge from a combined agent- and investor-oriented member coalition covered in the next observation.

OBSERVATION 9: AGENCY ISSUES

Once a cooperative is in place with physical assets and operating capital, it is natural for its management team to pursue growth in scale and scope of operation. Managing a cooperative profitably and sustainably is a matter of competent administration, logistics, and accounting. However, as markets evolve and cooperatives find themselves competing intensively for member patronage, management is apt to take a more proactive and offensive approach in setting strategy. With capable management, it is possible to generate significant firm value in following whatever strategy is put in place.

Paradoxically, success of this sort can be the downfall of a cooperative. As soon as a cooperative tries to provide members with liquidity through some form of earnings distribution, it is inevitable that members seek and expect continued earnings. With a focus on "earnings," a cooperative loses its essential character to focus on patron value. Additionally, without carefully designing equity management policies that maintain primary control and equity stake in the hands of current patrons, it is easy to end up with an intergenerational conflict, where members who are nearing retirement want to cash out their ownership stake. Alternatively, if the market value of a cooperative's assets exceed book value by a sufficient amount, it may be feasible to garner support for conversion.

CONCLUSION

These observations suggest real challenges for U.S. cooperatives in the future. Yet for almost one hundred years, these patron-led and -controlled cooperatives have met this challenge. In our view, their hybridization of "age-old" cooperative ideals (residual control rights in the form of "one person, one vote" and residual claim rights in the form of proportional distribution of benefits) and modern business organizational concepts (nonmember-business-generated permanent capital and vertical integration strategies) has fostered this accomplishment.

United States agricultural cooperatives have grown in assets controlled, revenues, market shares, and services provided each year since 1920 with one notable exception: the 1984–6 period. In 2009, the 2,389 agricultural cooperatives generated $170 billion in gross revenues, an increase from $100 billion in 2000. This continual growth suggests that the cooperative hybrid concept, which emerged during the tumultuous 1917–22 period, has continually adapted to its external environment and innovatively regenerated itself into a flexible, adaptive, and progressive form of group organization. The combination of principles drawn from the purist, non-stock oriented advocates and attributes from the pragmatic, stock cooperative promoters has informed the dynamic architecture of this set of U.S. cooperative hybrids, making it "a special kind of business."

CHAPTER 8

The Performance of Workers' Cooperatives[1]

Virginie Pérotin

INTRODUCTION

Workers' cooperatives are businesses owned and managed by their employees. Labor-managed businesses have existed since the 1830s, yet they remain one of the least well-known parts of the cooperative movement outside the specialized research community. The image of worker cooperatives has been marred by preconceived ideas that businesses run by their employees cannot work and must be rare, very small affairs that survive only in special industries. In this chapter, I present an overview of the key findings of international economics studies on labor-managed firms' performance and examine some of the implications for cooperative practice.

There exist many more worker cooperatives than most people think, even though the employee-owned firm is not a very common business form. For example, there are more than 25,000 worker cooperatives in Italy, several thousand in Spain, some 2,000 in France, and hundreds in many countries around the world. Worker cooperatives are found in most industries, including very capital-intensive ones as well as services, and traditional as well as high-technology sectors. Detailed comparative data available for a few countries also show that worker cooperatives tend to be larger on average than other firms, the vast majority of which are very small (for example, some 80% of all firms with at least one employee have fewer than ten employees in France and in the United States, but the figure is only 55% for French worker cooperatives).[2] The largest cooperative group owned by its workers – the Mondragon Cooperative

[1] Special thanks to Alberto Zevi, Lanfranco Senn, and other participants in the Conference on "The Cooperative Movement 1950–2010 ... and Beyond" (Bocconi University, Milan, October 2010), as well as to Mónica Gago, who provided insightful comments on an earlier version of the paper.
[2] The figures for France are for 2007 (see Fakhfakh, et al., 2012); the U.S. figure refers to 2004 (see U.S. Census Bureau at www.census.gov/epcd/www/smallbus.html, accessed on April 24, 2011). Comparative average sizes for Italian worker cooperatives and other firms are presented in Pencavel, et al. (2006). Burdín and Dean (2009) show that 64% of all firms in Uruguay have fewer than six employees, but only 9% of worker cooperatives. A likely reason for the greater size of worker cooperatives is that it takes several people to form a cooperative. Italy, France, and

Corporation in the Spanish Basque Country – employs some 85,000 people around the world. Worker cooperatives have often operated for considerably longer than a century, and a number of firms created in the late nineteenth century are still trading today. This descriptive evidence alone would suggest that workers' cooperatives are capable of performing reasonably well in market economies.

Unfavorable preconceptions about worker cooperatives come from the fact that cooperatives practice a form of economic democracy that many observers regard as unlikely to work. The concept of labor-managed firms turns on its head a fundamental feature, the bureaucratic hierarchy, of what most people think of as a firm. For this reason, the performance of worker cooperatives has been a thorny issue for more than a century among economists. Employee-run businesses are a minority form of firm, and many economists have thought the reason must be that labor-managed firms are less efficient, and generally less viable, than other firms. As a result, much of economists' interest has focused on the comparative efficiency of worker cooperatives relative to that of conventional capitalist firms. Fortunately, a few studies have looked at factors that make certain worker cooperatives more successful than others.[3]

The period we are examining – 1950 to 2010 – happens to correspond to that of the modern economics literature on labor-managed firms. In that time, a large share of that literature has been concerned with the performance of workers' cooperatives, several aspects of which relate to their efficiency. There are primarily two threads to that body of research. In the last three decades, a number of empirical papers have examined worker cooperatives' performance relative to that of conventional firms, investigating, for example, whether cooperatives are more or less productive than other businesses. Another set of studies has focused on cooperatives' overall ability to survive, that is, to achieve a measure of institutional sustainability. Several theorists have argued that perverse incentives built into the labor-managed firm model inevitably lead to the firm's demise, whether by underinvestment or degeneration to the capitalist form. These hypotheses have generated a small body of empirical work examining the survival record of workers' cooperatives.

Perhaps more fundamentally, the theoretical models of the labor-managed firm that predict underinvestment and degeneration have implications for the choice of constitutional structure for workers' cooperatives. In particular, these theories point to the central role of capital ownership and profit allocation

Uruguay legally require worker cooperatives to have certain minimum sizes, though in all three cases the required minimum has been decreasing in recent decades. There exist few very large worker cooperatives, but it is unclearr there is a larger proportion of very large firms among firms in general than among worker cooperatives.

[3] Because the profit-maximizing, investor-owned firm is the reference model to which the cooperative is compared, worker cooperatives are effectively compared to all types of private for-profit firms in these studies, though it might be interesting to compare worker cooperatives with more specific groups of conventional businesses that may share some characteristics with worker cooperatives, such as self-employment (as with family businesses) as well as with other types of cooperatives.

arrangements in determining the success or failure of this business form and can be discussed in the light of existing cooperative practice.

Comparatively little economics research can be found regarding the factors that make some worker cooperatives more successful than others with the same basic structure. The studies concerned have focused on the features that make worker cooperatives different from conventional firms, in order to assess whether the special features of labor-managed firms hamper or instead enhance their performance. Thus, the studies look at the proportion of employees with formal rights to participate in decisions and the share of profit they will receive, for example, and examine their effect on the firm's performance. I will cover this aspect of the literature first, along with comparative empirical studies of labor-managed and conventional firm performance that use the same methodological approach. Although the underinvestment and degeneration hypotheses have generated a large theoretical literature and many ad hoc discussions of empirical observations, much confusion remains regarding these hypotheses, and little rigorous empirical work on them has been done. I will summarize the theoretical hypotheses and extend the discussion of these issues to different types of evidence: thus, I will consider comparisons of the institutional arrangements to be found among workers' cooperatives in Italy, Mondragon (Spain), and France (Alzola, et al., 2010) before providing some evidence on survival and employment.

In order to accommodate evidence from countries that have multiple forms of firms fully owned by their employees, and to focus my institutional discussion of ownership and profit allocation arrangements, I will use a broad definition of a worker cooperative based on cooperative principles. Unless otherwise specified, a worker cooperative (or a labor-managed firm) in this chapter is a firm owned and managed by its employees, where the bulk of the capital is owned by employees (whether individually or collectively), all employees are eligible to apply for membership and a majority are members, and each member has one vote. Beyond this, the firms we will be looking at may have tradable or non-tradable shares, collectively owned capital, and so on.[4] As we will see, the details of these financial arrangements have important implications for institutional viability and firm survival.

For conventional firms, performance is commonly measured by financial success – for example, profit or return on assets. However, in worker cooperatives, pay is endogenous (Pencavel, 2001) and not analytically distinct from profit,[5] whereas in conventional firms pay is a cost bearing negatively on returns.

---

[4] I will not cover the case of Yugoslavia, where firms were socially owned and managed by their employees. More generally, the chapter will look primarily at industrialized countries, with a few references to the empirical studies that compare employee-owned firms to other ownership forms in transition economies.

[5] Depending on the tax regimes applying to pay and profit, members of worker cooperatives may choose to increase pay or to distribute more profit to themselves in a given year (pay increases do not necessarily have the same permanent character in worker cooperatives as in conventional firms,

Profitability is therefore not an appropriate measure of performance for employee-owned firms and is not comparable across the two ownership categories. Productivity, on the other hand, is a measure of performance more strictly related to the economic notion of productive efficiency, can be compared across firm types, and is an appropriate measure to test theoretical hypotheses that predict that labor-managed firms will be more (or less) efficient than conventional firms. Here I will look primarily at total factor productivity, which takes into account both labor and capital inputs. The objectives of cooperators, key theoretical hypotheses on labor-managed firms, and the policy debates also suggest that a broader view of performance is appropriate. Firm survival is a measure implied by the hypotheses that underinvestment and/or degeneration will lead to the demise of all labor-managed firms. In addition, both investment and job creation or preservation are especially interesting in today's recessionary context and relate to externalities to individual firms' behavior that are relevant to public policy. As Craig and Pencavel (1993) have shown, it is likely that employment as well as pay is an objective pursued by members of a labor-managed firm. I will therefore look at investment and employment in addition to total factor productivity and firm survival.

For the most part, the empirical studies I will refer to use cross-sectional data (i.e., data on many firms but only in one year) or short panels (i.e., data covering the same firms for several years) because consistent time-series and long panels are rare. This means that time dynamics can only occasionally be examined. However, the literature I review has different strengths. It covers a number of countries and types of worker-managed firms. Several of the studies use large samples of firms in a range of industries (especially recently) so that the issues can be put in the perspective of the practices of hundreds of businesses operating in a variety of contexts. In addition, the strong econometric tradition in this area means that considerable attention has been paid to controlling for possible confounding factors, reverse causality issues, and so on, so that the bulk of the evidence is solid.

The section on institutional sustainability looks at studies investigating factors that increase the productivity of workers' cooperatives and estimations of the comparative productivity of labor-managed and conventional firms. The section on job preservation and survival looks at institutional sustainability issues, including underinvestment and degeneration to the capitalist form. The evidence regarding employment and firm survival is presented later, and conclusions are drawn at the end of the chapter.

---

as worker members may decide to cut pay in subsequent years – see p. 28). A study of large and medium-sized Italian cooperatives carried out by Centrostudi Legacoop shows that in manufacturing and construction, their accounting profit would have been 13.0% higher in 2007 if pay increases approved by the AGM once operating surplus was known had been included in the profit appearing on the balance sheet. Among social cooperatives, the figure was 49.9% (Centrostudi Legacoop, 2009).

PRODUCTIVITY

A substantial body of literature developed from the late 1970s to test the proposition that several forms of employee participation that are practiced in workers' cooperatives had positive effects on productivity. Although that literature has been dominated by studies of employee participation in conventional firms, several papers, especially early on, examined the effects of different levels of worker participation among worker cooperatives, thus providing us with tests of whether performance is improved or hampered by different practices in some of the areas that are crucial for worker cooperatives. Another small group of studies compared the productivity of conventional and labor-managed firms with the help of data sets including both types of firms.

Factors Increasing Productivity among Worker Cooperatives

The theory behind the hypothesis that employee participation increases productivity is well known and can be summarized as follows.[6] In conditions of asymmetric information, uncertainty, and incomplete contracts, employee involvement in decision making improves the quality of information flows and decisions and may contribute to retaining employees by providing a "voice" alternative to the "exit" option and by internalizing employees' interests in decisions. This, in turn, may make it easier to implement decisions. Participation in decisions also may contribute to fostering intrinsic motivation (see, e.g., Frey and Jegen, 2005) by increasing employees' perceptions of being valued and treated with dignity as well as their sense of autonomy at work.

Participation in the economic returns of the firm, whether by receiving profit-related bonuses and/or dividends on capital shares (and, where relevant, capital gains), makes employees' income (and possibly wealth) dependent on good firm performance. This is thought to provide incentives to work harder and better, to share information with management and coworkers, and to invest in human capital and train others. The collective nature of returns participation in employee-owned firms also may encourage cooperation and team work. Having participation in both decision making and economic returns should further increase organizational effectiveness and productivity by providing incentives to make decisions consistent with firm profitability, and by offering employees opportunities to release relevant information as well as a way to check moral hazard on the part of managers in decisions that affect employees.[7]

Against these optimistic hypotheses, it has been argued that the collective nature of the incentives provided by profit participation promotes free-riding

---

[6] See, e.g., Blinder, 1990; Ben-Ner and Jones, 1995; Bonin, et al., 1993; Kruse and Blasi, 1997; Dow, 2003; and Addison, 2005 for reviews.

[7] "Moral hazard" refers to cases in which management may make decisions consistent with their own interests (and/or, in conventional firms, with investors' interests) but detrimental to other employees' interests.

rather than increased effort, although in the context of a firm, where the game among employees is normally repeated, a cooperative equilibrium may emerge (FitzRoy and Kraft, 1987).[8] It has also been contended that managers' incentives are diluted by employee ownership and profit sharing, and that conflicts, slow and ill-advised decision making, and coordination problems may beset employee-run firms.

Several early studies tested these hypotheses by estimating production functions on data from worker cooperatives that practiced different degrees of participation in decisions, profit, and capital ownership. In particular, a series of studies used three data sets from the U.K., France, and Italy, respectively (see, in particular, Jones, 1982; Defourny, Estrin, and Jones, 1985; and Estrin, Jones, and Svejnar, 1987). The British data set concerned some 150 long-established U.K. worker cooperatives in the printing, clothing, and footwear industries, observed every five years in 1948–68. The second data set covered around 550 French worker cooperatives in manufacturing, construction, and services observed in 1978–9. The third one included annual information on 150 Italian manufacturing and construction worker cooperatives observed in 1976–80.[9] The general approach was to augment the production function by inserting variables measuring the level of each form of participation, so that each of those effects could be estimated while taking into account the employment and capital levels of the firm as well as its industry and other relevant controls, such as the age of the firm. The extent of participation in decision making was measured with the proportion of cooperative members among employees (or, in some of the estimations for the U.K., the proportion of workers on the board of directors). The average amount of profit allocated to each worker (or, in the Italian data set, profit per employee) measured the level of profit sharing, and the average individually owned capital stake per worker represented the level of participation in ownership (in all three sets of cooperatives, only limited dividends were paid on capital, and membership shares were paid back at nominal value when the member left the firm; the bulk of capital was accumulated in collective ownership). Some of these studies also controlled for the level of collectively owned capital. Various functional forms for the production function were tested for. In the later studies in the series, the estimation methods took into account both the simultaneous determination of the input and output levels and the possibility that levels of participation were endogenous (so that estimated effects might be biased by reverse causality if, for example, more productive firms paid higher profit-sharing bonuses, or if more workers were inclined to join a prosperous cooperative). These issues were appropriately handled with Instrumental Variables estimation and firm-specific fixed effects where possible,

---

[8] Anecdotal as well as statistical evidence actually point to increased peer pressure in participatory firms (Kruse, et al., 2004).

[9] The whole series of early studies using these data sets is reviewed in Conte and Svejnar (1990) and in Doucouliagos (1995).

though the nature of the French data set limited the availability of good instruments.

In the three countries, the studies found that increased profit sharing was associated with higher total factor productivity, though some of the estimated effect still might have been due to reverse causality, in the French case in particular. Increased participation in decision making, in the form of a higher proportion of employees being cooperative members, was found to increase productivity in both France and Italy, but not in the U.K. cooperatives. However, in the U.K. case, there was some evidence that a greater proportion of workers on the board was associated with higher productivity, suggesting once again that greater participation in decision making improves performance. The level of individually owned capital per worker was found to improve productivity in the French and Italian cases but not in the British one, where the average stake per worker was very low. In the British cooperatives, however, higher individual capital stakes were associated with higher productivity when there were high proportions of workers on the board and of members among the workforce, suggesting some complementarity between participation in decisions and in ownership, as suggested by the theory. When the level of collectively owned capital per employee was included in the equation, it was found to be unrelated to productivity in the U.K. and French cooperatives, and negatively associated with productivity in Italy, though this last result was sensitive to specification. A later study by Estrin and Jones (1995), using the French data set, explicitly modeled the decision to join in an open membership cooperative and estimated equations determining the membership rate and individual capital stake in the cooperative jointly with the production function, in order to remedy the reverse causality problems that potentially biased earlier estimations of the effects of these two forms of participation on productivity. The findings of this study confirmed the earlier results, showing that both increased participation in the governance of the cooperative and greater capital commitment on the part of members are associated with productivity increases, independently of reverse causality effects.

The pivotal role of participation in decisions is confirmed by several studies of North American employee-owned firms, including, in particular, very early studies of the plywood cooperatives of the U.S. Pacific Northwest (reviewed, e.g., in Conte, 1982, and in Conte and Svejnar, 1990) and a more recent study of the compared performance of a 90% employee-owned firm set up as an ESOP (employee stock ownership plan) with matched conventional firms (Ros, 2003). These studies investigated the possible effects of participation in decision making (measured by identifying firm practices or by looking at workers' perceptions of the extent of their participation collected with employee surveys) and capital ownership or profit sharing on employees' attitudes, including commitment, motivation and job satisfaction, and/or effort in cooperatives.[10] Their findings

---

[10] See also Kruse and Blasi (1997) for a review of the evidence on these issues in part-employee-owned firms from studies in psychology and sociology as well as economics.

suggest that participation in decision making is associated with greater employee commitment, satisfaction, motivation, and effort. In contrast, ownership or profit participation may have narrower effects and some of these effects could be dependent on the presence of participation in decision making. These findings seem to imply that, at least in cooperatives, the hypothesized complementarity between participation in governance and profit may be verified for the effects of participation in profit or ownership, which may require participation in governance in order to obtain, but not necessarily for those of participation in decisions, which may stand alone. This interpretation of the evidence is consistent with the findings on the U.K. cooperatives reviewed previously and is echoed in Pencavel (2001).

The finding that participation in decision making increases efficiency as well as job satisfaction is confirmed by a more recent study investigating nearly 1,000 firms in Spain, including about 60 worker cooperatives (Bayo-Moriones, et al., 2003). Interestingly, however, the favorable estimated effect did not extend to measures of employee behavior, like absenteeism or industrial action, examined in the study; but the study did not consider forms of participation that are important to cooperatives, such as employee representation on the board of directors.

The evidence to date, therefore, is remarkably consistent in showing that the key feature of worker cooperatives, increased worker participation, never causes performance to deteriorate in these firms, contrary to many theoretical predictions. Across countries, firm samples, and methodologies, studies find that greater participation in governance is a factor of increased productive efficiency in worker cooperatives, both in itself and perhaps in boosting the incentive effects of participation in ownership and/or profit. More large-scale studies of these issues with panels of worker cooperatives would be useful in order to evaluate how solid the very early results are in relation to individually and collectively owned capital, for example, and to look at the different aspects of participation in worker cooperatives more systematically.

Participatory practices are not always comparable across firm types. For example, capital shares often have different characteristics and confer different rights in cooperatives and conventional firms. Several studies have instead taken advantage of the availability of comparative data to focus on the compared productivity of worker cooperatives and conventional firms overall, without looking at the details of participatory practices.

Compared Productivity of Worker Cooperatives and Conventional Firms

The studies of Italian, British, and French cooperatives we have just looked at were reviewed, along with studies of the productivity effects of participatory practices in conventional firms, in a meta-analysis by Doucouliagos (1995). His key finding is that employee participation in decision making and in profit have greater positive productivity effects in worker cooperatives than in conventional firms. He notes, however, that in the case of participation in governance, this is probably because there is more participation in cooperatives, whereas the greater effect found for profit sharing in cooperatives is independent of the size of the bonus.[11] It is possible that the greater productivity effect of profit sharing in cooperatives is due to the presence of greater participation in decision making in these firms. In contrast, the modest positive effects of employee ownership are not found to be statistically different in cooperatives and in other firms. This is consistent with the findings of Bayo-Moriones and colleagues (2003) that the same level of participation in decision making had the same effect in worker cooperatives and in conventional firms, and that the fact of being a cooperative did not affect productivity in and of itself independently from governance participation. Ros (2003) similarly found that once the level of participation was controlled for, the firm's being employee-owned had no extra effect on employee effort.

These results suggest that we should expect cooperatives to be more productive overall than conventional firms, both because they involve higher levels of participation in governance and because this feature may make profit sharing, which is also present in many conventional firms, more effective in raising productivity for cooperatives than for conventional firms. Even if they work more productively, however, cooperative members may well decide not to work as hard as they can. If the cooperative's objectives function is the utility of the representative or the median member, and members have a normal income-leisure trade-off,[12] output need not be maximized at a given level of employment and capital, even if employment does not enter the objectives function of the cooperative.[13] This implies that worker cooperatives, even if they are more productively efficient than conventional firms for the same input levels, may not appear more productive or even appear less productive if the labor input is measured as the level of employment (or even as the number of hours worked, if we cannot measure effort).

Five studies have estimated production functions on comparative samples including both workers' cooperatives and conventional firms from the United States (Berman and Berman, 1989, and Craig and Pencavel, 1995), Italy (Estrin, 1991, and Jones, 2007), and France (Fakhfakh, et al., 2012). Four of these studies used samples of cooperatives and conventional firms matched by size and industry and/or technology. Berman and Berman's data comprised 144 observations on 37 plywood plants in the U.S. Pacific Northwest, including ten cooperatives, seven former cooperatives, and 19 conventional plants. The plants were observed at five-year intervals during the period 1958–77. Craig and

---

[11] The meta-analysis pools together results of studies measuring governance and other forms of participation in different ways, and in which the average level of participation, if it is measured, varies (see Doucouliagos, 1995).

[12] That is, if they dislike effort and like leisure as well as income.

[13] This is the model proposed by Jensen and Meckling (1976) for the owner-manager of a conventional firm, who maximizes her utility but not profit because she prefers to spend some of the potential profit in getting benefits in kind from the firm.

Pencavel used an unbalanced panel of 170 observations on 34 plywood mills in the same region (seven cooperatives, seven unionized conventional mills, and eight nonunionized ones) observed every two years in 1968–86. Estrin's Italian sample included 49 cooperatives and 35 private firms in light manufacturing in Tuscany and Emilia Romagna, matched by industry and size and observed annually in 1981–5. Jones's research included 26 cooperatives and 51 conventional firms in construction in the same Italian regions, observed annually in 1981–9. The fifth study, on French firms, used data on two representative samples of conventional firms with 20 employees or more merged with information on all the worker cooperatives in the same size band. The resulting data sets were an unbalanced panel of 431 cooperatives and 6,456 conventional firms in construction, manufacturing, and services (seven industries) with about 19,600 annual observations in 1987–90; and an unbalanced panel of 166 cooperatives and 2,266 conventional firms in four manufacturing industries in 1989–96, with about 15,300 observations.

Three of the studies estimated Cobb-Douglas production functions and the other two (Jones, 2007, and Fakhfakh, et al., 2012) used translog specifications. Most of the estimations used Instrumental Variables/Random effects in order to take into account the simultaneous determination of input and output levels. Fakhfakh and colleagues (2012) also used System Generalized Moments Method (System-GMM) estimation for some specifications, which provides the most robust treatment of endogeneity issues (e.g., if cooperatives exist or survive mostly in subindustries that are most favorable to cooperative production).

When worker cooperatives and conventional firms were constrained to have the same production function, four of the studies (Berman and Berman, 1989; Estrin, 1991; Craig and Pencavel, 1995; and Fakhfakh, et al., 2012) found no significant difference in total factor productivity between the two groups of firms, although Fakhfakh and colleagues found some evidence that cooperatives may be more productive in certain industries. The fifth study (Jones, 2007) found differences that were not consistent across specifications and estimation methods. However, cooperatives and conventional firms do not have the same production function. Four of the studies tested for this and found the functions estimated for the two groups of firms to be statistically significantly different; and Jones (2007) found significant firm-specific fixed effects that may reflect technological differences between the groups. As Estrin (1991) put it, the two types of firms organize production differently. This is consistent with the hypothesis that the effects of the different types of participation practiced in cooperatives are reflected not only in greater output at all input levels with the same factor elasticities[14] (disembodied effects) but also in different elasticities (embodied effects).[15]

---

[14] Factor elasticity refers to the percentage change in output associated with a 1% increase in one of the inputs (capital or labor) only.

[15] Fakhfakh, et al. (2012) use the properties of the translog production function, in which factor elasticities and marginal products vary with input levels, to show that differences in estimated

In order to find out whether one group is more productive, Craig and Pencavel (1995) computed the output predicted by the functions estimated for cooperatives and for other firms at the mean point of each group's sample. They found that the predicted output was higher at both mean sample points with the function estimated for cooperatives. Fakhfakh and colleagues (2012) computed, for each sample firm, the output levels that would be predicted with the parameters estimated for the cooperatives and with the parameters estimated for the conventional firms, and tested whether the two levels were the same on average for each sample and in each industry. In all industries and with both data sets, the output predicted for worker cooperatives with their current inputs was the same with both sets of parameters or higher with the parameters estimated for cooperatives. However, with both data sets, there were several industries in which, as in Pencavel and Craig, the predicted output for conventional firms was higher with the parameters estimated for the cooperative sample. In other words, if conventional firms organized production in the same way as the cooperatives, they might produce more with their current average input levels in these industries.

Few economists expected the explosion of employee ownership that marked the transition to market systems in former centrally planned economies in the 1990s. In many transition countries, mass privatization programs resulted in an unprecedented incidence of employee ownership, with many firms in which nonmanagerial employees owned the majority of capital (Earle and Estrin, 1998). However, it has been shown that majority employee ownership in the transition tended not to be associated with corresponding levels of employee control, or participation in governance, and that as a rule control remained in the hands of managers (see Jones, 2004). In addition, employees' shares may not have been very liquid and profitability may have been low or nonexistent. This pattern may explain the findings of research on employee ownership in these economies. Employee-owned firms have been included in studies examining the effect of privatization on total factor productivity. Endogeneity issues are crucial in this area, since privatization may have targeted better- or worse-performing firms in the first place. In their review of the empirical literature on the effects of privatization, Estrin and colleagues (2009) identify seven studies that estimate the effects of employee ownership, among other ownership forms, on total factor productivity and handle endogeneity robustly. Of these studies, six found employee ownership to have no statistically significant effect on total factor productivity in Central and Eastern Europe and Confederation of Independent States (CIS) countries, and one study on Estonia found a positive effect.[16]

---

elasticities between the two groups are not simply explained by differences in factor demands, and can therefore be attributed to the effects of participation on the production function.

[16] Although it is hardly a triumph for worker ownership, this evidence is strikingly at odds with the predictions regarding the effects of employee ownership in the transition literature. As Estrin, et al. (2009) remark, their findings are more favorable to employee ownership than reviews that included studies in which endogeneity was not adequately taken into account in the econometric analysis.

Altogether, the evidence is again remarkably consistent across countries, types of labor-managed firms, economic circumstances and time periods, and with methodologically robust studies. Worker cooperatives are never found to be less productive than conventional firms[17] and may be more productive. The key factor explaining this productivity seems to be members' involvement in governance, which boosts productivity in and of itself as well as by improving the incentive effects of participation in the economic returns of the firm. Consistently equal or greater total factor productivity is a key element for competitiveness.

INSTITUTIONAL SUSTAINABILITY

One of the recurring questions regarding worker cooperatives has been why the firm type is so rare in market economies, especially if it is at least as productive as conventional firms, as the evidence suggests. For a long time, the widely accepted answer was that labor-managed firms are not institutionally viable – it was argued that there are incentives built into the structure of the organization that make it unsustainable. Two models, in particular, have dominated the debate: the underinvestment/self-extinction hypothesis put forward, with variants, by Furubotn and Pejovich (e.g., 1970) and Vanek (1977), and degeneration to the capitalist form, which was analyzed by Ben-Ner (1984) and Miyazaki (1984). Both hypotheses were put forward to explain phenomena that had been observed among labor-managed firms, and both provided key insights into the crucial importance of capital ownership and profit allocation arrangements to the institutional viability of workers' cooperatives. As we will see, existing types of labor-managed firms have provided different solutions to both potential problems. It is, therefore, of interest to summarize each hypothesis and examine its implications in the light of cooperative practice and evidence.

Underinvestment

This hypothesis generated much discussion and critique until the mid-1990s (see Uvalić, 1992, and Dow, 2003, for reviews). At the heart of the hypothesis is the truncation of property rights associated with collective capital ownership. When members of a cooperative with collectively owned capital leave the firm, they cannot receive a share of the present value of future profits generated by investment their work has helped finance, as owners of capitalist firms can by selling their shares. If it relies on internal finance, an income-maximizing, labor-managed firm where capital is owned collectively will, therefore, have an incentive not to invest, or to invest only in projects with inefficiently high short-term

---

[17] Megginson and Netter (2002) review studies that find employee ownership to have negative effects on performance, but the group of papers they review includes studies that do not deal appropriately with endogeneity (Estrin, et al., 2009) so that these effects probably pick up lower prior performance among firms that were privatized with employee ownership.

returns. The firm may even consume the collectively owned capital instead, and "self-extinguish," bringing its scale down to one member if its technology is characterized by constant returns to scale, or to an inefficiently small scale (i.e., with increasing returns) otherwise. This is a much simplified presentation of the hypothesis, and a number of assumptions that are necessary for the model to work (e.g., regarding the lifetime of capital equipment, the opportunity cost of capital) have been thoroughly questioned. Descriptive evidence suggests worker cooperatives with collectively owned capital assess investment projects with similar time horizons as conventional firms (Bartlett, et al., 1992; Robinson and Wilson, 1993). However, the insights of the theory are, first, that it may be tempting for cooperative members not to increase capital that will go to future generations of workers and, second, that far from accumulating capital, members who have access to capital accumulated by previous generations may instead be tempted to demutualize and appropriate that capital if they are allowed to do so. Indeed, the demutualization of cooperatives of other kinds, where demutualization was authorized by legislation, such as that of many British building societies, suggests that the temptation can be real.

The solution favored by many economists is to have a market for membership rights, so that shares are tradable, and if that market is reasonably efficient members can receive a share of the present value of future returns when they leave the cooperative.[18] Such a market may be difficult to organize, since, as Putterman (1984), Dow (2003), and others have argued, membership rights in the case of a labor-managed firm are tied with particular skills, and so on. In practice, many employee-owned firms that resulted from privatization were organized in a way that provided tradable rights to the returns to capital and control, though not exactly membership in the "bundled" cooperative sense, where both capital ownership and membership of a one-member, one-vote firm were merged in membership shares. In such firms, the stock was purchased by the employees and its value depended on the valuation of the company. Examples include many employee-owned firms in transition countries and the worker-owned bus companies that resulted from privatization in the 1990s in the U.K. A common pattern among such companies is that after a few years, especially if the firm is successful, worker members sell the company to a conventional owner. This process was observed even among the American plywood cooperatives of the Pacific Northwest, where there was a limited market for membership shares, in that shares were advertised in local newspapers but membership was subject to acceptance by the existing members and seemed underpriced (Pencavel, 2001).

It is, of course, debatable whether this kind of institutional instability represents a problem – after all, if cooperators are successful entrepreneurs and can retire comfortably thanks to the success of the cooperative, there is nothing

---

[18] As Estrin and Jones (1992) note, however, many economists in the past also have argued in favor of collective capital ownership, which may in particular strengthen cooperative advantages, such as commitment to certain values, and in this way decrease the risk of degeneration.

wrong there. It is, however, a potential issue for the movement as a whole, and also for public authorities if the cooperatives have received any tax concessions or subsidies. The key element here is the value of the share, which is both the solution to the investment incentive and the source of the incentive to sell off. Shares with a high value also require setting up arrangements for prospective members to pay for their shares by installments, in order to preserve an open membership, and for the payment of the shares of departing members over a period of time, in order to avoid potential decapitalization problems when a whole generation retires (Berman, 1982). Protection against selling out may be afforded by systems in which employees' shares are held in trust, as in some U.S. ESOPs, and generally by systems that allow the capital of members that sell shares and/or leave the firm to remain in the firm.

An alternative solution to the underinvestment issue, which was proposed by Vanek (1977), is one that actually has been in operation at least since the Second World War in worker cooperatives in France and Italy and also was adopted in the Mondragon system (Alzola, et al., 2010) – mandatory collective capital accumulation. In these cooperatives, part of the capital is owned individually, but attracts limited returns and, in Italy and in France, the individual membership shares are paid back at their nominal values. Another part of the capital (often the bulk of the capital) is owned collectively and may not be split among the members of the cooperative, even if the firm is wound up – in that case, the net assets devolve to another cooperative, a cooperative institution, or a charity (this provision is sometimes called an "asset lock"). This setup ensures institutional stability[19] but creates potential underinvestment incentives. However, in all three cases, the law or, in Mondragon's case, the cooperative group's own

---

[19] It has been said that some of the old-style British cooperatives, in which collective assets could not be split *except* in the case of dissolution, were wound up for the purpose of appropriating accumulated capital. However, the figures presented by Jones (1982) suggest that the demise of that part of the U.K. cooperative movement may have been due at least as much to the absence of new cooperative creations.

It is often remarked that the institutional stability provided by a full asset lock relies on a forced sacrifice on the part of those cooperators that leave the firm. However, it also allows new cooperators to enjoy the use of capital accumulated by previous generations – in this conception, the cooperative is a kind of public good to be used by successive generations of employees. In itself, this system may create other incentive problems, in that members of cooperatives that have very large reserves accumulated by earlier generations may be tempted by the complacency of *rentier* behavior (as Zevi put it) expecting the money to work for them. In the Mondragon system, incoming members pay a nonrefundable fee toward the collectively owned capital (Alzola, et al., 2010). This may ensure greater commitment on the part of members, as may other systems proposed in Zevi (2005) to keep stable resources in the firm while offering members appropriate incentives. More generally, Conte and Ye (1995) suggest that intergenerational financial arrangements of the kind already practiced by Mondragon can resolve underinvestment issues. Mondragon, the Italian, and the French worker cooperatives also all provide for individually owned capital accumulation over the years an individual member is employed in the firm (Alzola, et al., ibid.). In any case, a full asset lock need not prohibit the firm from leaving the cooperative form – this could be allowed, for example, provided the owners of the new firm buy back the collectively owned capital.

articles of association specify that a minimum percentage of profit has to be plowed back into the firm every year, and adds to the portion of capital that is collectively owned (Alzola, et al., 2010). The little rigorous empirical evidence there is on this issue suggests there is no underinvestment in these cooperatives. Estrin and Jones (1998) estimated an investment equation on a balanced panel of 270 French worker cooperatives observed in 1970–9. The equation is estimated robustly by GMM in first differences in order to deal with potential serial correlation and heteroskedasticity and includes time fixed effects. These authors found that the share of collective capital in the firm's assets had no effect on investment, but that investment might be financially constrained by the limitations on access to equity finance (individually owned capital). Gago and colleagues (2008) estimated investment functions by GMM on a 16-year unbalanced panel (1989–2004) comprising some 190,000 observations on conventional firms and 1,900 on worker cooperatives in French manufacturing. Their preliminary findings indicated that French worker cooperatives did not invest less than conventional firms, all else being equal, nor were the cooperatives more financially constrained than other firms. These findings are consistent with the investment equation estimated by Pencavel and colleagues (2006) on a long panel (1982–94) of some 2,000 worker cooperatives and 150,000 conventional firms in Italy, which indicates that investment in cooperatives and conventional firms reacts in the same way to product market shocks.

Although French worker cooperatives do not underinvest, it is unclear that this is entirely due to the existence of a mandatory plow-back rule. Navarra (2009) finds that the 60 worker cooperatives in the Italian province of Ravenna on which she has annual data for the period 2000–5 (in addition to interview and employee survey data for one third of the cooperatives in 2007), systematically plow back a considerably larger share of profit than the required minimum. This is consistent with figures presented in Alzola et al. (2010) that indicate that the bulk of worker cooperatives' profit is plowed back in Italy, in part due to Italian regulation and requirements to benefit from tax concessions. Anecdotal evidence suggests that profit plow-back is a little lower in French cooperatives, but still considerably higher than the legally required minimum. Fakhfakh and colleagues (2012) compared the mean annual rate of growth of fixed assets (i.e., investment) in worker cooperatives and conventional firms, using their two data sets (one covering 1987–90 and seven industries in manufacturing, construction, and services, and the other covering 1989–96 and manufacturing) with information on some 7,000 French firms, about 500 of which were worker cooperatives. With both data sets, they found that annual investment was always at least as large in the cooperatives as in conventional firms (in three out of seven industries in the first data set, cooperative investment was statistically significantly higher than in conventional firms, and there was no difference in any of the other industries studied). They also found no evidence that the cooperatives systematically produced with increasing returns to scale nor that they produced at a smaller scale than conventional firms.[20] Zevi (2005) argues that, far from having an inefficiently short time horizon, the members of worker cooperatives are first concerned with job security at a decent level of pay and thus plow-back profit in order to ensure the growth that will guarantee them jobs. This concern for long-term job stability, and in some cases, for the continued existence of the firm, may actually give cooperative members a longer time horizon than many conventional firms where managers are subject to short-term capital market pressures.

Degeneration to the Capitalist Form

Among the critiques of the underinvestment model, it was pointed out that a worker cooperative that employed nonmembers who did not share in profits would not underinvest (see discussion in Stephen, 1982). However, the use of hired employees has been at the center of another issue of institutional sustainability – degeneration to the capitalist form. The process modeled by Ben-Ner (1984) functions roughly as follows.[21] If an income-maximizing labor-managed firm is allowed to hire nonmember employees who do not get a share of the firm's profit, members will have an incentive to replace retiring and resigning members by nonmembers. A nonmember employee will produce the same marginal revenue product as a member would but will only be paid a wage, leaving more profit to share among the remaining members. Little by little, the cooperative will have a lower and lower proportion of members and an increasing proportion of nonmembers among its labor force. It will eventually become a conventional capitalist firm in which a minority of members exploit the majority of the workforce.[22] Ben-Ner notes that this process may not operate or may even be reversed if members are more productive than nonmembers because they participate in profit and decisions. Pencavel (2012) also notes that degeneration may not happen if nonmembers perform work that is distinct from members and remains necessary because of a complementarity between the two types of work.

The degeneration models were inspired by empirical observation, and clear evidence of it is presented, for example, by Russell (1995) for Israeli worker cooperatives and by Jones (1982) for early U.S cooperatives. Pencavel (2001, 2012) discusses some recent U.S. cases. Both profit sharing among members and shares that attract dividends or can be sold at a higher price than they were

---

[20] There is a larger proportion of medium-sized and large firms, and a lower proportion of small and very small ones, among workers' cooperatives than among conventional firms in France (Fakhfakh, et al., 2012) as in Italy (Pencavel, et al., 2006) and Uruguay (Burdín and Dean, 2009), a phenomenon already reported by Ben-Ner (1988) for France, the U.K., and Sweden in the early 1980s.

[21] Miyazaki (1984) proposes a different framework to explain degeneration, which applies only to systems in which unemployed members of the cooperative remain members.

[22] This is a very limited definition, for the purposes of this chapter. There is a more qualitative process of degeneration that has to do with democracy among members, which I am not covering here.

bought for provide incentives for degeneration (Estrin and Jones, 1992). If capital shares become expensive, it will also become easier to exclude new members (Russell, 1995). The proportion of nonmanagerial workers owning shares in firms that were employee-owned immediately after privatization dramatically decreased in the majority of employee-owned firms in transition countries (Jones, 2004). Kalmi (2004) shows that in the case of Estonia, this reduction in the proportion of employee-owners was achieved by means of a degeneration process of the type analyzed by Ben-Ner, where managers excluded new employees from share ownership. The obvious solution is to prohibit the habitual hiring of nonmember employees; however, a strict policy of this type may be too rigid. Most cooperatives in France, for example, have new employees go through a probation period of, say, six months before they get a permanent contract and apply for membership. Reviewing arrangements in some U.S. forestry cooperatives, Pencavel (2001) also noted the imbalances potentially introduced in voting patterns for decisions involving short-term versus long-term trade-offs by admitting to full membership rights employees who have just joined the firm and not fully paid their membership fee. In addition, hiring nonmembers may make it possible to pay employees with special skills substantially more than members.

The practices of French, Mondragon, and Italian worker cooperatives, all of which allow employment of nonmembers, provide different solutions to the problem (Alzola, et al., 2010) even though they may not have been adopted for this reason. French worker cooperatives, by law, split the share of profit allocated to labor (as opposed to mandatory allocations to collective capital and the share of profit paid out as dividends on individually owned capital shares) among members and nonmember employees on the same terms (CG-SCOP, 2003). These terms, in keeping with cooperative principles, typically consist in a profit bonus proportional to the individual worker's pay or hours worked in the cooperative (as with the "cooperative divi" or patronage-based payment). Together with the limited dividends paid on capital shares that do not appreciate in value, this setup eliminates the incentives for degeneration identified by Ben-Ner and Miyazaki. Estrin and Jones's (1992) findings confirm that French worker cooperatives do not exhibit degeneration, even though the percentage of members among the workforce varies over the life of a cooperative.[23] Although Italian worker cooperatives can in principle pay a share of profit to members only (again as patronage payments, as opposed to dividends paid on capital shares) legal caps on the amount that can be paid to individual workers in this way and tax concessions attached to plow-back mean that cooperatives seem to have policies of plowing back most profits and/or offering profit sharing to members and nonmembers alike (Zevi, 1982; Alzola, et al., 2010). These

---

[23] That percentage is likely to drop, in particular, during periods of growth, before new employees become members. The French setup, however, gives employees few incentives to become members, and many cooperatives have resorted to adopting a rule that requires all employees to apply for membership after a certain time with the firm.

policies are also consistent with a central concern for growth perceived as a way to ensure job security – an objective that would unite members and nonmembers (Zevi, 2005). The solution adopted by the Mondragon group is to limit the percentage of nonmembers allowed in the workforce to a predefined maximum (Alzola, et al., 2010). The maximum percentage of hired employees allowed for worker cooperatives to enjoy tax benefits in Uruguay seems to have had a similar effect, and Burdín and Dean (2009) do not find evidence of degeneration when they estimate a membership rate equation for all the worker cooperatives of that country observed in 1996–2005. Mondragon also has recently created a category of "temporary members" who have temporary membership rights and duties, in order to be able not to offer new members the absolute job security normally attached to membership during the recession, without degenerating.

Judging from the rules in force in many worker cooperatives, it therefore seems that under certain sets of rules used by the most successful Western European cooperatives, labor-managed firms are unlikely to disappear by underinvesting and can avoid degeneration. The little available evidence on cooperative survival will be presented in the next section. Increasingly, available evidence also points to worker cooperatives' concern with employment stability, a point that might explain the pattern of capital accumulation over and above the legal minimum (Zevi, 2005). In addition to her evidence on capital accumulation, Navarra (2009) also presents evidence in support of her argument that accumulating collectively owned capital is a form of collective insurance. Accumulating collective resources in this way allows cooperatives that consider employment stability a priority to provide more stable income to their members. Evidence on worker cooperatives' pay and employment adjustments to the business cycle will also be presented in the next section.

JOB PRESERVATION AND SURVIVAL

Pay and Employment Adjustments

Part of the reason why the economics literature on labor-managed firms focused so much effort on institutional stability for several decades comes from the model of the income-maximizing Illyrian firm. In this model, the need to maximize income per member leads to the well-known "perverse supply response," in which output price increases lead the cooperative to cut employment (see discussion in, e.g., Bonin and Putterman, 1987). The perverse supply response disappears if employment is included in worker cooperatives' objectives, whether as one of the arguments in a utility function or in the form of a labor supply constraint. As Craig and Pencavel (1993) show with data on the U.S. plywood cooperatives, the cooperatives behave as if both income and employment are relevant to their objectives. This is confirmed by Burdin and Dean's (2010) work on worker cooperatives from Uruguay.

Labor-managed firms are able to adjust pay in downturns in order to preserve employment, because the same people – the members – will decide the allocation of future profits, so that a commitment to increase pay later when market conditions improve, which would not be credible coming from a conventional employer, is incentive compatible in a cooperative. Similarly, worker cooperatives can increase pay in upturns knowing they may decide to cut pay again should market conditions worsen. Using their data set on U.S. plywood cooperatives and conventional firms, Craig and Pencavel (1992) show that employment and hours worked in the cooperatives are uncorrelated with movements in output prices, while there is an almost unit elasticity of pay with respect to the output price. Conventional firms do the opposite. Cooperatives also increase production in response to an increase in output price, though by less than conventional mills. In other words, the worker cooperative does not respond perversely and adjusts pay rather than employment in response to changing market conditions. Cooperative members bear financial risk rather than employment risk. Pencavel and colleagues (2006) estimated wage and employment (and capital – see p. 22 above) equations by fixed effects and Instrumental Variables (in first differences) respectively using a matched employer-worker panel data set covering 13 years of information on some 2,000 workers' cooperatives, 150,000 conventional workplaces, and about 13,000 individual workers per year in Italy. The worker cooperatives are found to adjust pay rather than employment to demand shocks, whereas conventional firms adjust employment both in response to wage changes and to demand shocks. In Italy, as in the U.S. plywood cooperatives, employment is more stable in the cooperatives. Similar results were obtained by Burdín and Dean (2009) with monthly data on the entire population of firms in Uruguay in 1996–2005, on which they estimated pay and employment equations by IV (in first differences) and fixed effects respectively. Worker cooperatives were found to adjust members' pay more than conventional firms in response to output price changes (though not nonmembers' pay) but not employment (whether for members or nonmembers, which suggests the bulk of the risk is borne by members' pay). Conventional firms were found to cut employment in response to a rise in pay, whereas members' pay and employment move in the same direction for cooperatives, and cooperatives adjusted employment less and more slowly to recession.

The available evidence, which is quite robust, is therefore once again remarkably consistent. It indicates that worker cooperatives adjust pay (at least for members) rather than employment to changing market conditions and generally preserve jobs better. Navarra (2009) suggests the need to ensure against market downturns motivates the high rate of profit plow-back. Accumulated collective capital will thus be drawn on by the cooperatives to weather unfavorable market conditions, in order to avoid the pay cuts that might otherwise be necessary to preserve jobs. These findings are consistent with earlier evidence from Italy and Spain (Bartlett, 1994). Descriptive evidence on Italy in the 1970s (Zevi, 1982) and France in the 1980s and 1990s (Fakhfakh, et al., 2012) also shows worker cooperatives preserving or even creating jobs in years in which conventional firms in the same industries cut jobs. In transition countries, the studies reviewed by Estrin and colleagues (2009) find that employee ownership has no effect on employment (contrary to predictions that employee owners were going to keep too high levels of employment), but these studies also find that privatization was generally associated with increases in employment rather than cuts as predicted.

It would be interesting to examine separately what happens to members and nonmembers when market conditions deteriorate. Mondragon offers complete job security to members (except for the recently created category of temporary members) who are redeployed in other cooperatives of the group if necessary. At various times in the group's history, pay has been cut in order to preserve jobs. Nonmembers have been massively laid off in the recession that followed the financial crisis of 2008, when Mondragon cut 10,000 jobs, but members' pay also has been cut (e.g., in Eroski for two years in a row). Other workers' cooperatives may also have cut nonmembers' jobs. Media reports on the John Lewis Partnership's response to the recession in late 2009 and early 2010 suggested that members' jobs may be cut.[24] Both Mondragon and John Lewis are very large employee-owned organizations, in which monitoring managers may sometimes be difficult for members. In addition, John Lewis is co-managed by senior management and other employees, so that managers have greater statutory power over governance than in classic workers' cooperatives. An interesting question for research would be whether there is an order of priority between absorbing possible losses with collectively owned capital, cutting non-members' jobs, and cutting members' pay and members' jobs – and if so, whether that order, and employment policy generally, is related to the governance of the cooperative.

Survival

Worker cooperatives in the U.K., France, and Italy have often exhibited considerable longevity, with a number of firms surviving for more than a century (Jones, 1982; Estrin and Jones, 1992; Pérotin, 2004). However, little comparable evidence exists regarding failure rates, and as yet very few econometric studies have looked at the conditions under which worker cooperatives survive or die. In France, annual death rates averaged 10% for worker cooperatives and 11% for conventional firms in 1979–2002 (Pérotin, 2006) but were 11% for both groups of firms over the 1979–98 period. Ben-Ner (1988) shows death rates of one-third less for worker cooperatives in France (6.9% in 1976–83) and the U.K. (6.3% in 1976–81) than among conventional firms (10.0% in 1980–3 in France and 10.5% in 1974–82 in the U.K.). Overall, the patchy evidence reviewed by Dow (2003) suggests that labor-managed firms probably survive better than conventional firms. The only comparative estimate of a causal hazard function model for worker cooperatives and conventional firms is Burdín's

---

[24] See, e.g., reports in *The Guardian* by Julia Finch in September–October 2009 (available on www. guardian.co.uk/business/2009/sep/30/john-lewis-call-centre-jobs, accessed on April 27, 2012) and by Julia Finch and Zoe Wood in March 2010 (available on www.guardian.co.uk/business/2010/mar/11/john-lewis-staff-share-bonus, accessed on April 27, 2012).

(2010), which confirms this with a data set comprising 22,315 firms including 243 worker cooperatives observed from April 1996 to December 2005 in Uruguay. His Cox proportional hazard estimates show the cooperatives to have lower hazard rates, all else being equal, than conventional firms. In addition, he finds the cooperatives have lower hazard rates than conventional firms specifically in industries where rates of worker supervision and of labor turnover are high, suggesting labor-managed firms have a specific advantage in these industries, but relatively higher hazards in industries with higher inequality (which may reflect greater skills heterogeneity). No difference between the hazards of cooperatives and conventional firms is found in industries with high investment rates.

The riskiest years in a worker cooperative's life seem to be the early years, as with conventional firms. However, hazard functions estimates for Israel, Atlantic Canada, and France suggest that the riskiest year for worker cooperatives may not be the first, as with conventional firms, but may happen later, after two to five years, so that cooperatives are characterized by a "liability of adolescence" (Staber, 1993; Russell, 1995; Pérotin, 2004).[25] The mean survival hazard estimated on the basis of a Cox proportional hazard model was 9.2 years for Israeli cooperatives but 18 for those of Atlantic Canada. Pérotin (2004) constructs nonparametric hazard curves for the 2,740 worker cooperatives created in France in 1977–93, 1,660 of which closed down during the period, and finds that in the first eight years or so of a firm's life, cooperatives created from scratch have the highest hazard rates, followed by rescue employee take-overs of failing firms, followed by cooperatives formed by an employee buy-out of a sound conventional firm. However, in the few years that follow, the order is reversed, with the highest hazards found among conversions of sound firms, followed by rescues, and last by cooperatives created from scratch. The origin of the firm may therefore affect the timing of the failure risk at least as much as its level. Studies on other countries and with data covering longer time periods may or may not confirm this in the future.

Following the sociological and economics literatures, Burdín, (2010), Staber (1989), and Russell (1995) all focus on external factors such as the dynamics of organizational demography and the business cycle in explaining hazards, and Pérotin (2006) on these factors to explain death rates. Both Staber (1989) and Pérotin (2006) find that the number of existing worker cooperatives affects their failure risk, though the findings of the two studies are not comparable and suggest effects in opposite directions. Finally, Pérotin (2006) estimates equations explaining the annual number of firms closing down in France for conventional firms and workers' cooperatives in 1981–2002 and finds the two equations are not statistically different. In particular, deaths among both types of firms respond in the same way to the business cycle, which suggests that fears that worker cooperatives disappear when market conditions are good (Ben-Ner,

---

[25] This pattern could result from financing problems experienced by young cooperatives relying entirely on profit plow-backs at a time when growth is needed.

1988) are unfounded. It is unfortunate that there is very little research to date on the relationship between individual cooperatives' characteristics, such as their start-up size or capital intensity or growth rates, which might tell us whether, for example, the widespread notion that worker cooperatives' difficulty in accessing external finance is a serious liability is verified over time.

CONCLUSIONS

This overview of the empirical evidence on the performance of worker cooperatives suggests both that worker cooperatives perform well in comparison with conventional firms, and that the features that make them special – worker participation and unusual arrangements for the ownership of capital – are part of their strength. Contrary to popular thinking and to the pessimistic predictions of some theorists, solid, consistent evidence across countries, systems, and time periods shows that worker cooperatives are at least as productive as conventional firms, and more productive in some areas. The more participatory cooperatives are, the more productive they tend to be. The temptation to consume capital accumulated by previous generations, demutualize, sell out successful cooperatives to conventional owners, or degenerate by restricting membership (about which the theoretical literature has had such useful insights), all have solutions that were adopted by different types of worker cooperatives around the world, assisted by legislation. That legislation has not protected workers' cooperatives, but rather enabled them to avoid perverse incentives (just as legislation protects minority shareholders' rights in conventional firms, for example). And the little we know about the survival record suggests that these solutions work.

Among the possible solutions are measures like asset locks and collective accumulation of capital that have been looked at with suspicion by generations of economists. Such measures do not seem to hamper productivity by dampening incentives – some of the same cooperatives that have adopted these particular measures are found to be more productive (as the French cooperatives) or to preserve jobs better (as the Italian cooperatives) than conventional firms. This, to me, seems to imply that we have given too much importance, in this literature, to issues of income over issues of job security and, more broadly, empowerment in worker cooperatives. Employment in a labor-managed firm is not the same thing as employment in a conventional one. In a labor-managed firm, members participate in the decisions that affect their unemployment and income risks. They are considerably better protected against the moral hazard potentially attached to management decisions over investment, strategy, or even human resource policies. This may explain why participation in governance is so important to the performance of workers' cooperatives (though these results have to be updated) rather than the monetary incentives we have focused on for so long. It is also a fact that workers' participation in profit and in decisions makes it possible for worker cooperatives to adjust pay rather than employment in response to demand shocks.

In this sense, there is no trade-off between cooperative principles and economic, or indeed social, performance, though not necessarily in the naive sense of a "win-win" business case for participation – profit may not be higher in more participatory cooperatives, but the firms may produce more and preserve their members' jobs better. One of the things that has become apparent in the course of this overview is that we have very little empirical economics work looking at what makes certain cooperatives more successful than others with the same structure.

The recent empirical literature has focused, correctly, on establishing comparative results that systematically put the cooperatives in the context of all other firms, and a lot more of this type of research remains to be done, as large representative data sets have only recently become available. For example, worker cooperatives may need to be compared with more specific segments of the firm population and other types of cooperatives. However, now that a lot of the groundwork has been done, we also need to compare worker cooperatives among themselves again, to look at those cooperative-specific features and to investigate those differences that may tell us more about the way forward. We need to know how cooperative specificities relate to success. One area about which we know little as yet is that of cooperative expansion, subsidiaries, and external growth. A lot has been happening in this area, which has raised important issues, for example, in Mondragon when the membership decided to bring into the cooperative fold noncooperative subsidiaries that had been acquired by external growth. Cooperative expansion, whether by creating new firms or subsidiaries or by external growth, has long been identified as an issue that is potentially more difficult and more important to tackle than cooperative survival (Pérotin, 2006). In this respect, numbers alone should make it clear that the Italian case has a lot to teach to other countries. Comparative research investigating different types of growth and examining the role of specialized support structures like the Italian *consorzi* may help us find out in particular whether cooperative specificities can help to handle this challenge.

References

Addison, John T. (2005). "The Determinants of Firm Performance: Unions, Works Councils and Employee Involvement/High-Performance Work Practices," *Scottish Journal of Political Economy*, 52(3): 406–50.

Alzola, Izaskun, Saioa Arando, Fathi Fakhfakh, Fred Freundlich, Mónica Gago, Virginie Pérotin, and Alberto Zevi. (2010, July). *Are Labour-Managed Firms All the Same? A Comparison of Incentives for Growth, Democracy and Institutional Sustainability in the Constitutions of Worker Cooperatives in Mondragon, Italy and France*. Paper presented at the 15th World Congress of the International Association for the Economics of Participation, Paris.

Bartlett, Will. (1994). "Employment in Small Firms: Are Cooperatives Different? Evidence from Southern Europe," in J. Atkinson and D. Storey (eds.), *Employment: The Small Firm and the Labour Market* (New York: Routledge), pp. 256–87.

Bartlett, Will, John Cable, Saul Estrin, Derek C. Jones, and Stephen C. Smith. (1992). "Labor-Managed and Private Firms in North Central Italy: An Empirical Comparison," *Industrial and Labor Relations Review*, 46(1): 103–18.

Bayo Moriones, José Alberto, Pedro Javier Galilea Salvatierra, and Javier Merino Díaz de Cerio. (2003). "Participation, Cooperatives and Performance: An Analysis of Spanish Manufacturing Firms," in Takao Kato and Jeff Pliskin (eds.), *Advances in the Economic Analysis of Participatory and Labor-Managed Firms. Vol. 7*, The Determinants of the Incidence and the Effects of Participatory Organizations (Oxford: Elsevier Science), pp. 31–56.

Ben-Ner, Avner. (1988). "Comparative Empirical Observations on Worker-Owned and Capitalist Firms," *International Journal of Industrial Organization*, 6: 7–31.

Ben-Ner, Avner. (1984). "On the Stability of the Cooperative Form of Organization," *Journal of Comparative Economics*, 8(3): 247–60.

Ben-Ner, Avner, and Derek C. Jones. (1995). "Employee Participation, Ownership and Productivity: A New Theoretical Framework," *Industrial Relations*, 34(4): 532–54.

Berman, Katrina V. (1982). "The United States of America: A Co-operative Model for Worker Management," in F. Stephen (ed.), *The Performance of Labour-Managed Firms* (London: Macmillan), pp. 74–98.

Berman, Katrina V., and Matthew D. Berman. (1989). "An Empirical Test of the Theory of the Labor-Managed Firm," *Journal of Comparative Economics*, 13: 281–300.

Blinder, Alan S. (ed.). (1990). *Paying for Productivity* (Washington, DC: The Brookings Institution).

Bonin, John, Derek C. Jones, and Louis Putterman. (1993). "Theoretical and Empirical Studies of Producer Cooperatives: Will Ever the Twain Meet?" *Journal of Economic Literature*, 31: 1290–320.

Bonin, John, and Louis Putterman. (1987). *Economics of Cooperatives and the Labor-Managed Economy* (New York: Harwood).

Burdín, Gabriel. (2010). *Survivability of Worker Cooperatives Compared with Capitalist Firms and Its Determinants: Evidence from Uruguay*. Paper presented at the 15th World Congress of the International Association for the Economics of Participation, Paris.

Burdín, Gabriel, and Andrés Dean. (2010). *Revisiting the Objectives of Worker Cooperatives: An Empirical Assessment*. Paper presented at the 15th World Congress of the International Association for the Economics of Participation, Paris.

Burdín, Gabriel, and Andrés Dean. (2009). "New Evidence on Wages and Employment in Worker Cooperatives Compared with Capitalist Firms." *Journal of Comparative Economics*, 37: 517–33.

Centrostudi Legacoop. (2009). *Aspetti quantitativi e qualitativi della cooperazione italiana* (Milan, Italy: Geco).

CG-SCOP. (2003). *Guide juridique des SCOP* (Paris: Scop Edit).

Conte, Michael A. (1982). "Participation and Performance in US Labour-Managed Firms," in F. Stephen (ed.), *The Performance of Labour-Managed Firms* (London: Macmillan), pp. 213–38.

Conte, Michael A., and Meng-Hua Ye. (1995). "An Overlapping Generations Model of Investment in Labor-Managed Firms," *Advances in the Economic Analysis of Participatory and Labor-Managed Firms*, 5: 159–73.

Conte, Michael A., and Jan Svejnar. (1990). "The Performance Effect of Employee Ownership Plans," in A. S. Blinder (ed.), *Paying for Productivity: A Look at the Evidence* (Washington, DC: Brookings Institution Press), pp. 143–72.

Craig, Ben, and John Pencavel. (1995). "Participation and Productivity: A Comparison of Worker Cooperatives and Conventional Firms in the Plywood Industry," *Brookings Papers: Microeconomics*, 121–74.

Craig, Ben, and John Pencavel. (1993). "The Objectives of Worker Cooperatives," *Journal of Comparative Economics*, 17: 288–308.

Craig, Ben, and John Pencavel. (1992). "The Behavior of Worker Cooperatives: The Plywood Companies of the Pacific Northwest," *American Economic Review*, 82(5): 1083–1105.

Defourny, Jacques, Saul Estrin, and Derek C Jones. (1985). "The Effects of Workers' Participation on Enterprise Performance: Empirical Evidence from French Cooperatives," *International Journal of Industrial Organization*, 3: 197–217.

Doucouliagos, Chris. (1995). "Worker Participation and Productivity in Labor-Managed and Participatory Capitalist Firms: A Meta-Analysis," *Industrial and Labor Relations Review*, 49(1): 58–78.

Dow, Gregory K. (2003). *Governing the Firm: Workers' Control in Theory and Practice* (Cambridge, UK: Cambridge University Press).

Earle, John S., and Saul Estrin. (1998). "Workers' Self-Management in Transition Economies," in Will Bartlett and Milica Uvalić (eds.), *Advances in the Economic Analysis of Participatory and Labor-Managed Firms*, 6: 3–28.

Estrin, Saul. (1991). "Some Reflections on Self-Management, Social Choice, and Reform in Eastern Europe," *Journal of Comparative Economics*, 15: 349–66.

Estrin, Saul, Jan Hanousek, Evžen Kočenda, and Jan Svejnar. (2009). "The Effects of Privatization and Ownership in Transition Economies," *Journal of Economic Literature*, 47(3): 699–728.

Estrin, Saul, and Derek C. Jones. (1998). "The Determinants of Investment in Employee-Owned Firms: Evidence from France," *Economic Analysis*, 1(1): 17–28.

Estrin, Saul, and Derek C. Jones. (1995). "Workers' Participation, Employee Ownership and Productivity: Results from French Producer Cooperatives," in Derek C. Jones and Jan Svejnar (eds.), *Advances in the Economic Analysis of Participatory and Labor-Managed Firms*, 5: 3–24.

Estrin, Saul, and Derek C. Jones. (1992). "The Viability of Employee-Owned Firms: Evidence from France," *Industrial and Labor Relations Review*, 45(2): 323–38.

Estrin, Saul, Derek C. Jones, and Jan Svejnar. (1987). "The Productivity Effects of Worker Participation: Producer Cooperatives in Western Economies," *Journal of Comparative Economics*, 11(1): 40–61.

Fakhfakh, Fathi, Virginie Pérotin, and Mónica Gago. (2012). "Productivity, Capital and Labor in Labor-Managed and Conventional Firms," *Industrial and Labor Relations Review*, forthcoming.

FitzRoy, Felix, and Kornelius Kraft. (1987). "Cooperation, Productivity and Profit Sharing," *Quarterly Journal of Economics*, 102(1): 23–35.

Frey, Bruno S., and Reto Jegen. (2005). "Motivation Crowding Theory," *Journal of Economic Surveys*, 15(5): 589–611.

Furubotn, Eirek G., and Svetozar Pejovich. (1970). "Property Rights and the Behaviour of the Firm in a Socialist State: The Example of Yugoslavia," *Zeitschrift für Nationalökonomie*, 30(3–4): 431–54.

Gago, Mónica, Virginie Pérotin, and Fathi Fakhfakh. (2008). "*Is the Investment Decision Different in Cooperatives?*" Paper presented at the 14th IAFEP World Congress, Clinton, New York.

Jensen, Michael, and William Meckling. (1976). "Theory of the Firm: Managerial Behavior, Agency Costs and Ownership Structure," *Journal of Financial Economics*, 3: 305–60.

Jones, Derek C. (2007). "The Productive Efficiency of Italian Producer Cooperatives: Evidence from Conventional and Cooperative Firms," in Sonja Novkovic and Vania Sena (eds.), *Advances in the Economic Analysis of Participatory and Labor-Managed Firms*. Vol. 9, Cooperative Firms in Global Markets: Incidence, Viability and Economic Performance (Bingley, UK: Emerald), pp. 3–28.

Jones, Derek C. (2004). "Ownership and Participation: A Review of Empirical Evidence for Transition Economies," in Virginie Pérotin and Andrew Robinson (eds.), *Advances in the Economic Analysis of Participatory and Labor-Managed Firms*. Vol. 8, Employee Participation, Firm Performance and Survival (Bingley, UK: Emerald), pp. 171–209.

Jones, Derek C. (1982). "British Producer Cooperatives, 1948–1968: Productivity and Organizational Structure," in D. C. Jones and J. Svejnar (eds.), *Participatory and Self-Managed Firms* (Lexington, MA: Lexington Books), pp. 175–98.

Jones, Derek C. (1982). "The United States of America: A Survey of Producer Co-operative Performance," in F. Stephen (ed.), *The Performance of Labour-Managed Firms* (London: Macmillan), pp. 53–73.

Kalmi, Panu. (2004). "Exclusion from Employee Ownership: Evidence from Estonian Case Studies," in Virginie Pérotin and Andrew Robinson (eds.), *Advances in the Economic Analysis of Participatory and Labor-Managed Firms*. Vol. 8, Employee Participation, Firm Performance and Survival (Bingley, UK: Emerald), pp. 35–65.

Kruse, Douglas, and Joseph Blasi. (1997). "Employee Ownership, Employee Attitudes, and Firm Performance: A Review of the Evidence," in Daniel J. B. Mitchell, David Lewin, and Mahmood Zaidi (eds.), *Handbook of Human Resource Management* (Greenwich, CT: JAI Press), pp. 113–51.

Kruse, Douglas, Richard Freeman, Joseph Blasi, Robert Buchele, Adria Scharf, Loren Rodgers, and Chris Mackin. (2004). "Motivating Employee Owners in ESOP Firms: Human Resource Policies and Company Performance," in Virginie Pérotin and Andrew Robinson (eds.), *Advances in the Economic Analysis of Participatory and Labor-Managed Firms*. Vol. 8, Employee Participation, Firm Performance and Survival (New York: Elsevier), pp. 101–28.

Maietta, Ornella Wanda, and Vania Sena. (2004). "Profit Sharing, Technical Efficiency Change and Finance Constraints," in Virginie Pérotin and Andrew Robinson (eds.), *Advances in the Economic Analysis of Participatory and Labor-Managed Firms*. Vol. 8, Employee Participation, Firm Performance and Survival (Bingley, UK: Emerald), pp. 149–67.

Megginson, W., and J. M. Netter. (2002). "From State to Market: A Survey of Empirical Studies on Privatization," *Journal of Economic Literature*, 39: 321–89.

Miyazaki, Hajime. (1984). "On Success and Dissolution of the Labor-Managed Firm in the Capitalist Economy," *Journal of Political Economy*, 94(5): 909–31.

Navarra, Cecilia. (2009). *Collective Accumulation of Capital in Italian Worker Cooperatives between Employment Insurance and "We-Rationality": An Empirical Investigation*. EURICSE Working Paper.

Pencavel, John. (2012). "Worker Cooperatives and Democratic Governance," forthcoming in Grandori (ed.), *Handbook of Economic Organization* (Aldershot: Edward Elgar).

Pencavel, John. (2001). *Worker Participation: Lessons from the Worker Co-ops of the Pacific Northwest* (New York: Russell Sage Foundation).

Pencavel, John, Luigi Pistaferri, and Fabiano Schivardi. (2006). "Wages, Employment and Capital in Capitalist and Worker-Owned Firms," *Industrial and Labor Relations Review*, 60(1): 23–44.

Pérotin, Virginie. (2006). "Entry, Exit and the Business Cycle: Are Cooperatives Different?" *Journal of Comparative Economics*, 34: 295–316.

Pérotin, Virginie. (2004). "Early Cooperative Survival: The Liability of Adolescence," in Virginie Pérotin and Andrew Robinson (eds.), *Advances in the Economic Analysis of Participatory and Labor-Managed Firms*. Vol. 8, Employee Participation, Firm Performance and Survival (Bingley, UK: Emerald), pp. 67–86.

Putterman, Louis. (1984). "On Some Recent Explanations of Why Capital Hires Labor," *Economic Inquiry*, 22: 171–87.

Robinson, Andrew, and Nick Wilson. (1993). "Co-operatives vs. Private Firms: An Empirical Comparison of Co-operatives and Private Small Firms in Britain," *International Business Review*, 2(3): 281–96.

Ros, Agustin J. (2003). "Do ESOPs Motivate Employees? Worker Effort, Monitoring and Participation in Employee Stock Ownership Plans," in Takao Kato and Jeffrey Pliskin (eds.), *Advances in the Economic Analysis of Participatory and Labor-Managed Firms*. Vol. 7, The Determinants of the Incidence and the Effects of Participatory Organizations (Bingley, UK: Emerald), pp. 83–103.

Russell, Raymond. (1995). *Utopia in Zion: The Israeli Experience with Worker Cooperatives* (Albany, NY: State University of New York Press).

Russell, Raymond, and Robert Hanneman. (1995). "The Formation and Dissolution of Worker Cooperatives in Israel, 1924–1992," in Raymond Russell, *Utopia in Zion: The Israeli Experience with Worker Cooperatives* (Albany, NY: State University of New York Press), pp. 57–95.

Staber, Udo. (1993). "Worker Cooperatives and the Business Cycle: Are Cooperatives the Answer to Unemployment?" *American Journal of Economics and Sociology*, 52(2): 129–43.

Staber, Udo. (1989). "Age-Dependence and Historical Effects on the Failure Rates of Worker Cooperatives: An Event-History Analysis," *Economic and Industrial Democracy*, 10: 59–80.

Stephen, Frank. (1982). "The Economic Theory of the Labour-Managed Firm," in F. Stephen (ed.), *The Performance of Labour-Managed Firms* (London: Macmillan), pp. 3–26.

Uvalić, Milica. (1992). *Investment and Property Rights in Yugoslavia* (Cambridge, UK: Cambridge University Press).

Vanek, Jaroslav. (1977). *The Labor-Managed Economy* (Ithaca, NY: Cornell University Press).

Zevi, Alberto. (2005). "Il finanziamento delle cooperative," in E. Mazzoli and S. Zamagni, *Verso una nuova toria della cooperazione* (Bologna, Italy: Il Mulino), pp. 293–332.

Zevi, Alberto. (1982). "The Performance of Italian Producer Cooperatives," in D. C. Jones and J. Svejnar (eds.), *Participatory and Self-Managed Firms* (Lexington, MA: Lexington Books), pp. 239–51.

CHAPTER 9

Organization: Top Down or Bottom Up? The Organizational Development of Consumer Cooperatives, 1950–2000

Espen Ekberg

Cooperative enterprises are commonly regarded as a distinct form of economic enterprise.[1] They are equally defined and are generally recognized by their adherence to a common set of officially stated cooperative values and principles.[2] Despite these defining characteristics, co-ops vary substantially in terms of how they actually organize their business operations. This variation is not only caused by the fact that co-ops operate within very different sectors of the economy – from banking and insurance to farming, fisheries, housing, different types of services industries, and retailing. Substantial variations also exist within different cooperative subgroups. Moreover, these variations, I will argue, have become gradually more pronounced during the second half of the twentieth century. An obvious yet underexplored question is why and how this development has come about. This chapter investigates this issue through a study of the organizational development of consumer cooperative enterprises in Western Europe in the period from 1950 to the turn of the millennium.

After their emergence in the mid-nineteenth century, most consumer cooperative enterprises became organized on a federal basis. Small, local co-ops were the operating units while national associations were set up to serve various common functions. Compared with the hierarchical structures of the modern business enterprise, the governance structure of these federal organizations was "inverted"; the local co-ops operated as the "parent companies," owning and controlling the central organizations, which then became the "daughter companies." Put differently, the cooperative enterprises were governed from the bottom up. The economic development of these organizations was generally quite positive. Although local failures were common, by the interwar years, the cooperative form of enterprise had advanced markedly in

[1] Parts of this paper draw extensively on my unpublished Ph.D thesis, Espen Ekberg, "Consumer Co-operatives and the Transformation of Modern Food Retailing: A Comparative Study of the Norwegian and British Consumer Co-operatives 1950–2002" (Det humanistiske fakultet, Universitetet i Oslo, 2008).

[2] As spelled out in International Co-operative Alliance, *Statement on the Co-operative Identity*, www.ica.coop/coop/principles-revisions.html.

many markets and penetrated large regions of the world (see especially Chapters 1 and 2 in this book).

Gradually, however, and with increasing pace from the 1950s and 1960s onward, the common organizational pattern characterizing most consumer co-ops started to splinter. Faced with increasing competitive pressure from large, centralized, and integrated retail chains, many co-ops saw the need to reform the structure of their organizations. From a situation where co-ops had been organized along fairly similar lines, a myriad of organizational forms developed (see also Chapters 3 and 4 in this book). Parallel to these developments, the economic fortunes of the consumer co-ops started seriously to diverge. Many co-ops started to experience substantial economic difficulties. Entire cooperative movements simply collapsed or became radically marginalized. In other countries and in other markets, however, consumer cooperative businesses continued to thrive.

The aim of this chapter is to investigate why and how this divergent organizational development unfolded and to briefly discuss how it may have affected the divergent economic development of the consumer co-ops. The chapter is organized in four main parts. First, I discuss how and why the federal model favored by most national consumer cooperative organizations came under increasing pressure from the 1950s onward. I show how one specific factor, namely, the increasing growth of multiple retailers, directly or indirectly caused a general drive within consumer cooperatives to reform how their business operations were organized. In the second part, I analyze how the common challenge represented by the advance of the multiple retailer was met with a variety of strategic responses by the consumer cooperatives. I identify three overall strategies, leading to three distinct organizational models: a "federal," a "nonfederal," and a "hybrid" model. In the third section, I discuss briefly how these divergent organizational approaches may have affected the parallel, divergent economic development of different consumer cooperatives. The aim here is not to provide a comprehensive answer to why Western European consumer co-ops developed so differently during the postwar years, but simply to discuss the possible role played by the choice of organizational models in the developments taking place. The final part of the chapter provides conclusions and discusses possible avenues for further research.

CONSUMER COOPERATIVES AND THE MULTIPLE RETAILERS

Together with agricultural and financial cooperatives, consumer cooperatives make up the backbone of the international cooperative movement.[3] In their

---

[3] In a listing of the 300 largest cooperative enterprises (in terms of turnover and total assets), developed by the International Co-operative Alliance, 40 percent were various financial cooperatives (insurance, banking, diversified financial and credit unions), 33 percent were agricultural cooperatives, while 25 percent were wholesale and retail cooperatives, see Garry Cronan, "The Global 300 Project – Measuring Cooperative Performance and Difference," *Review of International Co-operation*, 100, no. 1 (2007). It needs to be emphasized that a substantial portion

original form, consumer cooperatives were established to secure the interest of the consumers in the retail market, and they did so primarily by opening retail stores owned and controlled by the consumers as members.[4] As these organizations developed their strength locally, national secondary cooperatives were established to take care of common functions. Of these common functions, wholesaling was the most important. Hence, British retail societies established a common wholesale business, the Co-operative Wholesale Society (CWS), in 1863. Five years later a similar organization was set up in Scotland, the Scottish Co-operative Wholesale Society (SCWS). By 1911 federal models had been developed in all major European consumer cooperatives.[5] The majority of these federal organizations also developed a substantial manufacturing business, and in some countries they took on educational and ideological functions as well. Hence, when the NKL, a Norwegian cooperative federation, was formed in 1906, it was consigned to establishing a "close connection between educational work and commercial activities."[6] In other countries, commercial and ideological functions were organizationally separated. In Britain, a separate Co-operative Union was formed in 1869 as a second national federation, owned by both English and Scottish retail societies.[7]

The federal model turned out to be a successful recipe for most consumer cooperative enterprises. Across Western Europe, consumer co-ops gradually managed to gain substantial market share in their respective home markets. By the interwar years, co-ops were firmly established as an important alternative to the dominant forms of private food retailing. A major advantage held by the co-ops was their ability – through the federal structure – to combine local control and local market knowledge with national wholesaling, procurement, marketing, and even, to some extent, national production. In an industry still largely

---

of this share is made up of so-called retailer cooperatives. *Retailer cooperatives* are co-ops owned by regular retailers, and not by consumers, and hence are distinctly different from the consumer cooperative movement. Typical examples include Conad (Italy), Edeka (Germany), and E.Leclerc (France).

[4] As already indicated, the chapter focuses exclusively on consumer co-ops. It should be noted, however, that in common usage the term *retail cooperative* (not to be confused with retailer cooperative, see footnote 3) is often used interchangeably with *consumer cooperative*. For the purpose of variation, I apply both types of expressions throughout the paper.

[5] Johann Brazda and Robert Schediwy (eds.), *Consumer Cooperatives in a Changing World*, Vols. 1 and 2 (Geneva: International Co-operative Alliance, 1989); Niels Finn Christensen, "Between Farmers and Workers: Consumer Cooperation in Denmark, 1850–1940," in Ellen Furlough and Carl Strikwerda (eds.), *Consumers against Capitalism? Consumer Cooperation in Europe, North America and Japan, 1840–1990* (Lanham, MD: Rowman & Littlefield, 1999).

[6] Cited in Even Lange, et al., *Organisert kjØpekraft. Forbrukesamvirkets historie i Norge* (Oslo: Pax, 2006), p. 91. This combination of commercial and ideological functions was typical also of the Danish, Swedish, and Finnish national associations (Fællesforeningen for Danmarks Brugsforeninger [FDB], Kooperativa Förbundet [KF], and Suomen Osuuskauppojen Keskuskunta [SOK]), all formed around 1900.

[7] Desmond Flanagan, *A Centenary Story of the Co-operative Union of Great Britain and Ireland* (Manchester: Co-operative Union, 1969). Two-tired federal structures were also originally operated in Germany, France, Austria, Italy, and the Netherlands.

dominated by small, independent retailers, these scale advantages obviously provided the co-ops with a strong competitive edge.

Gradually, however, and with intensified strength from the 1950s onward, the cooperative market position came under attack. After almost one hundred years of more or less unbroken expansion, an increasing number of cooperatives had to accept substantial losses in market share and a gradual decline in membership. One of the major reasons was the intensified growth of an alternative form of retail organization, the multiple retailer, or the private retail chain.[8] By definition, the multiples (usually called chain stores in the United States) were retail enterprises operating ten or more branches under centralized control.[9] Often they held several hundred branches under centralized governance, and they operated them on a standardized basis. In order to reap the full potential for scale economies in buying, and to better coordinate the flow of goods into the large number of shops operated, they also integrated backward into wholesaling (and, in some instances, into production as well). Operating consistently on these three basic principles – centralization of control, standardization of operational procedures, and integration of the distribution function – the multiple chains soon gained a clear competitive advantage against the co-ops. Most importantly, the chains managed to handle huge volumes of trade at reduced costs, making way for dramatically increased efficiency and productivity of operations. In truth, the advance of these retailers did not proceed at an even pace across Western Europe. While multiples controlled about a fifth of the British retail trade in 1960, and about 10 percent of the market in Switzerland and the Netherlands, in countries such as Austria, Italy, Norway, and Finland the multiple share was still diminutive.[10] Gradually, however, the retail chains started to make their presence felt in these countries too.

Clearly, many of the organizational principles applied by the multiples from the 1950s onward already had been applied by the co-ops. Generally, however, the co-ops had not managed to reap the benefits of centralization, standardization, and integration to the same extent as the multiples now did. The reasons for this were many. First, although the various national cooperative

---

[8] The reasons were, of course, many and complex. One of the most visible changes in the postwar retail industry that fundamentally challenged the market position of the co-ops was the growth of supermarket and hypermarket retailing. A second challenge came from the increasing affluence and decreasing popular involvement of the postwar consumer, a trend directly challenging traditional virtues of the cooperative alternative. Since the main purpose of this chapter is to understand the divergent organizational pattern developing among consumer co-ops during the postwar era, I focus here on the organizational challenges presented by the rise of the multiples. A broader analysis is provided in Ekberg, "Consumer Co-operatives and the Transformation of Modern Food Retailing: A Comparative Study of the Norwegian and British Consumer Co-operatives 1950–2002."

[9] James B. Jefferys, *Retail Trading in Britain 1850–1950: A Study of Trends in Retailing with Special Reference to the Development of Co-operative, Multiple Shop and Department Store Method of Trading* (Cambridge: Cambridge University Press, Economic and Social Studies, 1954).

[10] James B. Jefferys and Derek Knee, *Retailing in Europe: Present Structure and Future Trends* (London: Macmillan, 1962), p. 65.

movements taken together indeed operated on a large scale, the organizational structure of the co-op remained grounded in the decentralized, small-scale, and fully independent cooperative societies. The structure of the co-ops thus remained genuinely a decentralized structure, governed in full from the bottom up. Second, despite the establishment of large, national wholesaling organizations, the level of integration between these federal wholesaling societies and the retail societies remained limited. The retail societies and the wholesale societies remained separate organizational units. The societies traded with their wholesalers on similar lines as they traded with other wholesalers, delivering their orders independently and stocking an uncoordinated variety of different products. Hence, while the retail and the wholesale units were integrated through ownership, they were not integrated operationally. Third and finally, even if all societies were part of the wider cooperative movement, the retail operations were controlled locally, and the level of standardization across society boundaries remained limited. Indeed, some standardization had been introduced, and, as Jefferys remarked in the British case, "multiple shop techniques of controlling the activities of these branches" were increasingly applied.[11] But the overall picture of the Western European co-ops was one of fragmentation, where local retail societies governed their local trading units according to their particular principles and traditions.

Compared with the multiples, the level of standardization, centralization, and integration was, therefore, much lower within the co-op movement. This was a situation increasingly recognized by cooperative leaders throughout the 1950s and 1960s. The 1960 International Co-operative Alliance (ICA) congress in Lausanne was fully devoted to the question of structural reform, and within most national movements, the need for the retail societies to join forces in larger trading units was widely recognized – and debated. In the U.K., where the multiples had made substantial progress since the interwar years, the co-ops set up an independent inquiry commission in 1955, with the "responsibility of surveying the whole field of cooperative production and marketing, both wholesale and retail."[12] The increasing competitive threat from the multiples was the main motive. As noted in the stenographic report from the congress appointing the commission:

this congress notes the changing pattern in retail distribution in Great Britain with the continued growth of large scale retailing under national control, and ... agrees in principle that more decisive action is necessary if progress is to be made towards securing the outmost advantage from co-operative productive resources.[13]

[11] Jefferys, *Retail Trading in Britain 1850–1950: A Study of Trends in Retailing with Special Reference to the Development of Co-operative, Multiple Shop and Department Store Method of Trading*, p. 54.
[12] Co-operative Union, *Report of the 86th Annual Co-operative Congress in the Usher Hall Edinburgh May 30th, 31st, June 1st and 2nd, 1955* (Manchester: Co-operative Union, 1955), p. 331. See also Friberg et al., in this volume.
[13] Ibid.

Along similar lines, in Germany, the 1963 congress of the *Zentralverband Deutscher Konsumgenossenschaften* established a separate Reform Commission to sketch out a new organizational structure for the consumer cooperative movement. Again, the increasing competitive threat from the multiples seems to have been the main motive. Even if the German co-ops in the period from 1950 to the beginning of the sixties had increased their market shares in the grocery segment from 6 to roughly 9 percent, the expansion of the multiples had been much more pronounced. Although these retailers, like the co-op, controlled 6 percent of the market in 1950, their share had surpassed 18 percent by 1964. By this point the cooperative share was on a clear downward trend, having peaked in 1957, while the multiple share was steadily increasing.[14] According to the president of the British Society for Co-operative Studies, W. P. Watkins, reporting in retrospect on the German development in the *Society for Co-operative Studies Bulletin*, the Germans at this point considered it "imperative to readjust relations between the primary societies and the central federations, notably by rationalizing overlapping functions such as warehousing, and vesting in the central bodies certain overriding powers in the formulation and application of policy."[15]

Fear of the superiority of the multiple form of retailing also was pushing forward reform in countries where this type of retailing had made only limited headway. As Patricia Battilani has shown, the multiple form of retailing had hardly made any inroads whatsoever in the Italian retail market by the 1960s. Nevertheless, the rise of the multiples in other countries indirectly pushed forward organizational reform within the Italian movement as well. When the Italians, from the 1960s onward, started on a process of radical modernization of their retail stores and their overall organizational structure, it was, as argued by Battillani, "dictated by the fear that entry of large size Italian industrial companies and foreign capitals into the retail sector would have rendered traditional retail shops marginal within a few years and endangered the presences of the consumer cooperatives." As she further states, the organizational models on which the modernization process rested were directly "inspired ... from western European firms."[16]

A somewhat similar story may be told in the Norwegian case. Multiple retailers were practically nonexistent in the early 1960s. Despite this, the consumer co-ops had already started on a process of substantial modernization of their organizational structure. In contrast to the Italian case, the major source of inspiration for the Norwegians came not from European but from U.S.

---

[14] All figures from Johann Brazda (ed.), *The Consumer Co-operatives in Germany*. Vol. 1, *Consumer Cooperatives in a Changing World* (Geneva: International Co-operative Alliance, 1989), p. 183.

[15] W.P. Watkins, "Consumers' Cooperation in the Federal German Republic – The Latest Phase," *Society for Cooperative Studies Bulletin*, 27 (1976), p. 24.

[16] Patrizia Battilani, "How to Beat Competition without Losing Cooperative Identity: The Case of Italian Consumer Cooperatives," in ACTA of the International Congress (ed.), *Consumerism versus Capitalism? Cooperatives Seen from an International Comparative Perspective* (Gent: Amsab Institute of Social History, 2005), p. 118.

enterprises, and particularly the independent chain store model practiced by many American retail firms. Leading representatives of the Norwegian movement made numerous trips to the United States at the end of the 1940s and the beginning of the 1950s to study American retailing practices. These trips were part of a broader trend of European retailers traveling to the United States to learn more about the American way of organizing and managing retail operations.[17] Although many European visitors studying American retailing were impressed by the dissemination of the self-service system and the size of the retail stores, the reports written by the NKL management were largely focused on how the American system of distribution serving the stores was organized. In a series of articles in the internal magazine *Forbrukeren (The Consumer)*, leading NKL manager Knut Moe argued that the important thing to be learned from the American retail industry was not the particularities of how the individual stores or warehouses were operated and run, but rather how the different links in the chain of distribution were treated as an integrated system.[18] On this basis, a series of groundbreaking organizational reforms were implemented by the Norwegian cooperators from the early 1950s onward.

By the early 1960s, awareness gradually spread among cooperators across Western Europe that the structure of their movement was inadequate to meet the future challenges of multiple retailing. Although scale economies and integrated distribution had been obtained in some areas and by some societies, the core organizational feature of the movement was still its numerous, small, independent retail societies operating one or a few branches. The massive growth of the multiples, either directly or indirectly, caused an increasing questioning of the adequacy of the decentralized federal structure on which the consumer cooperatives rested. The question became not whether changes had to be made, but rather how the co-ops could best adapt. As it turned out, the responses, despite being reactions to a similar threat, varied greatly between different national consumer cooperative movements. The next section looks into these divergent responses in more detail.

SIMILAR CHALLENGE – DIVERGENT OUTCOMES: THE
CONSUMER COOPERATIVES' RESPONSE TO THE CHALLENGE
FROM THE MULTIPLES

How did Western European consumer cooperatives respond to the enforced growth of the multiple retailers? The short answer is: quite differently. As we

---

[17] See, e.g., Harm G. Schröter, "The Americanisation of Distribution and Its Limits: The Case of the German Retail System, 1950–1975," *European Review of History: Revue europeenne d'histoire*, 15, no. 4 (2008); Matthias Kipping and Ove Bjarnar, *The Americanisation of European Business: The Marshall Plan and the Transfer of U.S. Management Models* (New York: Routledge, 1998).

[18] Knut Moe, "Strømlinjeformet vareomsetning. Artikkel 1. Amerikansk engroshandel i matvarebransjen," *Forbrukeren*, 10, no. 4 (1955); "Strømlinjeformet vareomsetning. Artikkel 2. Amerikansk engroshandel i matvarebransjen," *Forbrukeren*, 10, no. 5/6 (1955).

have just seen, most co-ops either directly or indirectly realized the need to radically reform the way their business operations were organized. The ultimate result of the reorganization processes varied, however, between different national consumer co-ops. Some co-ops focused primarily on merging small, local societies into larger regional units and integrating and standardizing operations through different forms of contracting. A second overall strategy was to combine mergers of independent retail societies with the development of a standardized and integrated retailing business under the centralized control of the national federal organizations, typically the national wholesale federation. Finally, a third approach consisted of merging all independent societies, as well as the national federal organizations, into one fully centralized, integrated, and standardized national cooperative enterprise.

THE NONFEDERAL MODEL

The most radical approach taken to face the competitive threat from the multiples was to merge all independent consumer cooperative societies, and their national federals, into one organizational unit. In such instances, the federal structure was abandoned altogether and replaced by a fully centralized, integrated, and standardized national enterprise. The result was what may be termed a "nonfederal model."

In most instances, such a solution was the result of immediate and grave economic difficulties. A prominent example is the consumer cooperatives in Austria. On June 22, 1978, the large majority of Austrian retail societies, their national federals, and all subsidiaries and production enterprises merged to form Konsum Austria as a single, national cooperative enterprise. The new enterprise comprised 96 percent of total cooperative sales as well as all cooperative wholesaling and production. It is evident that the final decision to establish Konsum Austria was motivated by substantial economic difficulties. As reported in retrospect by the Austrian cooperative researcher Robert Schediwy in a 1996 article in the *Review of International Co-operation*, "the solution of mergers on a grand scale forming the giant 'Konsum Austria' had to be envisaged, if one did not want to run the risk of sizeable regional bankruptcies which would have been highly detrimental to the whole movement."[19]

A similar story may be told of the neighboring German movement. In 1981, a majority of the German retail societies had become part of the Coop AG. The reasons for the merger were largely the same as those pushing forward the Austrian merger. The market position of the German co-ops had declined steadily since the late 1950s. The co-ops, it seemed, simply could not compete with the expanding multiples. Although multiple stores and co-ops held approximately the same share of the grocery retail market in 1950, fifteen years later the

---

[19] Robert Schediwy, "The Decline and Fall of Konsum Austria," *Review of International Co-operation*, 89, no. 2 (1996).

multiple share was more than twice as large as that of the co-ops.[20] Several attempts were made throughout the 1960s to reform the structure of the co-ops, but they largely failed to bring an end to the ongoing process of absolute and relative market decline. Moreover, the majority of retail co-ops, as well as the federal wholesaler GEG, were increasingly running huge losses. In 1973–4 alone, accumulated losses within the retail co-ops amounted to almost 90 million deutsche marks, while total losses at the national federals were 100 million. In addition, the retail societies owed 600 million marks in debt.[21] On these grounds, it soon became clear that more drastic measures were necessary to save the consumer co-ops from total collapse. Gradually, a total merger of all consumer cooperatives and their national federals was envisaged and carried through, and the Coop AG was formed. Motivated by the prospect of being able to amass new and much needed capital, the Germans also decided to abandon the cooperative organizational form, turning the merged organization into a limited liability company.[22]

THE HYBRID MODEL

A second, less drastic approach taken by Western European consumer co-ops to fight off the increasing competitive threat from the multiple retailers was to combine an amalgamation of societies into larger units with the establishment of commercial operations under the centralized control of the national wholesaler. In co-ops opting for this approach, the federal model was sustained, but the operations of the retail societies were supplemented with a fully integrated national retail/wholesale enterprise operating alongside the federal structure. This "hybrid model" was often the result in countries where the leading management of the national federals ideally would want to create a fully integrated unit, but where opposition from local and regional societies instead caused the development of compromise solutions.

A typical example of such a development can be found in the case of the U.K. co-ops. The prospects of creating a single national society – a Co-op Great Britain – had been a persistent feature of the structural debates in the British cooperative movement since the chief secretary of the cooperative union, J. C. Grace, in 1906 launched the idea of amalgamating all independent retail societies into one national society. The idea was later repeated on several occasions, but it failed to receive the necessary support from the retail societies. Instead, centralization was achieved through a gradual reduction in the number of

---

[20] Figures from Brazda, *The Consumer Co-operatives in Germany*, p. 183.

[21] Figures from ibid., pp. 200–3.

[22] It should be noted that not all German consumer co-ops joined the Co-op Zentrale. Most prominently, the Dortmund-Kassel Co-op – Germany's biggest consumer cooperative at the time of the merger – stayed out. The same was true for Co-op Schleswig-Holstein and the co-op Nordbayern Genossenschaft, both large societies with turnover in the 450 million plus range. Some middle-sized, and also some very small, societies also stayed out of the new national enterprise.

societies. From a starting point in 1960 of 859 independent societies, by 1990 the number had been reduced to seventy-seven. Ten years later, forty-seven cooperative retail units were in operation.

This development toward increased centralization did not break with the overall federal structure on which the movement rested. The centralization process solely concerned the retail level and did not involve any major alterations in the trading relationship between the retail societies and the national wholesalers. As some of the societies became increasingly large, however, they started to integrate backward, strengthening their wholesaling operations by building new warehouses and developing new organizational capabilities in buying and merchandizing. The federal structure, characterized by a clear division of labor between the retailing operations of the retail societies and the wholesaling operations of the national wholesalers, thus became gradually more confused.

Furthermore, increased confusion was caused by the fact that a substantial part of the reduction in the number of retail societies did not come from amalgamations of two or more retail societies into a larger unit. Rather, it came from societies transferring their engagements to their national wholesaler. The first step in this direction was taken with the formation of the Co-operative Retail Society (CRS) in 1934 (originally called CWS Retail Society Limited), a separate retail unit partly owned by the Co-operative Wholesale Society (CWS). The original intention with the establishment of CRS was to use it as a vehicle to expand cooperative trade into areas where such trade was still limited, the so-called cooperative deserts. As it turned out, however, the society primarily grew by taking over ailing retail co-ops. By 1985, a total of 172 retail societies had transferred their engagements to this society. In addition, from the 1970s onward, the CWS also started to develop its own internal retail arm. Growing according to the CRS formula of taking over ailing retail societies, this branch soon became a major contender to the CRS. By 1992 the CWS was not only the movement's prime wholesaler and merchandiser but also had become the largest retailer, controlling close to 27 percent of the movement's retail trade.

By the mid-1990s, the organizational structure of the British consumer cooperative movement had become extremely complex. One large retail society and one large wholesale and production society controlled the majority of cooperative retail trade. The movement operated two separate buying groups. Several regional societies also operated fully independent distribution and wholesaling facilities. The structure remained built partly on the traditional division of labor between local retail societies and national wholesaling and partly on the principle of total centralization, as represented by the CWS retail-wholesale operations. Hence, it was neither a top-down nor a bottom-up structure, but rather a form of hybrid.

This structure was radically reformed when the CWS and CRS merged in 2000 to form the Co-operative Group.[23] Later, three of the largest British

---

[23] See Friberg et al., in the present volume.

regional societies also joined the merger, and by 2009, 85 percent of total consumer cooperative trade in the U.K. was in the hands of the one single society. From the turn of the millennium onward, the British movement developed from a distinctive hybrid structure toward a fully centralized, non-federal model.

In other countries, the hybrid structure proved to be more consistent. In Denmark, the national cooperative union and wholesale association, FDB, integrated forward into retailing by merging with the large Hovedstadens Brugsforening (the Capital's Co-op) in 1973.[24] The merger turned the FDB into a large retailer, alongside its role as manufacturer and wholesaler for the still large number of remaining independent societies. Later it expanded its retailing activities by developing its own retail chains as well as by acquiring existing private chains. By 2010, the FDB controlled about 65 percent of total cooperative retail trade. A similar development was seen in Sweden in 1992, where KF, in cooperation with some selected retail societies, most prominently the Stockholm Cooperative Society, merged to form a common retailing enterprise, the KDAB, controlled by the national association. The merger followed a protracted debate on whether to create Co-op Sweden as a single national society. However, a full merger failed. The new enterprise managed to take control of about half of the total retail trade in the movement, while the remaining share remained in control of independent retail societies.[25] This share has remained stable into the new millennium.

In both Sweden and Denmark, and up until very recently in the U.K., the end result of their postwar structural adjustments was the development of a "hybrid federal model," relying partly on the traditional federal structure and partly on a fully centralized cooperative enterprise operating a substantial portion of the cooperative trade. The evolution of these hybrid structures was largely the result of failed attempts by the federal management to create fully integrated national cooperative societies. Local opposition simply remained too substantial. Many local and regional cooperators were unwilling to dispose of their local decision-making authority. A genuine concern about the democratic consequences of a full merger was also clearly present. This attitude was well expressed by the director of the Lincoln Cooperative Society writing in a 1995 issue of the *Journal of Co-operative Studies*:

Do we want a single, rigid command structure or do we want local management which can take account of local knowledge and cultures? A Single National Society could be reasonably successful in purely financial terms if we could find the right directors and executives and if we could be ruthless enough. But it would quickly become

[24] An overview is provided by Aage Büchert, *Forræderiet mod en god idè* (KØbenhavn: Vindrose, 1992). See also "Starting Signal for Co-op Denmark," *Review of International Co-operation*, 64, no. 4 (1971).

[25] See Friberg et al., in the present volume. See also Hugo Kylebäck, *Federation eller Konsum Sverige? Konsumentkooperativ förändringsprocess Del 3 1985–1995* (Göteborg: Novum Grafiska AB, 1999).

unrecognizable from the other national multiples. The notion of democratic control would disappear along with all our other principles.[26]

The end result of this and similar attitudes was that a full-blown merger of all cooperative trade into one unit became difficult to achieve, and the effort to centralize, standardize, and integrate the federal model on which the cooperative retail operations initially had been based ended in different types of hybrid structures. When the CRS and the CWS finally decided to merge in 2000, and create something close to a Co-op Great Britain, it was, as in the Austrian and German cases, largely a consequence of the severe economic difficulties experienced by the two societies, and especially by the CRS.

THE FEDERAL MODEL

A third solution to the challenge represented by the multiple retailers developed in countries where the co-op movement concentrated on merging small, local societies into larger regional units and on integrating and standardizing operations through different forms of contracting. These contracts secured loyalty from the independent societies toward the national wholesaler and helped standardize cooperative retail operations across the boundaries of the individual societies. At the same time, they secured at least some form of local or regional control over the retail operation. Generally, in cooperative organizations opting for this strategy, the national federals stayed out of retailing and the traditional division of labor between local retail units and national wholesale and manufacturing associations was largely upheld. Overall, the basic federal model on which most co-ops had rested throughout their history remained intact.

A typical example of such an organizational approach can be found in the development of the Norwegian movement. In the immediate postwar years, the Norwegian co-op movement had implemented several changes in how their wholesaling operation was organized. These processes continued throughout the century. Most prominently, after having experienced a dramatic economic crisis during the 1980s, the movement radically reorganized its total system of distribution. But instead of opting for a full merger, as the Swedish and Danish federal management did, the Norwegians remained dedicated to the federal model. Within the course of a few years, the regional warehousing structure of the NKL was "rationalized" and all NKL buying was centralized in the Oslo headquarters. Buying was made the sole responsibility of the national association, while the retail societies focused on their role as retailers. To guide the NKL negotiators, now buying on behalf of the retail societies, a carefully planned standardized assortment was developed.

This model, of course, implied substantial functional centralization, but it did not part with the basic federal structure. Local retail societies continued to own

---

[26] Alan Middleton, "Independence and Unity," *Journal of Co-operative Studies*, no. 83 (1995), p. 17.

and operate their stores. All the major changes had to be accepted by the NKL annual meeting, controlled by the retail societies. Finally, the division of labor between the NKL as the movement's wholesaler and the retail operations of the cooperative societies was upheld.[27] A continuous challenge with the model was to keep the independent retail societies dedicated to the centralized and standardized system. As a means to help sustain the necessary loyalty and discipline, the NKL, in collaboration with the retail societies, developed a comprehensive internal system of contractual arrangements and incentives. This proved vital in ensuring that the federal structure was kept tightly integrated and that all societies adhered to the standardized operational procedures developed. As such, it simply made possible the efficient operation of a fully integrated, standardized, and centralized food chain within the structure of a federal organizational model.

Consumer co-ops in other countries developed similar models. In Finland, the development of the Finnish S-cooperative movement was consistently based on a federal organizational structure. After having been on a more or less continuous decline throughout the 1970s and 1980s, the market position of Finnish consumer cooperative food trade rose remarkably through the 1990s. From a 16 percent share in 1990, the movement garnered more than 31 percent control by 2002. Throughout this process of expansion, the federal structure was kept intact, consisting in 2005 of twenty-two regional cooperatives and nineteen local co-ops, with the SOK as their common wholesaler. The SOK also took on some business operations on its own, but the organization's primary function remained that of a wholesaler, to lead and develop the entire group and to coordinate its operations.[28] Along similar lines, the remarkable postwar expansion of the Italian consumer co-ops took place within a basic federal structure. Or, as Tito Menzani and Vera Zamagni have argued, it evolved within a distinct network structure based, on the one hand, on independent retail co-ops and, on the other hand, on a strong, national wholesale consortium "that on one side provides the product strategy of the retailing cooperatives and on the other side coordinates manufacturing firms."[29] Alongside improved capitalization, this "vertical network" was, according to Menzani and Zamagni, a key factor in explaining the progress of Italian consumer co-ops from the 1970s onward.

Why did the co-ops in these countries hold on to the basic federal organizational model? One probable hypothesis could be that the cooperators in these countries were more inclined to defend the virtues of local authority and democratic governance. Existing evidence does not, however, suggest that, for example, the Norwegian cooperators were more democratic than the British. In fact, comparative studies have shown that Norwegian cooperators throughout the second half of the twentieth century spent much less time than the British

---

[27] Apart from a series of largely unsuccessful attempts by the NKL to expand into non-food retailing.
[28] SOK. (various years). *Annual Report.*
[29] T. Menzani and V. Zamagni, "Cooperative Networks in the Italian Economy," *Enterprise & Society*, 11, no. 1 (2010), p. 114.

worrying about their members' democratic participation. Instead, they focused on strengthening their members' loyalty and economic involvement in their local co-op.[30] Alternatively, one could make the claim that the organizations stuck to the federal model because they were generally less economically strained than those that abandoned the federal structure. But the economic crisis affecting both the Finnish and the Norwegian movement during the 1970s and 1980s was far from trivial. In both countries market shares were evaporating. Profits declined, and in some years the two movements had to accept substantial losses. In Norway, during the 1980s, membership decreased for the first time in the history of the organization. Despite these problems, the central leadership chose to stick with the federal structure when contemplating how to stop the decline and stimulate new growth.

Thus, a more promising explanation seems to lie in the level of the central management. In Norway, both Knut Moe, who was the leading manager of the NKL from 1950 to 1980, and Rolf Rønning, who as CEO of the NKL pushed forward the massive reorganization process of the 1990s, were in strong favor of the basic federal structure on which the co-op rested. Instead of viewing it as a hindrance to competiveness, they saw it as an advantage. Along similar lines, the central leadership of the Italian movement, commenting on the British national merger discussion during the 1990s, expressed strict adherence to the federal model, noting how the Italian movement "is a federation of societies who have still individual sovereignty but are members of and assisted by the service and advice of the National Association of Consumer Co-operatives."[31]

After having been organized in a fairly similar manner until the 1950s, the postwar period saw Western European consumer co-ops develop their organizations in a variety of different directions. Some stayed with the basic federal model, while others abandoned it, either partly or fully. While this was happening, the economic fortunes of the Western European consumer cooperatives started to diverge quite dramatically. Was there any relationship between these parallel processes of organizational and economic divergence? Put differently, was there one organizational model more suitable to counter the competitive threat from the multiples than others? The subsequent discussion provides some speculative reflections.

ORGANIZATIONAL STRUCTURE AND COMPETITIVENESS IN WESTERN EUROPEAN CONSUMER COOPERATIVES

Despite various attempts to reform their organizational models, from the 1950s onward the consumer cooperative form of trade started to lose ground in many countries. By 1990, the cooperatives in the Netherlands, Belgium, France,

---

[30] See Ekberg, "Consumer Co-operatives and the Transformation of Modern Food Retailing: A Comparative Study of the Norwegian and British Consumer Co-operatives 1950–2002," pp. 254–8.

[31] Guiseppe Fabretti, "Italian Experience," *Journal of Co-operative Studies*, no. 83 (1995), p. 30.

Austria, and Germany had largely collapsed. In other countries, cooperatives had to accept a dramatic decline in market share. In Britain, the co-op's share of the food retail market declined from about 20 percent in the mid-1950s to 6 percent by the turn of the millennium. In Sweden, the co-ops experienced a 15 percent decline in their market share during the 1990s alone.[32]

In other countries, however, the consumer cooperative form of trade fared much better. In countries such as Norway, Finland, Italy, Switzerland, and Denmark, co-ops managed to defend, and in some instances even dramatically increase, their share of the market. Also in Portugal and Spain, consumer co-ops managed to grasp quite substantial market shares. Hence, despite the fact that the cooperative form of business was marginalized in many Western European countries, some national consumer co-ops managed to defend and even strengthen their market positions.

Understanding how this divergent economic development came about is clearly one of the major tasks for historians of the consumer cooperative movement. Some attempts have been made, but much research remains to be done before a definitive answer can be provided. What is evident from the available literature is that the specific federal organizational structure of the co-ops has been of substantial importance in explaining what happened. Moreover, the dominant view in the literature seems to be that the federal model was a disadvantage for the co-ops as they struggled to meet the increasing competition from the centralized, top-down structure of the multiple retailers, and hence was a major factor in explaining the economic problems experienced by so many consumer co-ops during the postwar period. The following quotation from Schediwy is illustrative:

an organization that functions top-down with a central headquarters that sees to it that the subsidiaries are all working well ... certainly offers practical advantages over a central organization that is owned by a multitude of "parent" co-operatives who jealously try and protect their independent sphere of action. Central organizations of this second type nearly always have to struggle with the problem that they are in the end risk-bearers for the whole movement. . . . But they still have very few rights in ensuring the grass-roots level is working properly. All this may be justified in terms of "this is the price that has to be paid for more economic democracy." But in some cases this price is simply too high to be paid.[33]

Although this claim may be true at a general level, it does not correlate well with the actual experiences of Western European consumer cooperatives during the postwar period. From the considerations above, one would expect that consumer co-ops choosing to stick with a federal model would be the ones that

[32] As Friberg et al., show in this volume, the recorded market shares of both the Swedish and U.K. co-ops have, for various reasons, strengthened again somewhat in recent years. Figures from Ekberg, "Consumer Co-operatives and the Transformation of Modern Food Retailing: A Comparative Study of the Norwegian and British Consumer Co-operatives 1950–2002," p. 199.
[33] Robert Schediwy, "International Co-Operation between Consumer Co-Operatives," *Yearbook of Co-operative Enterprises* (1990), p. 119.

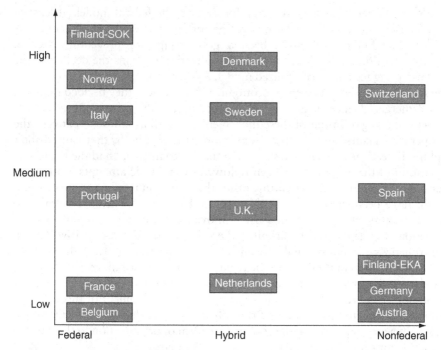

FIGURE 9.1 Organizational structure and economic performance among Western European consumer cooperatives

would experience economic problems, while co-ops replacing the federal structure with a partly or fully centralized and integrated model would fare better. But the organizational and economic history of consumer cooperation in Western Europe tells a different story. Figure 9.1 provides a simple illustration of the point. It plots Western European consumer cooperatives according to two criteria: their choice of overall organizational model (vertical axis) and their economic performance, roughly estimated in terms of market shares by 2000 (horizontal axis).[34]

Although the overall picture is, indeed, quite blurred, what seems clear is that there is no distinct relationship between choice of federal model and economic decline among consumer co-ops. Rather, if there is a tendency, it is an inverted one: consumer co-ops sticking to the federal model generally have fared rather well, while co-ops opting for the nonfederal model, with some exceptions, have declined or simply collapsed.[35] The experiences of the hybrid forms are more mixed, but generally they also have fared less well than the federal co-ops.

[34] Note that the figure is intended as an approximate illustration of the relationship between choice of organizational model and economic performance and does not rely on precise statistical estimation.

[35] Another example of this relationship is the Cooperative Retailing System in western Canada, see Brett Fairbairn, *Living the Dream: Membership and Marketing in the Co-operative Retailing System* (Saskatchewan: University of Saskatchewan, 2003).

Hence, rather than being a recipe for decline, the federal model, at least in many cases, seems to have been a recipe for success. And, on the contrary, seldom has full centralization been a good recipe for preventing decline. Clearly this does not mean that such centralization explains the decline of the co-ops opting for a fully centralized model. As mentioned, both the German and the Austrian movements were in economic trouble before they decided to go for a full merger. Hence, it is more likely that it was the factors preceding the structural reorganization of these movements, as well as failures to govern the cooperative giants, and not the organizational model itself, that caused their failure. Indeed, as Schediwy has noted in the Austrian case, "had the big rescue operation of the mega merger been followed by energetic attempts at modernizing, stream-lining and cost-cutting inside the new giant retailing cooperative, it might have been successful. But this did not happen."[36] The substantial economic success of the integrated Swiss movement, as well as recent positive development trends seen in Britain (where by 2009 the Co-operative Group controlled 85 percent of total consumer cooperative trade), also indicates that full centralization in itself cannot be regarded a reason for failure. On the other hand, there are at least some reasons to believe that the federal model has played an important part in shaping the largely positive development of those organizations sticking to this structure. Primarily it may have done so by facilitating a more efficient adaptation of the cooperative form of organization to the parallel demands for centralization, integration, and standardization.

One would perhaps expect that organizations opting for high or full centralization of cooperative trade also would be better positioned to integrate and standardize their operations. Historical evidence, however, tells us otherwise. It seems that too much centralization too fast often created fundamental organizational challenges. Large regional societies tended to develop their own store formats; they often practiced separate marketing schemes and operated independent distribution and wholesaling facilities. In particular, the development of hybrid forms frequently resulted in very complex organizational structures where responsibilities, managerial authority, and democratic governance were mixed together in extremely confusing ways. Although forward integration by the wholesalers increased the level of centralized control over the retailing function, it remained difficult to efficiently integrate the overall co-op movement and develop a coherent and standardized national strategy. National buying and national marketing – elements central to the success of the multiples – became a difficult, if not an impossible, strategic option.

In organizations sustaining a basic federal structure, where the centralization proceeded at a gradual pace and where the national wholesaler largely stayed out of retailing, the dynamics were different. A more modest, average size of the retail societies facilitated a gradual increase in the overall, national coordination of cooperative trade. It made possible the development of similar store formats

---

[36] Schediwy, "The Decline and Fall of Konsum Austria," p. 63.

across society structures and ensured that national marketing campaigns were embraced by all societies. And although many of the largest societies that eventually were established within these organizations were inclined to trade independently of their national wholesaler, trading loyalty could be secured through various forms of contracting and incentive systems. The overall governance structure also remained comparatively simple and straightforward. Organizations opting for more limited degrees, or at least a slower pace, of centralization, as well as upholding a strict division of labor between the retail and the wholesale level, seem to have been in a better position to align the demands for centralized operations with those of standardization and integration.

In these ways, the federal structure favored by many of the most successful Western European consumer cooperatives in the second half of the twentieth century may have helped these organizations to more efficiently counter the competitive advantages of the multiple retail chains. Instead of copying the multiples, they developed their own competitive advantages within the boundaries of the federal structure. By combining local control of retail operations within independent retail societies with substantial centralization, standardization, and integration of common functions such as wholesaling, distribution, buying, and marketing, these organizations managed to counter the major benefits held by the chain store organizations, without having to fully sacrifice the parallel benefits of local control, local market knowledge, and local accountability.

CONCLUSION AND FURTHER RESEARCH

The organizational history of cooperative enterprises in the last half of the twentieth century is thus a rich and important history of divergence. It is also a history of mixed economic fortunes. This chapter has sought to account for this development by way of a comparative study of the organizational development of Western European consumer co-ops in the period from 1950 to the turn of the millennium. I have analyzed the driving forces behind the organizational reforms taking place within most consumer cooperative enterprises during this period, described and discussed the divergent responses, and also discussed briefly the consequences of these responses for the economic fortunes of the various national consumer co-ops.

The intensified growth of multiple retailing from the 1950s onward brought to the forefront a reconsideration of the federal organizational model that most consumer co-ops used. The challenge from the multiples, however, was perceived and acted upon differently by different national consumer cooperative movements. From a situation where most national consumer co-ops were organized fairly similarly, a variety of organizational forms developed. Analyzing these divergent organizational responses, I have shown how decisions to abandon the federal model altogether and replace it with a fully centralized structure often were preceded by severe economic difficulties. In organizations developing so-called hybrid models, the federal management was frequently in favor of full centralization. These plans were countered, however, by managers and members at the local and regional levels, determined to sustain their authority. Finally, in some co-ops, the traditional federal model was sustained. Here, full centralization was often never even envisaged. The overall attitude in these organizations seems to have been that the federal model was, in fact, an advantage in meeting the competitive threat of the multiples, given that it could be adapted to the necessary demands for centralization, standardization, and integration.

The final section has discussed the relationship between these divergent organizational trends and the economic outcomes for the Western European co-ops. Existing research has tended to relate the decline of the cooperative form of trade in many countries in the period after the Second World War to inherent inefficiencies of the federal model. These studies have failed to recognize, however, that most of the co-ops that were successful during this period were, in fact, those that continued to be organized as federals. On the other hand, many of the co-ops that abandoned the federal model and opted for full centralization experienced decline and even total collapse. The reasons for this somewhat surprising picture are not easy to comprehend. Clearly, the overall decline of the fully centralized co-ops often was caused by factors preceding the actual establishment of the "nonfederal" structure. Hence, the role of the organizational model itself in explaining the decline of these co-ops is by no means straightforward. As concerns the more successful federal co-ops, however, one of their major advantages seems to have been their ability to develop an organizational structure combining the traditional federal virtues of local control and local market knowledge with substantial centralization of common functions such as marketing, buying, and wholesaling. The organizational structure applied by these organizations seems to have played an important part in shaping their success.

These results need to be used cautiously because the postwar development of some Western European consumer co-ops diverged quite fundamentally from the overall trend just presented. As shown in Figure 9.1 , not all federally organized consumer co-ops were successful. Moreover, some co-ops, such as the Danish, combining a traditional federal structure with a fully centralized model – what I have termed a "hybrid structure" – also were successful. It is also clear that some co-ops abandoning the federal structure altogether and opting for a fully centralized model developed successfully. The Swiss movement is a case in point, as is the promising trends within the U.K. movement that have followed the major mergers from 2000 onward. What this sort of counterevidence indicates is that the question of survival or decline among consumer co-ops is a complex issue that needs to be analyzed from several different perspectives. Although organizational structure obviously played an important role in what happened, a series of other factors also were important.

Future research should focus more systematically than that done so far on these complex forces. Factors such as the role of leadership, of organizational culture, and of the varied political and ideological affiliations of consumer cooperative enterprises need to be taken more fully into account. The varied ability of national cooperative enterprises to secure necessary financing is another issue that has received only limited attention in the literature. The legal framework for cooperative trade, the specific structure and historical development of national retailing industries, as well as the role of geography and demography in shaping the retail markets of various countries also need to be analyzed. Still, I hope the present analysis has taken a firm step toward the goal of providing a better understanding of how and why the consumer cooperatives have evolved in the years since World War II.

Sources and References

Battilani, Patrizia. (2005). "How to Beat Competition without Losing Co-operative Identity: The Case of Italian Consumer Co-operatives," in ACTA of the International Congress (ed.), *Consumerism Versus Capitalism? Co-operatives Seen from an International Comparative Perspective* (Gent: Amsab Institute of Social History).

Brazda, Johann (ed.). (1989). "The Consumer Co-operatives in Germany," in Johann Brazda and Robert Schediwy (eds.), *Consumer Co-operatives in a Changing World*, Vol. 1 (Geneva: International Co-operative Alliance).

Brazda, Johann, and Robert Schediwy (eds.). (1989). *Consumer Co-operatives in a Changing World*, Vols. 1 and 2 (Geneva: International Co-operative Alliance).

Büchert, Aage. (1992). *Forræderiet Mod En God Idè* (København: Vindrose).

(1971). "Starting Signal for Co-op Denmark," *Review of International Co-operation*, 64(4).

Christensen, Niels Finn. (1999). "Between Farmers and Workers: Consumer Cooperation in Denmark, 1850–1940," in Ellen Furlough and Carl Strikwerda (eds.), *Consumers against Capitalism? Consumer Cooperation in Europe, North America and Japan, 1840–1990* (Lanham, MD: Rowman & Littlefield).

Co-operative Union. (1955). *Report of the 86th Annual Co-operative Congress in the Usher Hall Edinburgh May 30th, 31st, June 1st and 2nd, 1955* (Manchester: Co-operative Union).

Cronan, Garry. (2007). "The Global 300 Project – Measuring Co-operative Performance and Difference," *Review of International Co-operation*, 100(1).

Ekberg, Espen. (2008). *Consumer Co-operatives and the Transformation of Modern Food Retailing: A Comparative Study of the Norwegian and British Consumer Co-operatives 1950–2002* (Det humanistiske fakultet, Universitetet i Oslo).

Fabretti, Guiseppe. (1995). "Italian Experience," *Journal of Co-operative Studies*, no. 83.

Fairbairn, Brett. (2003). *Living the Dream: Membership and Marketing in the Co-operative Retailing System* (Saskatchewan: University of Saskatchewan).

Flanagan, Desmond. (1969). *A Centenary Story of the Co-operative Union of Great Britain and Ireland* (Manchester: Co-operative Union).

International Co-operative Alliance. *Statement on the Co-operative Identity*, www.ica.coop/coop/principles-revisions.html.

Jefferys, James B. (1954). *Retail Trading in Britain 1850–1950: A Study of Trends in Retailing with Special Reference to the Development of Co-operative, Multiple Shop and Department Store Method of Trading* (Cambridge: Cambridge University Press, Economic and Social Studies).

Jefferys, James B., and Derek Knee. (1962). *Retailing in Europe: Present Structure and Future Trends* (London: Macmillan).

Kipping, Matthias, and Ove Bjarnar. (1998). *The Americanisation of European Business: The Marshall Plan and the Transfer of Us Management Models* (New York: Routledge).

Kylebäck, Hugo. (1999). *Federation Eller Konsum Sverige? Konsumentkooperativ Förändringsprocess Del 3 1985–1995* (Göteborg: Novum Grafiska AB).

Lange, Even, Espen Ekberg, Eivind Merok, Iselin Theien, and Jon Vatnaland. (2006). *Organisert Kjøpekraft. Forbrukesamvirkets Historie I Norge* (Oslo: Pax).

Menzani, T., and V. Zamagni. (2010). "Cooperative Networks in the Italian Economy," *Enterprise & Society*, 11(1): 98–127.

Middleton, Alan. (1995). "Independence and Unity," *Journal of Co-operative Studies*, no. 83.

Moe, Knut. (1955). "Strømlinjeformet Vareomsetning. Artikkel 1. Amerikansk Engroshandel I Matvarebransjen." *Forbrukeren*, 10(4).

(1955). "Strømlinjeformet Vareomsetning. Artikkel 2. Amerikansk Engroshandel I Matvarebransjen." *Forbrukeren*, 10(5/6).

Schediwy, Robert. (1996). "The Decline and Fall of Konsum Austria," *Review of International Co-operation*, 89(2): 62–8.

(1990). "International Co-operation between Consumer Co-operatives." *Yearbook of Co-operative Enterprises*.

Schröter, Harm G. (2008). "The Americanisation of Distribution and Its Limits: The Case of the German Retail System, 1950–1975," *European Review of History: Revue europeenne d'histoire*, 15(4): 445 –58.

SOK. (various years). *Annual Report*.

Watkins, W. P. (1976). "Consumers' Co-operation in the Federal German Republic – The Latest Phase," *Society for Co-operative Studies Bulletin*, 27: 2–42.

CHAPTER 10

The Politics of Commercial Dynamics: Cooperative Adaptations to Postwar Consumerism in the United Kingdom and Sweden, 1950–2010

Katarina Friberg, Rachael Vorberg-Rugh, Anthony Webster, and John Wilson

INTRODUCTION

Listening to a speech by Philip Blond, a leading adviser to the new Conservative Prime Minister, delegates to the 2010 Co-operative Congress could only reflect upon the transformation of the British cooperative movement. While cooperators were accustomed to occupying the margins of national political life, in the summer of 2010 cooperatives were headline news. To the surprise of many across the political spectrum, Prime Minister David Cameron made the mutualization of public services a central theme of his 2010 election campaign, and it became a priority of the subsequent Tory-led coalition government.[1] The interest expressed by Blond and Cameron signaled a remarkable change in the movement's fortunes since the dark years of the 1980s, when business elites and politicians broadly agreed that British cooperation was no longer relevant.

In contrast to its nineteenth- and early-twentieth-century heyday, since the 1950s U.K. consumer cooperatives had experienced a prolonged commercial decline, paralleled by a vastly reduced political and cultural status that reached a nadir under the Conservative government of Margaret Thatcher (1979–90). Thatcher and her party regarded the cooperative movement and mutual business models as Victorian anachronisms with little relevance to modern consumer society. At the same time, large retail multiples such as Sainsbury's, Tesco, and ASDA rapidly extended their presence, while the Co-operative Wholesale Society (CWS) and retail cooperative societies suffered a substantial loss of market share, from 21 percent in the mid-1960s to around 4 percent by century's end. Membership, which had once accounted for nearly half of all British households, fell to around 8 percent in 2000.[2]

---

[1] On recent Conservative interest in cooperatives, see: "Cameron in 'Co-op Vision' to Free City Poor," *Yorkshire Post* (November 9, 2007); M. Ivens, "Cameron's Tactical Blond Moment," *Sunday Times* [London] (November 29, 2009), p. 23; A. Stratton, "New Tory Campaign Backs Co-operatives in Bid to Woo Voters," *Guardian* [London] (February 16, 2010), p. 11.

[2] S. Yeo, *A Chapter in the Making of a Successful Co-operative Business: The Co-operative Wholesale Society 1973–2001* (Manchester: Zeebra Publishing, 2002), p. 35; E. Ekberg, *Consumer Co-operatives and the Transformation of Modern Food Retailing: A Comparative*

This depressing outlook was not exclusive to Britain. By the 1990s, consumer cooperation was either extinct or in decline in Belgium, France, Germany, Austria, and the Netherlands.[3] Even in parts of Europe where cooperatives fared better, such as Scandinavia, retreat was still evident. Cooperative societies in Norway, which were more successful than most in holding off the challenge of the multiple retailers, still suffered a loss of market share in the 1980s.[4] Consumer cooperatives in Sweden, the comparator in this study, also saw a significant, though less dramatic, decline in market share, from 25.7 percent in 1962 to 17.5 percent in 2004.[5] Although competition from other retailers was less acute in the initial postwar period, by the end of the 1960s, Kooperativa Förbundet (KF, the Swedish wholesale society and trade association) and retail societies were losing ground to ICA (Central Wholesale Union, an association of private food retailers). Concerns over the issues facing the cooperative sector led politicians, mainly social democrats and members of Centerpartiet (the former Farmers' Party), to establish a cross-party commission in the mid-1970s. Although this resulted in important tax concessions for Swedish cooperatives in the 1980s, the final decades of the twentieth century saw continued decline in market share.[6]

In the first decade of the twenty-first century, however, British and Swedish cooperatives reversed their commercial fortunes. In Britain, the change was accompanied and facilitated by major structural changes in the consumer cooperative sector. In 2001, CWS and its subsidiaries, the Co-operative Bank and the Co-operative Insurance Society (CIS), united with their former rival, Co-operative Retail Services (CRS), to become the Co-operative Group.[7] The remaining independent societies also joined the Co-operative Retail Trading Group (CRTG, founded by CWS in 1993), consolidating for the first time ever all of the British movement's food-buying and marketing functions into a single operation.[8] Additional mergers, especially with United Cooperatives (2007), and the acquisitions of private multiple retailers Alldays (2003) and Somerfield (2008) increased commercial strength. By 2010, consumer cooperatives' share of the food retail market had doubled to around 8 percent.

Study of the Norwegian and British Consumer Co-operatives, 1950–2002 (University of Oslo, 2008), p. 16.

[3] Ekberg, *Consumer Co-operatives*, p. 9.

[4] Ekberg, "Consumer Co-operation and the Transformation of Modern Food Retailing: The British and Norwegian Consumer Co-operative Movement in Comparison, 1950–2002" in L. Black and N. Robertson (eds.), *Consumerism and the Co-operative Movement in Modern British History: Taking Stock* (Manchester: Manchester University Press, 2009), pp. 51–68, p. 60.

[5] SOU 1979:62; Kooperativ Årsbok. H. Kylebäck, *Varuhandeln i Sverige under 1900-talet* (Göteborg, 2004); International Co-operative Alliance, *Statistics and Information on European Co-operatives* (Geneva: ICA, 1999); NAF International Group 1999, Data on NAF Owners, KF Annual Reports 2001–2009. Thanks to E. Ekberg for providing these statistics.

[6] See Table 10.1.

[7] Yeo, *A Chapter*, pp. 22–4.

[8] See www.crtg.coop/index.cfm/item_id:3/about_CRTG/ (accessed February 1, 2010).

Although the Co-operative Group remains primarily identified with food retailing, since the 1990s the Co-operative Bank and CIS have become increasingly important in generating profits.[9] Graham Melmoth, chief executive in 1996–2002, led radical changes in the Group's business and marketing strategies, emphasizing integration of its "cooperative family of businesses." These efforts were underpinned by a coordinated recasting of cooperative values and principles for modern circumstances, building on traditions of leadership in Fair Trade products and "ethical" business, an approach ultimately encapsulated in the Report of the Co-operative Commission, published in January 2001.[10] This signaled revival in the Group's commercial fortunes and an enhancement of its political profile.

Similarly, although Swedish cooperatives had experienced declining market share, in the twenty-first century there is evidence of modest recovery, with market share reaching 21.4 percent in 2007.[11] As in Britain, Swedish cooperatives implemented internal reform and structural integration, with KF taking over the operations of several regional retail societies. In both Britain and Sweden, consumer cooperatives shifted away from producing the goods they sold, with both CWS and KF selling off their manufacturing operations in the 1990s and outsourcing the production of cooperative branded goods.[12] Other efforts at reorganization were less successful, however. For example, Co-op Norden (a company created by the Swedish, Norwegian, and Danish cooperative unions in 2002, in response to the potential threat of international competitors in the retail sector) was abandoned by 2008.[13]

A major difference between the Swedish and British cases has been a reluctance in the former to restore cooperative identity to the core of the organizational and business strategies. Although a modernized version of the dividend was introduced in Sweden in 2010, most changes after the late 1990s were not badged as distinctly cooperative.[14] Nor have Swedish cooperatives attracted the same degree of interest from the center-right government of Prime Minister Fredrik Reinfeldt (2006–present) as was the case in Cameron's "Big Society." Although Swedish consumer cooperatives received some

[9] Yeo, *A Chapter*, pp. 24–6.
[10] *The Co-operative Advantage: Creating a Successful Family of Co-operative Businesses* (2001).
[11] SOU 1979: 62; Kooperativ Årsbok. H. Kylebäck, *Varuhandeln i Sverige under 1900-talet* (Göteborg, 2004); International Co-operative Alliance, *Statistics and Information on European Co-operatives* (Geneva: ICA, 1999); NAF International Group 1999, Data on NAF Owners, KF Annual Reports 2001–2009. Thanks to E. Ekberg for providing these statistics.
[12] E. Giertz and B. U. Strömberg. *Samverkan till egen nytta. Boken om konsumentkooperativ idé och verklighet i Sverige* (Stockholm: Prisma, 1999), pp. 174–7.
[13] Beck-Friis Ulrika, *Kooperation i framkant?* (Studentlitteratur and Öhrlings: Price Waterhouse Coopers, 2009), p. 31.
[14] "Nu inför vi medlemsåterbäring!," in *Mersmak* 11:2010. The headline in the member/customer paper *Mersmak* was "Now We Introduce Dividend for Members." Note: It used *introduce*, not *reintroduce*. They could not write reintroduce, since it was not dividend in the old sense where the economy of the member household was linked to that of the retail society. The new dividend was a fixed percent on purchases.

attention in the 1990s from politicians interested in the "Third Sector," or social economy, this has since receded. Indeed, indifference may prove problematic for KF, as a revision of the Association Act, the legal framework for cooperatives, is now being considered.

This chapter will compare and evaluate the business strategies of the British and Swedish consumer cooperative movements in an era of growing consumer spending power and increased competition from larger and increasingly multi-national investor-led retail corporations. It is a comparison of efforts to modernize commercial organizations created in the period before the huge expansion of incomes and consumer demand which characterized many national economies in Western Europe and North America after 1945. In this context, we define *modernization* as a process of adapting structure and strategy to the challenges of a rapidly changing external environment, accommodating both changing consumer habits and radically different competition. Specifically, this involves the adoption of more rigorous business accounting and marketing practices, centralized coordination of buying and distribution, and the recruitment of professionals capable of managing this kind of organization. As such, it is a study of the evolving business strategies of CWS/Co-operative Group and KF in facing the challenges of modernization since 1950.

The dearth of cross-national comparative cooperative studies has been recognized – indeed, it is a key reason for the publication of this volume. Ekberg's comparison of Britain and Norway, which offers an important example of the insights gained from such analysis, highlights the dangers of assuming a common European narrative of cooperative "rise and decline." In Ekberg's analysis (which concludes in 2002), Norway's successes are contrasted with the decline of cooperative fortunes in Britain.[15] As noted, however, the recent revitalization of the British movement suggests that the "narrative of decline" also requires revision, whilst the Swedish cooperative movement presents a less straightforward success story than the Norwegian experience.

Britain and Sweden are compelling subjects for comparative study, as much for their differences as for their similarities. In both countries, the dominant organizational form was consumer cooperation, with cooperatives commencing the 1950s with significant capital, a large share of the retail food market, and substantial memberships. Both CWS and KF were large business enterprises with extensive distribution networks and significant manufacturing operations, and in comparison to other European movements, they suffered little wartime damage. However, there were profound differences, especially in the political and commercial environments in which they operated. It will be argued that these differences resulted in some divergence in their modernization strategies. A key difference between the U.K. and Swedish movements is structural. In Britain,

---

[15] Ekberg, *Consumer Co-operatives*, pp. 9–11. See also K. Friberg, *Workings of Co-operation: A Comparative Study of Consumer Co-operative Organisations, Britain and Sweden 1860 to 1970* (Växjö: Växjö University Press, 2005), where organizational differences in Sweden and Britain are studied and analyzed from a local retail society perspective.

the policy and commercial wings of national cooperative organization (the Co-operative Union [renamed Co-operatives UK in 2002] and CWS/Group respectively) developed separately, each enjoying a high degree of autonomy. Conversely, in Sweden these functions were merged in KF from an early stage in the movement's development, providing one reason for comparison.

Furthermore, in Britain cooperatives function within a highly competitive market economy, and are tied to parliamentary politics at a national level through the Co-operative Party, formed in 1917 and directly affiliated with the Labour Party. In contrast, the Swedish cooperative movement has a history of political nonalignment in that country's social democratic political and economic tradition. To what extent did the contrasting internal political environments of the two cooperative movements, and the external national and international political contexts within which their businesses operated, assist or hamper strategic initiatives? Although efforts to reform business practice began early in the period under scrutiny in both countries, there were differences in the success achieved. The reforms pursued differed in the two cases, but both were driven by increasingly problematic commercial and political contexts. Moreover, the dynamics of both the internal and external environments of the two cooperative movements played a central part in the differing outcomes.

The chapter begins with a review of the historic development of cooperative business in the two countries prior to 1950, focusing especially on the respective relationships enjoyed by CWS and KF with the local and regional societies they served. This sets the scene for examination of the internal politics of both cooperative movements, and the evolution of external political relationships in this period, particularly with the state, major political parties, and commercial rivals. Later the chapter assesses the main developments affecting the movements as the period unfolded, identifying key factors that determined the similarities and differences between the two cooperative businesses.

BRITISH AND SWEDISH COOPERATIVE MODELS, 1860–1950

To understand the differences between British and Swedish modernization strategies in the late twentieth century, it is essential to trace the relationships that developed between the central commercial organizing bodies and local cooperative societies. As noted, a major organizational difference was that, from 1904, KF was both union and wholesale society, while in Britain the two functions were vested in separate organizations, the Co-operative Union and CWS. The roots of this difference lay in the emergence of cooperative societies in Britain and their developing relationship with CWS after its establishment in 1863. In Britain, several factors shaped both the development of cooperative business and its ability to implement internal reform. First, the high period of cooperative formation from the late 1840s occurred in a society already much changed by accelerating industrialization. In the earlier phase of industrialization, cooperative society formation was sporadic, with a high rate of failure stemming from violent economic fluctuations and problems associated with their uncertain legal status.[16]

By the 1840s and 1850s, however, cooperative societies emerged in larger numbers, based on organizational principles (the Rochdale model) that proved to be more durable than earlier ones. Significantly, cooperative societies grew fastest in the most industrialized areas of Britain, particularly the north of England, where population was densely concentrated in urbanizing localities that already supported a complex business ecology of markets and local stores with which the new cooperatives had to compete. These developments have been described by various historians, especially the rapid development of small stores and grocery shops in the early nineteenth century.[17] Jefferys and Alexander have argued that 1850 marked a watershed in the development of British retailing, with the advent of advertising, branding and packaging of goods, more sophisticated systems of distribution and procurement, and culminating in the development of larger department stores and multiple chains.[18]

This competitive environment shaped the ideology and strategy of many of the new cooperative societies. Local societies had to compete for customers and were also obliged to secure reliable and affordable supplies for their stores. Purvis's study of cooperative retailers in the northeast of England in the 1860s and 1870s shows that local societies tried to spread risk by procuring supplies from a range of wholesale suppliers, thereby keeping costs as low as possible and minimizing the danger of private trader-inspired wholesaling boycotts.[19] Such strategies of local entrenchment became even more important later in the century, when private traders began to organize politically against cooperative societies.[20] In this context, the development of social and cultural activities by local cooperatives took on a practical as well as an ideological importance. Festivals, reading rooms, and the creation of a vibrant social life for members ensured consumer loyalty to the local store, building a substantial body of local

---

[16] See G. D. H. Cole, *A Century of Co-operation* (London: Allen & Unwin, 1944), chapter 2.

[17] See D. Hodson, "'The Municipal Store': Adaptation and Development in the Retail Markets of Nineteenth Century Industrial Lancashire," *Business History*, 40, no. 4 (1998), pp. 94–114; R. Scola, "Food Markets and Shops in Manchester 1770–1870," *Journal of Historical Geography* 1, no. 2 (1975), pp. 153–68; J. Blackman, "The Food Supply of an Industrial Town: A Study of Sheffield's Public Markets 1780–1900," *Business History*, 5, no. 2 (1963), pp. 83–97; Blackman, "The Development of the Retail Grocery Trade in the Nineteenth Century," *Business History*, 9, no. 2 (1967), pp. 110–17; M. Winstanley, *The Shopkeeper's World 1830–1914* (Manchester: Manchester Univeristy Press, 1983), pp. 2–19.

[18] J. Jefferys, *Retail Trading in Britain, 1858–1950* (Cambridge: Cambridge University Press, 1954); D. Alexander, *Retail Trading in England during the Industrial Revolution* (London: Oxford University Press, 1970); N. Alexander and G. Akehurst, "Introduction: The Emergence of Modern Retailing, 1750–1950," *Business History*, 40, no. 4 (1998), pp. 1–15.

[19] M. Purvis, "Stocking the Store: Co-operative Retailers in North East England and Systems of Wholesale Supply circa 1860–1877," *Business History*, 40, no. 4 (1998), pp. 55–78, p. 62.

[20] Winstanley, *The Shopkeepers World*, pp. 83–9; A. Bonner, *British Co-operation* (Manchester: Co-operative Union, 1961), pp. 111–12.

activists to defend the local co-op should this prove necessary.[21] Consequently, British cooperative societies developed a powerful sense of localism and independence, merging appreciation of the need to be competitive with a desire to maintain local support and activism through sociocultural initiatives and the "divi."[22] This independence was signaled by the speed with which societies developed a range of services, either on their own or in cooperation with other societies, but seldom with CWS.[23] For instance, the 1893 *Co-operative Directory* list of business functions commonly carried on by societies included drapery, tailoring and shoe repair departments, bakeries, corn milling, ironmongery, and jewelry.[24]

This tradition of independence had profound implications for the relationships between local societies and CWS. The motives for establishing CWS included an ideological aim to create a self-enclosed system of supply which was independent of the market, alongside the aim of ensuring at least one reliable source of produce in the volatile wholesaling environment of the mid-nineteenth century. By the 1860s, the latter was particularly influential, especially among those societies that joined CWS. From the start, however, there were major differences over its role. For those who organized CWS, the aim was to become the principal, and preferably the only, supplier of commodities to local cooperative societies. These leaders saw CWS as a national and international giant, becoming a major manufacturer as well as the key commercial intermediary between producer and consumer cooperatives. Thus, CWS would become the effective commercial leader of cooperation in England and Wales, with its counterpart, the Scottish Co-operative Wholesale Society (SCWS, founded in 1868), performing this role north of the border.[25] The movement's newspapers, *The Co-operator* and its successor, the *Co-operative News*, argued that it was the duty of cooperative member societies to buy as much as possible from CWS. By the 1870s, the *News* regularly attacked societies for their small purchases from CWS, seeking to embarrass them into buying more.[26] The figures were indeed shocking. Among the worst culprits was none other than the Rochdale Pioneers.[27]

[21] P. Gurney, *Co-operative Culture and the Politics of Consumption in England 1870–1930* (Manchester: Manchester University Press, 1996), pp. 199–201. See also N. Robertson, *The Co-operative Movement and Communities in Britain, 1914–1960, Minding Their Own Business* (Ashgate, 2010).

[22] James McKendrick, "Northern Letter," *Co-operative News*, 6 (February 6, 1875), p. 67.

[23] Friberg, *Workings of Co-operation*, part 1.

[24] *Co-operative Directory* (Manchester: Co-operative Union, 1893), p. 9.

[25] See J. Kinloch & J. Butt, *History of the Scottish Co-operative Wholesale Society Limited* (Glasgow: CWS, 1981).

[26] For example, "The Trade of the Wholesale," *Co-operative News*, 7 (April 6, 1876), p. 175.

[27] "The Wholesale and the Retail Societies," *Co-operative News*, 10 (March 15, 1879), p. 171. The article showed that the Rochdale Pioneers' Society's purchases from CWS amounted to only 16 percent by value of Rochdale Pioneers' sales.

CWS found that producer cooperatives generated friction.[28] Throughout the 1870s, CWS promoted producer cooperatives by selling their produce to consumer societies and providing overdrafts and loans to these ventures through CWS Bank (established in 1872). However, as many of these producer cooperatives failed, CWS suffered heavy losses.[29] In June 1881, £32,000 of these debts had to be written off,[30] causing some member societies to rebel against what they saw as an irresponsible use of their funds.[31]

In reality, CWS was unable either to render the mass of local societies sufficiently commercially dependent upon itself, or assert enough political authority to achieve the position of leadership to which it aspired. This remained the case throughout the organization's history, partly accounting for the failure of numerous initiatives to reform cooperative business practices in England, and later in Britain. This impaired capacity to lead was exacerbated by divisions in cooperative organization on the national stage. The Co-operative Union, established in 1869 as the movement's advisory body and sponsor of the national Co-operative Congress, provided a forum for, and potential leadership of, rival strategies to those offered by CWS.[32] Further dispersal of power followed the creation of CWS Retail Society in 1927, as a quasi-independent body empowered to establish CWS retail branches where local societies had yet to emerge.[33] After the Second World War, renamed Co-operative Retail Services Limited (CRS), this organization grew from being a rescue service for struggling retail cooperatives to become a rival to the CWS. Thus, British cooperation evolved as a dysfunctional business federation from the late nineteenth century, characterized by separation of powers at the national level, combined with a loose commercial structure in which there were fundamental differences between the center and local societies about the purpose of CWS.

The situation in Sweden was different. In spite of a measure of industrialization in several parts of the country by the late nineteenth century, Sweden remained a rural society of small, geographically dispersed communities. Local cooperative societies consequently emerged in a less competitive environment than that experienced by their British counterparts. The lack of a developed distribution system in rural and newly industrialized areas benefited traders connected with

---

[28] On nineteenth-century producer cooperatives, see B. Jones, *Co-operative Production* (Oxford: Clarendon Press, 1894); and Cole, *Century of Co-operation*, particularly pp. 148–78, 197–215.

[29] In 1878, for example, it was reported that CWS had lost £7,351-0s-3d on its loans and investments in the Eccleshill Coal Company. Minutes of General & Branch quarterly Meetings, December 1878, Committee's Report (printed), Minutes of the General Committee of CWS 1878, Vol. 5, pp. 69–74, New Century Hall, Manchester.

[30] Minutes of General Quarterly Meeting, Manchester, June 18, 1881, Minutes of the General Committee of CWS, Vol. 6, pp. 143–4.

[31] For example, motion to quarterly general meeting of CWS, June 18, 1881, adopted by the Newcastle branch, but coming from one of its local societies: "That in future no loans or overdrafts be allowed to other than distributive co-operative societies or to societies whose shares are held by such societies."

[32] Bonner, pp. 821–83.

[33] Ibid., p. 171.

their localities' major industrial firms, resulting in a developed truck system.[34] Following an initial burst of cooperative society formation in the 1860s, characterized by levels of failure similar to those experienced in the "pre-Rochdale" phase in Britain, a successful period of cooperative development followed in the 1890s, when more than two hundred societies were established.[35]

Although the new wave of local cooperatives proved more durable than their predecessors, initial attempts to form federal cooperative wholesale societies failed, until the establishment of KF, the Swedish Co-operative Union, in 1899. Legal changes allowed KF to add cooperative wholesaling to its remit in 1904. When in 1907 the regional wholesale society in Gävle (an industrial town north of Stockholm) amalgamated with KF's wholesale operation, KF became Sweden's sole national cooperative wholesaler.[36] During the next two decades, KF became the center and commercial leader of the movement, with more than nine hundred member societies by 1914.[37]

KF enjoyed several advantages over CWS. First, being the political/ideological center of the movement, as well as its commercial leader, KF avoided the dispersal of political power which hampered CWS. In 1914, the KF congress decided to admit only consumer cooperatives (retail and insurance) as members, thereby improving distribution efficiency but restricting the scope of union activities.[38] Second, as both union and wholesaler, it was easier for KF's leadership to implement reforms through the KF-organized Co-operative Congress. Between 1905 and 1910, the secretary of KF, Martin Sundell, and his team developed an organizational and financial system that tied the member societies to KF. This resulted in a strict (and ultimately successful) savings and distribution system that increased KF's capital resources. This was reinforced in 1918, when KF introduced the "kontokurranten" system, whereby member societies' funds were placed with KF to expedite payment for goods. By the 1950s, KF had also introduced a joint budget planning system for all member societies. These reforms improved the financial situation of the member societies, while simultaneously increasing KF's control. In 1923 KF established Svenska Hushållsföreningen to save member societies in financial difficulties, an association that worked intimately with KF, unlike CRS's growing tension with CWS.[39]

---

[34] A. Gjöres, *Svensk kooperation före åttiotalet* (Stockholm: Kooperativa Förbundets Bokförlag, 1919).

[35] R. Schewidy, "The Consumer Co-operatives in Sweden," in J. Brazda and R. Schewidy (eds.), *Consumer Co-operatives in a Changing World*, Vol. 1 (Geneva: ICA, 1989), pp. 229–340, pp. 236–7.

[36] W. Sjölin, Med förenade krafter (Stockholm: Kooperativa Förbundets Bokförlag, 1949); Johansson Tore, *"Samhällets spelregler i föränding – kooperativ lagstiftning"* (Kooperativ Årsbok, 1999).

[37] O. Ruin, *Kooperativa Forbundet 1899–1929* (Lund, 1960), p. 23.

[38] Ibid., p. 22.

[39] G. W. Silverstolpe, *En Krönikebok. Den svenska konsumentkooperationens väg* (Stockholm: Kooperativa Förbundets Bokförlag, 1944), pp. 134, 139; Sun-Joon Hwang, *Folkrörelse eller affärsföretag: Den svenska konsumentkooperationen 1945–1990* (Stockholm: Stockholms universitet, 1995), pp. 39, 51.

Although Swedish cooperative societies faced competition from private retailers and wholesalers, it was far less intense than that experienced by their British counterparts. Individual retailers and their associations tried to stop cooperative expansion, but in the 1940s they joined forces in a retail and wholesale association called Hakonbolaget, later reorganized as ICA. Furthermore, it was not until the 1980s that ICA overtook cooperative societies in market share.[40] Although competition in the wholesale sector was much tougher, boycotts against KF and individual cooperative societies were rebuffed by successful KF campaigns against monopolies and trusts in the 1920s and 1930s, strengthening the position of KF within the movement.

Apart from these commercial differences, there were also important divergences in the external political relations of the respective movements. During the late nineteenth century, British cooperation eschewed any specific political loyalties, though its leaders lobbied Parliament for laws to protect societies from fraud. The Industrial and Provident Societies Acts of 1852 and 1862 laid the foundations for individual society membership, safeguarding societies against the dangers of majority shareholding and establishing the legal basis for federal societies like CWS.[41] Of crucial importance to the movement's politicization, however, were the Free Trade debates of the first years of the twentieth century. As a major international trader, CWS supported free trade, while cooperative members saw it as a way to keep food prices low.[42]

The creation of the Labour Party in 1900 also shaped the political strategies of British cooperation. The roots of cooperation in Owenite socialism formed a natural affinity between cooperators and the socialist and labor organizations which emerged from the 1880s. Two elements of this emergent socialist/labor movement, however, hampered the relationship between cooperation and the new Labour Party. First, the dominance of Labour by Fabian ideas generated ideological differences. While Beatrice and Sydney Webb saw an important role for cooperatives in their strategy for socialism, alongside trade unions and the state, other Labour Party strategists regarded the state as the principal agent for the establishment of a socialist society. Cooperation's role would recede as the state became the main provider of education, health care, pensions, and economic management. Thus, cooperation, with its tradition of voluntarism and preference for civil society over the state, sat uneasily alongside such statist blueprints for creating a new society. This tension effectively marginalized cooperative ideas in the development of Labour Party policy.

A second problem arose from the central position of the trade unions as the founders and financiers of the Labour Party. It elevated the worker and producer

[40] Kylebäck Hugo, *Konsumentkooperation i strukturomvandling 1946–1960* (Kungälv, 1983), pp. 52, 62–4; Kylebäck Hugo, *Varuhandel i Sverige under 1900-talet* (Göteborg, 2004).
[41] Bonner, pp. 66–74.
[42] On cooperative involvement in debates over free trade, see F. Trentmann, *Free Trade Nation: Commerce, Consumption, and Civil Society in Modern Britain* (Oxford: Oxford University Press, 2008).

above the consumer in Labour ideology. The latter's concerns became secondary priorities in planning the new socialist order. Although cooperation had its merits in the earlier stages of industrial development, it was considered incapable of delivering the ultimate transition to a socialist order. Some trade unionists also believed that cooperative societies were just another set of employers, whose commercial interest depended upon exploiting workers. Such ideological differences further weakened the purchase of cooperative ideas on Labour Party thinking. This was exacerbated by the creation of the Co-operative Party in 1917, in response to cooperative concerns about the wartime government's policies on rationing, conscription, and taxation.[43]

Following the war, there was an uneasy reconciliation as the Co-operative Party sought to be an "honest broker" between the movement and the Labour Party;[44] however, the Co-operative Party and movement became merely a faction within the Labour Party with limited influence.[45] Thus marginalized, the cooperative movement struggled to influence policy when Labour was in power. Indeed, in some ways, the post-1945 expansion of the welfare state and public sector by Labour governments limited the scope for cooperative initiatives and expansion. Some Labour politicians were also unsympathetic to the participatory traditions of the cooperative movement, as became clear in the Co-operative Commission of the late 1950s. Also, by siding with Labour, the cooperative movement limited its options for developing alliances with other political parties, most notably the Conservative Party. When British cooperatives began to lose market share from the 1950s on, their political base was consequently so limited that governmental support was not forthcoming.

Conversely, the Swedish movement continued its policy of partisan nonalignment, notwithstanding the large number of cooperators with Social Democratic sympathies, and the fact that many cooperative leaders were active in the Swedish SAP (Socialdemokratiska Arbetarpartiet). This latent pro-SAP tendency was advantageous to Swedish cooperation, especially at a local level, where cooperative leaders were often members of city councils. But the nonpartisan cooperative tradition allowed workable relations across the political spectrum. Indeed, unlike the British case, no cooperative organization in Sweden ever promoted socialism (or nationalization); rather, like the majority of Social Democrats, they supported a mixed business community. In this environment,

---

[43] Ibid., pp. 169–92, 208–14; Sidney Pollard, "The Foundation of the Co-operative Party," in A. Briggs and J. Saville (eds.), *Essays in Labour History, 1886–1923* (London: Macmillan, 1971); T. Adams, "The Formation of the Co-operative Party Re-considered," *International Review of Social History*, 32 (1987), pp. 48–68.

[44] David Stewart, "'A Party within a Party'? The Co-operative Party-Labour Party Alliance and the Formation of the Social Democratic Party, 1974–81," in Anthony Webster, Linda Shaw, John K. Walton, Alyson Brown, and David Stewart (eds.), *The Hidden Alternative: Co-operative Values, Past, Present and Future* (Manchester: Manchester University Press, 2011), pp. 137–56.

[45] See K. Manton, "The Labour Party and the Co-op, 1918–58," *Historical Research*, 82, no. 218 (November 2009), pp. 756–78; and Manton, "The Labour Party and Retail Distribution, 1919–58," *Labour History Review*, 73, no. 3 (December 2008), pp. 269–86.

most political parties accepted cooperatives as part of the mixed economy that developed in Sweden between the 1930s and 1970s. No cooperative party was formed, while KF's political role was confined to representation on government commissions and comments on proposed legislation.[46] Conversely, it is significant that no political party ever sought to establish a supportive legal framework for cooperation. Apart from the first Association Act of 1895, Sweden has never had cooperative legislation protective of a specific cooperative identity.[47] Nonetheless, during the twentieth century, the internal balance of politics within the Swedish cooperative movement, together with careful management of external political relationships, served the cooperative movement in Sweden better than its British counterpart's approach served that in Britain, especially in dealing with tougher competition.

CONTRASTING COOPERATIVE MODERNIZATION STRATEGIES AND THE CHALLENGE OF THE NEW CONSUMERISM, 1950–2010

The Swedish movement entered the postwar era better placed than its British counterpart to deal with the increased competition and changing consumer demand that would emerge in the ensuing decades. Led by Albin Johansson (KF's chief executive and chair of the board, 1924–59) and Henry Nilsson, a KF senior manager, a modernization plan was developed in the mid-1940s. This plan proposed the rapid development of self-service stores, an American innovation of the interwar period.[48] The numbers of these rose from four in 1947 to 2,896 by 1960, while traditional stores declined from 6,576 to 2,767.[49] Market share initially held up well, and from the mid-1960s on, KF implemented a new management and marketing strategy for its member societies, including similar shop fronts, a common symbol (the eternity sign), and the development of the Domus department stores in which KF influenced the range of products and services offered.[50]

Although centralization in distribution and marketing had been evident since the early 1950s, Johansson and other KF leaders believed it could be improved. In particular, Johansson wanted to reorganize the warehouse system with a network of KF-controlled supply depots to serve the stores directly. Resistance from regional societies[51] led to the scheme being adapted to give members

---

[46] See Ruin, 1960, pp. 133–70; Hwang, 1995, pp. 131–44.

[47] Johansson, 1999; Friberg, *Workings of Co-operation*, part 1.

[48] Schewidy, "The Consumer Co-operatives in Sweden," pp. 276–78.

[49] H. Kylebäck, *Konsumentkooperation i strukturomvandling 1946–1960* (Kungälv, 1983), p. 101.

[50] Kylebäck, 1983, pp. 103–15; L. Brunnström, *Det svenska folkhemsbygget: Om Kooperativa Förbundets arkitektkontor* (Stockholm: Arkitektur Förlag, 2004), pp. 188–233. The KF architect's office designed cooperative stores from the 1930s, but it was in 1960, when Konsum was established as the store name for self-services shops and Domus as the name for cooperative department stores, that co-ops all over the country started to look the same.

[51] Schewidy, pp. 280–1; Kylebäck, 1983, pp. 118–35; Hwang, 1995, pp. 38–45.

greater control, creating tensions between KF and its constituents.[52] During the next thirty years, KF tried to achieve greater integration into what it called "Co-op Sweden," but opposition stalled this process until 1992.[53]

Partly because of these internal conflicts and abortive reforms, KF and Swedish retail cooperatives lost market share from the end of the 1970s, principally to ICA. Ironically, ICA had reorganized its own warehouses and supply depots along similar lines to Johansson's plan, creating the foundation for an increase in market share.[54] Even though KF membership increased significantly from the mid-1960s, sales did not keep pace, prompting the view that "the Co-op" was losing touch with its consumers.[55]

KF's response to this challenge began in the mid-1970s, when with the regional societies it implemented a series of reforms, including some bold decisions about its range of products. Three Consumer Congresses (1971, 1976, and 1983) launched policies leading to new product lines, including generic goods, textiles, furniture, and organic products. In addition to "rationalizing" the range of goods, a new marketing strategy was adopted which emphasized traditional cooperative traits: high-quality produce without frills, simple design, low price, limited promotion, and straightforward consumer information.[56] However, complaints from some members and competition with the sophisticated marketing of rival chains in the 1980s forced KF and the retail societies to stock other brands alongside the cooperative goods.[57] KF also introduced three new brands in the 1990s: *Signum* (high-quality products); *Blåvitt* (low price, good quality) and finally *Änglamark* (the cooperative's own organic range of products) within which Fair Trade tea and coffee were introduced in 1997.[58] Organic products were particularly successful, with KF's market share in this area rising to 44 percent by 2004.[59]

Notwithstanding these successes, by the mid-1980s KF leaders concluded that only reforms as radical as those of the 1950s/1960s could reverse decline. The aim was to decentralize and reform all areas of the business. A new element was the involvement of outside consultants. Significantly, the 1980s reforms eschewed the educational dimension which had been prominent in the changes of the 1950s. Nevertheless, they gave KF new powers to control developments within the movement, leading to greater emphasis on food. Responding to immediate financial difficulties, KF sold its remaining manufacturing operations, outsourcing the supply of cooperative brand goods. As previously noted, by the 1990s KF had persuaded member societies to accept its centralization strategies,

---

[52] Kylebäck om lagerhusplanen ...; Hwang, 1995, pp. 38–45.
[53] Hwang, 1995, pp. 58–70.
[54] H. Kylebäck Hugo, *Konsumentkooperation i strukturomvanding 1960–1985* (Kungälv, 1989).
[55] Giertz and Strömberg, pp. 156–7.
[56] Ibid., pp. 127–30.
[57] Ibid., pp. 160–1. See also *Konsumetkongressen*, 1983.
[58] Ibid., pp. 176–7.
[59] Beck-Friis, 2009, p. 27.

following the surrender to KF by several struggling regional societies of all commercial activities.[60]

The crisis that beset Swedish cooperation in the second half of the 1970s worried politicians, because of the important role the movement had played in Swedish life since the nineteenth century. Some sought legal assistance to regenerate the sector. In 1976 a Parliamentary commission on cooperation was established to evaluate the social and economic roles of cooperatives (retail, wholesale, production, insurance, agriculture, funeral care, housing, etc.), with representatives from most parties (except the Communists), together with cooperative leaders, including those from KF.[61] A debate followed about the reasons for decline. Although complete consensus was probably unachievable, key factors were identified in the report, published in 1981. It was agreed that one problem was the legal prohibition against government-controlled pension funds investing in cooperative businesses, even though they could purchase private company stocks quoted on the stock exchange. Proposed tax benefits for the cooperative sector divided the commission, principally because they might be seen as preferential treatment. Nonetheless, following the review, new tax privileges were granted to Swedish cooperatives, most notably the right to deduct certain interest payments on share capital, where such payments were reinvested in cooperative shares.[62] This limited but significant concession, while hardly decisive in the stabilization of Swedish cooperation, reflected the strong cross-party desire to revive the cooperative sector.

Some elements of the postwar Swedish story were also evident in Britain, most notably abortive reform strategies resisted by dissident regional retail societies and flawed leadership. As in Sweden, however, there was optimism in the 1950s. Not only did the consumer cooperative share of retail sales (see Table 10.1) remain stable until at least the mid-1960s,[63] but CWS and local cooperatives stole a march on the private sector by pioneering self-service stores, 60 percent of which were cooperative-owned by 1957.[64] However, national and local managers failed to recognize that a self-service revolution required major changes in cooperative stores, and the creation of a sophisticated and centralized distribution system to maximize potential economies of scale.[65] Part of the problem was resistance from regional/local cooperative societies. As in Sweden during 1950s, local British retail cooperative leaders saw centralization as a threat to their autonomy. Some also saw self-service as a challenge to the cooperative ideal that

[60] H. Kylebäck., *Federation eller Konsum Sverige? Konsumentkooperativ förändringsprocess Del 3 1985–1995* (Göteborg, 1999), pp. 67–89.

[61] *Kooperationen i samhället Huvudbetänkande av kooperationsutredningen*, SOU 1981:60.

[62] Schewidy, p. 316.

[63] L. Sparks, "Consumer Co-operation in the UK 1945–93: Part 1. Review and Prospects," *Journal of Co-operative Studies*, 79 (1994), pp. 1–63, figure 3.3, p. 25.

[64] Ekberg, "Consumer Co-operation," p. 50.

[65] G. Shaw & A. Alexander, "British Co-operative Societies as Retail Innovators: Interpreting the Early Stages of the Self Service Revolution," *Business History*, 50, no. 1 (2008), pp. 62–78, pp. 74–5.

TABLE 10.1 *U.K. and Swedish Cooperative Share of Retail Trade (%)*

	U.K.	Sweden
1900	15	
1950	23	
1960	21	25.7 (1962)
1970	15	21.3
1980	12	22
1990	5.5	20.3
2000	4.4	18.5
2010	8.0	21.4 (2007)

Sources: Data for U.K. supplied by Professor Jim Quinn from research conducted in *The Grocer*. Data for Sweden was supplied by E. Ekberg.

a visit to the store was as much about social interaction as it was about consumption. As one cooperative activist put it in the early 1960s: "We do not want a situation in which people simply come in and collect their goods and then we forget all about them."[66]

The stymieing of the self-service revolution was merely the first of numerous abortive attempts to modernize the British cooperative movement between the late 1950s and the 1980s. In the mid-1950s, an independent commission was set up to evaluate how British cooperation should change to meet the demands of full employment, rising incomes, and an expanding consumer market. Labour's links with the movement resulted in Hugh Gaitskell and Tony Crosland playing a leading role in the commission's deliberations. Its recommendations, published in 1958, were far-reaching, calling for better-educated managers, a reduction in the number of regional and local societies, and a change in CWS's function. The latter required that CWS move away from selling produce to local cooperatives and move toward undertaking the purchase of commodities for them. In essence, the report wanted British cooperation to become more like the multiple chain stores and supermarkets against which it competed. Notions of cooperative democracy were scorned, perhaps unsurprisingly in light of the long-standing Labour prejudices described earlier. The goal was to have larger, more modern, professionally designed stores, along with an expansion into the dry goods sector through large department stores. Significantly, on this last point, the commission was influenced by visits to Sweden, especially to the Domus department stores.[67]

[66] Ekberg, *Consumer Co-operatives*, p. 86.
[67] L. Black, "'Trying to Sell a Parcel of Politics with a Parcel of Groceries': The Co-operative Independent Commission (CIC) and Consumerism in Britain," in Black and Robertson, *Consumerism and the Co-operative Movement in Modern British History*, pp. 33–50.

Implementation of these reforms was only partly successful in the 1960s, despite the best efforts of the Joint Rationalization Committee.[68] Indeed, changes during the 1960s, 1970s, and 1980s tended to be thrust upon the movement by adverse events (as in the merger of SCWS and CWS in 1973, when the former's financial difficulties threw them together). In the 1970s, CWS moved directly into retailing, a move that antagonized regional societies and CRS. During the same period, CWS slowly developed an individual membership system which would eventually produce significant benefits. By the 1980s, the Co-operative Bank had introduced free banking to current account holders, as part of a package of policies that would lead to the ethical banking and trading strategies of the 1990s. As food market share continued to fall in the 1980s, a sense of inevitable doom prevailed, epitomized by the expression used by older and more cynical CWS officials: "t'll see me out!" Table 10.1 reveals this trajectory of decline from the 1950s, with market share falling by the turn of the millennium to just 4.4 percent.

Why were efforts to rationalize and reform so ineffectual? An important reason has been identified by Ekberg, who notes that the internal political obstacles to coordinated reform within the cooperative movement became even more intractable in the postwar period. This seems surprising at first glance, especially given the merger trend among local societies which resulted in their number falling from more than five hundred during the Second World War to just forty-two by 2002.[69] One might expect this to make it easier for CWS to secure reform through persuasion. Furthermore, the decline of the movement's active membership also might be expected to have weakened resistance to change, allowing cooperatives to operate more like the capitalist organizations they aspired to supplant.[70] But Ekberg shows that the emergence of large and relatively well-resourced regional cooperatives inspired an even stronger sense of independence from CWS.[71] Indeed, retail societies developed their own wholesale activities to rival those of CWS, just as CWS had branched out into retailing. But they were following a policy destined to fail, since it led to inefficient replication of functions, curtailing their ability to take advantage of mass, national-scale buying in bulk. The ingrained spirit of regional and local independence, and a lukewarm – and occasionally hostile – attitude toward CWS which had characterized relations within the movement since the formation of CWS in 1863, lived on. It is little wonder that efforts at reform foundered.

Nevertheless, CWS cannot be absolved from responsibility for this predicament. One senior insider from the 1970s notes numerous internal problems in

[68] F. Muller, "The Consumer Co-operatives in Great Britain," in Brazda and Schewidy, *Consumer Co-operatives in a Changing World*, Vol. 1, pp. 50–136, pp. 85–98.
[69] Ekberg, "Consumer Co-operation," p. 59.
[70] This erosion of the cooperatives as centers of social and political activism is well recorded in J. K. Walton, "The Post-War Decline of the British Retail Co-Operative Movement: Nature, Causes and Consequences," in Black and Roberston, *Consumerism and the Co-operative Movement in Modern British History*, pp. 13–31.
[71] Ekberg, *Consumer Co-operatives*, p. 300.

the management structure – the attitudes of senior managers, the lack of outside talent, difficulties in relations between the member-elected board and senior managers, and conflicts between key national bodies within the cooperative movement.[72] On the last point, clashes between CRS and CWS, and contradictory polices and strategies pursued by the Co-operative Bank and CIS, made the development of a cohesive policy impossible. During that time, several CWS insiders described the short, gentle, ten-minute stroll from the CIS building to New Century Hall (where CWS was located) as "the longest walk in Manchester."

How then did the revival of cooperative fortunes come about after the mid-1990s? This period saw CWS disposing of its manufacturing activities, merging with CRS (in 2001), and promoting a merger momentum that delivered sufficient power to the center to allow real change to begin. This momentum also prompted the merger in 2001 of CIS and the Co-operative Bank, to form Co-operative Financial Services, building further on the "ethical banker" platform devised a decade earlier. Similarly, a new branding program was launched, based on the movement's time-honored values of ethical trading combined with a new retail strategy focusing on the convenience store sector. In the process, a hostile takeover attempt was beaten off.[73] By the late-1990s, profits were rising, though, as shown in Figure 10.1, they were based largely on the success of the Bank, rather than retail. Nonetheless, a more cohesive "family of cooperative businesses," based on a distinctly cooperative ideological foundation, had been forged, in concert with the revival of a member-based dividend scheme in 2005 that proved extremely popular. By 2010, the acquisition of Somerfields and merger with Britannia completed an astonishing revival of British cooperation's fortunes.

This regeneration of British cooperation was made possible by changes in the internal political dynamics of the movement over a prolonged period – what could be termed a "falling toward the center." First, the paradoxical decline of cooperative businesses was an essential ingredient in the commercial recovery of the 1990s/2000s. As market share and profitability dwindled in the 1980s (see Table 10.1), mergers and takeovers of the regional societies gathered pace, led by CWS. This helped remove opponents and obstacles to change. Second, after the 1970s, senior managers who were unsympathetic to change were gradually replaced by new people who recognized that reform was essential, in the process forging closer and more effective relations between the board and management. By the end of the 1980s, the internal structures and personnel were in place for a fresh reform initiative to be launched.

Conversely, little of British cooperation's revival owed much to the external political environment. Labour politicians' efforts to lead reform in the

---

[72] Interview with Sir Graham Melmoth, September 8, 2010.
[73] John F. Wilson, "Co-operativism Meets City Ethics: The 1997 Lanica Take-over Bid for CWS," in A. Webster, J. Walton, and D. Stewart (eds.), *Hidden Alternatives* (Manchester: Manchester University Press, 2011), pp. 16–36

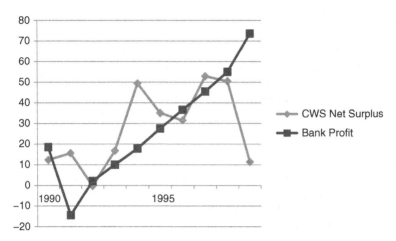

FIGURE 10.1 CWS profits and Co-operative Bank profits, 1990–1999 (£million)
Source: CWS *Annual Reports*, 1900–1999.

commission of the 1950s had been unsuccessful, largely because of their indifference to the values and traditions of cooperation. They really wanted to turn
the co-op into a retail organization run on strictly capitalist lines. Nor did the
policies of Labour governments much benefit cooperation. Although the Blair
government supported the changes of the late 1990s, cooperative ideas were
largely ignored by New Labour ideologists, for all their talk of "A Third Way."
Moreover, during the Thatcher era, the cooperative movement's traditional
allegiance to Labour had alienated free market Conservatives, who enthusiasti-
cally promoted demutualization (see Chapter 5 in this book). Consequently,
there are signs that the new Co-operative Group is reassessing its allegiance to
Labour, or at least widening the net of political engagement. In the run-up to the
General Election of 2010, the Group worked with other mutuals in promoting
the sector to all the main political parties through "MUTUO," a joint pressure
group established for this purpose. Although the Co-operative Party's link with
Labour continues, the new coalition government, with its commitment to a "Big
Society" in which cooperatives and mutuals will theoretically help fill the gap left
by a retreating public sector, has made overtures to cooperation that would have
been unthinkable twenty years ago. Perhaps, at last, the external political
environment is becoming more hospitable to the cause of British cooperation.

CONCLUSIONS

In drawing together the principal themes of this comparative study, the two
types of cooperative ideology must be clearly differentiated. The Swedish movement was always characterized by a tradition of member household-orientated
distribution and related ideology, while the British cooperative movement was
more closely associated with socialism and a civil society tradition. These

ideological differences help explain how the varying responses were shaped in the 1950s and 1960s and in the period of 1990–2010. The major difference was that KF and the retail societies in Sweden made significant changes in management and marketing much earlier, while in the U.K. such changes were suggested but not executed for several decades. Consequently, by the 1990s, the need to reform was much more urgent in the U.K., as reflected in the 1997 takeover bid. The overwhelming defeat of this bid provided the leadership with an opportunity to reimpose the values and principles of cooperation, while simultaneously implementing radical commercial and organizational strategies for a twenty-first-century renaissance. In Sweden, reform was more influenced by an investor-led, 1980s concept of corporate change, prompting an overhaul of the system twenty years earlier than in Britain.[74] Interestingly, Sven-Åke Böök, who researched and provided the necessary material for revaluating the International Co-operative Alliance's statement of cooperative principles in 1995, remained a marginal figure in Sweden.[75] This resulted in his departure as head of Kooperativa Institutet (the Co-operative Research Institute). Meanwhile Melmoth, who served as the Alliance's president when the *Statement on the Co-operative Identity* was published, was able to drive through his values-driven program in the U.K. with very little resistance.

Until the 1950s, both movements enjoyed strong market shares, extensive memberships, and abundant capital resources, some of which was invested in self-service stores. By the 1990s and 2000s, they had modernized operations by centralizing management and streamlining links between distribution and retail. Although the CWS imitated KF's regional warehousing model, it is significant that they both settled on the same solution to this supply-chain challenge. Ultimately, though, external competitive pressures were more influential than internal problems in moving both organizations toward "rationalization." In the 1990s, CWS and KF abandoned manufacturing to specialize in retail, largely because of the need to compete in an increasingly globalized market. The focus on retailing was linked with branding initiatives associated with "ethical trading," providing a distinctive marketing strategy that has been sustained, and even imitated by rivals.

As well as similarities, however, there were also significant differences, not the least of which was in the political environments in which the movements operated. There was a stark contrast between Anglo-Saxon liberalism and the Swedish commitment to a social democratic "mixed economy." Swedish political parties tended to display toward KF a kind of benign neutrality, characterized by mild approval bordering on indifference. Party attitudes in Britain were more complex. Both Conservatives and Labour were suspicious of cooperation. Indeed, latent hostility existed in both camps, arising from Labour's statist

[74] O. Holm, *Organisation i Dissonans – konsumtrörelse I brytningstid* (Stockholm: Timbro, 1989); T. Eliasson, *KONSUM i det nya landet* (Stockholm: Rabén & Sjögren, 1989).

[75] Interview with Sven-Åke Böök; see also International Co-operative Alliance, *Statement on the Co-operative Identity*, ICA Web site, www.ica.coop/coop/principles.html (accessed March 1, 2011).

socialism on the left and the Conservatives' belief in the market on the right (at least until the recent Conservative conversion to the "Big Society"). The Swedes' practical preference for central authority helped KF's moves to strengthen its position within the cooperative movement. Although many CWS leaders wanted to centralize and streamline operations as early as the late nineteenth century, they were unable to persuade local and regional societies that this was in their mutual interest, until the crisis decades of the 1980s and 1990s obliged societies to accept a strategy of consolidation.

Of course, KF was helped by its role as a combined cooperative union and wholesaler, an advantage not shared by CWS. A traditional ideological belief in "rationalization" stimulated faster modernization in KF during the 1960s, a process assisted by the concentration of Swedish cooperation's activities in food and household goods retailing. Conversely, CWS historically maintained a much more diverse range of activities, from financial services to funeral care, travel agents, property, and garages. Implementing effective reorganization was always going to be more problematic, especially given the devolution of power to the organizational structures that ran these different activities. In the long run, however, this diversity, and the profits it generated, provided the resources for modernization. The political environments in both countries played insignificant roles in fashioning these responses, a situation that reflects the primacy of commercial dynamics as the essential catalyst that drove through change.

Conclusion: The Decisive Factors of Cooperatives' Future – Their Nature, Longevity, Role, and Environment

Patrizia Battilani and Harm G. Schröter

The task of this book is to provide an overview of the development of cooperative enterprise in the world after 1950. There are two main reasons for doing so. First, co-ops did not simply dwindle away and vanish from mature economies, as predicted by many scholars. On the contrary, based on their remarkable performance during the financial crisis in 2008, they have become more attractive and have attracted more attention than ever before. Thus, it is worthwhile to examine this special kind of enterprise. Second, although there is quite a bit of literature on several aspects of cooperative economics as well as many studies on single regions or countries, there still is relatively little research comparing international trends in this sector. In a globalized world, international trends are becoming increasingly important, and consequently, an overview is necessary.

The editors have selected the issues to explore because of their importance, representativeness, or innovation. All aspects of these issues, including problems, limitations, and failures, have been taken into account. Nevertheless, everything could not be covered. We provide no special information on Africa and Latin America; even though the literature on the evolution of cooperatives in these continents has been growing since the turn of the century, it is still difficult to find in-depth contributions. Nor do we cover the role and impact of outstanding managers, politicians, or health care, to point out only a few issues. Choices had to be made for this volume; there are far more issues than we could deal with in a few pages. Therefore, we have chosen to concentrate on three major areas, each one representing a set of problems that needs to be dealt with in the future of the co-op-movement: the special nature of co-ops, their longevity as a species, and the impact of their environment upon them, and vice versa.

THE SPECIAL NATURE OF CO-OPS

Few years ago Yair Levi and Peter Davis labeled cooperatives as the *"enfants terribles"* of economics because they are too economically oriented to be included in the nonprofit sector and too socially oriented to be considered as economic for-profit organizations (Levi and Davis, 2008). Although we, as the editors, do not think of co-ops as "terrible children" and prefer to refer to them as a "special kind of business," Levi and Davis were right. Co-ops are enterprises, that is, organizations designed to make money, but at the same time they are jointly owned and democratically organized. They are ruled by their members, applying the "one person, one vote" rule. Although profits are shared according to the amount of use by members – for instance, in consumers co-ops, in direct relation to the sum of purchases within one year – voting rights are not according to size of turnover or use but to the simple existence of membership. An important economic share of a co-op does not lead to a corresponding influence on it. Members vote directly or indirectly on all important issues, including managers and their work, though in most cases they do so indirectly through their elected representatives. In co-ops, democratic governance is applied.

This democratic structure is, according to many economists, detrimental to profit generation. The combination of these contradicting ideas represents the *dual nature* of co-ops. Consequently, co-ops are both democratic and enterprises. Many authors have elaborated on this issue; therefore, we want to point to new insights and developments.

The contributors to this volume agree with the view that a functioning democracy is indispensable for co-ops. According to Kramper, it was the loss of democracy that caused the failure of consumer co-ops in some European countries and insurance co-ops in Japan. For Ekberg, it was the democratic (bottom-up) co-ops that survived, while the change to top-down decision making caused an economic upswing in the short term but collapse in the long run. Thus, the ideas fostered in some quarters of the co-op movement during the 1970s and later, to the effect that co-ops have to reduce member participation in order to centralize and stay competitive, have been evaluated and dismissed again – but this time on a global scale.

Many researchers consider the democratic structure and, by definition, inflexible ownership of co-ops to present a disadvantage compared to the investor-owned business (IOB). Murray E. Fulton suggested that co-ops suffer from inefficiencies "because co-operatives are often formed to pursue multiple objectives."[1] In other words, it is their dual nature that puts them at a disadvantage compared to IOBs. However, it has been stated before, and is stated again in this volume (see Zamagni),[2] that these deficiencies can easily be compensated for by the intrinsic motivation of the co-op members. Furthermore, Pérotin shows that

---

[1] Murray E. Fulton, "Traditional versus New Generation Cooperatives," in Christopher D. Merrett and Norman Walzer (eds.), *A Cooperative Approach to Local Economic Development* (Westport, 2001), pp. 11–24, p. 14.

[2] In order not to bore the reader with a repeated "in this volume," we use only the names of our contributors to refer to their contributions in this book. Only references to other publications are provided in full; otherwise, the contributor's name refers to the material in this volume.

employee participation in decision making and in profit distribution has greater positive productivity effects in worker cooperatives than in conventional firms.

Working for one's own benefit is, indeed, the ultimate stimulus! Endowed with such consent, co-ops need much less administration and supervision, and therefore can produce their products or services at the same or even lower costs than IOBs.

Johnston Birchall and Richard Simmons suggest in their *Mutual Incentives Theory* a "participation chain" that links *motivation* and *mobilization* of members directly to *resources*.[3] They connect the attitude of members directly with the economic results of their co-op. Problems may emerge when democracy is no longer sufficiently practiced or members, for other reasons, no longer feel committed. In such a case, motivation switches from an intrinsic to a secondary one, entailing that there are only minor differences left between the co-op and an IOB.

Many authors take one or several more steps. In their arguments, they surpass the line of the economy and enterprise by addressing issues such as personal dignity and happiness as well as the social and political services co-ops render to society. Vera Zamagni wrote: "The comparative advantage of cooperation lies in putting the dignity and the relational component of people at the center of economic activity." Cooperatives are said to be "formed and kept alive by the decision of people who put positive liberty . . . at the top of their scale of values."[4] Members of co-ops have no reason to feel exploited. With less injustice done to single persons, co-ops promote more peaceful societies. This argument already builds a bridge between the single individual, on the one hand, and society on the other. Because co-ops involve democratic rule and control, they act as schools for democracy – free of charge for society. The co-ops thus play a role in one of the most important trends in global society since World War II: the move toward democratic rule and away from various forms of authoritarian centralization and exploitation. Co-ops teach their members practical mutual solidarity and, in doing so, represent a type of glue for any society. The economic argument in favor of co-ops points to the fact that they help to construct and maintain an economic middle class of society, which is an essential element for a functioning democracy. Thus, the existence of co-ops offers a variety of different advantages for the society in which they are active. Because of these advantages, delivered without charge, and the economic disadvantages of the co-op model, some authors have demanded compensation in the form of special co-op laws, beneficial for this kind of enterprise.

Democracy within co-ops can become endangered in several ways. History has shown that the first, and in most cases the second, generation of members

[3] Johnston Birchall and Richard Simmons, "What Motivates Members to Participate in Cooperative and Mutual Businesses? A Theoretical Model and Some Findings," in *Annals of Public and Cooperative Economics*, 75, no. 3 (2004), pp. 465–95.
[4] Stefano Zamagni and Vera Zamagni, *Cooperative Enterprise: Facing the Challenge of Globalization* (Cheltenham/Northampton, 2010), p. 28.

feel committed to the co-op model. Problems start with the third and later generations which, for instance, no longer bother using their voting rights. Probably everybody would agree that a democracy is a strange one when the execution of voting rights falls below 10 percent of the electorate. Co-ops may become big enterprises, and quite often they do, but they need to organize in some way to keep their members' participation and avoid a sort of management tyranny.

Another principal challenge is foreign direct investment (FDI). With FDI, whether it represents the takeover of an existing enterprise or a greenfield investment, the initiative comes from the investor. Although FDI is the best (safest) course for IOBs, for a co-op, the most natural way is to associate new members in other countries. However, many legal obstacles make that strategy unworkable. Furthermore, even if those obstacles were removed, the differences in language and culture could complicate the relationship among the members, and consequently the management, of such an undertaking. In other words, the co-op style of globalization needs a strong cultural integration, because members play a central role.

Until now, the creation of transnational cooperatives has been tested only in Europe. In 2003, as part of the European integration process, the EU introduced the possibility for co-ops to incorporate at the European level instead of that of a single state, like it did with IOBs in the case of *Societas Europaea*.[5] It took three years to have the co-op regulation implemented by all European national states. In 2006, Copemic, the first SCE-European cooperative society, was set up by the European retailer co-ops. To date no more than twenty SCEs have been created. However, what deserves attention is the fact that, at least in some cases, the setting up of an SCE has been motivated by the desire to create a European network of members who share the values of the founders – that is, to create a true transnational co-op.[6]

As a matter of fact, to address cross-border activities, cooperatives still prefer to use the possibility of establishing an IOB. The Swiss Migros did so and failed with its FDI even in the regions surrounding Switzerland. Others, however, have succeeded, the most striking example being Mondragon. Mondragon, a Spanish (Basque) co-op, owns producing enterprises on nearly all continents. Parts of these are organized as co-ops, and others as IOBs. Mondragon seems to have managed to square the circle and remain a co-op, but it represents an exception to the rule. Some co-ops in Italy, such as Conserve Italia (a food-processing co-op with plants in France and Spain and trading companies in Germany and the U.K.) and Sacmi (a group manufacturing machines with plants in twenty-three different countries), have also become international, but usually by setting up or buying IOBs.

---

[5] Regulation 1435/2003 on the Statute for European Cooperative Society (SCE).

[6] See, for example, the experience of Nova SCE and ESCOOP reported in *Study on the Implementation of the Regulation 1435/2003 on the Statute for European Cooperative Society (SCE)* – Contract No. SI2.ACPROCE029211200 of October 8, 2009.

This latter solution – which, from the point of view of the co-op movement, is a second-best solution – exposes a co-op on a series of critical fronts. The very idea of co-ops is self-aid and initiative (democracy). Any FDI by a co-op needs to inject into the acquired enterprise trust, initiative, and commitment. If this cannot be done, the FDI will remain an alien part of the co-op's body. This need generally applies to all acquisitions of co-ops, but usually it is more easily met within a country where mentalities are known and are often more similar to each other than those between countries. Geert Hofstede's research showed that human beings as economic actors do not react to identical incentives in the same way; they react in ways shaped by the culture in which they live. In his path-breaking book *Scale and Scope*, the business historian Alfred D. Chandler pointed to different ways of organizing a capitalist society, exploring substantial differences between the United States, the U.K., and Germany. The topic was deepened by the sociologists Peter Hall and David Soskice. These authors have in common a focus on IOBs in highly developed Western countries. Behavior and values differed significantly between these countries, reflecting, of course, ideas about democracy and control. If there are already substantial differences between these Western states, where do African or East Asian ones fit in? A far-flung network of affiliated IOBs all over the world is, by definition, a threat to the core idea of co-ops: democracy including control and responsibility based on equal terms of all actors. Co-ops, however, have a third choice, apart from the setting up of an SE, which is possible only within the EU, or the acquisitions of IOBs. Networking is another way to address cross-border activities. In a globalizing economy, international networks become ever more important. As with all minorities, co-ops in different countries have a special mutual trust toward each other – a feeling from which non-cooperatives are excluded – and that can make it easier for co-ops to form networks. During the last decades, the formation of networks has been deeply analyzed. In Italy, for instance, such networks have been recognized as one of the main reasons for the flourishing of co-ops. Networking for co-ops has become very attractive because it allows them to merge large company size (and the cost reduction associated with it) with the ability to cater to local needs.

Some practices introduced since the millennium also question or even threaten democracy within co-ops. Chaddad and Cook mentioned the possibility of outside investment into co-ops. When investment and membership, which represents democratic voting and control, are separated, little difference remains between co-ops and IOBs. The same applies to voting according to economic weight rather than by person. When such rules are accepted, it becomes difficult to find significant differences between co-ops and IOBs.

THE LONGEVITY OF CO-OPS AS A SPECIES

Comparative studies on the survival rates of co-ops and IOBs show only small differences, and those are usually in favor of co-ops (see, e.g., Pérotin). Nevertheless, the idea of a decline of the cooperative model is widespread, even in some of the countries (e.g., Germany) where cooperatives have just begun their development. This line of reasoning suggests that co-ops may be bound to a life cycle.[7]

The idea of the life cycle is that all products live for a certain amount of time. They thrive and grow quantitatively when they are young; they mature without much further expansion; and, when demand slackens, their life span, after a phase of decline, finally ends. Raymond Vernon held that this idea can also be applied to organizational structures and enterprises by showing that FDI can be explained partly by the life-cycle approach.[8] Since the idea and movement for modern co-ops started in the United Kingdom, Germany, France, and Denmark, and since co-ops in some decades also declined in at least two of these countries, the idea of comparing the development of co-ops to the life cycle is by no means far-fetched. In contrast to Germany and partly to the U.K., there was no similar decline or stagnation in Mediterranean countries or in the emerging nations of the Asian continent, for instance, India and South Korea (for the latter country, see the essay by Jung and Rösner). Therefore, if we try fitting the life-cycle theory to co-ops, we surely have to take into account the many different cycles to be found in many countries and regions, and identify which characteristics of cooperatives are subject to a life cycle.

Testing the life-cycle idea is not just an issue of theory and analysis that will give us a better understanding of the nature of co-ops; the life-cycle idea also has practical implications. It may help to identify the place of co-ops in their developmental path within the cycle. In a case in which they are in decline, the cycle idea may help them to organize a relaunch that could prolong the cycle. It may also help co-ops in developing countries to decide what they can learn from the more advanced ones and what they had better exclude from such transfers.

The first aspect we should take into consideration is the sectors in which co-ops have traditionally flourished. At the beginning, co-ops were rooted, above all, in agriculture, retailing, and finance. However, during the last decades, both the number of co-ops and the number of members have declined in the agricultural sector. Zamagni showed, in her contribution to this volume, a decline of 40 percent in members and 44 percent in co-ops in this sector within about twenty years in the United States. In manufacturing, cooperatives have always had, and still have, a marginal role, so it is not surprising that the decline in agriculture has not been accompanied by development in the manufacturing sector. Furthermore, in the traditional service sector (e.g., retailing), co-ops have shown no clear pattern. Consumer co-ops declined in Germany and in France, but were successful in Italy, while retailer co-ops increased their market share

---

[7] Murray Fulton suggested to apply the product cycle to single co-ops (Fulton, in Merrett and Walzer).

[8] Raymond Vernon, "International Investment and International Trade in the Product Cycle," in Raymond Vernon, "The Product Cycle Hypothesis in a New Environment," *Oxford Bulletin of Economics and Statistics*, 41 (1979), pp. 255–67.

everywhere. In conclusion, European co-ops in the retail sector seem to share a single characteristic, namely, growth in size. (One can see the trends of consumer co-ops in different countries by comparing the essays by Ekberg and Kramper with the one by Friberg, Vorberg-Rugh, Webster, and Wilson in this volume). In well-off countries, the novelty of the last decade has been the emergence of co-ops in new service sectors, for instance, in personal services, as Zamagni showed in her contribution. On the contrary, in the newly industrialized and developing countries, co-ops have continued to be important in more traditional sectors, such as agriculture, insurance, and finance. All of this suggests the existence of a life cycle with respect to the sectors in which co-ops can flourish. Given the fact that co-ops are less suitable for manufacturing, the pattern of specialization seems to be connected with the stage of development of each country. Therefore, in developing or newly industrialized countries, most co-ops are set up in agriculture, insurance, or retailing, while in the richest nations they have to spread into personal or business services in order to retain an important role in their economies.

The second aspect we would like to take into consideration is that of ideal inspiration or, even better, of the aims pursued by members who decide to join a cooperative. Quoting McPherson in this volume, we should bear in mind that "the sources for the cooperative values are very complex, derived from history, many community situations, cultural understandings, bodies of thought, and economic circumstances." However, it is a matter of fact that for many decades co-ops have been designed for self-aid and to improve the standard of living of the poor. This conviction was strong not only in Europe but also in the United States, where other ideals and goals maintained a central role within the cooperative movement. Consequently, we can suggest that when the average income has risen and a certain higher level of living is granted, either through successful self-aid or a generous welfare state, there is no good reason for co-ops to exist anymore; their very success will have terminated their life span. However, the emergence of the affluent society has changed the needs pattern, rather than terminating co-ops. Members of the new generations can join co-ops to improve their human capital and their entrepreneurship talent if they are workers, as well as to buy healthy food if they are consumers. In conclusion, in respect to members' ideals and needs, co-ops seem to be strictly bound to the life-cycle model. Furthermore, the ability of the cooperative movement to define a new pattern of ideal inspirations and goals is crucial not only for the survival but, above all, for the flourishing of the co-ops. Ideologies matter. Values matter. Culture matters for cooperatives, as for other institutions.

THE ROLE OF CO-OPS IN A COUNTRY'S ECONOMY

A long-standing tradition in economic thought holds that co-ops are a tool to overcome deficiencies of a not-yet-mature market. They fill a gap, but when markets are fully functioning, there are no important gaps any longer and co-ops are no longer necessary (see Kramper, and Chaddad and Cook). Furthermore, their growth is constrained by their limited access to fresh capital; co-ops cannot offer new shares on the stock exchange like (listed) IOBs. During the last decades, many financial co-ops demutualized for this reason (Battilani and Schröter). In case commitment of members is no longer granted, a free-rider problem may occur. Since a minimum investment is enough to obtain voting rights, further investment may be withheld by some.[9] This interpretation relies on the idea of the life cycle.

A very peculiar life cycle is the one experienced by co-ops in the former communist countries where the majority of members dismissed the idea of co-ops as soon as possible after the authoritarian system collapsed. For them co-ops were part and parcel of communism and, consequently, simply undesirable. In theory they would have been perfect vehicles for improvement, but neither theory nor the practical efforts of the ICA had a significant impact on experience-hardened peasants.

As you can see from the examples of demutualization and the evolution of co-ops in Eastern Europe, many features of cooperatives can be connected to the life-cycle model. Thus: Are co-ops and their special form of enterprise in general in decline or even doomed?

The answer, we believe, is no. The evidence indicates that life cycles can be prolonged and products can be relaunched in many ways. Co-ops can be set up in new sectors, cooperatives' goals can be reformulated in order to cater to the needs of a new generation of members, and institutional innovations can overcome the capital shortage. Even when markets become efficient, co-ops can guarantee more "intrinsic motivations" than IOBs in those sectors where interpersonal relationships between producer and client are crucial. Indeed, there are indicators of a co-op revival and of an ability to start new phases of their life cycles even in the West. Since the beginning of the new millennium, many small co-ops have been founded in Europe (Friberg, Vorberg-Rugh, Webster, and Wilson). Co-ops survived the financial crisis of 2008–9 much better than IOBs. Co-ops tend to take fewer risks than other enterprises, and although their slowness and risk aversion are usually mocked by IOBs, those factors made them relatively resistant to the crisis. In the long-term perspective, they might be the better choice, especially in case the trend toward globalization, speed in decision making, and short-term focus continues.

It also can be argued that the "decline in co-ops" can be questioned not from a democratic, but from an economic, point of view. Zamagni showed that although co-ops declined in numbers of both members and co-ops in U.S. agriculture, their share of the market remained stable. There was centralization of enterprise, but no decline of performance in the sector. Finally, the new generation cooperatives (NGCs) in the United States and the cooperative groups in Europe surely represent a relaunch of the cooperative idea. New generation

---

[9] Michael L. Cook, "The Future of U.S. Agricultural Cooperatives: A Neo-Institutional Approach," *American Journal of Agricultural Economics*, 77 (1995), pp. 1153–9, p. 1156.

co-ops (NGCs) are, in short, more capitalistic than traditional co-ops (Chaddad and Cook, and Zamagni). They exist only in the agricultural sector of North America. The NGCs require a substantial amount of investment by members, the investment takes the form of shares, and these shares are tradable. Shares are sold and bought exclusively among members, and membership is closed. Members own delivery rights, on the one hand, and have delivery obligations on the other. In most NGCs, democratic control remains in place: NGCs are co-ops that apply the democratic rules of "one member, one vote," regardless of economic weight. Critics have argued that the NGC is a perverted form of a co-op, designed to enrich the rich. Closed membership means a closed shop, excluding the have-nots, whose enrichment represented the very concept of the cooperative idea. The NGC's precondition for the necessary heavy investment shows that it is designed exclusively for the well-to-do person, another issue that has little to do with the initial ideas of the Rochdale and other founders: self-aid to overcome poverty with the help of morally superior enterprise. Nonetheless, the NGCs indicate how flexible the co-op institution can be and demonstrate how the process of social evolution in the economy has produced yet another new form of cooperative economic organization.

Also in Europe, institutional innovation has brought forth the approval of a new set of laws. Recall the Italian experience where, in 1983, a new bill was passed[10] that granted cooperatives permission to own fully or to have a majority stake in a capitalist corporation. This law allowed the largest cooperatives to attract capital from the market in a variety of ways, including being quoted on the stock exchange. Another step in the direction of multiplying the financial resources for cooperatives was provided by Law 59, approved in 1992, which allowed cooperatives to have members who only supplied capital (*socio sovventore*) and to issue special preferred shares (*azioni a partecipazione cooperativa*). The use of these instruments was crucial for the creation of large cooperative groups and modified the typical cooperative networks. Of course, the same criticisms listed in the previous discussion of NGCs can be applied to the Italian cooperative groups, but so can the argument for this group being another example of continued experimentation with new forms of organization.

Probably both sides are right: the traditionalists and the initiators of a relaunch. One needs to acknowledge a strategic split in the movement. In advanced economies, co-ops are no longer (or not only) an instrument for promoting the poor but, instead, promote the (indispensable in all democracies) middle class, or even better for empowering members regardless of their social status. In less well-to-do countries, they still fulfill their traditional role: helping the poor in the economic, personal (dignity!), and political dimensions to become persons who, through self-aid, enable themselves to obtain a better

---

[10] The Law No. 72, June 1983, known as the Visentini Law, after the name of the minister who produced it.

standard of living as well as an improved recognition in society. Society, on the other hand, is supported by co-op members' activities concerning economic and political self-rule and self-control (democracy!) and their growing economic contributions to the state (tax and other commitments).

Consequently, our evaluation endorses a modified and improved version of the life-cycle concept, differentiated according to countries or regions. In conclusion, co-ops, like other forms of enterprise, need to change their organizational structures, goals, ideals, and inspirations over time and enter into new sectors to face the challenges of the modern world.

CO-OPS AND THEIR ENVIRONMENT

Already the differentiation of the life cycle according to countries has indicated the importance of the environment for co-ops. Culture, policy, and law are decisive elements for all enterprise, and so, too, for co-ops.

In the second half of the twentieth century, cooperatives have followed at least three distinct paths of development, largely attributable to the economic and cultural models adopted by different countries. The first path characterized nations where command economies emerged. In the former Soviet Union, Eastern Europe, India, China, and many African countries, a state-centric model of co-ops prevailed (see the Hoyt and Menzani essay). There the cooperatives became one of the many tools used by the central state to control economic processes. State-centric cooperatives emerged along with state-owned enterprises. Generally speaking, the socialist and communist states, following the path of Soviet Russia, created many co-ops especially in the agrarian sector. They were initiated and governed from above, and this top-down approach was in stark contrast to the ideas of democracy and self-control.

During the last two decades of the twentieth century, when many of those countries began the transition toward the market economy, not only state-owned enterprises but also cooperatives started to be converted. In the Soviet Union and Eastern Europe, the transformation took the form of demutualization; in China after 1978, communes were dissolved; and in many African countries, state-centric co-ops went bankrupt as soon as international competition became stronger. On the contrary, in India, where the command economy was abandoned much more slowly, governments stimulated old co-ops to refocus on the basis of the Western model. In both China and Africa, the disposal of the old-style co-ops was soon followed by the setting up of a new generation of undertakings conducting economic functions similar to those of traditional Western cooperatives.

Altogether, during the last thirty years, the state-centric cooperatives have gradually disappeared. Culture and legislation that had played a crucial role in their affirmation also remained decisive for their conversion and in determining their dismantling or renaissance.

The second path characterized nations with strong trade unions like Germany, Scandinavia, as well as the United Kingdom and some other Western European countries. Until the 1960s, co-ops in those countries enjoyed a favorable environment. Many who were not members perceived co-ops as the morally better enterprises. Co-ops received this premium label because they were said not to "exploit" their workers or customers. Since the workers or customers owned the respective co-ops themselves, exploitation was excluded. The workers' movement supported co-ops for this reason. For instance, the highest trade union leader of West Germany in the 1950s said, "co-ops have laid the foundations of new economic ethics and for a new economic order. Their weight and influence will grow in the future."[11] From the 1970s onward, however, co-ops became less fashionable than before in those countries. Higher income per capita and functioning markets caused people to conclude that co-ops were less important now than they were earlier. And those co-ops that were doing well, for instance, in the financial sector, often were not perceived as co-ops but as "normal" IOBs. Although co-ops in fact remained economically important, they became less and less visible. The leaders and followers of the co-op movement and its national organizations did not properly understand the importance of good will and ideological empathy in modern societies and did not react with campaigns against the prevailing view of co-ops as IOBs.

The much colder societal climate for co-ops since the 1970s has caused political advocates of IOBs to attack cooperative-protecting laws. But even before that, during more positive phases, laws did not always promote co-ops. For instance, during the 1950s, West Germany created a rule preventing retail co-ops from collecting a substantial surplus during a year for distribution of these profits to their members at the end of the year. One reason was to stop a transfer of nonmembers to members, after retail co-ops had been opened by law to all customers. Although the intention behind the law was good, the law undermined the support of retail co-ops. The new rule allowed no more than 2 percent of the member's turnover to be given back. A substantial distribution by their consumer's co-op at the end of the year was traditionally an important issue for poor families. They could repay their debts, make larger acquisitions (e.g., furniture), and had the means with which to celebrate Christmas and the New Year. Mothers, especially, looked at this additional income as a means for covering extraordinary expenses. But the 2 percent did not represent a large sum. In consequence, the traditional close relationship between co-ops and worker-families was undermined. In many cases, females were apparently less interested in co-op decision making (including, among other issues, on the amount distributed at the end of the year), which also weakened the co-op's democracy. The law was intended to be beneficial for the poor, providing them their rebates at once, but the small amount of additional money the new rule represented was not recognized. Law does not always meet the intentions of its creators.

---

[11] Willi Richter, "Wegbereiter einer neuen Wirtschaftsordnung," in Zentralverband Deutscher Konsumgenossenschaften (ed.), *Wirtschaft für den Verbraucher* (Hamburg, 1957), p. 134 ff.

At that same time, a significantly different environment existed in some of the other countries mentioned, for instance, in the United States.[12] The perceived difference was in the way of thinking; in the European countries, co-ops had always been near to the worker's movement, and the ideas of solidarity and mutual aid were strong, while in America, the benefits-for-members aspects were underlined.

This brings us to the third path of development of cooperative enterprise, which characterized countries where the links between trade unions and co-ops remained weak. This was the case not only for the United States, but also for Japan as well as Italy, Spain, Denmark, and many others. In all those countries, the flourishing of co-ops was stimulated by a multitude of ideal inspirations which could be only partially connected to trade unions. Hence, in those countries, the decline of the worker movement ideals affected neither the development nor the image of co-ops. Nevertheless, a problem of redefining the role and aims of this form of enterprise emerged as a pressing issue in these countries, too, above all as a consequence of the deep economic and social transformations of the last few decades.

So far we have described how institutional arrangements as well as prevailing economic cultures have shaped co-ops. Now we would like to focus on legislation to analyze how it has contributed to the institutional viability of co-ops. Looking at the history of IOBs, one can find a wide range of legislative measures aimed at ensuring their proper functioning, for instance, the protection given to minority shareholders' rights or the definition of rules and procedures to be adopted in issuing IPOs (initial public offerings). Something similar happened with co-ops regarding the underinvestment issue. The literature on cooperative enterprises traditionally has identified undercapitalization as one of the typical weaknesses of co-ops. In this connection, we can mention the contribution by Furubotn and Pejovich in 1970, who underlined the manner in which the inadequate capitalization of cooperatives limited their growth potentialities. This was said to be due to the lack of a market for cooperative shares, in which the expected future flows of profits could increase their value for the shareholders. According to this approach, the members tended to privilege strategies maximizing returns over the short term of their expected presence in the cooperative, because they were in no position to cash the capital gains on the shares when they left. The works by Ward and Vanek between 1975 and 1977 reached similar conclusions, saying that the members tended to keep investments low because the target of cooperatives was to maximize the income of the working members while keeping returns on capital as low as possible. The laws on cooperatives in each country have tried to address this problem in

---

[12] Focusing on these differences, important voices understood co-ops as a primarily *European* issue – in contrast to the rest of the world – and mainly in contrast to the United States. For instance, in 1957, Fritz Baade, one of the most influential German economists of his time, labeled co-ops as the *European form* of defining the balance between order and freedom in the economy. Baade, *Weltmacht Verbraucher*, S. 19.

many ways, sometimes following the suggestions of economists, and sometimes simply by adopting a pragmatic solution without theoretical assumptions.

In many transition countries, as well as in the U.K., the solution adopted for worker-owned companies has been to create a market for membership rights. However, many such undertakings converted into IOBs after a few years. So far a legislative contest creating a market for membership rights has not proven favorable to the cooperatives, despite the support of many economists. An alternative solution to the underinvestment issue has been the mandatory collective capital accumulation adopted at least since the Second World War in France, Italy, and in the Mondragon system. In these countries, the underinvestment problem was particularly pressing because in each cooperative, part of the capital was owned individually and another part was owned collectively and could not be split among the members. In all three countries, laws or cooperatives' statutes have tried to foster capital accumulation and investment by stating that a percentage of profit has to be ploughed back into the firm every year and added to the portion of capital that is collectively owned. Often mandatory collective capital accumulation is accompanied by other kinds of incentives, for instance, tax exemption of retained earnings set aside in indivisible reserves. The empirical evidence so far available proves that mandatory accumulation has had a positive impact. These issues are deeply analyzed by Pérotin in this volume.

In conclusion, in looking at the second half of the twentieth century, it emerges that environment, or even better culture and legislation, have shaped cooperative undertakings in many ways. The extreme example is the invention of state-centric cooperatives in command economies, but even in countries in which co-ops generally continued to follow the ICA principles, legislation has played a crucial role because, in some cases, it has helped co-ops to avoid perverse incentives, while in others it has encouraged them to become similar to IOBs. One can say that, like IOBs, cooperative undertakings need a coherent set of rules to be institutionally and economically viable. This "Conclusion" has shown that the three issues dealt with in this volume – the special nature of co-ops, their longevity as a species, and the impact of the environment on them – are interdependent: the species will not survive if the special nature of co-ops becomes seriously undermined. The contributions in this volume, however, indicate that this has not happened and is unlikely to happen in the future. This special kind of business will doubtless continue to evolve and to maintain an important position in a rapidly changing world economy.

Statement on the Cooperative Identity

Definition

A co-operative is an autonomous association of persons united voluntarily to meet their common economic, social, and cultural needs and aspirations through a jointly owned and democratically controlled enterprise.

Values

Co-operatives are based on the values of self-help, self-responsibility, democracy, equality, equity, and solidarity. In the tradition of their founders, co-operative members believe in the ethical values of honesty, openness, social responsibility, and caring for others.

Principles

The co-operative principles are guidelines by which co-operatives put their values into practice.

1st Principle: Voluntary and Open Membership

Co-operatives are voluntary organizations, open to all persons able to use their services and willing to accept the responsibilities of membership, without gender, social, racial, political, or religious discrimination.

2nd Principle: Democratic Member Control

Co-operatives are democratic organizations controlled by their members, who actively participate in setting their policies and making decisions. Men and women serving as elected representatives are accountable to the membership. In primary co-operatives members have equal voting rights (one member, one vote) and co-operatives at other levels are also organized in a democratic manner.

3rd Principle: Member Economic Participation

Members contribute equitably to, and democratically control, the capital of their co-operative. At least part of that capital is usually the common property of the co-operative. Members usually receive limited compensation, if any, on capital subscribed as a condition of membership. Members allocate surpluses for any or all of the following purposes: developing their co-operative, possibly by setting up reserves, part of which at least would be indivisible; benefiting members in proportion to their transactions with the co-operative; and supporting other activities approved by the membership.

4th Principle: Autonomy and Independence

Co-operatives are autonomous, self-help organizations controlled by their members. If they enter to agreements with other organizations, including governments, or raise capital from external sources, they do so on terms that ensure democratic control by their members and maintain their co-operative autonomy.

5th Principle: Education, Training and Information

Co-operatives provide education and training for their members, elected representatives, managers, and employees so they can contribute effectively to the development of their co-operatives. They inform the general public – particularly young people and opinion leaders – about the nature and benefits of co-operation.

6th Principle: Co-operation among Co-operatives

Co-operatives serve their members most effectively and strengthen the co-operative movement by working together through local, national, regional, and international structures.

7th Principle: Concern for Community

Co-operatives work for the sustainable development of their communities through policies approved by their members.

Source: ICA Web site (www.ica.coop/coop/principles.html).

APPENDIX II

Figures on the Cooperative Movement Worldwide

Comparison of Ownership as Percentage of Total Population

Region	Cooperative Members (%)	Direct Shareholders (%)
Africa	7.4	1.3
Americas	19.4	9.2
Asia Pacific	13.8	4.4
Europe	16.0	7.5
World	13.8	5.0

Source: Ed Mayo, *Global Business Ownership* (Manchester: Cooperative UK Limited, 2012), p. 13, tab. 2.

Comparison of Ownership in Selected Countries

Country	Cooperative Members	Percentage of Population (%)	Direct Shareholders	Percentage of Population (%)
Brazil	8,252,410	4.4	3,123,425	1.7
Canada	11,000,000	33.7	12,396,020	38
China	160,000,000	12.2	78,318,000	6
Finland	3,164,226	60.1	761,674	14.5
Germany	20,509,973	24.9	10,317,000	12.5
Ghana	2,400,000	10.7	345,000	1.5
India	242,000,000	21.8	21,794,832	2
Japan	17,000,000	13.3	39,284,500	30.7
Kenya	8,507,000	23.1	110,000	0.3
S. Korea	7,600,000	15.7	4,441,000	9.2
Portugal	2,000,000	18.9	323,237	3.1
Spain	6,960,870	15.8	2,152,969	4.9
U.K.	12,800,000	21.1	9,060,260	14.9
USA	120,000,000	40.2	62,880,000	21.1

Source: Ed Mayo, *Global Business Ownership* (Manchester: Cooperative UK Limited, 2012), p. 13f, table 3.

Index

Printed in the United States
by Baker & Taylor Publisher Services